Profits,
Priests,
and
Princes

PETER MINOWITZ

Profits, Priests, and Princes

Adam Smith's Emancipation of
Economics from Politics and Religion

STANFORD UNIVERSITY PRESS

STANFORD, CALIFORNIA 1993

Stanford University Press
Stanford, California

© 1993 by the Board of Trustees of the
Leland Stanford Junior University

Printed in the United States of America

CIP data are at the end of the book

For Max

Acknowledgments

I AM INDEBTED to Professor Harvey C. Mansfield, Jr., of Harvard University, for supervising the dissertation from which this book is derived and for shepherding my scholarly career with prudence, patience, and graciousness. His appreciation of scholarly detail blends magically with his appreciation of the things that matter to people who are not scholars. He strives always to keep his thinking fresh and his writing vigorous.

The late Professor Judith N. Shklar—who served as an examiner and as a second adviser—encouraged me when I most needed encouragement and provided crucial suggestions as the dissertation neared completion.

I would never have contemplated a doctorate in political science were it not for the all-around excellence of the political scientists with whom I studied at Middlebury College: Murray Dry, Russell Leng, Paul Nelson, and David Rosenberg. My interest in Adam Smith, kindled initially by Paul Nelson, was rekindled in graduate school by Stephen Holmes, whose enthusiasm for the study of Smith I share and whose learning and intellectual acuity I emulate.

My parents both possess an irrepressible curiosity and an unequivocal respect for learning; I hope this book is worthy of being counted among their grandchildren. Several scholars—Chris Bobonich, Chip Carey, Murray Dry, Ralph Hancock, Gordon Hylton, and Jim Stoner—have distinguished themselves as friends and colleagues over the entire course of the project. I would also like to commend Susan Carriere, who aided me in checking quotations, along with a group of outstanding editors at

Stanford University Press: Grant Barnes, Peter J. Kahn, Barbara O'Neil Phillips, and Norris Pope.

There remain individuals to whom I am indebted for a variety of benefits, including comments upon chapters, edifying conversations, and assistance with translating and word processing. In this regard, let me mention Paul Bator, Leslie Bethard, Francis Canavan, S.J., Ted Chiappari, Kevin Conlin, Martin Cook, Diane Cranor, Constantine Danopoulos, Veronica Davey, John Dunlap, Nancy Ellis, John Fells, John Ferejohn, Janet Flammang, Ian Fugate, Nancy Hammerman, Eric Hanson, Phillip Kain, Elisabeth Langby, Timothy J. Lukes, Jo Burr Margadant, Marsha McCoy, Debbie Minowitz, Judy Minowitz, Fred Mueller, Michael Myers, Steve Nahmias, Tim O'Keefe, Becky and Brad Osgood, Thomas Pangle, Fred Parrella, Patricia Peterson, Jody Reis-Johnson, Joan Robins, Marc Stier, William Sundstrom, Steve Sweeting, Cindy Taft, Donald Urrabazo, and George Von der Muhll.

For financial and administrative support, I would like to thank Santa Clara University and the H.B. Earhart Foundation; special thanks are due to the John M. Olin Foundation, which funded a one-year leave that enabled me to complete the initial revisions.

P.M.

Contents

A Note to the Reader

Editions and Abbreviations for Smith's Works

Citations to Adam Smith are to the Glasgow Edition of the Works and Correspondence of Adam Smith, published by Oxford University Press. The *Correspondence* volume was published in 1977 and edited by E. C. Mossner and I. S. Ross. In the text and notes, I have abbreviated the remaining volumes of Smith's works as follows:

EPS   *Essays on Philosophical Subjects.* Ed. W. P. D. Wightman, J. C. Bryce, and I. S. Ross. Oxford: Oxford Univ. Press, 1980.

LJA   *Lectures on Jurisprudence,* Report of 1762–63. Ed. R. L. Meek, D. D. Raphael, and P. G. Stein. Oxford: Oxford Univ. Press, 1978.

LJB   *Lectures on Jurisprudence,* Report of 1766. Ed. R. L. Meek, D. D. Raphael, and P. G. Stein. Oxford: Oxford Univ. Press, 1978. These lectures were initially published in 1896, edited by Edwin Cannan.

LRBL   *Lectures on Rhetoric and Belles Lettres.* Ed. J. C. Bryce. Oxford: Oxford Univ. Press, 1983.

TMS   *The Theory of Moral Sentiments.* Ed. D. D. Raphael and A. L. Macfie. Oxford: Oxford Univ. Press, 1976.

WN   *An Inquiry into the Nature and Causes of the Wealth of Nations.* Ed. R. H. Campbell, A. S. Skinner, and W. B. Todd. Oxford: Oxford Univ. Press, 1976.

Languages	"Considerations Concerning the First Formation of Languages." This essay was first published in 1761 in *The Philological Miscellany*, and was later appended to the fourth edition of *TMS*; it is reprinted in *LRBL*.

I employ the following short titles to specify works included in *EPS*:

Astronomy	"The Principles which lead and direct Philosophical Enquiries; illustrated by the History of Astronomy."
Imitative Arts	"Of the Nature of that Imitation which takes place in what are called the Imitative Arts."
Letter	"A Letter to the Authors of the *Edinburgh Review*."
Logics	"The Principles which lead and direct Philosophical Enquiries; illustrated by the History of the Ancient Logics and Metaphysics."
Physics	"The Principles which lead and direct Philosophical Enquiries; illustrated by the History of the Ancient Physics."

Abbreviations are also used for two frequently cited works of David Hume:

ICHU	*An Inquiry Concerning Human Understanding.* Ed. C. Handel. Indianapolis, IN: Bobbs-Merrill, 1955.
ICPM	*An Inquiry Concerning the Principles of Morals.* Ed. C. Handel. Indianapolis, IN: Bobbs-Merrill, 1957.

Explanation of Citation Forms

My citations to Smith's works specify paragraph numbers and sectional divisions rather than page numbers. These formulas appear atop each page of the Oxford series to facilitate the locating of passages. *WN* is divided into five "Books," subdivided into chapters which are in turn sometimes subdivided into numbered "Parts" and "Articles" and/or unnumbered sections, all of which are sequentially labeled by the Oxford editors. Book numbers appear as capitalized roman numerals, chapter numbers as uncapitalized roman numerals, smaller subdivisions as uncapitalized letters, and paragraphs as arabic numerals. For example:

WN III.iv.10 = Book 3, Chapter 4, paragraph 10.
WN IV.vii.c.80 = Book 4, Chapter 7, Part 3, paragraph 80.
WN V.i.a.22 = Book 5, Chapter 1, Part 1, paragraph 22.
WN V.i.f.23 = Book 5, Chapter 1, Part 3, Article 2, paragraph 23.

TMS is divided into "Parts" (rather than "Books"), which are in turn sometimes subdivided into "Sections" before being further subdivided into chapters (a few "Sections" are not further subdivided). Following the Oxford editors, Part numbers appear as capitalized roman numerals; Section numbers, where they occur, appear as uncapitalized roman numerals; Chapter and paragraph numbers appear as arabic numerals. For example:

> *TMS* I.iii.2.1 = Part 1, Section 3, Chapter 2, paragraph 1.
> *TMS* III.2.33 = Part 3, Chapter 2, paragraph 33.
> *TMS* VI.iii.28 = Part 6, Section 3, paragraph 28.

Smith's other writings are cited simply by title and paragraph, except for the Astronomy and Imitative Arts essays, which Smith divided into sections designated by roman numerals.

A Note on Emphases

Unless otherwise indicated, emphases (italics) have been added and were not utilized by the original authors.

Profits,
Priests,
and
Princes

CHAPTER ONE

Introduction

The whole is a riddle, an enigma, an inexplicable mystery.
—Hume, *The Natural History of Religion*

THE DEMISE OF COMMUNISM has precipitated praise of Adam Smith along with criticism of Karl Marx, but both authors are judged with more enthusiasm than they are studied. This is especially unfortunate in a time rife with speculations about "the end of history." Even today, however, there is vastly more attention paid to Marx's words than to Smith's, and many people are unaware of the dialectical prowess Smith's works display in blending reform with conservation, optimism with pessimism, indignation with resignation, confidence with doubt, rhetoric with science, action with reflection, excellence with equality, discipline with liberty, reason with emotion, history with nature, and benevolence with self-interest.

Smith is famous for two related innovations, one theoretical, his launching of a new discipline (economics), and one more practical, his powerful argument for laissez-faire policies. There is insufficient awareness, however, of the disparagement of politics and religion that accompanied his innovations. Smith here builds on the work of various modern philosophers—Machiavelli, Bacon, Grotius, Hobbes, Pufendorf, Locke, Montesquieu, Hutcheson, Hume, and Rousseau—but the disparagement is more pronounced, anticipating the Marxian vision of religion and the state as "superstructure" that will "wither away" with the coming of communism.

"Politics" and "religion" are general terms that require further specification. Regarding religion, Smith is a severe, but usually tactful, critic of Christianity and, derivatively, of the other biblical religions (Judaism and

Islam). Although there are variations within and between these religions, the main branches are united theologically (for example, in worshiping a Creator-God who reveals Himself to human beings) as well as historically (for example, in regarding Moses as a prophet and the Old Testament as a sacred book). And although Smith's condemnations of medieval Catholicism could hardly be more explicit, he applies the term "sect" to Christianity as a whole (*TMS* III.6.1) and ignores the distinctions between (and within) Catholic and Protestant theologies. Smith's first book, *The Theory of Moral Sentiments*, suggests that he has substituted deism or natural religion for revealed religion, but even these seem to wither away in his magnum opus.

"Politics" is an even looser term than is "religion," and Smith's posture toward it is more complex. One may nevertheless discern two broad types of anti-political messages. The first consists of Smith's efforts to elevate wealth, security, and bodily comfort as social ends, to encourage "bourgeois" virtues in opposition to more heroic ideals, to dismiss the fulfillment available through political participation, to promote the free market by constricting the activities of government, and to demote national identity and self-sufficiency for the sake of international trade. The second, a more theoretical type of disparagement, comes to light when one takes a broad view of the questions Smith poses and the techniques he uses to answer them. Whereas the categorization, analysis, and evaluation of the different forms of government were the central tasks of ancient political philosophy and substantial components of modern political philosophy prior to Smith, these activities almost disappear from the political economy of *The Wealth of Nations* and the moral philosophy of *The Theory of Moral Sentiments*. On a more general level, Smith tends to replace normative political philosophy with social science (for example, empirically based modeling and system building); he tends to replace the quest for timeless, natural standards with a quasi-materialistic philosophy of history.[1]

Politics and religion share much that made them targets for Smith and Marx. God is the ruler of the universe, and one's conception of divine rule may provide analogies for human rule; neither Smith nor Marx encourages people to bow before gods and kings. In analyzing society and history, both authors implicitly deny that human individuals have made contributions analogous to the sudden, willful creations of the biblical God. And both hope that people will no longer strive to join God in Heaven or to live on this earth as prophets or tyrants. For Smith, politics and religion are arenas where the stakes are too great, and the "corruption" engendered by the worship of wealth is preferable to the corruption engendered by the linkage of religion, faction, and fanaticism. When one encounters the majestic language of politics and religion in Smith, one is likely to find that this language is being employed to accentuate economic messages.

Despite the economic discourses of seventeenth- and eighteenth-century authors Antoine de Montchrétien, Thomas Mun, William Petty, Josiah Child, Samuel Pufendorf, John Locke, Pierre de Boisguillebert, Dudley North, Nicholas Barbon, Charles Davenant, Richard Cantillon, Francis Hutcheson, François Quesnay, David Hume, Sir James Steuart, Victor Mirabeau, Josiah Tucker, Mercier de la Rivière, A. R. J. Turgot, and Abbé Galiani, Smith is universally regarded as the founder of modern economics.[2] Smith's impact is usually explained by invoking the depth, comprehensiveness, coherence, and analytical rigor of *The Wealth of Nations*. It is also widely acknowledged, however, that only with David Ricardo's *The Principles of Political Economy and Taxation* (published in 1817) was political economy purged of its historical, philosophical, theological, and moral strands to produce an abstract, mathematically rigorous investigation that mimicked physics in uncovering empirical laws that operate with "iron necessity."[3] This evolution peaked in the present century, with the conversion of political economy into economics. In examining Smith, I hope to illuminate the relationships between economics and the older disciplines and to illustrate the ways in which *The Wealth of Nations* invited and facilitated the continued narrowing of political economy.[4]

Beyond his contributions to political economy, Smith was an adept psychologist and sociologist. He may consequently be considered as a founder of modern social science—whose development has been spearheaded by economics—and perhaps even as an architect of modern society.[5] Economics is the only social science for which Nobel Prizes are awarded; it is the most mathematical and positivistic of the social sciences; and it is the most heavily funded by government agencies such as the National Science Foundation. Economics and other social sciences, moreover, dominate society to an extent hardly imaginable two hundred years ago—for example, in public administration, teacher education, business schools, law schools, policy institutes, and think tanks. Economists are prominent in policy making, and the terminology of political debates borrows freely from economic concepts: trade-offs, productivity, efficiency, cost-benefit analysis, deficits, interest rates, inflation, indexing, bracket creep, tax loopholes, the balance of trade, and so on. Ronald Reagan invoked an economic construct—the "misery index"—to batter Jimmy Carter, and Bill Clinton used a broader array of "economic indicators" to defeat George Bush. The Gross National Product is regarded as a chief indicator of national well-being, despite the procedural muddles involved in calculating it and the dubiousness of identifying well-being with the annual value of "goods and services"—including cigarettes, alcohol, prisons, litigation costs, and pornography, and excluding any work that is unpaid.[6] Woe to the politician who presides over or condones a recession, i.e., a GNP that shrinks during two successive quarters.

In the years since World War II, the behaviorist revolution has fueled the attempt to apply economic techniques throughout the social sciences. Within political science, a field founded by economists—social-choice theory—has recently exploded in prominence. Even political philosophy is today infused with economic theory. Rawls's *A Theory of Justice*, a work hailed by many as a revival of political philosophy from its twentieth-century slumbers, turns crucially on such concepts as the "indifference curve," "chain connection," and Pareto optimality. Economists A. K. Sen, W. J. Baumol, and K. J. Arrow are each cited by Rawls more frequently than Plato, Machiavelli, Hobbes, Montesquieu, *The Federalist*, and Tocqueville combined. The only moral or political philosophy that Rawls considers seriously as an alternative is utilitarianism, another philosophy thoroughly blended with economics. Within jurisprudence, Richard Posner's "law and economics" school stands as the "conservative" equivalent to the neo-Marxist "critical legal studies" movement.

For many years, criticism of the independence of economics as a discipline came primarily from Marxists, "political economists" seeking to unmask the sinister relations of domination and exploitation that underlie the apparently scientific categories of mainstream (i.e., neoclassical) economics. Thus, Irving Kristol identifies the "effort to reestablish the premodern sovereignty of political, moral, and religious values over economic life" with radical economics.[7] Radical economists, however, are not interested in reviving premodern thought in general or premodern political philosophy in particular. As a rule, they ignore or reject Aristotle, whose architectonic political science treated acquisition as a means to "the good life" defined in terms of moral and intellectual virtue. One can say with even more confidence that they do not wish to reintroduce the soul and the otherworldly, to put sexual and religious liberty at risk, or to encourage elites (for example, the pious, the wise, or the wealthy) to claim a right to dominate society. Kristol's statement is also belied by the example of George Gilder, a leading "supply side" theorist, who tries to infuse economics with concern for God, the soul, courage, and sacrifice.

Criticism from the "conservative" wing of the economics profession—the Austrian school—laments the exclusion of the political from political economy even less than the mainstream does. Politically, it leans toward libertarianism; economically, it is averse even to macroeconomics (Kirzner, pp. 118–19).

The relationship between politics and economics in Smith has received much greater scholarly attention than his treatment of religion. The discrepancy is not difficult to explain. On the one hand, Smith's great book—*The Wealth of Nations*—is a work of political economy, not of philosophy or theology, and it devotes little explicit attention to religion. On the other hand, contemporary scholars are more interested in economics and politics than in religion, more passionate about "interests" than about salvation. As we will see, however, the ideas that made Smith famous are partially derived from his ideas about religion.

Although Smith is ultimately concerned with the question of "the whole" (Physics 9), it is notoriously difficult to understand Smith's corpus as a whole. If there has been a central theme to Smith scholarship, it is *"das Adam Smith Problem,"* a phrase employed by an earlier generation of German scholars to denote the glaring contradiction between the central themes of Smith's two books: self-interest in *The Wealth of Nations* and "sympathy" in *The Theory of Moral Sentiments*. Recent scholarship supposes that the two books can easily be rendered consistent.[8] Raphael and Macfie, the editors of the Oxford edition of *The Theory of Moral Sentiments*, put the matter strongly, labeling the *Problem* "a pseudo-problem based on ignorance and misunderstanding" (*TMS*, p. 20). The problem, however, needs to be reconsidered.

According to Albert Hirschman, Smith's exposition and defense of the free market "turned out to be riddled with so many intellectual puzzles that sorting and solving them occupied generations of economists" (p. 112). There are puzzles in other areas that have barely been recognized, let alone solved. We will explore a hitherto neglected series of contradictions regarding religious matters, especially the status of God, the soul, and the afterlife. I shall also try to shed new light on perhaps the central paradox: the desirability of "wealth and greatness," the ends of political economy. Contradictions exist within each of the two books as well as between them.

It is occasionally suggested that the paradoxes and contradictions reflect either carelessness or a change in opinion between the early (1759) *Theory of Moral Sentiments* and the late (1776) *Wealth of Nations*. Most scholars have shied away from such suggestions, with good reason. For one thing, both books were meticulously composed, edited, and revised through five or more editions in Smith's lifetime.[9] The penultimate edition of *The Theory of Moral Sentiments* was indeed published in 1790, the year of Smith's death, and fourteen years after *The Wealth of*

Nations; the revisions, though not insubstantial, indicate no reversals on major questions.

Smith's thinking, furthermore, is systematic and rigorous as a matter of principle. Smith presents his ideas as "systems" and stresses the kinship between systems and machines.[10] A machine is "a little system created to perform, as well as to connect together, in reality, those different movements and effects which the artist has occasion for"; a system is "an imaginary machine invented to connect together in the fancy those different movements and effects which are already in reality performed" (Astronomy IV.19). Although the wheels of a machine may turn in opposite directions,[11] it will not function unless its parts cohere. Philosophy, according to Smith, attempts to render nature coherent (II.12).[12]

How, then, can the paradoxes in Smith's writings be explained? Why have some of them escaped scholarly attention? These questions cannot be answered without reference to Smith's comprehensiveness, eclecticism, and rhetoric. Although some "parts" receive disproportionate attention, Smith's corpus does convey a view of "the whole"—of the cosmos and of humanity's place in it—and "the whole" is difficult to fathom.[13] Modern scholars, given their specialized training, are likely to find some of the subject matter Smith covers inaccessible. Smith is also remarkably eclectic. He incorporates physics blended from Descartes and Newton; metaphysics from Epicureans, Stoics, Deists, and Hobbes; philosophy of history from Montesquieu and Rousseau; moral psychology from Plato, Mandeville, Hutcheson, and Hume; rhetoric and moral virtues from Aristotle; epistemology from Berkeley and Hume; political doctrines from Locke, Montesquieu, and Hume; jurisprudence from Grotius, Pufendorf, and Hutcheson; economic theory from mercantilists and Physiocrats. Viner labels Smith "*the* great eclectic."[14]

Smith's pervasive employment of rhetoric also helps explain the paradoxes and their insufficient appreciation by scholars. Although the depiction of systems and machines would not require rhetoric, the persuasion of human beings may require it. There is no doubt that Smith acknowledges the potential discrepancy between what is true and what is persuasive: the truth may not always persuade, and what persuades may not always be true. In Winch's words, Smith was "a master of the art of equipoise" whose "rhetorical" and "didactic" aims are difficult to untangle.[15]

In a long footnote to one of his posthumously published essays, Smith ridicules the suggestion that Plato's writings contain "a double doctrine," that "they were intended to seem to mean one thing, while at bottom they meant a very different" thing. Smith says this is something "which the writings of no man in his senses ever were, or ever could be intended to do" (Logics 3). This remark prompts W. P. D. Wightman, the editor of the recent Oxford edition of Smith's essays, to introduce a footnote asserting that the "coexistence of esoteric and exoteric writings is pretty well attested among men far from being 'out of their senses' " (*EPS*, p. 122n9). None other than Karl Marx repeatedly alleges that Smith conveyed both "esoteric" and "exoteric" messages.[16] In one of the fuller statements, Marx says that Smith

> with much naivety, lives in a permanent contradiction. On the one hand he tracks down the inner relations of economic categories or the hidden structure of the bourgeois economic system. On the other hand, and close by, he sets down the apparent relations given in the manifestations of competition, as they appear to the unscientific observer or to any one interested and confined in the process of bourgeois production.[17]

For Marx, the exoteric Smith is the bourgeois ideologist and the esoteric Smith is the scientific critic who anticipates Marxian doctrines. Robert Paul Wolff, a philosopher with formidable skills as a mathematical economist, has argued that *Capital* itself is "a work of high literary art whose dominant metaphors, ironic structure, and authorial voice subserve a deliberate philosophical purpose"; irony is communication "that employs an utterance with a double meaning, to which correspond two audiences."[18]

Given Smith's ridicule of a Platonic "double doctrine," however, one should hesitate to suggest that Smith practiced esoteric writing; Smith certainly gives the impression of being a "man in his senses." Even if Smith does not convey two cleanly differentiated doctrines—esoteric and exoteric—his writing strategy is subtle and complex. Smith employs rhetoric on behalf of doctrines and practices that are salutary even though the doctrines may be false and the practices may have blemishes that he renders obscure but not invisible.[19] Smith himself argues that "no system, how well soever in other respects supported, has ever been able to gain any general credit on the world, whose connecting principles were not such as were familiar to all mankind" (Astronomy II.12). One is tempted to suggest that the cruder interpretations of Smith, and perhaps even certain intellectual "blinders" worn by subsequent economists, can be traced to the exoteric Smith; his esoteric doctrines would then be the complexities and qualifications that he quietly acknowledges, his tribute to the Socratic distinction between seeking wisdom and finding it. Many of the Smithian contradictions derive from the provocative vestiges, scattered through his writings, of traditional perspectives (both classical and Christian) that clash with his primary messages. The whole is greater than the sum of the parts.

The controversies about esotericism, however, cannot be resolved *a priori.* Assessing Smith's rhetoric requires careful attention to the form as well as the content of his writings, and the relevant texts will be incorporated in succeeding chapters to enable the reader to reach an informed judgment.

In his correspondence, Smith explicitly acknowledges, at least regarding certain religious matters, that one should be circumspect when writing for publication. In a letter to Smith, David Hume wrote of his *Dialogues Concerning Natural Religion* that "nothing can be more cautiously or artfully written." Despite the alleged caution, Smith strenuously opposed even the posthumous publication of these dialogues. As he wrote to William Strahan, the publisher, "Tho' finely written I could have wished [it] had remained in Manuscript to be communicated only to a few people."[20] A letter by Smith about Hume's death was published in *Scots Magazine* and later appended to Hume's brief autobiographical preface to *An Inquiry Concerning Human Understanding*. After describing the nobility of Hume's manner as he died, Smith praised him for "approaching as nearly to the idea of a perfectly wise and virtuous man, as perhaps the nature of human frailty will permit."[21] Such praise of a philosopher widely suspected of atheism was apparently inflammatory; Smith wrote later to Andreas Holt that this brief and "I thought . . . very harmless sheet" had brought him "ten times more abuse than the very violent attack I had made upon the whole commercial system of Great Britain" (#208, October 1780). If true, one may infer that Smith's other writings, insofar as they combat religion, combat it subtly; we will see that the atheism of *The Wealth of Nations* is uncompromising but unobtrusive. If Smith's professed caution regarding religion led him to address it with delicacy, we should not be surprised that scholarly interest in his treatment of religion has been minimal, and that the "Adam Smith Problem" has been uncovered almost exclusively in non-religious matters.[22]

Let me now sketch what will be conveyed in the pages that follow: a solution to the recast "Problem." Sympathy is indeed as prominent in *The Theory of Moral Sentiments* as self-interest is in *The Wealth of Nations*, but it is obvious that both books are animated by the project of harmonizing individual and society. The most profound difference between the two books is that the proposed reconciliation in *The Theory of Moral Sentiments* is steeped in religion. In *The Theory of Moral Sentiments*, God is almost omnipresent; in *The Wealth of Nations*, God is never mentioned. In the former, "Providence" is responsible for the original division of land; in the latter, holdings were "acquired or usurped." In the former, biblical and Christian teachings are briefly considered; in the latter, the Bible is ignored or trivialized. The former stresses the contributions that belief in an afterlife can make to morality, happiness, and dignity; the latter describes only a "debased" vision of the afterlife.

The most innovative feature of *The Wealth of Nations* is its providing a secular account of individual, society, and cosmos that tries to reorient humanity to a godless universe. In place of a moral philosophy that remains dependent on God and the afterlife, it consolidates a new science of the past, present, and future that blends human hopes and fears in such a way as to obviate the need for divine support. The book's psychological foundation is the individual's ceaseless desire to "better his condition," a desire caused by his never being "perfectly and completely satisfied with his situation" (*WN* II.iii.28). Despite this alleged dissatisfaction, Smith tries to impart a quasi-Stoic resignation to the ills of this world without acknowledging any prospect for a better life in heaven. The difficulties inherent in this project provide an opening for Marx's revolutionary critique of bourgeois economics and the bourgeois world.

In the absence of a more systematic exposition of the immense literature on Smith, I shall briefly situate my approach with reference to two excellent and influential studies that take opposing views about Smith's belittlement of politics and that represent two poles of interpretive approach, textual and historical. Despite (or perhaps because of) their hermeneutical commitments, neither pays adequate attention to Smith's stance regarding the horizons within which thought is embedded, a stance that will be scrutinized in the chapters that follow.

Joseph Cropsey's *Polity and Economy* (1957) broke new ground in analyzing Smith's place in the philosophic tradition, especially his debt to Hobbes. The book concludes by suggesting that Smith's defense of capitalism cannot be fathomed without regard to his views on religion, but pays scant attention to most of Smith's discussions of religion. In this work and in two later articles, Cropsey also sketches Smith's contribution to "the deflection of political philosophy toward economics,"[23] adding powerful suggestions about the philosophical "fissure" that separates Smith and Marx. Cropsey's book, however, is insufficiently attentive to Smith's rhetoric. For example, the first chapter is entitled "The General Foundations of Smith's System," but the book never considers why Smith neither began by presenting these foundations nor proceeded to elaborate them fully. The last chapter, "The Problem of Smith's Intention," ignores Smith's remarks about intention in general and his own in particular.

Donald Winch, in *Adam Smith's Politics: An Essay in Historiographic Revision* (1978), attempts to rescue Smith from interpreters—Cropsey along with Robert Cumming, William Grampp, and Sheldon

Wolin—who view Smith primarily from "the liberal capitalist perspective" and thereby transport his teachings about politics into a context alien to the eighteenth century. Drawing on the contextualist methodology pioneered by Quentin Skinner and John Pocock, Winch tries to provide a genuinely historical understanding of Smith.[24] Winch is especially critical of the view that *The Wealth of Nations* represents the "eclipse" of politics by economics, "an episode . . . along a road which runs from Locke to Marx."[25] Winch, by examining Smith's views on some salient political controversies in eighteenth-century Britain—standing armies, the public debt, the American Revolution—concludes that "Smith has a 'politics' which is far from being trivial" (*Smith's Politics*, p. 23). Winch's careful attention to the wording of Smith's texts and to the immediate historical context requires the "deflection" thesis to be reformulated—but not discarded. Winch's approach will help neutralize the impulse to distort Smith for partisan purposes (p. 183), but it may sacrifice the forest to save the trees. Without fathoming Smith's contribution to the deflection, one cannot adequately adjudicate the disputes between Smith and Marx, for what is most inadequate in Marx—the reduction of philosophy to the analysis of history's "line of march" or "economic law of motion"—is anticipated but not consummated by Smith.

Winch uncovers much carelessness in the Smith literature, but Winch too has to rely on presuppositions that are far from evident. One cannot fault Winch for attempting to recover "what Smith can legitimately be said to have intended, rather than . . . what he might be said to have anticipated or foreshadowed" (p. 1). But when Winch asserts that *The Wealth of Nations* is "quintessentially a work of the eighteenth century" (pp. 2, 165), he seems to overlook what Smith "intended" by titling his works, and describing their respective subjects, in ways that point well beyond the confines of the eighteenth century. In articulating "*the* theory of moral sentiments," furthermore, Smith compares, judges, and synthesizes more than a dozen representatives of a two-thousand-year tradition. Smith acknowledges circumstances that are "necessary and therefore always the same" in addition to those that are "transitory, occasional, or accidental" (*WN* V.ii.c.6). And despite his numerous and profound acknowledgments of historical change, including its impact on the development of moral sentiments and scientific theories, Smith speaks freely about the experiences of "all ages."[26] It is not easy to specify an era to which Smith's thought "quintessentially" belongs.

Winch stumbles into an epistemological no-man's-land, moreover, when he reformulates his purpose as elucidating "what it would be conceivable for Smith, or someone fairly like him, to maintain, rather than what later generations would like him to have maintained" (*Smith's Politics*, 5). The historical approach here seems to be a thoroughly philosophical one: what kind of knowledge is necessary to determine what it was "conceivable" for Smith to maintain? Worse still, how can we determine what someone "fairly like him" might have thought? In a later article, Winch suggests the appropriateness of working "initially, from text to context, rather than vice versa" ("Smith's 'enduring particular result,' " p. 269), and the chapters that follow will place Smith's texts in the limelight.

I shall emphasize the texts Smith intended to convey to posterity—his published works, especially the two books, and his posthumously published *Essays on Philosophical Subjects*.[27] These texts alone (along with a few letters) have come down to us as written in his own hand. Notorious for his concern with privacy, Smith, with great forethought and determination, arranged to have all his unpublished papers (save the aforementioned philosophical essays) burned before his death.[28] Student lecture notes for Smith's lectures at Glasgow University on jurisprudence (two versions) and rhetoric were subsequently discovered and are now available as part of the Oxford edition of Smith's works. I shall not draw heavily on the lectures, for several reasons. First, insofar as one is interested in the ideological reorientations Smith intended to promote, one should have recourse primarily to writings he intended others to read. Historically, these lectures have had nothing resembling the influence of the published writings. The jurisprudence volume edited by Edwin Cannan (*LJB*) was not published until 1896; the longer version (*LJA*) was published only in 1978; the rhetoric lectures were first published in 1963. Second, resort to the lectures may desensitize the reader to the complexity and subtlety of the published writings. The lectures provide clues to the missing pieces of Smith's account of the "whole," but there are many such clues in Smith's writings.[29] Third, contemporary scholars interested in Smith's politics have paid close attention to the jurisprudence lectures.[30] With adequate attention given to Smith's writings, the lectures are of course a valuable supplement.

Interest in Adam Smith among scholars with a more partisan bent has also been on the upsurge, but they run into some of the same difficulties as Cropsey and Winch. Michael Novak, in *The Spirit of Democratic Capitalism*, stresses the compatibility of Christianity and capitalism. Whatever the merits of his criticisms of Marxism and liberation theology, Novak's projection of a wholehearted alliance of Smith, capitalism, and Christianity cannot withstand a careful examination of Smith's writings. Irving Kristol's "Adam Smith and the Spirit of Capitalism" does a better job of grasping Smith's "melioristic" spirit and the clash between

Smith's two books, but underestimates the degree to which Smith saw economics as "a substitute for moral and political philosophy" (*Reflections*, pp. 158, 173). Robert Heilbroner, finally, has provided many shrewd observations about Smith and the obfuscating "veil" of economic ideology, but he is more a prisoner of that ideology—especially its Marxist variant—than he realizes.

The first half of this book will address the issue that divides Cropsey and Winch: Smith's "deflection of political philosophy toward economics." The word "deflection" is most appropriate, for it is clear that neither politics nor political philosophy disappears in Smith. "Deflection" likewise implies a departure from previous theorists. When contrasted with ancient and medieval philosophers, many modern thinkers may seem to elevate economics and demote politics; but Smith's departure is more radical than that of Machiavelli, Bacon, Grotius, Hobbes, Pufendorf, Locke, Montesquieu, Hutcheson, Hume, and Rousseau.[31] Many features of the Smithian deflection are consummated by philosophers like Bentham and economists like Ricardo. The remaining features are consummated by that great critic of Bentham and Ricardo, Karl Marx.

The most obvious dimension of the deflection is the tendency, prominent in many modern theories of society, to use economic ends such as wealth, security, and bodily comfort to define the identity and the purposes of human association. Among the "political" alternatives, one might include virtue (especially courage and liberality), solidarity, nobility, independence, glory, empire, and what Smith calls "heroic spirit" (*LJB* 333).[32] Smith radicalizes the tendency first by taking the primacy of the economic ends more or less for granted (rather than arguing on their behalf) and second by inaugurating a sophisticated new science devoted to their procurement. Chapter 2 begins with a systematic exploration of Smith's exaltation of the economic ends. The bulk of the chapter examines Smith's treatment (or non-treatment) of forms of government and his coolness toward the republican ideal of civic participation.

The theme of Chapter 3 is justice. Smith's account of justice in *The Wealth of Nations* treats government largely as a means of protecting property, and involves a quasi-materialistic philosophy of history that obviates both the need and the possibility of normative inquiry. Smith's account of the "circumstances which naturally introduce subordination" replaces the concern of the ancients to evaluate the merits of competing claims to rule and the concern of the social-contract theorists to specify formal conditions of legitimacy. His historical account of the "administration of justice" replaces Thomistic natural law and modern natural right along with ancient attempts to derive justice from a philosophical dialectic. In *The Theory of Moral Sentiments*, Smith also links justice with equality, self-interest, and a Lockean view of the ends of government. Instead of employing philosophy to justify or defend such an account, however, Smith employs social psychology and "natural jurisprudence" to explain its popularity.[33]

Chapter 4 explores Smith's complex analysis of human psychology. Smith emphasizes economic longings at the expense of political longings—the desire for comfort, ease, security, and wealth rather than for ruling, self-sufficiency, and glory. Although he acknowledges the power of these political impulses, he subtly attempts to encourage the economic; for example, he subordinates the longing for "honor" and "superiority" partly by converting it into the longing for esteem. In explaining such crucial phenomena as exchange value, the division of labor, and the commercial "disposition," however, Smith portrays a human nature characterized by a complex interplay of impulses. Bourgeois virtue nevertheless becomes the ideal for human character, in opposition to the "passion for present enjoyment," grasping ambition, love, contemplation, Epicurean asceticism, and Stoic resignation.

Chapter 5 addresses the international ramifications of *homo economicus* and of Smith's political economy as a whole. In critiquing mercantilism, Smith encourages international trade rather than national self-sufficiency, commerce rather than war and empire. Citizenship recedes and cosmopolitanism grows. Smith occasionally speaks of these tendencies as a chronicler rather than an advocate, however, and his advocacy is balanced by vestiges of older views. He also concedes that the liberty and the individualism conducive to economic progress must occasionally yield to military necessities. Socioeconomic progress, moreover, though it renders "civilized" societies secure from "barbarian" invasion, necessitates the increasing diversion of resources to military applications, and introduces weapons of increasing destructiveness.

Chapter 6, "The Invisible Hand," provides an introduction to Smith's theology and its relevance for politics, history, psychology, and economics. Though famous as an economic concept, the "invisible hand" was first employed by Smith in theological contexts that laid the groundwork for a secular explanation of religion. Smith's discussion of the invisible hand in *The Theory of Moral Sentiments*, moreover, occasions the criticisms of "wealth and greatness" that point to the heart of the "Adam Smith Problem." In all of its contexts, the invisible hand mediates between the individual and the whole, social and cosmic. Smith raises and quietly answers questions regarding the purposes and procedures of the invisible phenomena that guide human beings. Contrary to the popular impression, however, the invisible hand ultimately serves to denigrate the individual and to exalt the species.

The next two chapters examine Smith's treatment of religion in *The*

Wealth of Nations. Chapter 7 shows that Smith quietly but unequivocally rejects the central tenets of Christianity: God, the soul, the Messiah, the afterlife, revelation, and the Bible. His use of key religious terms (for example, "piety" and "the sacred") serves either to corrupt them by appropriating them as economic categories or to ridicule the Church's claim to embody them. *The Wealth of Nations* provides an overview of the history of Western civilization that excludes not only divine contributions but even the secular equivalents of phenomena such as prophecy and dogma. Smith thus effaces the historical contributions of philosophers as well as prophets (especially Jesus). Chapter 8 explores the theological-political nexus suggested by Smith's thematic investigation of religion in Book V. Smith's discussion here of religious "establishment" and persecution incorporates his most comprehensive analysis of authority. Smith denounces the medieval Church as "the most formidable combination that was ever formed . . . against the liberty, reason, and happiness of mankind" (*WN* V.i.g.24), but he explains both the problem and the solution in economic terms (subsistence, self-interest, and management). Though Smith praises certain presbyterian clergy, his analysis of the Reformation confirms that he rejects Christian theology as a whole, not just Catholicism. The atheism of *The Wealth of Nations* runs so deep that Smith abandons even civil religion—dogmas and ceremonies recommended for their social utility.

The final chapters on Smith examine *The Theory of Moral Sentiments*, where religion is treated more sympathetically. Chapter 9 shows that the book abandons the biblical God for the deist God and disparages the central moral precepts of Jesus. The ambiguities in Smith's account of the purposes of the deist God, furthermore, push the book toward atheism. The chapter concludes by examining Smith's account of the afterlife, which is praised for its contribution to human happiness and morality; Smith concedes the utility of certain doctrines of the afterlife, but not their truth. Chapter 10 argues that Smith's examination of the "mechanism within" that generates moral judgments serves both to explain and to replace revealed religion. Smith's "natural jurisprudence" likewise illustrates his erasure of divine law, and the "impartial spectator" serves as a substitute for God and priest: Smith depicts a morality based on human rather than divine approval. The chapter concludes by exploring Smith's complex account of virtues and vices (especially benevolence and pride), to clarify his posture toward Christianity and antiquity.

The final chapter examines the withering of religion and politics in the thought of Karl Marx, and speculates about capitalism and communism at the "end of history."

CHAPTER TWO

The Ends and Forms of Government

Economic Ends: Subsistence and Prosperity

Smith identifies the form of inquiry embodied in *The Wealth of Nations* as the science of "political oeconomy," a branch of "the system of civil government" (*WN* IV.ix.38) and of "the science of a statesman or legislator."[1] Political economy is thus subordinate to politics, at least formally. Unlike political philosophy, however, political economy is not a vehicle for deliberating about the proper ends of politics. Smith's presentation of political economy suggests that it takes certain ends as given: "The great object of the political oeconomy of every country, is to encrease the riches and power of that country" (II.v.31). Smith criticizes the different systems of political economy, both mercantile and agricultural, because they fail to further "the great purpose" they "mean to promote"—leading society "towards real wealth and greatness" (IV.ix.50). Nowhere does Smith comprehensively evaluate the status of "wealth and greatness" as the ends of public life. By emphasizing the "causes" of wealth rather than its "nature," Smith further mutes the question of its desirability.

Subsistence and prosperity dominate the horizons of *The Wealth of Nations*, though not always conspicuously. The book abounds with references to "commodities" and to the produce of society's land and labor, and its title mentions neither greatness nor power. The definition that begins the discussion of "systems of political oeconomy" in Book IV presents the political as the means to the economic: "considered as a branch of the science of a statesman or legislator," political economy aims to promote revenue and subsistence, to "enrich" the people and the sovereign (IV.Intro.1). Smith defines wealth or riches as "necessaries, conveniencies, and amusements" (I.v.1), and the first sentence of the work addresses the procurement of "the necessaries and conveniencies of life"; Smith later specifies "subsistence and conveniencies" as food, clothing, and lodging.[2] Even in *The Theory of Moral Sentiments*, Smith, in alluding to the "advantages the subjects of a well-governed state enjoy," says only that such subjects are better lodged, clothed, and fed (*TMS* IV.1.11).

The amount of textual attention Smith devotes to various subjects is itself quite suggestive. The longest chapter of *The Wealth of Nations* is the eleventh chapter of Book I, "Of the Rent of Land." A major focus of this chapter is food, "the first of all necessaries" (I.xi.g.28, IV.v.a.8), "the principal part of the riches of the world" (I.xi.c.36). This chapter includes a notoriously long digression, "Variations in the Value of Silver." The length of this digression contrasts strikingly with the brevity of Smith's examination in the second chapter of "the propensity to truck, barter, and exchange"—the propensity that "gives occasion to" the division of labor. Smith hints that this propensity is a "necessary consequence of the faculties of reason and speech" rather than one of human nature's "original principles." But because this question "belongs not to our present subject," Smith excludes it from further consideration (I.ii.1,2). The disparity between Smith's exploration of human nature and his exploration of the value of silver distinguishes *The Wealth of Nations* from other books that have achieved worldwide fame for their philosophical reflections on human society.

Smith's manner of presentation is similarly suggestive in the famous paragraph elaborating "the desire of bettering our condition," arguably the psychological linchpin of the whole book. Between womb and tomb, Smith writes,

> there is scarce perhaps a single instant in which any man is so perfectly and completely satisfied with his situation, as to be without any wish of alteration or improvement, of any kind. An augmentation of fortune is the means by which the greater part of men propose and wish to better their condition. It is the means the most vulgar and the most obvious. (*WN* II.iii.28)

About the pursuit of wealth as a means of bettering one's condition, Smith says only that it is the most "vulgar" and "obvious" means. The wording suggests the existence of less vulgar and obvious notions of human betterment, but Smith does not identify them.[3] The science of political economy moves within the horizon of the vulgar interpretation.

Smith's system of natural liberty is "the obvious and simple system"; the duties of the sovereign under it, spelled out in Book V, are "plain and intelligible to common understandings" (IV.ix.51). If social goals were more exalted, governmental responsibilities might be "plain and intelligible" only to uncommon minds.

The casual eclipse of other human ends by prosperity takes myriad forms in *The Wealth of Nations*. Smith identifies the "greatest of all improvements" as the development of roads, canals, and navigable rivers; the "greatest of all publick advantages" is "the compleat improvement and cultivation of the country" (I.xi.b.5, I.xi.l.12); a "great society" is one with a large population (I.viii.57). Smith's perspective is economic when describing bad things as well as good things. Bankruptcy is "perhaps the greatest and most humiliating calamity which can befall an innocent man" (II.iii.29); the North American colonial governments that instituted paper currencies whose payment was not exigible for a period of several years committed "an act of such violent injustice, as has scarce, perhaps, been attempted by the government of any other country which pretended to be free" (II.ii.100). Almost without exception, Smith in *The Wealth of Nations* employs such rhetoric only to impart the seriousness and splendor generally associated with religion and politics to economic phenomena.[4]

The only reference in Smith's writings to "natural law" is in an economic context: in criticizing primogeniture, Smith invokes "the natural law of succession" (adopted by the Romans), which divides an inheritance equally among a family's children. Although this natural law tends to prevail when property is "considered as the means only of subsistence and enjoyment," Smith concedes that primogeniture made sense during precarious times when land was "considered as the means, not of subsistence merely, but of power and protection" (the feudal landlord was "a sort of petty prince"). Primogeniture, in conjunction with entails, operated as a major retardant to economic progress; although primogeniture clashes with the "interest" even of noble families, their "pride" has prevented its disappearance (III.ii.3–7). Natural law thus stands, with "subsistence," "enjoyment," "interest," equality, and economic progress, in tension with pride—the preeminently political passion—and the feudal fusion of politics and economics whereby land was the means to "power and protection."[5]

Virtue and Progress

The above sketch hardly exhausts the examples that reveal the more or less surreptitious triumph of the "economic" outlook. The triumph of this outlook, however, coexists with numerous instances of its eclipse by more traditional notions. This paradox could be encompassed by the "Adam Smith Problem," with the proviso that the tension between outlooks is present within *The Wealth of Nations* itself, and even within *The Theory of Moral Sentiments*.

The Wealth of Nations incorporates material way beyond the purview of contemporary economics, not to say contemporary social science as a whole: the "essential . . . character of human nature," the appropriateness of the tripartite division of ancient Greek philosophy, the contrast between ancient and modern battle, the rise and fall of the medieval Church, and the fate of the "intellectual, social, and martial virtues." These subjects, however, are addressed only in the final book of *The Wealth of Nations*, a book whose title—"Of the Revenue of the Sovereign or Commonwealth"—is forthrightly pecuniary. Smith whets his readers' appetite for these subjects with the prosaic conclusion of Book IV: the proper performance of the "several duties of the sovereign necessarily supposes a certain expence; and this expence again necessarily requires a certain revenue to support it." The first chapter of Book V will explain

> what are the necessary expences of the sovereign or common-wealth; and which of those expences ought to be defrayed by the general contribution of the whole society; and which of them, by that of some particular part only, or of some particular members of the society. (*WN* IV.ix.52)

This chapter nevertheless conveys an almost Aristotelian concern for human perfection. In elaborating the duties of the sovereign regarding education, Smith states that preventing the spread of the "mental mutilation, deformity, and wretchedness" entailed by cowardice deserves "the most serious attention of government," even apart from the consequences for societal defense (V.i.f.60). In the succeeding paragraph, Smith makes the same claim about "gross ignorance and stupidity":

> A man, without the proper use of the intellectual faculties of a man, is, if possible, more contemptible than even a coward, and seems to be mutilated and deformed in a still more essential part of the character of human nature. (*WN* V.i.f.61)

Such a concern with the "essential" character of human nature is alien to contemporary economics and political science, and limits the kinship of Smith's thought with the liberalism of Locke, Bentham, Kant, Rawls, Nozick, and even J. S. Mill. By identifying virtue as an end rather than a means, Smith departs even from the "civic humanists" inspired by Machiavelli. But *The Wealth of Nations* as a whole serves to efface the possible obligation of government to promote human perfection. The above passages may therefore be conceived as a vestigial Aristotelian check on the lower limits of character deformation. Smith recommends that government try to prevent gross cowardice and stupidity; he says nothing about promoting the peaks of courage and intelligence.[6]

These Aristotelian lamentations come at the very conclusion of the section on education, capping Smith's famous portrayal of the debilitating effects of the division of labor (in a commercial society) on the intellectual, social, and martial virtues—"all the nobler parts of the human character"—of the "great body" of the people (*WN* V.i.f.49–51). He proceeds to indicate how the government may "facilitate," "encourage," and "even impose" the acquisition of basic skills in reading, writing, and arithmetic: parish schools emphasizing geometry and mechanics rather than Latin; prizes for children who excel; examination as a prerequisite for entering a corporation or a trade (V.i.f.54–57). This program is clearly in the spirit of a Lockean rather than Aristotelian regime. As if to emphasize the contrast with antiquity, Smith then illustrates how the Greek and Roman republics promoted "martial spirit" by a similar combination of facilitating, encouraging, and "even . . . imposing" their military and gymnastic exercises (V.i.f.58). The discussion of character and virtue appears as a digression illuminating the martial superiority of the ancients.[7] Although conceding the efficacy of ancient gymnastic education, Smith goes out of his way (challenging "the very respectable authority" of Plato, Aristotle, Polybius, and Montesquieu) to disparage the efficacy of education in "music": despite their musical training, the Greeks had morals inferior to those of the Romans, who lacked musical education (V.i.f.39–40).[8] To explain the superiority of Roman morals in "private life," Smith ultimately invokes the structure of their court system (f.44). It seems that "social and moral duties" (f.39)—but not military duties—are promoted indirectly, without pedagogy.

It is difficult to assess Smith's sympathy for the Aristotelian vision that government should cultivate moral virtue because he addresses such matters (in *The Wealth of Nations*) more as a historian than as a philosopher. As a historian, furthermore, he combines an abstract theory of social development—the so-called four-stages theory—with recapitulations of actual history. Smith seems to treat the development of human society through hunting/fishing, herding (pasturage), agriculture, and commerce (trade and manufacturing) as a "natural progress" to opulence, "improvement," and "civilization."[9] The decay of civic virtue entailed by the division of labor is thus a noxious side effect of the *natural* path of social development.[10]

There are other puzzles about the four-stages theory. It is difficult to determine the status of ancient Greece and Rome at their peaks: they might seem to be civilized but not commercial. In a "commercial society," Smith tells us, "every man . . . lives by exchanging, or becomes in some measure a merchant" (I.iv.1). This was not the case in Greece and Rome, and the "great body" of the people was not debilitated by the division of labor. Smith intimates at least one reason for this anomaly: slavery. Citizens of the ancient republics were discouraged from engaging in manufacturing and foreign trade, which were either prohibited or carried on by slaves (IV.ix.47). Feudal society too was built on a type of enslavement that continued in Russia and eastern Europe (III.ii.8). The commercial civilization of western Europe, however, was marred by a phenomenon comparable to slavery: the common people being burdened by a labor "so constant and so severe, that it leaves them little leisure and less inclination to apply to, or even to think of any thing else" (V.i.f.53).[11] Perhaps compensating for the vestige of slavery in modern civilization is the "universal opulence" (I.i.10) that emerges where the mass of people have the opportunity and therefore the incentive to "better their condition" by inventiveness and sheer effort (II.iii.28, IV.ix.47, III.ii.9).

Pinning Smith down on these matters is difficult for several reasons: he does not systematically articulate the four-stages theory; he nowhere (even in the lectures) supplies a comprehensive evaluation of the different stages; he portrays the developmental path with an air of inevitability; he says little about the agricultural phase, which might seem to be an attractive mean between the desperate poverty of a hunting society—which in effect enslaves people to the grim struggle for survival—and a capitalistic frenzy. Although men in each of the first three stages are both warriors and statesmen, and engage in varied occupations that keep the mind active, they lack "that improved and refined understanding" possible in a civilized stage (V.i.f.51). All of the stages seem flawed, and one is left with the economist's task of contemplating trade-offs. As shall be demonstrated in Chapter 5, the development of civilization is also accompanied by a tragic military dialectic. Unlike Marx, Smith does not predict an end to fundamental "contradictions," and leaves them as food for his more philosophical readers.

Forms of Government

> The great question which in all Ages has disturbed Mankind, and brought on them the greatest part of those Mischiefs which have ruined cities, depopulated countries, and disorder'd the Peace of the World, has been, not whether there be Power in the world, nor whence it came, but who should have it. . . . If this remains disputable, all the rest will be to very little purpose.   —Locke, *First Treatise of Government*

Classical political philosophy, according to Leo Strauss, was the quest for the best regime (*politeia*), regime being "the order, the form, which gives society its character," a specific way of life that "depends decisively on the predominance of human beings of a certain type."[12] Central to the classical enterprise were the depiction, analysis, and ranking of different forms of government: for example, monarchy, aristocracy, democracy, oligarchy, and their variants. The whole question becomes less important beginning with Machiavelli, who explicitly narrows the classical typology.[13] This tendency in modern political philosophy peaks with Marx, who understands politics as superstructure and who predicts the coming of a stateless world society where the administration of things will replace "political rule over men."[14] Unlike Marx, Smith treats the political realm as permanent. None of Smith's writings, however, endorse a ruling class or extol a particular set of political institutions; none of them directly evaluate or even categorize the different forms of government. Smith anticipates, but does not consummate, the Marxian endeavor to replace the quest for the best regime by a philosophy of history emphasizing the mode of production or subsistence.

The modern philosophers who de-emphasized the regime may have had various objectives in view: to augment individual liberty by separating state and society, to promote less exalted but more attainable ends for politics, to combat war and faction, to discourage the pretensions of elites (for example, "gentlemen" and priests) claiming a title to rule, or to de-emphasize the variety of social ends and the possibilities for choice among them. Although Hobbes and Locke both posit modest ends that oblige all governments, Locke devotes still less space to analyzing and evaluating the different forms of government. Montesquieu, like Smith, smiles upon commerce and looks to history and geography rather than to the formalisms of the social contract, but *The Spirit of the Laws* is dominated (especially in the early books) by the comparison of regimes.[15] Even Hutcheson, Hume, and Ferguson compare and evaluate forms of government.[16] Unlike *The Wealth of Nations*, Sir James Steuart's *An Inquiry into the Principles of Political Oeconomy* (1767) features a chapter investigating the effect of "forms of government" on commerce (p. 211) and begins with a chapter entitled "The Government of Mankind."

In *The Wealth of Nations*, Smith never presents a typology of regimes, much less an evaluation of the different forms of government. In his jurisprudence lectures, Smith does distinguish monarchy, aristocracy, and democracy as the "three generall classes, or distinct forms" of government, defined by the locus of the sovereign's powers—legislative, judicial, and federative/executive (*LJA* iv.1–3). Only once in *The Wealth of Nations*, however, does Smith ever refer to the three types together. Not surprisingly, the focus is pecuniary: he examines the suitability of each type for deriving revenue from mercantile projects (*WN* V.ii.a.4). Only once does Smith frame his policy recommendations with an eye to differences necessitated by variations in the "form of government"—in the final Part of Book V, chapter 1, "Of the Expence of supporting the Dignity of the Sovereign."[17] This discussion occupies half a page; the first three Parts occupy over 120 pages. May we infer a demotion of the dignity of the sovereign and therewith of politics?

As is typical of Smith, the innovations that pervade the bulk of his work are contradicted by the vestigial remarks—or "danglers"—that embody a more traditional perspective.[18] Smith's abandonment of the quest for the best regime coexists with remarks that suggest its traditional primacy. Thus, his suggestion that the "nature" of its government "forms the character of every nation" (*WN* IV.vii.b.52) evokes the primacy accorded by Plato and Aristotle to the regime.[19] Smith's passing reference to "the ideal republick described in the laws of Plato" (III.ii.9) makes one wonder why Smith does not speculate about the best regime; his reference to "the study of politics,—of the several systems of civil government, their advantages and disadvantages" (*TMS* IV.1.11) makes one wonder why he did not undertake to compare the various forms of government.

Political Constraint Versus Natural Liberty

Smith's system of natural liberty is notorious for constricting the sphere in which government may direct the activities of individuals, especially economic activities. *The Wealth of Nations* is a critique of mercantilism, whose "essence" is "restraint and regulation" (IV.ix.3), and the essence of government seems to be its capacity for compelling its subjects "to act according to some certain plan or system" (III.iii.8). Smith thus stresses that large-scale plans or projects are difficult to execute and are generally unnecessary; the economy constitutes a more or less independent "system."[20] The concluding paragraph of Smith's first chapter, "Of the Division of Labour," articulates the stunning complexity of the activities necessary to provide the commodities routinely enjoyed by even an ordinary laborer (I.i.11). The second chapter begins by arguing that the division of labor "is not originally the effect of any human wisdom, which foresees and intends that general opulence to which it gives occasion" (I.ii.1). The chief task of *The Wealth of Nations*, however, is demonstrating that the social complexity necessary for advancing opulence occurs without individuals attempting to "superintend" or direct the economy as a whole. Smith shows us that nature's wisdom, "the system of natural liberty," benefits the human species by properly unleashing the human individual's wisdom in pursuing self-interest. Smith seems to exclude the classical vision of a part of society aspiring to shape the whole of society.

Nature, which Smith generally identifies with the way things operate "of their own accord," appears frequently within *The Wealth of Nations* as an authority that constrains or preempts human deliberation and choice. Book I is entitled "Of the Causes of Improvement in the productive Powers of Labour, and of the Order according to which its Produce is *naturally* distributed among the different Ranks of the People." It is easy to overlook the gravity of the assumption that wealth is distributed by nature rather than by human decision.[21] That assumption is challenged by Aristotle (who in this respect is less teleological than Smith) as well as Marx. Smith goes so far as to describe money as a means by which "every individual in the society has his subsistence, conveniencies, and amusements, regularly distributed to him in their proper proportions" (II.ii.13).[22] The core of Smith's economic analysis is his investigation of "the rules which men naturally observe" in exchanging commodities (I.iv.12). It is unclear whether these rules operate with the "iron necessity" and detailed predictability of the economic laws described by Say, Malthus, Ricardo, and Marx.[23]

If the natural economic patterns were fully self-actualizing, of course, there would be no need for Smith to extol them, and the system of natural liberty would have been widely in place. Nature's system of political economy partakes of the ambiguity that surrounds Smith's account of the "natural progress of opulence," "natural" levels of wages, prices, profits, and rents, and the "natural balance of employments."[24] The natural state of affairs is not merely the desirable state of affairs, but it is less than a "necessary" state of affairs.[25] For all the methodological sophistication of contemporary economics, the same ambivalence characterizes its notions of the free market and "perfect competition."

There remains, therefore, a substantial role for government.[26] Economic progress has political preconditions: during the feudal era, for example, the natural progress of opulence was retarded because of the absence of "order and good government" and the "liberty and security of individuals" (*WN* III.iii.12). Opulence requires and Smith extols the government's "securing to every man the fruits of his own industry" (IV.vii.c.54).[27] While Smith thus stresses equal security for the fruits of labor, he is indifferent to the liberal version of equality according to which all must consent to government, not to say the Rousseauean version according to which all must participate in ongoing legislation. Smith bandies about the terms "sovereign" and "sovereignty" as if no possible question could be raised about who is or should be sovereign in human society. In effect, Smith reduces sovereignty to the actual locus of societal authority.[28]

Republicanism

In the lectures, Smith labels aristocracy and democracy as republican forms of government (*LJA* iv.1–3). In *The Wealth of Nations*, Smith uses the term "republican" without defining it. Smith does, however, seem to specify characteristics of the American colonies that render their "manners" and governments "more republican" than those of Britain: they enjoy the liberty (except regarding foreign trade) "to manage their own affairs their own way"; this liberty is secured (as in Britain) by a representative assembly, possessing sole prerogative to tax, which prevents abuses from the executive; their assemblies are perhaps more "influenced by the inclinations of their constituents"; there is no hereditary nobility; there is more equality (IV.vii.b.51). This depiction is empirical rather than formal, and it does not raise, let alone answer, the question of the general desirability of republican versus non-republican government. The context, furthermore, is economic: Smith is trying to explain the economic success of the British colonies compared with the colonies of Spain, Portugal, and France, whose "absolute governments" reproduce the governments of the mother countries.[29] The particular problem is the abuse of the discretionary powers delegated by absolute governments to their subordinate officials, especially in the provinces. Unlike such subordinates, the sovereign "can never have either interest or inclination to pervert the order of justice, or to oppress the great body of the people" (IV.vii.c.52). Smith explains later that "even a bad sovereign . . . knows that the permanent grandeur of his family depends upon the prosperity of his people, and he will never knowingly ruin that prosperity for the sake of any momentary interest of his own" (V.ii.k.74). Perhaps Smith speaks here with a touch of irony, intending to exhort more than to depict, but no republican could be so complacent about monarchy.

Some scholars nevertheless attribute to Smith an endorsement of republicanism (especially in its British form).[30] They have perhaps been inspired by a remark of the Earl of Buchan, described by John Rae as Smith's "pupil and lifelong friend":

> He [Smith] approached to republicanism in his political principles, and considered a commonwealth as the platform for the monarchy, hereditary succession in the chief magistrate being necessary only to prevent the commonwealth from being shaken by ambition or absolute dominion introduced by the consequences of contending factions. (Rae, p. 124)

No such endorsement is present in Smith's writings, though the lectures contain a detailed and sympathetic analysis of English political institutions (*LJA* v.5–31): "Here is a happy mixture of all the different forms of government properly restrained and a perfect security to liberty and property" (*LJB* 63).

Alone among the thinkers commented upon by Smith, Rousseau is treated as a partisan of republicanism. In 1755, Smith anonymously published a letter in the *Edinburgh Review* discussing, among other things, Rousseau's *Second Discourse*. Smith suggests that the book exhibits "the true spirit of a republican carried a little too far" (Letter 12). Rousseau's *Social Contract* was first published in 1762, three years after *The Theory of Moral Sentiments* and fourteen years before *The Wealth of Nations*. We do not know if Smith read it, but its spirit clashes profoundly with that of Smith's writings, compared to which it is brimming with political philosophy. The question of legitimacy that dominates Rousseau's book is not raised in any of Smith's writings. Smith ignores most of the book's central concerns: the social contract, the evaluation of different regimes, the desirability of small societies, the emphasis on *moeurs* and therewith on the "censor," the looming figure of the lawgiver, the necessity of civil religion, the contemptibility of finance and the bourgeoisie. Rousseau's vision of "moral freedom"—living only under a law that you give to yourself—must not be confused with Smith's praise of the liberty possessed by colonists "to manage their own affairs their own way": Smith praises this liberty for its contribution to rapid economic progress (*WN* IV.vii.b.4,51). And whereas Rousseau exalts independence and self-sufficiency, especially with respect to "commodities" and "consideration,"[31] Smith exalts dependence on others for both commodities and consideration (the morality of *The Theory of Moral Sentiments* is built on the quest for esteem). Although Smith in the letter shows some sympathy for Rousseau, and absorbs much of the *Second Discourse* into his own writings,[32] Rousseau is never mentioned or alluded to in either of Smith's books.[33] Smith and Rousseau were contemporaries who, despite a shared philosophical background and large areas of agreement, set philosophy on separate paths. *The Wealth of Nations* gave birth to the classical economics of Say, Malthus, and Ricardo, and fueled the utilitarianism of Bentham and James Mill. Rousseau's thought gave birth to German idealism, the philosophy of freedom,[34] which eclipsed *The Theory of Moral Sentiments*. The two strands were reunited, however, in Marx's synthesis of political economy and Hegel.

Freedom, Despotism, and the Natural Aristocracy

The Wealth of Nations only minimally invokes the three forms of government. With difficulty, however, one can pull from it a classificatory scheme for governments: a spectrum ranging from the "legal and free" to the "arbitrary and violent" or "despotical" (IV.vii.b.52, II.ii.94).[35] Free government has a certain kinship with republican government. Britain and its American colonies (IV.vii.b.52, c.74) are models of "legal and free" government, and the ancient republics of Greece and Rome were home to "free people[s]" (V.i.f.39–41).[36] Smith also suggests that a "free country" is one in which citizens either exercise legislative power or elect the legislators. Ironically, Smith provides this elaboration in order to show that slaves may be better off (and therefore more productive) under an "arbitrary" government because its magistrates, compared with those of a "free" government, are more likely to interfere with the subjects' property (*WN* IV.vii.b.54).[37] A free country, like a republic, is thus characterized by the restrained nature of the executive power; "in the progress of despotism the authority of the executive power gradually absorbs that of every other power in the state" (V.i.d.16).

Perhaps Smith's most important allusion to the free-despotic spectrum is his claim that

> those exertions of the natural liberty of a few individuals, which might endanger the security of the whole society, are, and ought to be, restrained by the laws of all governments; of the most free, as well as of the most despotical. (*WN* II.ii.94)

Natural liberty, though usually a paramount aim of law, thus gives way even under free governments to the "security of the whole."[38] This priority of security over liberty may contribute to Smith's unconcern with sovereignty, consent, participation, and the whole question of the regime. Smith goes so far (following Montesquieu) as to identify the liberty of the individual with "the sense which he has of his own security" (V.i.b.25).[39] Smith faults absolute governments such as those of Spain and Portugal for their deleterious effect on economic progress,[40] but he smiles on "civilized monarchies" (France) and conducts no Lockean diatribe against absolute monarchy. One must agree with Winch that for Smith (following Hume) "personal liberty, seen as the regular and impartial administration of justice, and the security of property and contracts, was compatible with many different forms of government, except those that were purely despotic and arbitrary."[41]

In a remarkable passage from *The Theory of Moral Sentiments*, Smith simultaneously deflates the majesty of kings and asserts the primacy of the end: "Kings are the servants of the people, to be obeyed, resisted, deposed, or punished, as the public conveniency may require" (*TMS* I.iii.2.3). Kings are popular servants in that they are to be held accountable to the common good. But how are the "servants" to be instructed?

Smith nowhere insists on mechanisms by which the public will may be formulated, voiced, or provided with institutional power. He allows that kings can be "resisted" or "deposed," but never provides a detailed specification of the Lockean "right of resisting."[42]

The liberty Smith tries to insulate against governmental encroachment means especially the ability to dispose freely of one's labor and capital.[43] Taxation, however, is a "badge" of liberty: though "subject" to government, the payer owns property and is therefore not a slave (*WN* V.ii.g.11).[44] Being subject to government is thus a mean between the extremes of subjection and independence. Taxation is a badge of liberty because there is no liberation from subjection to government; property rights, along with protection against enslavement by conquerors, come at a price.

The non-egalitarian side of Smith's account of political freedom emerges in his discussion of the American Revolution: the "stability and duration . . . of free development" depend on the power of "the natural aristocracy" to pursue "importance" (IV.vii.c.74). But who is this "natural aristocracy," and what are the grounds and ends of their rule? Such an aristocracy, it seems, is neither hereditary (III.ii.6, V.i.b.9) nor defined by virtue. It is composed of the "leading men," those "ambitious and high-spirited men" who "draw the sword in defence of their own importance" (IV.vii.c.74), the "principal people," perhaps the "principal nobility and gentry" (V.i.a.41). One may infer that a stable free government, by allowing the natural aristocracy to pursue importance, substitutes a free market in ambition for the hereditary monopoly of a traditional aristocracy.

Given Smith's sympathy for "commercial society," it is surprising that he so sharply distinguishes the "natural aristocracy" from the commercial classes. Government by an "exclusive company of merchants" is "perhaps, the worst of all governments" (IV.vii.b.11); "no two characters seem more inconsistent than those of trader and sovereign" (V.ii.a.7); "merchants and manufacturers . . . neither are, nor ought to be the rulers of mankind" (IV.iii.c.9).[45] One of the flaws that disqualifies a merchant council for governing is that the mercantile profession necessarily lacks "that sort of authority which naturally over-awes the people, and without force commands their willing obedience"; as a result, the council employs "military and despotical" means (IV.vii.c.104). Given that the natural for Smith is the "usual" and the "ordinary" rather than the fruit of "violence" and "artifice," we may infer that a "natural" aristocracy rules gently.[46] Because Smith is elsewhere so insistent about the preferability of "management and persuasion" to "force and violence" as instruments of government (V.i.g.19), we might expect him to be more of a partisan of free government and its natural aristocracy: even Hume argues moderately on its behalf.[47]

In *The Theory of Moral Sentiments*, Smith looks with Newtonian eyes on the class structure of society, seeking to determine the correlation of forces:

> Every independent state is divided into many different orders and societies, each of which has its own particular powers, privileges, and immunities. . . . Upon the manner in which any state is divided into the different orders and societies which compose it, and upon the particular distribution which has been made of their respective powers, privileges, and immunities, depends, what is called, the constitution of that particular state. (*TMS* VI.ii.2.7–8)

Smith proceeds to identify constitution with "form of government" (VI.ii.2.11), and this is as close as he comes to the classical notion of regime. Some orders may have more power than others, but Smith is uninterested in the virtues that might justify their claim to rule.[48]

The only remark in *The Wealth of Nations* bearing on the general desirability of a particular form of government comes at the very conclusion, where Smith indicates that "rancorous and virulent factions" are "inseparable from small democracies" (*WN* V.iii.90).[49] One wonders about the implications for Smith's praise of the colonists' liberty "to manage their own affairs their own way" (IV.vii.b.51) and his insistence that "every man, as long as he does not violate the laws of justice" be "left perfectly free to pursue his own interest his own way" (IV.ix.51). Given Smith's indulgence of the natural aristocracy (who pursue "importance" via a "share in the management of public affairs"), we may suppose that he prefers "the great body of people" to be occupied with bettering their material condition and thereby insulated from the intoxicating elixirs of politics. In a "barbarous" society, "every man is . . . in some measure a statesman" (V.i.f.51). In a commercial society, the division of labor prevails in politics as well as in economics.[50]

Founding

Dugald Stewart, in his well-known 1793 commentary on Smith, supplies a plausible rationale for what we have identified as Smith's turning away from the question of the regime. Stewart says that Smith, along with Quesnay and Turgot,

> aimed at the improvement of society—not by delineating plans of new constitutions, but by enlightening the policy of actual legislators. Such speculations, while they are more essentially and more extensively useful

than any others, have no tendency to unhinge established institutions or to inflame the passions of the multitude.[51]

The ancients, Stewart claims, focused on the "comparison of the different forms of government," whereas the moderns "investigate those universal principles of justice and expediency, which ought, under every form of government, to regulate the social order." Stewart proceeds to defend this modern approach by alleging that happiness depends "not on the share which the people possesses . . . in the enactment of laws, but on the equity and expediency of the laws that are enacted."[52]

Stewart is doubtless correct in implying that Smith is more concerned with legislation, what we today call public policy, than with the principles that would guide founders or constitution writers. Smith's focus, furthermore, is surely on the "equity and expediency" of laws, not the identity of the legislators. Compared to many of his modern predecessors, moreover, Smith seems especially reluctant "to unhinge established institutions or to inflame the passions of the multitude." The titles of Smith's works are of a detached, scientific character: an "inquiry" into wealth's nature and causes, a "theory of moral sentiments," the "principles which lead and direct philosophical enquiries." Each of Smith's two great published writings is presented as a "system," i.e., as "an imaginary machine invented to connect together in the fancy those different movements and effects which are *already in reality performed*" (Astronomy IV.19).

Although Smith intransigently attacks the prevailing system of political economy, he does not challenge forms of government or even political institutions.[53] And as the alternative both to mercantilism, which forcibly favors the town at the expense of the country, and to agricultural political economy, which forcibly favors the country at the expense of the town, Smith's system denigrates political choice in the name of nature. Indeed, with the systems "of preference or of restraint . . . taken away, the obvious and simple system of natural liberty establishes itself of its own accord" (*WN* IV.ix.51), i.e., naturally. To drive home the naturalness of the system one last time, Smith ends Book IV by indicating that Book V, wherein natural liberty is expounded, "will *naturally* be divided into three chapters" (IV.ix.52). The natural system, of course, had never been actualized, and Smith admits the utopian character of his proposals for perfect freedom of trade, for uniting Britain with its colonies, and for the best alternative (dismembering the empire) to the latter. Smith, however, remains a picture of sobriety even when describing "Utopia" and playing "the visionary."[54]

Rousseau would condemn Stewart's belittlement of popular participation in lawmaking, but Stewart would respond that Rousseau's writings display the unwholesome "tendency to unhinge established institutions or to inflame the passions of the multitude." Smith's final remark on Rousseau (in the letter) hints at a similar concern. Smith says that the Dedication of the *Discourse* is "an agreeable, animated, and I believe too, a just panegyric, [which] expresses that ardent and passionate esteem which it becomes a good citizen to entertain for the government of his country and the character of his countrymen" (Letter 16). This concluding praise is rhetorically suggestive of Smith's conservatism. The Dedication, first of all, is irrelevant to the Rousseauean themes Smith had discussed: the blessings of the state of nature, the gradual development of society from naturally asocial (but compassionate) individuals, government as the tool of the rich, and Rousseau's debt to Mandeville (11–12).[55] Smith concludes by calling attention to the rhetorical "style" that enabled Rousseau to purge Mandeville's principles of their disgraceful "tendency to corruption and licentiousness" and by translating long passages of Rousseau to illustrate the "rhetoric and description" that pervade the *Discourse* (12–16). How, then, could Smith have overlooked the exaggerated tone of Rousseau's praise of Geneva? Smith proceeds to generalize, asserting that "a good citizen" should express an "ardent and passionate esteem . . . for the government of his country." This implies that a good citizen who happens not to live under a good regime is obliged to lie. Although Smith strives to temper the more "ardent and passionate" forms of patriotism, it is Smith—not Rousseau—who treats the government of his country (and government in general) with kid gloves.

As we have seen, Smith combines his discussion of Rousseau's rhetoric with a rhetorical treatment of Rousseau.[56] Something similar occurs in the thematic discussion of Mandeville (*TMS* VII.ii.4), where Smith's remarks about the potency of Mandeville's rhetoric tacitly invite reflection about the potency of his own rhetoric. It is Smith, not Rousseau, who uses rhetoric to purge Mandeville's principles of their "tendency to corruption and licentiousness." Despite Smith's great debt to Mandeville, he is—like Rousseau—never mentioned, quoted, or even alluded to in *The Wealth of Nations*. The dry, systematic tone of Smith's works distinguishes them from the works of both Mandeville and Rousseau, making them less suitable for stirring up popular sentiments and more suitable for inaugurating new sciences.

On behalf of the approach identified by Stewart as "modern," one could add that the opportunities to employ policy science are as ubiquitous as the opportunities to employ regime science are rare. In the words of Adam Ferguson,

> No constitution is formed by concert, no government is copied from a plan. . . . The seeds of every form are lodged in human nature; they spring up and ripen with the season.[57]

The prominence of "revolution," "founding," and "new form of government" in the chapter on colonies might suggest that Smith was impressed by the opportunities in colonies for large-scale experimentation and innovation. But it is precisely the continuities between colonies and the mother country—that colonists from a "civilized" country bring with them habits of subordination and "regular government" (in addition to knowledge of the arts)—that cause, in conjunction with abundance of land and the elevation of wages, the rapid progress (IV.vii.b.2–3). Smith later praises Europe for its contribution to "the education and great views" of the colonies' "active and enterprizing founders" (IV.vii.b.64). Apart from the other ironies surrounding this remark, Smith says nothing about the precise content of the education and great views, leaving one with the suspicion that they are limited to the habits characteristic of civilized colonists.

Smith, however, does not shrink from acknowledging instances of regime change in the recent historical record. He refers, conjoined with some approving phrases, to the British "government established by the Revolution" (*WN* V.iii.88). His rhetoric in depicting the Continental Congress in America is still more ebullient:

> From shopkeepers, tradesmen, and attornies, they are become statesmen and legislators, and are employed in contriving a new form of government for an extensive empire, which, they flatter themselves, will become, and which, indeed, seems very likely to become, one of the greatest and most formidable that ever was in the world. (*WN* IV.vii.c.75)

In *The Theory of Moral Sentiments*, Smith goes so far as to identify "the reformer and legislator of a great state" as "the greatest and noblest of all characters" (VI.ii.2.14). But what Smith gives with one hand, he often retracts with the other. He proceeds to warn about the dangers of "fanaticism" in political reform (VI.ii.2.15–17).[58] Smith likewise pairs his praise of the American revolutionaries—he also calls them "ambitious and high-spirited men" who have "chosen to draw the sword in defence of their own importance" (*WN* IV.vii.c.74)—with the following less flattering observation: having been previously intoxicated by "the little prizes which are to be found in what may be called the paltry raffle of colony faction," they can be bought off if admitted to "the wheel of the great state lottery of British politicks" (c.75). This paragraph, taken as a whole, seems to display what Haakonssen calls Smith's "perfect equipoise between irony and encomium."[59] Smith exudes an even more judicious equipoise when he articulates the general challenge of balancing improvement and order: "It often requires, perhaps, the highest effort of political wisdom to determine when a real patriot ought to support and endeavour to re-establish the authority of the old system, and when he ought to give way to the more daring, but often dangerous spirit of innovation" (*TMS* VI.ii.2.12).

Jurisprudence, Forms of Government, and History

Assessing Smith's contribution to the deflection of political philosophy to economics is complicated by the explicitly unfinished character of his philosophical enterprise. The "Advertisement" (i.e., preface) to the 1790 edition of *The Theory of Moral Sentiments* confirms that Smith intended to complete his corpus with a project analogous to political philosophy—"the theory of jurisprudence." He refers to the conclusion of the book, where he had promised to provide elsewhere an account of

> the general principles of law and government, and of the different revolutions they have undergone in the different ages and periods of society, not only in what concerns justice, but in what concerns police, revenue, and arms, and whatever else is the object of law. (*TMS* VII.iv.37)

Cropsey infers from this that Smith had nothing more to say about politics and political philosophy than what subsequently appeared in *The Wealth of Nations* (*Political Philosophy*, p. 58). Cropsey overlooks the 1790 preface where Smith apologizes for only having "partially executed" his project, "at least so far as concerns police, revenue, and arms."[60] That is, *The Wealth of Nations* accounts for governmental principles regarding these three "object[s] of law" but not justice.[61] In the jurisprudence lectures, Smith follows his presentation of the typology of regimes by a historical account of the development of government that fuses actual Western history with the more formalized four-stages theory to provide an account of "all the forms of government which have existed in the world" (*LJA* iv.113).[62]

As sketched in *The Theory of Moral Sentiments*, however, jurisprudence resembles Smith's political economy in failing to undertake a comprehensive deliberation about the ends of politics: jurisprudence addresses justice, police, revenue, arms, "and whatever else is the object of law" (Advert.2, VII.iv.37), but how are we to determine the proper objects of law? Smith's systematic account of governmental duties (*WN* V.i) ultimately invokes the necessities that impinge on societies as they develop along the four stages. Nowhere in *The Wealth of Nations* does he even raise the question of what constitutes the objects of law or refer to the four he identifies in *The Theory of Moral Sentiments* with jurisprudence.

According to *The Theory of Moral Sentiments*, "system[s] of positive law" emerge because of the circumstances that force magistrates to prevent people from harming each other; in a well-governed state, there will be judges guided by rules that are "in general, intended to coincide with those of natural justice" (VII.iv.36). Smith sketches four phenomena that may cause positive law to deviate from natural justice. One of these is the state's "constitution," i.e., "the interest of the government" (VII.iv.36). Natural jurisprudence thus incorporates the regime only as a "constitution" that may corrupt justice. Unlike Hobbes, Locke, Rousseau, and even Montesquieu, Smith eschews the quest for principles of natural right or justice with which to evaluate different regimes; unlike Aristotle, he does not treat differing notions of justice as concomitant with competing claims to rule.

Smith's natural jurisprudence, however, is in some respects strikingly ahistorical, at least when contrasted to ancient political philosophy. Natural jurisprudence elaborates the general principles that "ought" to ground "the laws of all nations."[63] Instead of the ancients' sensitivity to the variety of regimes and the different circumstances that bear on the choice among them, we see a universalistic theory that applies to every nation.[64] Still more striking is the following passage:

> But though empires, like all other works of men, have all hitherto proved mortal, yet every empire aims at immortality. Every constitution, therefore, which it is meant should be as permanent as the empire itself, ought to be convenient, not in certain circumstances only, but in all circumstances; or ought to be suited, not to those circumstances which are transitory, occasional, or accidental, but to those which are necessary and therefore always the same. (*WN* V.ii.c.6)

If political philosophy is a discipline that tries to guide the formation of constitutions, it would strive to accommodate itself to permanent rather than transitory circumstances, i.e., to nature rather than history. Political economy here mimics political philosophy: the dazzling statement about immortal empires and constitutions is provided to illustrate the proper means of taxing land-rent (V.ii.c.2–7).

Smith is quite explicit about the novelty of his approach to law. *The Theory of Moral Sentiments* introduces "natural jurisprudence" as "a particular science, of all sciences by far the most important, but hitherto, perhaps, the least cultivated" (VI.ii.Intro.2). More precisely, "it was very late in the world before any such general system was thought of, or before the philosophy of law was treated of by itself, and without regard to the particular institutions of any one nation." Smith suggests that the proper approach emerged only with Grotius (VII.iv.37). Like Smith, Grotius de-emphasizes forms of government[65] and expresses a heightened concern for international unity and peace.[66]

Smith faults "the ancient moralists"—Cicero, Aristotle, Plato—for not enumerating "those rules of natural equity which ought to be en-forced by the positive laws of every country"; Smith strangely asserts that the laws of Cicero and Plato are "laws of police, not of justice" (*TMS* VII.iv.37). In the lectures, Smith traces the concept of "police" to the Greek *politeia,* which previously referred to "the policey of civil govern-ment," but now "only means the regulation of the inferiour parts of government, *viz.* cleanliness, security, and cheapness or plenty" (*LJB* 203).[67] We may infer that Cicero and Plato were excessively attentive to the lofty concerns of the best *politeia* and insufficiently cosmopolitan. Natural jurisprudence can be universal only because Smith consciously restricts himself to an economistic notion of justice—safeguarding life, property, and contracts—whose enforcement is a more or less universal prerequisite of government. Insofar as Smith is concerned to make rec-ommendations about the less institutional side of *politeia*—way of life, moral sensibility, and so on—his orientation is likewise economic, favor-ing a society oriented toward "cheapness or plenty." He nevertheless concedes that questions about how to carry "dirt from the streets" and how to organize local constables are "too mean to be considered in a general discourse" on police (*LJB* 203).

CHAPTER THREE

Justice: Political Economy and Moral Philosophy

Justice and Political Economy

Smith's appeal for the system of natural liberty is partly an appeal for justice.[1] Smith's unleashing of self-interest is constrained or framed by justice: in explaining the system of natural liberty, Smith begins with the condition that "every man, *as long as he does not violate the laws of justice*, is left perfectly free to pursue his own interest his own way" (*WN* IV.ix.51). As H. J. Bitterman perceptively observes, however, Smith does not indicate what he means by "the laws of justice"—are they the laws of natural justice or simply the existing laws (p. 518)? Because Smith proceeds to elaborate the sovereign's duties to administer justice, we may assume the content of the laws of justice that limit self-interest is not open-ended. As we will see, however, Smith's historical approach ultimately serves to minimize the relevance of the distinction between natural and positive law: the necessary laws emerge more or less naturally, and Smith is more or less content with the necessary.

A Preliminary Comparison of Locke and Smith

The connection between natural liberty and justice is established partly by a Lockean-sounding argument about property and labor: "The property which every man has in his own labour, as it is the original foundation of all other property, so it is the most sacred and inviolable" (*WN* I.x.c.12). This appears to be a restatement of the famous claim, in Locke's chapter on property, that "every man has a property in his own person. . . . The labour of his body, and the work of his hands, we may say, are properly his" (*Second Treatise*, sec. 27). Unlike Locke's argument, Smith's has a relative form: property in labor is only the *most* sacred of the different kinds of property. Smith nowhere specifies the degree to which this form is sacred and inviolable, or the circumstances in which it may be overridden by other considerations. The most striking difference between the two authors, however, is in the way they mix normative and empirical concerns. For example, Smith provides much less argumentation in support of private property, both the general right to it and the validity (given the labor/property nexus) of its actual distribution. Unlike Smith, Locke invokes the "law of nature" to legitimate the acquisition of property by labor and ultimately makes the notorious claim that "men have agreed to a disproportionate and unequal possession of the earth" (sec. 50) and to "larger possessions" generally (sec. 36). Locke suggests that positive laws have only "settled the property which labour and industry began" and that even between nations land has been divided consensually (secs. 38, 45, 50). Smith, by contrast, implies that the division in modern Europe is traceable to the fall of the Roman Empire, when the barbarian chiefs "acquired or usurped to themselves the greater part of the lands" (*WN* III.ii.1).[2]

Smith likewise appears more cynical or amoral than Locke about the implications of the labor/property nexus for the wage relation. Smith states that "in all arts and manufactures the greater part of the workmen stand in need of a *master* to advance them the materials of their work, and their wages and maintenance till it be compleated"; throughout Europe, "twenty workmen serve under a master for one that is independent" (*WN* I.viii.8,10). Smith describes this phenomenon without defending it or explaining its origin. Although "the natural recompence" of labor is its produce (I.viii.1), only in the "early and rude state" of society does "the whole produce of labour . . . always belong to the labourer": once land has been appropriated and stock accumulated, the owners of land and stock both take a cut.[3] Smith makes no attempt to demonstrate the justice of this sharing, though he seems more sympathetic to the claim of the stockowner than to that of the landlord.[4]

Regarding the so-called labor theory of value, Locke and Smith differ again as philosopher and economist. By grounding his arguments about private property, money, and inequality, Locke's formulations of the claim that labor "put the difference of value on everything"[5] are integral to his efforts to liberate acquisitiveness. Rather than argue for the liberation of acquisitiveness, Smith simply presupposes its desirability and builds a science to explain and facilitate it: Smith's labor theory of value unfolds to explain "the principles which regulate the exchangeable value of commodities" (*WN* I.iv.14). Smith's discussion of the land-lords' and capitalists' shares in the produce of labor begins in a chapter whose title—"Of the component Parts of the Price of Commodities" (I.vi)—uses the terminology of economics to mask a politically charged investigation.

Property, Justice, and the Ends of Government

Of the sovereign's various duties under the system of natural liberty, the administration of justice is the only one that directly involves a virtue. As will soon become clear, the reason for this is that justice is the virtue whose public realization is both most possible and most necessary. In explaining this duty of the sovereign, however, Smith refrains from answering or even raising the Socratic question, "What is justice?" Smith states that the sovereign's three duties under the system of natural liberty, though "of great importance," are "plain and intelligible to common understandings" (*WN* IV.ix.51). Although Plato and Aristotle begin their complex dialectical analyses of justice from opinion (*doxa*), their pursuit of knowledge leads them to venture further than Smith does from "common understandings." For Smith, the deficiencies of "human wisdom or knowledge" (IV.ix.51), once recognized, will not subvert either prosperity or justice.

The Article housing Smith's systematic examination of justice begins by identifying the duty to establish "an exact administration of justice" with protecting "every member of the society from the injustice or oppression of every other member" (V.i.b.1); there is no precise definition of injustice and oppression. The subsequent analysis of how the administration of justice varies in "the different periods of society," however, implies that injustice means "injury" to property, person, or reputation (b.1–2). This corresponds to what is identified in *The Theory of Moral Sentiments* as "mere justice"—not "hurting our neighbour," not violating our neighbor's person, estate, or reputation (II.ii.1.9)—and to Locke's "law of nature," which "teaches" that "no one ought to harm another in his life, health, liberty, or possessions" (*Second Treatise*, sec. 6). Locke and Smith differ, however, in that Locke's "law of nature" is argued as a moral imperative, whereas Smith simply explains the origins of the necessity that government prevent people from injuring one another. This necessity replaces the "ought" of Locke's law of nature. Smith eschews recourse to natural law, natural right, the social contract, or divine precept; he maintains the Lockean ends of government—protection of life and property—without the philosophical apparatus that Locke employs to justify them. Political economy simply defers to the historical and natural pressures that generally cause governments to protect life and property.

The whole discussion of governmental duties in the first chapter of Book V ("Of the Expences of the Sovereign or Commonwealth") is framed by questions of revenue and expense. The standards Smith employs in analyzing the administration of justice would seem to be the following: "exact" and "equal and impartial" (*WN* V.i.b.1,15,25). But the only deviations from those standards depicted in the section—labeled as "gross abuses" and "corrupt" (b.14–15)—are attributed to the patterns of judicial funding that naturally develop in a shepherd-stage society, where government derives substantial revenue from the fees paid by people who petition the courts (b.13). That is, corruption stems neither from defective opinions about what justice is nor from the defective characters of those who administer it. The remedy, moreover, fits the problem. Smith does not propose philosophical edification about the nature of justice or strategies for training judges. Instead, he explains how the administration of justice naturally improves as society develops. The increasing expense of defense necessitates taxes that are then available as an alternative source of judicial funding (b.17). Smith's recommendations for contemporary judicial administration are likewise centered on the question of funding: properly structured court fees (rather than revenues from general taxation) can defray the expenses without engendering "corruption" (b.20). Smith even suggests that the "present admirable constitution of the courts of justice of England" is the result of the emulation promoted by the funding system (b.21).

Smith's discussion of the separation of powers is likewise tied into the historical evolution of funding through the social stages:

> The separation of the judicial from the executive power seems originally to have arisen from the increasing business of the society, in consequence of its increasing improvement. The administration of justice became so laborious and so complicated a duty as to require the undivided attention of the persons to whom it was entrusted. (V.i.b.24)

As a result, the executive appointed a deputy to serve as judge (b.24). The circumstances of the natural development of society thus obviate the need (if not the possibility) of deep speculation or radical innovation. Smith does extol the separation of powers: unless judges are independent of the executive, they will be tempted to sacrifice justice, the "rights of a private man," to "the great interests of the state."[6] Perhaps nowhere else in his corpus does Smith express such a strong preference for a particular arrangement of political institutions. Smith's bold remarks are of course preceded by historical exposition. Smith likewise plays historian-economist (more than political philosopher) when addressing the institution of representation. Smith simply explains the origin of burgher representation in the large European monarchies: as cities grew in strength the sovereign could no longer tax them without their consent and they were allowed to send deputies to the general assemblies (III.iii.11). In a section added for the 1790 edition of *The Theory of Moral Sentiments*, Smith says that in "commercial countries, where the authority of law is always perfectly sufficient to protect the meanest man in the state," families naturally disperse (*TMS* VI.ii.1.13). The placement of the commas suggests a remarkable generalization: socioeconomic evolution suffices to render the protection of law universal within a society. Although this passage is not cited by Duncan Forbes, it supports his claim that (for Smith) "what matters is not the form of government, whether free or absolute, but the degree of civilization" (p. 198).

Government and Class Conflict

Smith's account of the origins of government in a way peaks with the assertion that "Civil government, so far as it is instituted for the security of property, is in reality instituted for the defence of the rich against the poor, or of those who have some property against those who have none at all" (*WN* V.i.b.12). To comprehend this claim, we must examine Smith's account of why and how government emerges. Smith finds the end or purpose of government in the origins of government, but by means of a philosophy of history rather than a social contract. Whereas Hume (and Smith in the lectures) explicitly rejects contract theory as ahistorical, Smith (in his books) does so only implicitly.[7] Like Montesquieu and Hume, Smith abandons the formalisms of contract theory; unlike them, he substitutes the new formalisms of economics. His account of government's origins has echoes of Rousseau and anticipations of Marx.

In the first social stage (hunting), there is "neither sovereign nor commonwealth" (*WN* V.i.a.2). Insofar as Smith provides an explanation of this, it comes in the discussion of justice: the natural causes of "subordination" are lacking because of poverty (V.i.b.7–8,11). That is, because there is no "valuable and extensive property" (i.e., property that "exceeds the value of two or three days labour"), inflicting injury brings no benefit, no "real or permanent advantage" to the perpetrator.[8] As a result, "tolerable" security is available without an "established magistrate or any regular administration of justice," i.e., without "civil government" (V.i.b.2).

This hunting stage calls to mind various versions of the state of nature: for Smith, mankind literally begins in an apolitical situation.

Smith combines the peaceful "state of nature" of Rousseau's *Second Discourse* with the necessitousness (but not the combativeness) of Hobbes's version; Smith adopts the anthropological approach of Rousseau rather than the hypothetical approach of Hobbes and Locke. In contrast to both Rousseau and Hobbes, the beginning point is not asocial—there is nothing in Smith about isolated individuals.[9] Although Smith and Rousseau share the anthropological emphasis, Smith retains teleology: the development along the four stages is natural, not the result of tragic accidents.[10] Unlike all three philosophers, however, Smith completely eschews recourse to a consciously formulated social contract to remedy the ills of the state of nature. The social contract is replaced by a detailed and systematic account of how property and government develop "naturally" with social evolution. The principle of consent disappears with the contract.[11] For Locke, "natural liberty" is "to be free from any superior power on earth, and not to be under the will or legislative authority of man." For Locke, natural liberty is also the premise for liberty in society: "to be under no other legislative power but that established by consent in the commonwealth" (*Second Treatise*, sec. 22). Smith's "natural liberty" is defined in terms of security and economic freedom and bears no reference to political consent.[12] Even Locke shows more interest than Smith does in the will, defining freedom under government as the "liberty to follow my own will in all things where the rule prescribes not, and not to be subject to the inconstant, uncertain, unknown, arbitrary will of another" (sec. 22).

In identifying government with oppression by the rich of the poor, however, Smith follows Rousseau. Smith's explanation of the peaceful character of hunting societies culminates in a famous and shocking passage:

> Wherever there is great property, there is great inequality. For one very rich man, there must be at least five hundred poor, and the affluence of the few supposes the indigence of the many. . . . It is only under the shelter of the civil magistrate that the owner of that valuable property, which is acquired by the labour of many years, or perhaps of many successive generations, can sleep a single night in security. He is at all times surrounded by unknown enemies, whom, though he never provoked, he can never appease, and from whose injustice he can be protected only by the powerful arm of the civil magistrate continually held up to chastise it. (*WN* V.i.b.2)

Smith here stops short of asserting that the wealth of the rich has been stolen from the poor. He states that the valuable property has been acquired by "the labour of many years," rather than, we suppose, by force or fraud; by not specifying whose labor is responsible, however, Smith begs the Marxian question about whether such wealth is just a congealed form of the surplus labor expropriated from slaves, serfs, or proletarians. Smith does proceed to assert that the "unknown enemies" of the rich have not been "provoked," and that the rich man is to be protected from their "injustice." The picture is further complicated by Smith's concluding claim that "Civil government, so far as it is instituted for the security of property, is in reality instituted for the defence of the rich against the poor, or of those who have some property against those who have none at all" (V.i.b.12).[13] This formulation raises first the question of to what degree, in Smith's account, government is "instituted" in a decisive, founding moment. Second, the summary statement refers only to government "so far as it is instituted for the security of property"; Smith does not specify how far. Third, the statement implies the possibility that government might protect the many rich who have some property against the few poor who have none, thus softening the earlier thesis that "the affluence of the few supposes the indigence of the many." The statement in fact concludes a description of how "men of inferior wealth," in order to protect their property, support the property of the richest (b.12).

In his letter to the *Edinburgh Review*, Smith says that according to both Rousseau and Mandeville, "those laws of justice, which maintain the present inequality amongst mankind, were originally the inventions of the cunning and the powerful, in order to maintain or to acquire an unnatural and unjust superiority over the rest of their fellow creatures" (Letter 11). Smith's investigation of the "causes or circumstances which naturally introduce subordination" (*WN* V.i.b.4) calls to mind the central theme of the *Second Discourse*, the "Origin and Foundations of Inequality among Men." The Academy question to which Rousseau responded, however, asked not only about the origin of inequality but whether it was "authorized by natural law." Rousseau's removal of the question about natural law is at first glance contradicted by Smith's explicit search for causes that "naturally" introduce subordination. But Smith too abandons natural law, mentioning it only once in his writings. Smith's examination of subordination, moreover, aims to illuminate the phenomena that spontaneously produce subordination in the various social stages, not to provide a moral basis for hierarchy. Rousseau, according to Smith, maintained that the superiority of the cunning and powerful is "unnatural" as well as "unjust." Smith's own account of subordination shows that subordination is natural, and avoids introducing a normative conception of justice that might be used to evaluate it.

Natural Authority and Subordination

Immediately after showing that property "requires" government, Smith explains how the subordination in turn required by government develops gradually and "naturally" with the growth of property (WN V.i.b.2–3). There are four "causes or circumstances which naturally introduce subordination, or which naturally, and antecedent to any civil institution, give some men some superiority over the greater part of their brethren" (b.4). The wording implies that the natural character of subordination is its antecedence to "any civil institution." One may infer that subordination results from neither conspiracy nor sudden violence.

The four causes are superiority of "personal qualifications," age, wealth, and birth. The first category comprises bodily excellence along with the mind's "wisdom, and virtue" (prudence, justice, fortitude, and moderation). After minimizing the authority conveyed by bodily traits unsupported by mental ones, Smith indicates that the latter can indeed yield great authority. Because these qualities are invisible and thus disputable, however, no society "has ever found it convenient" to base rank and subordination upon them (V.i.b.5). From a moral or philosophical point of view, wisdom and virtue would be the supreme entitlement (at least in comparison with the other three "circumstances") to rank or superiority; one thinks of philosopher-kings and Aristotelian gentlemen. The Machiavellianism of Smith's political economy is shown in his unwillingness to exhort on behalf of these unrealizable qualities, the Greek virtues: interest is surely a firmer foundation. According to *The Theory of Moral Sentiments*, "the great mob of mankind are the admirers and the worshipers . . . of wealth and greatness" as opposed to wisdom and virtue (*TMS* I.iii.3.2), which they are perhaps incapable of even discerning (VI.ii.1.20). As we have seen, *The Wealth of Nations* defers to the "vulgar" view—adopted by "the greater part of men"—that one betters one's condition by acquiring more wealth (II.iii.28).[14]

The second cause of subordination, age, is obviously "a plain and palpable quality which admits of no dispute"; it is the "sole foundation of rank and precedency" in a hunting society (WN V.i.b.6). The authority conveyed by superior wealth (the third cause), although large in "every age of society," peaks precisely in the first stage to admit "any considerable inequality of fortune," the shepherd stage.[15] Like the feudal barons and clergy described elsewhere in *The Wealth of Nations* (III.iv.5–7, V.i.g.22–25), a Tartar chief can only employ his material surplus in "maintaining" large numbers of people, who, depending "entirely upon him for their subsistence, must both obey his orders in war, and submit to his jurisdiction in peace"; he is necessarily both general and judge (V.i.b.7).

The authority conveyed by birth, needless to say, is for Smith largely derivative from that conveyed by fortune: it reflects a family's ancient superiority of fortune. "Upstart greatness is every where less respected than antient greatness" because a tradition of deference makes deference easier to bear (V.i.b.8). Apart from his wealth, the great shepherd or herdsman is "revered on account of the nobleness of his birth, and of the immemorial antiquity of his illustrious family" (b.11). Smith's lack of sympathy for hereditary nobility is illuminated by his dry observation that there has never been "a great family in the world whose illustration was entirely derived from the inheritance of wisdom and virtue" (b.9).[16] Whatever sympathy Smith might have with wisdom and virtue as titles to rule (*TMS* IV.2.1, III.5.9), he surely does not find them adequately embodied in traditional aristocracies.[17]

Birth and fortune are thus "the two circumstances which principally set one man above another . . . the principal causes which naturally establish authority and subordination among men." Their influence peaks in the shepherd stage, providing the great shepherd with a "natural authority." The two causes combine to procure for him both executive and judicial authority: because he can "command the united force" of more people than anyone else, individuals "naturally" follow his banner in war and generally appeal to him for protection and redress (V.i.b.11). The inequality of wealth thus "introduces some degree of that civil government which is indispensably necessary for its own preservation." It "seems to do this naturally" and "even independent of the consideration" of the necessity (b.12). Such consideration, however, operates subsequently to perpetuate subordination. The rich are of course interested in maintaining their superiority, and the "men of inferior wealth" recognize that they too have interests at stake and therefore cooperate with the rich. Smith describes these inferiors as "a sort of little nobility" with "their own little sovereign" and concludes by identifying civil government with "defence of the rich against the poor" (b.12). One is left wondering whether ordinary nobility and sovereignty are just a larger version of these phenomena.[18] Smith indicates that in feudal antiquity, the king "was little more than the greatest proprietor in his dominions" (III.iv.7).

Smith's attempt to explain authority as derivative "from the state of property and manners" (III.iv.8) may serve to demystify authority. James Harrington had written:

> Men are hung upon riches of necessity, and by the teeth; forasmuch as he who wants bread is his servant that will feed him. If a man thus feeds a whole people, they are under his empire.

After quoting this, Dumont perceptively comments that "Harrington deduces subordination from subsistence; he gives a modern view of a traditional situation."[19] By amplifying the modern view, Smith perhaps contributes to the erosion of the ideas that supported the traditional situation, even if Smith's language is less inflammatory than Harrington's. Smith's concept of the "natural aristocracy," at least when examined casually, would leave intact a minimal moral aura surrounding political authority, but *The Wealth of Nations* is stingy in supplying legitimizing support for aristocracy or monarchy. Although Burke proclaimed himself Smith's disciple, Smith contributed to the Enlightenment enterprise that Burke derided: tearing away life's "decent drapery" and "pleasing illusions."[20]

What, then, is the force of the "natural" in Smith's concept of natural authority and subordination? Authority would seem to be natural chiefly in the sense that it emerges of its own accord, without human plan or artifice: as we have seen, the greatest natural cause of subordination (wealth) introduces government "naturally," without "consideration" of government's necessity (V.i.b.12). Additionally, natural authority is neither begun nor exercised with violence, in contrast to merchant councils, which are "despotical" and "military" (IV.vii.c.104). Natural authority is likewise natural in that it supports "the natural progress" of things, the evolution of human society from hunting to commerce.[21]

One might fault Smith's whole attempt to provide a socioeconomic account of authority because it does not explain how the shepherd chief is able to control the large flocks: Smith slights the contribution of opinion. From "the easiness with which the many are governed by the few," Hume infers that "as force is always on the side of the governed, the governors have nothing to support them but opinion. It is, therefore, on opinion only that government is founded."[22] In asserting that "for Smith, as for Hume, opinion is the basis for government," Haakonssen overlooks the absence of such statements in Smith's books.[23]

For Smith, wisdom and virtue, although naturally causes of rank, are naturally the weakest of the causes. Smith's reliance on concepts like "natural authority" and "natural aristocracy" seems to clash with the basic postulate of liberalism that people are by nature free and equal. But Smith remains within the liberal framework by eschewing the proposition that people of superior wisdom and virtue possess a title to rule. He certainly leaves no place for Aristotle's natural slavery. His deflection of political philosophy also entails, however, abandonment of the necessity of consent that follows (for the contract theorists) from the premise of natural freedom and equality. In the end, both rule and freedom from rule are left without philosophical support. Into the breach steps outcome. Natural authority remains desirable or defensible because it is the efficient means to the subordination so necessary for human societies, at least for the last three stages. More accurately, it is desirable because it is necessary for the advance of society toward "wealth and greatness," the ends of political economy.[24]

In a passage added to the 1790 edition of *The Theory of Moral Sentiments*, Smith goes so far as to say that

> Nature has wisely judged that the distinction of ranks, the peace and order of society, would rest more securely upon the plain and palpable difference of birth and fortune, than upon the invisible and often uncertain difference of wisdom and virtue. The undistinguishing eyes of the great mob of mankind can well enough perceive the former: it is with difficulty that the nice discernment of the wise and the virtuous can sometimes distinguish the latter. In the order of all those recommendations, the benevolent wisdom of nature is equally evident. (VI.ii.1.20)

Thus, the result of nature's "benevolent wisdom" is that birth and fortune—unlike wisdom and virtue, which are invisible and uncertain—produce rank and therefore order. But nature itself is responsible for the weakness of wisdom and virtue; perhaps a truly wise and benevolent nature would have made wisdom and virtue more "plain and palpable."[25] Smith's whole corpus aims to impart resignation to such shortcomings, and generally presents nature as authoritative. More precisely, the standard is nature's "effectual truth," which is more supportive of preservation, propagation, and prosperity than of virtue, wisdom, and nobility.

Smith's account of the administration of justice is conspicuously silent regarding the existence of rank and subordination in the final stage. Presumably, fortune and birth still produce deference.[26] Smith's most comprehensive perspective on classes is that of the economist: he defines "the three great, original, and constituent orders of every civilized society" as those who "live by" rent, wages, or profit. Of these, it is the latter whose "plans and projects . . . regulate and direct all the most important operations of labor"; stock employed for profits "puts into motion the greater part of the useful labour of every society" (*WN* I.xi.p.8,10); the owners of "great mercantile capitals are necessarily the leaders and conductors of the whole industry of every nation" (IV.vii.c.61). This language, however, is accompanied by Smith's insistence that the interest of the capitalist class clashes with that of society as a whole (I.xi.p.10). *The Wealth of Nations* is indeed a ringing critique of the mercantilist policies foisted by the merchants and manufacturers whose political authority made them resemble an "overgrown standing army" (IV.ii.43). The "interests" of the other two orders mesh with society's, but these orders lack intellectual ability (I.xi.p.7–9). In other words, the three classes are equal insofar as they are all unqualified to be the ruling class.[27] One might speculate that only the political economist or the philosopher possesses both the wisdom to discern the common good and the virtue to pursue it (I.i.9, V.i.f.51).

The strongest general exhortation to equality in *The Wealth of Nations* sums up a critique of mercantilist restrictions on the wool trade:

> To hurt in any degree the interest of any one order of citizens, for no other purpose but to promote that of some other, is evidently contrary to that justice and equality of treatment which the sovereign owes to all the different orders of his subjects.[28]

We may perhaps infer that there exist no orders whose contribution to social well-being would justify special privileges.[29]

Smith emphasizes the administration of justice in one other context. He says that commerce and manufacturing are unlikely to flourish unless there is a "regular administration of justice," that is, unless people have a "certain degree of confidence in the justice of government" (*WN* V.iii.7). Needless to say, for Smith, the "justice of government" does not mean that the government is ruled by those who deserve to rule, or that the government gives to each his due, or that the government adheres to any particular distributive principle. Justice means that people feel "secure in the possession of their property," that contracts are legally enforced, and that the state is known to "be regularly employed" in enforcing debt payment (V.iii.7). This is the justice addressed by the political economist and essential to the system of natural liberty; because of its contribution to prosperity, Smith can substitute appeals to "interest" for philosophical explanation and exhortation.

Whereas the economic development of Spain and Portugal was hampered by their "irregular and partial administration of justice, which often protected the rich and powerful debtor from the pursuit of his injured creditor" (IV.vii.c.53), Great Britain's was especially enhanced by "that equal and impartial administration of justice which renders the rights of the meanest British subject respectable to the greatest, and which, by securing to every man the fruits of his own industry, gives the greatest and most effectual encouragement to every sort of industry" (IV.vii.c.54). Such equality is an intrinsic feature of the system of natural liberty, but Smith provides more assertions than arguments about its justice.[30] Although "civil government" was originally established to protect the rich against the poor, it may later function to protect the poor against the rich.

Justice and Moral Sentiments

An Overview of Smith's Moral Theory

We turn to *The Theory of Moral Sentiments* to remedy the incompleteness of the account of justice in *The Wealth of Nations*. Although the former has a great deal to say about justice, it is akin to the latter in linking justice with property and in eschewing a philosophical analysis of what justice *is*. This avoidance characterizes Smith's treatment of all the virtues, so we must begin with a summary of the book's general approach.

The Theory of Moral Sentiments is primarily an analysis of the nature and causes of moral sentiments; it is primarily a description. It is more a psychological treatise than an authoritative pronouncement about what is right and wrong: "The present inquiry is not concerning a matter of right, if I may say so, but concerning a matter of fact" (II.i.5.10).[31] Yet in identifying the "natural" forms of the moral mechanism, Smith does bring in a normative standard of a sort, especially since the mechanism's source is a more or less beneficent nature, more or less connected with a deity. Although its organizing theme is theoretical—uncovering "the nature and origins" of moral sentiments (VII.i)—the book is brimming with language meant to inspire virtue and nobility.

"Moral sentiments" are "principles by which nature has taught us to regulate our contempt or admiration" (III.2.35). Smith insists that moral judgments are ultimately derived from passion rather than reason: the "first perceptions of right and wrong" are the object of "immediate sense and feeling"; only sense and feeling can "render any particular object agreeable or disagreeable to the mind for its own sake" (VII.iii.2.7).[32] This is elaborated in a summary that Smith later provides of his system. Moral approbation is derived from four sources: "the sense of propriety," derived from "sympathy" with the agent's motives; "the sense of merit," derived from sympathy with the gratitude of others; conformity of action to the general rules by which these two forms of sympathy act; the beauty that action derives from its utility.[33] All but the third are sentiments, and the general rules of morality are derived by reason *from* sentiment.[34]

The theory of the impartial spectator enables an appeal beyond actual sentiments of approbation and disapprobation to "natural" sentiments, an appeal beyond praise and blame to the praiseworthy and blameworthy.[35] Virtue implies an "excellent and praise-worthy character," "the natural object of esteem, honour, and approbation" (VII.i.2); the "natural sense of praise-worthiness and blame-worthiness" is operationalized in the impartial spectator (III.2.32). The impartial spectator, identified by Smith with a wide variety of phrases, such as "the man within the breast" and "conscience," is first and foremost a spectator whose detachment neutralizes the individual's self-centeredness. His superiority to ordinary spectators seems to be a function of his being "cool," "candid," "consistent," and "properly informed" of conduct's "motive and circumstances" (VII.ii.4.10). Under the pressures of living with other people, the impartial spectator naturally emerges as what today would be called an internalized social conscience; our self-centeredness is tamed as we learn to look at ourselves from an outside, impartial point of view.[36] One may infer that almost all human beings would be capable of adopting this vantage point: neither divine enlightenment, deep study, nor special talent is necessary. In Campbell's words, the impartial spectator is distinguished not by his special qualities but by "his particular viewpoint: he represents the reactions of the ordinary person when he is in the position of a non-involved spectator" (p. 135).

To the extent that Smith reduces morality to what "the many" praise and blame, he would be labeled by Socrates as a sophist (Republic, 492b). At times, Smith approaches this, for his appeals to the impartial spectator are mixed with appeals to "every human heart," "every reasonable man," "every body," "our heart," and "any third person."[37] Smith concedes, however, that not everyone experiences the natural moral sentiments; though he describes the deviants in condemning language,[38] can he derive his condemnations from anything but sentiment? The complexity of Smith's posture regarding appeal beyond prevalent sentiments is best illustrated in the following passage:

> It is scarce agreeable to good morals, or even to good language, perhaps, to say that mere wealth and greatness, abstracted from merit and virtue, deserve our respect. We must acknowledge, however, that they almost constantly obtain it; and they may, therefore, be considered as, in some respects, the natural objects of it. (TMS I.iii.3.4)

The problem of appealing beyond actual sentiments to nature is an explicit theme in Part V of The Theory of Moral Sentiments, in which Smith shows that "custom and fashion" are the "chief causes of the many irregular and discordant opinions which prevail in different ages and nations concerning what is blameable or praise-worthy" (V.1.1). Smith argues, however, that moral sentiments are "founded on the strongest and most vigorous passions of human nature; and though they may be somewhat warpt, cannot be entirely perverted" (V.2.1). As in The Wealth of Nations, Smith expounds a philosophy of history that shows how "circumstances" naturally spawn human responses that are adaptive to them: "In general, the style of manners which takes place in any nation, may commonly upon the whole be said to be that which is most suitable to its situation" (V.2.13).[39] This formulation is of course full of qualifications: "in general," "commonly," "upon the whole." And Smith stresses that "particular usages" may "shock the plainest principles of right and wrong," as in the Greek practice of infanticide (V.2.14–15).

Such atrociousness could not prevail more broadly in a society, for the society would quickly perish (16). Smith also concedes there will be differences in moral tone between professions, countries, and social classes (V.2.3–5,10,13), but the greatest cleavage is that between the primitive ethic of self-denial/hardiness and the civilized ethic of humanity/sensibility (V.2.8–11).[40]

Justice and Mere Justice

Even in *The Theory of Moral Sentiments*, Smith does not systematically raise and answer the question, "What is justice?," suggesting that he may be content to draw on the generally understood meaning of the term. Although his usage consistently reinforces the linkage in *The Wealth of Nations* of injustice and injury (*TMS* II.ii.1.5), the definition of harm is more elaborate. Smith maintains the Lockean focus on life and property (III.3.37), but adds other components, for example, reputation (II.ii.1.9) and "personal rights"—what becomes "due" someone as a result of promises from others (II.ii.2.2).[41] Whether or not something counts as injustice seems to turn on the seriousness of the evil it inflicts, as measured by the resentment felt by the impartial spectator.[42] The "most sacred laws of justice" are thus those "which guard the life and person of our neighbour," followed by those guarding his property and possessions, and, lastly, those guarding his "personal rights" (II.ii.2.2). Once, however, Smith goes so far as to identify justice with the protection of our neighbor's "happiness" (VI.ii.Intro.2). The protection of person, estate, and reputation, furthermore, is but "mere justice" that does not seem deserving of reward because "it does no real positive good." Mere justice is "upon most occasions, but a negative virtue, and only hinders us from hurting our neighbour" (II.ii.1.9).

Only in Smith's analytic survey of the history of moral philosophy in Part VII does he elaborate the differences between the dominant concept of justice employed in *The Theory of Moral Sentiments* and the more expansive conceptions of the ancients. Smith beings by arguing that the word for justice in Greek and other languages has several different meanings, indicating that there exists "some natural affinity among those various significations." Smith presents a three-fold classification. First, justice means not inflicting any "positive harm" on person, estate, or reputation, a type of justice whose observance may be extorted by force. This is Aristotle's "commutative justice" and, moreover, the kind that "I have treated above" (VII.ii.1.10). Smith says nothing here about why in the body of the book he concerns himself with this justice and not the other types. The second sense of justice, sometimes called "distributive justice," consists in "proper beneficence, in the becoming use of what is our own" and thus "comprehends all the social virtues." In a footnote, Smith says that Aristotle's distributive justice is "somewhat different," entailing "the proper distribution of rewards from the public stock of a community" (VII.ii.1.10). Smith's decision here to employ a footnote, especially given the paucity of footnotes in *The Theory of Moral Sentiments*, suggests the distance he wishes to put between his own position and a more political approach to justice, especially Aristotle's famous examination of the justice of competing claims to rule. Smith's impartial spectator would surely have difficulty adjudicating the Aristotelian debate between the oligarch and the democrat.[43] As Macpherson says of Hobbes's treatment of distributive justice: "There is no room . . . for an assessment of the merit of different men in terms of the contribution they make to the purposes of the whole society or in terms of their needs as functioning parts of a social organism."[44] Smith's statement that "it is the end of jurisprudence to prescribe rules for the decisions of judges and arbiters" (*TMS* VII.iv.8) likewise suggests a debt to Hobbes's reduction of distributive justice to "the Justice of an Arbitrator" (*Leviathan*, ch.XV) and confirms the gulf between Smith's "natural jurisprudence" and classical political philosophy.

The third sense of justice is for Smith typified by Plato, according to whom justice means "exact and perfect propriety of conduct and behaviour" and includes commutative justice, distributive justice, and the other virtues—prudence, fortitude, and temperance (*TMS* VII.ii.1.10). Plato, of course, insists that reason is the faculty that determines "what ends are fit to be pursued, and what degree of relative value we ought to put upon each" (VII.ii.1.3). For Smith, on the contrary, only "immediate sense and feeling" can render an object "agreeable or disagreeable to the mind for its own sake" (VII.iii.2.7); more generally, Smith's criterion for determining how much value or esteem an object "may appear to deserve or to be naturally fitted for exciting" is the impartial spectator (VII.ii.2.10).

In the concluding section of *The Theory of Moral Sentiments*, Smith thus recounts but does not criticize conceptions of justice far broader than the one he adopts in the earlier portions of the book (and seventeen years later in the *The Wealth of Nations*). One may suggest several reasons for Smith's emphasis on "mere justice." Compared to the broader notions of justice, the realization of mere justice in society is both more possible and more necessary. It is more possible in part because its requirements can be more precisely delineated; it is more necessary because people generally demand that it be enforced. Smith in *The Theory of Moral Sentiments* both explains and extols the political enforcement of mere justice, just as *The Wealth of Nations* explains and extols the sovereign's duties to "administer" justice. On Smith's presentation, justice (i.e., "mere justice") is unique among the virtues in the extent to which its observance can be extorted by force and in the precision with which its obligations may be determined.[45] The violation of justice is the "proper object" of resentment and punishment, and "mankind" will "go along with" the use of force both to prevent injustice and to punish its perpetrators (*TMS* II.ii.1.5). Mere justice also is supported by a less exalted teleology than that associated with the ancients.

Justice and Punishment

The only provocation that warrants harming someone, in the eyes of the impartial spectator, is "attempted, or actually committed" injustice (*TMS* VI.ii.Intro.2). Smith's most comprehensive explanation of the legitimacy of punishment runs as follows:

> Among equals each individual is naturally, and antecedent to the institution of civil government, regarded as having a right both to defend himself from injuries, and to extract a certain degree of punishment for those which have been done to him. Every generous spectator not only approves of his conduct when he does this, but enters so far into his sentiments as often to be willing to assist him. (*TMS* II.ii.1.7)

At first glance this calls to mind the Lockean claim that everyone in the state of nature has the right to defend against and to punish the transgressors of the law of nature (a law prohibiting "harm" to life, liberty, health, or possessions); in Hobbes's state of nature, on the contrary, any violence pursuant to the natural right to self-preservation is justified. Regarding the content of the right, Smith sides with Locke rather than Hobbes, but in explaining or justifying it he departs from both. On Smith's formulation, the attribution of the right, rather than the right itself, is natural. Smith's use of the passive voice and his placement of a phrase between "naturally" and "regarded" obscures what I judge to be Smith's true meaning: human beings "naturally," *that is*, "antecedent to the institution of civil government," regard an individual who lives among equals as having a right to defend and punish. This interpretation is suggested by Smith's placement of the commas and by his other uses of the formulation "naturally, and antecedent to." Smith later interprets the claim that the moral faculties are the source of "natural" standards of right and wrong as meaning that the mind is "naturally," or "antecedent to all law and positive institution," endowed with these faculties (VII.iii.2.3). In *The Wealth of Nations*, as we saw, Smith explained the four causes that "naturally, and antecedent to any civil institution" introduce subordination (*WN* V.i.b.4). A natural condition "antecedent to the institution of civil government" corresponds to the state of nature, but Smith looks to it to find natural human judgments and circumstances rather than natural law or natural right. In his attempts to bolster the authority of moral judgments and to demonstrate that they are natural rather than conventional, Smith appropriates—but transforms— the terminology of contract theory.

Equality, Utility, and Self-Preference

Smith's maintaining characteristic theses of the contract theorists while abandoning the philosophical structures that support them is likewise manifest in his approach to equality. Whereas the contract theorists employ "the state of nature" to establish our natural equality, Smith (in the above passage) indicates only that the right to punish is attributed to equals: each individual "is regarded" as having the right to defend and punish "among equals." Smith's use of the passive voice accentuates that he does not here specify *who* regards individuals as having the right. The answer can only be "mankind" in the form of the impartial spectator. Smith fails to employ normative reasoning on behalf of equality here, just as *The Wealth of Nations* simply asserts that the administration of justice must be "equal and impartial." The necessity that the administration of justice be impartial, however, surely derives support from the necessity in *The Theory of Moral Sentiments* that the spectator be impartial in order to qualify as the voice of morality. In defining injustice as the inflicting of harm upon one's neighbor, Smith assumes that human individuals do not differ decisively in moral worth. The impartiality of the free market, despite or rather because of the impersonal character of money, likewise presupposes a certain equality among persons. As we shall now explore, Smith's complex doctrine of the impartial spectator is enmeshed in the question of equality: Smith's doctrine presupposes equality, and the impartial spectator teaches equality.

The overarching question of Smith's two great works is how the individual's interests and passions can be harmonized with those of other individuals. The prime function of the impartial spectator is to balance the needs and desires of the individual with those of other individuals, especially (but not exclusively) to counteract natural selfishness. Smith insists that "it is only by consulting this judge within . . . that we can ever make any proper comparison between our own interests and those of other people" (*TMS* III.3.1). As the chief theme or concept of *The Theory of Moral Sentiments*, the impartial spectator aptly addresses the concerns articulated in the famous opening sentence of the book:

How selfish soever man may be supposed, there are evidently some principles in his nature, which interest him in the fortune of others, and render
their happiness necessary to him, though he derives nothing from it, except
the pleasure of seeing it. (I.i.1.1)

Smith insists that only the impartial spectator can teach the individual
that he is "but one of the multitude, in no respect better than any other"
(III.3.4). Departing from the contract theorists who derive natural equality from the state of nature, Smith does not provide an argument that
every individual is "in no respect better than any other." He does not
appeal to revelation; he does not invoke Platonic *eidē*, an Aristotelian
telos, or natural law. We may infer that such philosophical and theological apparatus is superfluous because the necessary lessons are taught by
nature directly, through the impartial spectator. As an individual grows
up and lives in the company of others, there automatically grows in him
an impartial spectator or "man within" who enables the individual to
look at himself as others see him:[46] the impartial spectator thus corrects
the "natural misrepresentations of self-love" (III.3.4). Smith's avoidance
of authoritative appeal to reason or revelation is accompanied by his
demonstration of the natural pressures and circumstances that cause the
egalitarian message to be recognized and heeded.

Smith's approach threatens to deprive morality of its sanctity or authority. This approach is carried to an extreme in the account of the
origin of moral philosophy presented in *The Wealth of Nations*. The raw
material for moral philosophy is the "rules and maxims" for the conduct
of human life that are everywhere "laid down and approved of by common consent"; once there is writing, "wise men" chime in with "their
own sense . . . of proper and improper conduct"; taking its cue from
natural philosophy, moral philosophy attempts to arrange the maxims in
a "distinct or methodical order" or even to "connect them together by
one or more general principles, from which they were all deducible, like
effects from their natural causes" (*WN* V.i.f.25). This procedure is manifestly followed in *The Theory of Moral Sentiments*: our various approba-
tions are arranged and reduced to the three underlying principles (sympathy with propriety, sympathy with merit, the beauty of utility). But how
can this procedure allow the rules and maxims to possess any authority
beyond "common" approval? *The Wealth of Nations* goes still further in
attenuating the support that moral philosophy can derive from nature:
moral maxims are deduced from general principles as effects are deduced
from their "natural causes." Another dilemma posed by Smith's approach to moral philosophy is that his resort to writing implies some
weakness in the natural moral mechanism, just as actualization of "nat-

ural liberty" seems to require Smith's book on political economy. "Impartial spectator" and "the man within" are Smith's terms: they were not and are not common currency. Smith's "realism" also limits what his moral theory can offer to temper the abuses of international politics and even domestic factionalism (*TMS* III.3.42–43).

If individuals count equally, and there are no natural rights that adhere to individuals as such, under what circumstances can the welfare of many override that of one? On the one hand, Smith, as in *The Wealth of Nations* (II.ii.94, IV.v.b.39, V.ii.b.6), acknowledges that utilitarian regard for the whole may override the "ordinary" constraints of justice. It may be necessary and therefore "just," for example, that a sentinel who falls asleep be executed even though his act does not stimulate acute resentment—"when the preservation of an individual is inconsistent with the safety of a multitude, nothing can be more just than that the many should be preferred to the one" (*TMS* II.ii.3.11). We may infer that although the sleeping sentry does not arouse in people the resentment aroused by other capital offenses, the recognition of the necessity of severe punishment—based on the precedence of the many over the one—has permeated the criminal code.[47] And though Smith insists that in general it is unjust to inflict harm on someone who has committed no injustice, there are exceptions: "under the boisterous and stormy sky of war and faction," there may arise "the necessity of violating sometimes the property, and sometimes the life of our neighbour," against the usual precepts of justice and humanity (III.3.37).

Smith's impartial spectator nevertheless stops short of full utilitarianism:

> One individual must never prefer himself so much even to any other individual, as to hurt or injure that other, in order to benefit himself, though the benefit to the one should be much greater than the hurt or injury to the other. (III.3.6)

> There can be no proper motive for hurting our neighbour . . . which mankind will go along with, except just indignation for evil which that other has done to us. To disturb his happiness merely because it stands in the way of our own, to take from him what is of real use to him merely because it may be of equal or more use to us, or to indulge, in this manner, at the expense of other people, the natural preference which every man has for his own happiness above that of other people, is what no impartial spectator can go along with. (II.ii.2.1)

In the first passage, Smith simply asserts this "must," but the passage is surrounded by references to "the man within" (III.3.5,6), suggesting that Smith is but his mouthpiece. The second passage explicitly contextualizes the prohibition: mankind will not "go along with" unprovoked harm; no impartial spectator can "go along with" taking from others something even of greater use to you. Smith does not shrink from applying this doctrine to the tough question about rich and poor: "The poor man must neither defraud nor steal from the rich, though the acquisition might be much more beneficial to the one than the loss could be hurtful to the other"; the poor man is aware of "those sacred rules, upon the tolerable observation of which depends the whole security and peace of human society" (III.3.6). The impartial spectator's utilitarian recognition of the sacred rules thus balances his egalitarian recognition that the necessities of the poor are more important than the luxuries of the rich.[48]

The claim in the second passage that the impartial spectator combats "the natural preference which every man has for his own happiness" is followed immediately by a qualification: "Every man is, no doubt, by nature, first and principally recommended to his own care; and as he is fitter to take care of himself, than of any other person, it is fit and right that it should be so" (II.ii.2.1). As Smith insists throughout *The Theory of Moral Sentiments*, the impartial spectator does not demand pure altruism: although it leans against self-preference in order to combat the contrary tendencies of human nature, it also condones and even requires self-preference under the appropriate circumstances.[49] The passage quoted above is a particularly strong statement of the qualification. Smith leaves out the references to the impartial spectator and "the man within" that infused his presentation of the anti-selfish imperative, and employs strongly moral and philosophic language. The individual is "by nature" recommended "first and principally" to self-concern, and Smith goes beyond identifying this as a psychological imperative to judging it as "fit and right." Smith's argument on behalf of his judgment is as subtle as it is brief: you can care better for yourself than you can care for anyone else. Smith is not making the more usual liberal and egalitarian claim that you will be better cared for when you take care of yourself than when anyone else takes care of you.[50] The more usual version is employed in *The Wealth of Nations* during Smith's paean to the invisible hand (*WN* IV.ii.10).

As depicted by Smith, other people and therefore the impartial spectator naturally allow the individual that degree of self-preference associated with liberalism. People will "indulge" an individual's self-love

> so far as to allow him to be more anxious about, and to pursue with more earnest assiduity, his own happiness than that of any other person. . . . In the race for wealth, and honours, and preferments, he may run as hard as he can, and strain every nerve and every muscle, in order to outstrip all his

competitors. But if he should justle, or throw down any of them, the indulgence of the spectators is entirely at an end. It is a violation of fair play, which they cannot admit of. (*TMS* II.ii.2.1)

On Smith's account, our moral sentiments are thus programmed to support a framework of human action called for by liberal political philosophy. For example, we may suppose that the impartial spectator would look with sympathy upon the system of natural liberty, which leaves "every man, as long as he does not violate the laws of justice . . . perfectly free to pursue his own interest his own way" (*WN* IV.ix.51). The programming is implanted biologically and modified by the circumstances in which individuals develop. Just as, according to *The Wealth of Nations*, the administration of justice takes its character from the progress of society through the four stages, our "natural" moral sentiments emerge, more or less adaptively, from evolving social circumstances (*TMS* V.2.8,13,16).

Virtue and the Ends of Government

The liberal programming extends also to the posture of government toward virtue generally. In both of Smith's books, however, and especially in *The Theory of Moral Sentiments*, there are vestiges of the expansive classical vision of the ends of government: virtue, wisdom, and happiness. But the conclusion of *The Theory of Moral Sentiments*— where Smith promises to provide a theory of jurisprudence, of "the general principles of law and government" regarding justice, police, revenue, arms, and "whatever else is the object of law" (VII.iv.37)—expresses a narrower vision, reiterated in the 1790 preface when he states that *The Wealth of Nations* constitutes the promised treatment of police, revenue, and arms. Although Smith refers to "whatever else is the object of law," it is safe to say that his writings, along with the jurisprudence lectures, generally identify the ends of government as justice (i.e., "mere" justice), police, revenue, and arms.

The allusion to other objects is most apt, however, given the vestiges of a more expansive vision of government's ends. First, Smith writes that

All constitutions of government . . . are valued only in proportion as they tend to promote the happiness of those who live under them. This is their sole use and end. (*TMS* IV.1.11)

Characteristically, this remark appears not in a systematic investigation of the ends of government (there is no such investigation in *The Theory of Moral Sentiments*) but to illustrate the human propensity to become more intoxicated with the means that achieve ends than with the ends themselves. Smith asserts that the promotion of happiness is government's "sole use and end," but this assertion follows from a psychological generalization (about why constitutions "are valued") rather than a philosophical deduction (IV.1.11). Smith later elaborates the happiness at which governments should aim:

> What institutions of government could tend so much to promote the happiness of mankind as the general prevalence of wisdom and virtue? All government is but an imperfect remedy for the deficiency of these. (*TMS* IV.2.1)

The wording here implies that wisdom and virtue are eminently desirable as means to the happiness aimed at by government, but Smith stops short of insisting that they are ends in themselves. As in the above assertion about happiness, however, the context is psychological: Smith is explaining that wisdom and virtue derive a certain beauty from their facilitation of government (IV.2.1). There is no doubt that the ends of government as finally articulated in the book—justice, police, revenue, and arms—likewise contribute to human happiness, but what happened to the rest of wisdom and virtue?

Smith's most detailed exploration of the relation between high and low governmental ends comes in the paragraph immediately following the claim that "Among equals each individual is naturally . . . regarded as having a right both to defend himself from injuries" and to punish the perpetrator (II.ii.1.7). One may infer from Smith's account that whereas an individual may inflict harm on his equals only to prevent or avenge injuries, a "superior may, indeed, sometimes, with universal approbation, oblige those under his jurisdiction to behave, in this respect, with a certain degree of propriety to one another" (II.ii.1.8). Again, we see Smith condone the exception with an invocation of "universal approbation." The passage nevertheless implies that human moral sentiments are not simply liberal, that there are "superiors" who can oblige people to act with propriety. Smith proceeds immediately to specify the "respect" in which such compulsion is acceptable (or will be accepted):

> The laws of all civilized nations oblige parents to maintain their children, and children to maintain their parents, and impose upon men many other duties of beneficience. The civil magistrate is entrusted with the power not only of preserving the public peace by restraining injustice, but of promoting the prosperity of the commonwealth, by establishing good discipline, and by discouraging every sort of vice and impropriety; he may prescribe rules, therefore, which not only prohibit mutual injuries among fellow citizens, but command mutual good offices to a certain degree. (*TMS* II.ii.1.8)

As always, Smith's wording is meticulous. The whole passage merely illustrates the sense in which a superior may "with universal approbation" oblige propriety; laws of "all civilized nations" enforce familial duties; the magistrate "is entrusted with the power" to promote virtue. There seem to be two broad categories of governmental mandate: to preserve peace by restraining injustice and to promote prosperity by establishing "discipline" and "discouraging every sort of vice and impropriety." Perhaps the anti-liberal implications of allowing government to oppose "every sort of vice" are softened by the subservience of this mandate to the goal of "prosperity"—virtue enforced for the sake of the economy rather than for its own sake.[51] The virtue in question is likewise limited to beneficence, and the "good offices" can only be commanded "to a certain degree."

In concluding the discussion, Smith strikes a fine balance:

> Of all the duties of a law-giver, however, this, perhaps, is that which it requires the greatest delicacy and reserve to execute with propriety and judgment. To neglect it altogether exposes the commonwealth to many gross disorders and shocking enormities, and to push it too far is destructive of all liberty, security, and justice. (II.ii.1.8)

One suspects that the "delicacy and reserve" of the duty is reflected in the delicacy and reserve in Smith's exposition of it. In staking out a middle ground between licentiousness and tyranny, Smith reveals just how far he stands from the libertarianism of our day. The finely honed neutrality of the conclusion suggests that the sovereign's decision about how far to enforce virtue is more a matter of prudence than principle. We are left with the question of what circumstances may have prompted Smith in *The Wealth of Nations* to move so far from Aristotle, though even there he provides a countervailing dose of Aristotelian concern for the public promotion of the "essential parts" of human character (*WN* V.i.f.60–61). *The Theory of Moral Sentiments* contains almost nothing that directly suggests the system of natural liberty; the book says little about liberty of any kind.[52]

With respect to the question of to what degree law should be concerned with deeds rather than souls, Smith comes down more solidly on the liberal side. Nevertheless, he argues that even the attempt at injustice is properly punishable (*TMS* VI.ii.Intro.2) and that attempted murder (because our resentment of the crime is so high) should receive capital punishment (II.iii.2.4). Smith continues by arguing that acts of "gross negligence," even when they do not cause harm, constitute "real injustice" and may properly be punished, albeit within certain limits: executing someone in such an instance would itself violate "our natural sense of equity" (II.iii.2.8). Although punishment of attempted injustice is thus permissible, Smith insists that punishment not be applied to human "sentiments, thoughts, [and] intentions." Smith identifies this restriction as a "necessary rule of justice" and adds that punishing intentions would turn a trial into a tyrannical inquisition (II.iii.3.2–3). Regarding morality, as distinguished from legality, Smith approaches the Kantian exaltation of intention and the good will. He argues that it is an "irregularity" in our moral sentiments that the actual consequences of actions should have any influence on our moral judgments: "That the world judges by the event, and not by the design, has been in all ages the complaint, and is the great discouragement of virtue." Smith's explanation and evaluation of all this involve the most complex aspects of his teleology and theology (II.iii.3.1–2).[53] Unlike Kant, Smith blurs "is" and "ought" rather than sever them for the sake of the "ought."

The passages regarding the sovereign's mandate to enforce virtue are part of a section on the comparison of two basic virtues, "Of Justice and Benevolence" (II.ii). Part of the difference between the two virtues can be accounted for solely within the confines of moral philosophy, without reference to government. In order for giving to constitute the virtue of beneficence, it must be "free," not extorted by force, whereas justice (i.e., "mere justice") remains a virtue even when coerced (II.ii.1.3,5). Smith defends this distinction by appealing to mankind's general sentiments, to the impartial spectator. As Haakonssen explains, the distinction ultimately reflects two circumstances: that pain is more pungent than pleasure and that our "ordinary" state is closer to the peaks of enjoyment than to the depths of suffering.[54] Smith explicitly distinguishes justice's subjective status from that of the other social virtues—"we feel ourselves to be under a stricter obligation to act according to justice, than agreeably to friendship, charity, or generosity" (II.ii.1.5). Justice is likewise more coercible because its rules are far more accurate, and less subject to exception, than the rules of the other virtues (III.6.10–11).

The most important distinction between justice and beneficence, however, hinges on their differing necessity for the survival of society. Human beings are "fitted by nature" for society. When the assistance we require arises from love, gratitude, friendship, and esteem, society "flourishes and is happy" (II.ii.3.1). Society, however, can survive without flourishing:

> But though the necessary assistance should not be afforded from such generous and disinterested motives, though among the different members of the society there should be no mutual love and affection, the society, though less happy and agreeable, will not be dissolved. Society may subsist among different men, as among different merchants, from a sense of its

utility, without any mutual love or affection; and though no man in it should . . . be bound in gratitude to any other, it may still be upheld by a mercenary exchange of good offices according to an agreed valuation. (*TMS* II.ii.3.2)

The importance of this passage cannot be exaggerated, for in *The Wealth of Nations* Smith takes it for granted that society is glued together by the mercantile bond of utility rather than by love, gratitude, and friendship.[55] Smith does, however, state that no society can be "flourishing and happy" if those who live by labor, the "great body of the people," are so badly compensated for their work that they are "poor and miserable" (*WN* I.viii.36,43). Smith's many pleas on behalf of the laboring masses, conjoined with his prescriptions for increasing national wealth, may thus aim at making society as flourishing and happy as is feasible. In the "progressive state" of the economy, in which national wealth increases, "the condition of the labouring poor, of the great body of the people, seems to be the happiest and the most comfortable"; otherwise, that condition is either "hard" or "miserable" (I.viii.43). According to the passage from *The Theory of Moral Sentiments*, a society where gratitude and love do not prevail "may still be upheld by a mercenary exchange of good offices according to an agreed valuation"—hence the need for the science of exchange value provided in *The Wealth of Nations*.

Although society may "subsist" without "mutual love and affection," it cannot subsist, Smith continues, "among those who are at all times ready to hurt and injure one another." Even the gang of robbers and murderers will have to avoid robbing and murdering each other. Beneficence is thus "less essential to the existence of society than justice" (*TMS* II.ii.3.3). Human approval of using force and punishment on behalf of justice rather than beneficence thus reflects nature's ingenious effort "to raise and support" the "immense fabric of human society." Beneficence is like "the ornament which embellishes, not the foundation which supports the building"; it is recommended but not imposed. Justice, however, is "the main pillar that upholds the whole edifice" (II.ii.3.4). The perfection and the happiness of organized human life are thus less the concern of nature than is human survival—preservation and propagation.

Justice and Natural Jurisprudence

The emphasis on necessity pervades the discussion of natural jurisprudence that concludes *The Theory of Moral Sentiments*:

Every system of positive law may be regarded as a more or less imperfect attempt towards a system of natural jurisprudence. . . . As the violation of justice is what men will never submit to from one another, the public magistrate is under a necessity of employing the power of the commonwealth to enforce the practice of this virtue. Without this precaution, civil society would become a scene of bloodshed and disorder. (*TMS* VII.iv.36)

Natural jurisprudence is an inquiry into "the natural rules of justice independent of all positive institutions"; it attempts to provide "a theory of the general principles which ought to run through, and be the foundation of, the laws of all nations." As we have seen, Smith laments the late date at which "the philosophy of law was treated of by itself, and without regard to the particular institutions of any one nation" (VII.iv.37). On a quick reading, it sounds as if Smith were alleging that the distinction between natural and conventional justice is a recent discovery; one wonders what Smith finds lacking in the treatment of law in ancient and medieval political philosophy. Smith explains that Cicero's *Offices* and Aristotle's *Ethics* "treat of justice in the same general manner in which they treat of all the other virtues" (37). That is, they forsake the special precision with which justice, as distinct from the other virtues, may be determined (III.6.10–11). As we have seen, Plato and Cicero also fall short, providing laws of police, not of justice or "equity" (VII.iv.37); Smith achieves universality and precision for justice only by detaching it from politics, from the question of the regime. For Plato, Aristotle, and Cicero, of course, the laws aimed not only at a broader version of justice than Smith's "mere justice," but at other virtues as well. Consequently, a systematic, precise, and universal science of the laws was perhaps out of the question. Grotius, whom Smith identifies as a pioneer of natural jurisprudence, draws extensively on Plato, Aristotle, and Cicero, but anticipates Smith by elevating property at the expense of moral and intellectual virtue.[56] In Pocock's words, "the child of Jurisprudence is liberalism."[57]

Smith's natural jurisprudence, like his moral philosophy and political economy, reformulates the "ought" to bring it closer to the "is": natural jurisprudence is the science of the principles upon which civil and criminal law "either are or ought to be founded" (*TMS* VI.ii.Intro.2). Compared with the laws, not to mention the regimes, of the ancient philosophers, jurisprudence exists in much less tension with the realm of the necessary. Nay, it is spawned by an almost universal necessity: in all governments that possess "any considerable authority," the magistrate "undertakes to do justice to all" (VII.iv.36), i.e., Smith's "mere justice" of preventing harm and redressing injury. In a "well-governed" state there will in addition be appointed judges and prescribed rules for "regulating" their decisions. These rules are "in general, intended to coincide with those of natural justice," though the intention is not always actualized; nowhere "do the decisions of positive law coincide exactly, in every case, with the rules which the natural sense of justice would dictate" (36). There is a *telos*, but one that is more easily realized than the Aristotelian version. The easy actualizability of Smithian justice reflects the power with which nature supports human preservation, propagation, and prosperity, even though that power is manifested with complexity if not paradox in our "natural" moral sentiments.[58]

Smith specifies four sources of the possible disjunction between positive law and natural justice: the state's constitution, i.e., "the interest of the government"; "the interest of particular orders of men who tyrannize the government"; the "rudeness and barbarism" of a primitive people; a poor court system (VII.iv.36). The obstacle to the coincidence of natural and conventional justice thus may lie in interests or in institutions, but not in ignorance about what justice is. The place that might be occupied by incorrect opinions about justice is taken by the backwardness of sentiments in countries where "the rudeness and barbarism of the people hinder the natural sentiments of justice from arriving at that accuracy and precision which, in more civilized nations, they naturally attain to" (36). Smith thus replaces the ascent from opinion to knowledge with the civilized/savage matrix, just as in *The Wealth of Nations* he employs the four-stages theory rather than dialectical philosophy in determining the duties of the sovereign, including the administration of justice. At the end of *The Theory of Moral Sentiments*, Smith promises "another discourse" to provide "the general principles of law and government," focusing on their changes in the "different ages and periods of society." His last words are that he will now say no more about "the history of jurisprudence."

CHAPTER FOUR

'Homo Economicus'

THE DISCIPLINE OF ECONOMICS is frequently faulted today for its reliance on the concept of "economic man": a calculative being who "rationally" seeks to maximize its preference-satisfaction or utility. In general, economic models assume that money, the universal means to "goods and services," and leisure are our dominant goals. "Utility" is a more comprehensive term, leaving room for the obvious variety in what people pursue. As a rule, economists do not attempt to enlighten people about what goals they should seek. Rather than prescribe the genuine constituents of what is useful or good, they provide a framework for facilitating the efficient pursuit of wants or goals, however constituted; in the famous definition, economics studies the allocation of scarce resources to competing ends. Insofar as the discipline is genuinely neutral concerning the content of the competing ends, it is Machiavellian in helping everyone get what they want without regard to the goodness or moral character of what they want. Insofar as the discipline is not fully neutral regarding ends, it is Machiavellian in endorsing the end that most people want most of the time: material comfort. Like Machiavelli, economists generously counsel others about how to be selfish.

Friends as well as critics of "economic man" have held *The Wealth of Nations* partially responsible for his creation and his present status in the discipline. To some extent, Smith both describes human nature in such terms and encourages the associated character traits, but these tendencies coexist with broader perspectives. Smith acknowledges, encourages, and perhaps even exalts other dimensions of human character.

Not surprisingly, however, Smith's legacy reflects what could be called the "impetus" of his writings—the impressions his writings would tend to make when examined without special diligence—which is narrower than his full vision. The generally detached or "objective" tone of his prose anticipates the scientific posture so prominent among contemporary scholars, but missing today are the undercurrents of irony and ambiguity that call dominant values into question.

The equivalent to economic man in Smith's corpus is human nature insofar as it is constituted by the desire for commodities, ease, security, and bodily comfort. In this chapter, we will examine the ways Smith juggles economic man and "political man," who might be defined by his pursuit of such things as mastery, domination, glory, independence, and nobility. We will also examine the highly complex analysis of human psychology that reverberates through Smith's exposition of fundamental economic concepts such as the division of labor, the commercial "disposition," and exchange value.

Spiritedness and Appetite

Duncan Forbes diagnoses the following tension within Smith's thought: although man's desire to better his condition "leads naturally to increasing opulence," there is "another, unfailing principle, man's desire to dominate others and enforce his will, which brings it about that the progress of opulence will not diminish but tend to increase and worsen slavery" (p. 199). Forbes says little, however, to elaborate the psychology that underlies the two impulses—bettering one's condition and domination—or to explain how Smith tries to influence their mixing.

Smith's most systematic exploration of the relevant psychology comes in his discussion of the account of the soul presented in Plato's *Republic*. Smith identifies the first of the two irrational "faculties" of the soul with "what the schoolmen call the irascible part" (i.e., *thymos*). The correlative passions—"ambition, animosity, the love of honour and the dread of shame, the desire of victory, superiority, and revenge"—are founded in "pride and resentment" and associated with "spirit or natural fire" (*TMS* VII.ii.1.4). The second faculty (i.e., *epithymia*) is "founded in the love of pleasure, or in what the schoolmen called the concupiscible part of the soul," comprehending "all the appetites of the body, the love of ease and security, and of all sensual gratification." Despite the tendency of both sets of passions to rebel against reason, the soul's "governing principle," they both (according to Smith's Plato) are necessary. The concupiscible passions serve "to provide for the support and necessities of the body." The spirited passions serve "to defend us against injuries, to assert our rank and dignity in the world, to make us aim at what is noble and honourable." The former were regarded as the "more generous and noble" set of passions; when sculpted into the virtues of fortitude and magnanimity, they could function as "the auxiliaries of reason" to make their possessor "despise all dangers in the pursuit of what was honourable and noble" (VII.i.1.4–7). Given the general parallel in the *Republic* between city and soul/man, it is natural to associate spirit with politics and appetite with economics: spirit in the soul corresponds to the ruling guardian class of the city, appetite to the productive but subordinate class.[1] In the *Republic*, of course, the spirited guardians are ultimately subordinate to the true rulers, the philosopher-kings. But there is no place for the philosopher-kings in Smithian society or for their equivalent in the Smithian soul: Smith rejects the Platonic view that the passions are the "natural subject" of reason, that reason is the soul's "ruling principle," and that reason determines not only "the proper means for attaining any end, but also what ends are fit to be pursued" (*TMS* VII.ii.1.3–4). Smith never criticizes the Platonic account of spirit and appetite, and the terminology with which he describes the two faculties reverberates throughout his corpus. We may therefore suppose that Smith intended to analyze and even to direct the interplay between them, perhaps especially with a view to specifying the faculty that will assume the throne from which reason was expelled—rulership of the soul. At first glance, *The Wealth of Nations* seems to reflect the prominence of the economic traits and *The Theory of Moral Sentiments* of the political, but the full picture is more complex—we face another set of paradoxes related to the "Adam Smith Problem."

The desire to better one's condition, as presented in *The Wealth of Nations*, aims at objects characteristic of the appetitive faculty (as depicted in *The Theory of Moral Sentiments*)—at "ease," "security," and bodily gratification rather than at the honor, superiority, victory, and nobility associated with *thymos*. Because no one is ever "perfectly and completely satisfied with his situation," we are perpetually desirous of "bettering our condition"; for most of us, the betterment desired is increased wealth (*WN* II.iii.28). In the remaining uses of the phrase (bettering one's condition) in *The Wealth of Nations*, it is identified with "ease," "plenty," "opulence," "the conveniencies and elegancies of life," "wealth and prosperity," and "preservation."[2] There are, however, qualifications to this emphasis on ease and opulence. First, Smith brands wealth as only the most "obvious" and "vulgar" means of betterment. Second, Smith's most detailed elaboration of the principle identifies it as "the principle which prompts to save," capable of counterbalancing the principle prompting expense—"the passion for present enjoyment" (II.iii.28). The appetitive passions thus have a long-term as well as a short-term dimension. The "love of present ease and enjoyment," linked with the hatred of labor, is indeed the passion that prompts the poor to plunder (V.i.b.2).

These qualifications, however, do not suffice to dispel the shock that occurs when one turns to the sole discussion of "bettering our condition" in *The Theory of Moral Sentiments*. Smith begins by explaining that "we pursue riches and avoid poverty" chiefly out of concern for the "sentiments of mankind." Befitting the gravity of the theme, Smith proceeds to employ a rhetorical device he employs only rarely: posing and then answering searching questions.

> For to what purpose is all the toil and bustle of this world? What is the end of avarice and ambition, of the pursuit of wealth, of power, and pre-eminence? Is it to supply the necessities of nature? (*TMS* I.iii.2.1)

Smith answers that the wages of "the meanest labourer" can supply these necessities—"food and clothing, the comfort of a house, and of a family." Indeed, a careful examination of this laborer's "oeconomy" would show that a large portion of his wages is spent "upon conveniences, which may be regarded as superfluities, and that, upon extraordinary occasions, he can give something even to vanity and distinction." Smith winds up with a flourish:

> From whence, then, arises that emulation which runs through all the different ranks of men, and what are the advantages which we propose by that great purpose of human life which we call bettering our condition? To be observed, to be attended to, to be taken notice of with sympathy, complacency, and approbation, are all the advantages which we can propose to derive from it. It is the vanity, not the ease or the pleasure, which interests us. (*TMS* I.iii.2.1)

The attainment of "greatness" brings "observation and fellow-feeling," which compensate, "in the opinion of mankind,"

> all that toil, all that anxiety, all those mortifications, which must be undergone in pursuit of it; and what is of yet more consequence, all that leisure, all that ease, all that careless security, which are forfeited for ever by the acquisition. (*TMS* I.iii.2.1)

Scholars often quote this paragraph, but generally suppose the problem can be disposed of by pointing to the claim in *The Wealth of Nations* that for most of the wealthy, "the chief enjoyment of riches consists in the parade of riches" (I.xi.c.31). There are other passages in *The Wealth of Nations* where Smith admits vanity and the desire for admiration as important motivations,[3] but the overwhelming emphasis of the book is on wealth. The desire to better one's material condition seems to be the dominant, independent drive.

Necessity and Superfluity

Wealth, as defined in *The Wealth of Nations*, is constituted by "necessaries, conveniencies, and amusements" (I.v.1). In the very first sentence of the book, Smith identifies labor as the fund that supplies a nation with all the "necessaries and conveniencies" it consumes; the phrase, occasionally without "amusements," appears throughout. In one of the crucial passages on bettering one's condition, Smith distinguishes the situation in the feudal countryside, where people were defenseless and therefore content with "their necessary subsistence," from what happens when they are "secure of enjoying the fruits of their industry": they "naturally exert it to better their condition, and to acquire not only the necessaries, but the conveniencies and elegancies of life" (III.iii.12). One may infer that whatever the situation, people will strive to subsist and survive. Smith's balancing of the appetitive faculty with the spirited faculty hinges on the liberation of the pursuit for things beyond subsistence.

According to *The Theory of Moral Sentiments*, as we have seen, the toil and bustle of bettering one's condition are not for the sake of "the necessaries of nature"—food, clothing, a house, and a family. Even the "meanest" laborer, moreover, can afford "conveniencies," "superfluities," and some articles of "vanity and distinction." In *The Wealth of Nations*, Smith states that "after food, cloathing and lodging are the two great wants of mankind" (I.xi.c.2), and proceeds to explain how vanity enters into the quest for conveniences and amusements. Apart from food, human "wants and fancies" focus on "cloathing and lodging, household furniture, and what is called Equipage." Rich and poor consume the same quantity of food, although not the same quality. But their wardrobe and accommodations differ greatly in quantity as well as quality:

> The desire of food is limited in every man by the narrow capacity of the human stomach; but the desire of the conveniencies and ornaments of building, dress, equipage, and household furniture, seems to have no limit or certain boundary. . . . What is over and above satisfying the limited desire, is given for the amusement of those desires which cannot be satisfied, but seem to be altogether endless. (*WN* I.xi.c.7)

Whereas the desire for necessaries is thus finite and easily satisfied, the desire for conveniences and amusements is infinite. A society devoted to satisfying the insatiable desires will require unceasing economic growth.

Near the end of *The Wealth of Nations*, moreover, Smith concedes that even "necessary" is a changing concept: it is partially constituted by the desire for esteem and is therefore partly determined by custom. Necessities are not only those commodities "indispensably necessary for the support of life, but whatever the custom of the country renders it indecent for creditable people, even of the lowest order, to be without." Only what exceeds this is truly a luxury (V.ii.k.3). Such is the power of the human longing for esteem and, therefore, of custom as opposed to nature. In the sections of *The Theory of Moral Sentiments* added for the 1790 edition, Smith claims that the "necessaries and conveniencies" of the body "are always very easily supplied." Although external goods are "originally recommended to us" to supply these bodily needs, they are eventually pursued more for the respect and rank they bring (*TMS* VI.i.3).[4]

Avarice, Vanity, and Pride

The concessions in *The Wealth of Nations* to the yearning for esteem are rhetorically eclipsed by the overall emphasis on material opulence (and the related primacy of nature over convention). Even in the passages conceding the power of esteem, there is no hint of the plaintive questioning of the world's "toil and bustle." At least two explanations may be offered for the discrepancy. First, Smith's rhetorical elevation of wealth at the expense of esteem may promote social peace. The esteem and admiration that come from wealth are inherently relative—a "zero-sum game," in contemporary parlance: only some can enjoy them. Material goods, on the other hand, can be enjoyed in increasing amounts by an entire society, even if what fuels their pursuit is a competitive streak in human nature that both reveals and reflects the sublimated desire for esteem.[5] Indeed, the contemporary imperative of economic growth is often attributed to the perceived likelihood that once the "pie" has stopped growing, people will be more combative about how it is divided. A second explanation is that the readers' interest in the wealth of *nations* may be augmented by the book's relentless investigation of wealth's causes. In *The Theory of Moral Sentiments*, Smith suggests that the best way to "implant public virtue" is not to list the advantages enjoyed by subjects in a well-governed state—"that they are better lodged, . . . clothed [and] . . . fed"—but "to describe the great system of public police which procures these advantages" (*TMS* IV.1.11). The basic necessities are obviously not the most inspiring public goals. The presentation of the complex machinery at work to promote them appeals to another powerful human longing, what Smith calls "the spirit of system." A fascination with the mechanism of increasing national wealth, generated by Smith's "system of political economy," might eclipse the concern for wealth itself. What we have here, however, is a second-order displacement, insofar as wealth (along with "greatness") is pursued as a means to esteem and admiration rather than for its own sake.

The passage in *The Theory of Moral Sentiments* on bettering one's condition explains ambition, the quest for "power," as well as avarice, the quest for wealth (*TMS* I.iii.2.1). Indeed, Smith later indicates that the "objects of avarice and ambition differ only in their greatness. A miser is as furious about a halfpenny as a man of ambition about the conquest of a kingdom"; ambition is thus the pursuit of "great objects of self-interest" whose "loss or acquisition quite changes the rank of the person" (III.6.7). Political economy's status as a means to "wealth and greatness," "riches and power," suggests that political and economic ends are equally important. According to *The Theory of Moral Sentiments*, the pursuit of both ends (beyond necessities) is motivated by "vanity," not the desire for ease or pleasure. Being noticed and observed, enjoying "sympathy," "approbation," and "fellow-feeling," is what counterbalances the ill effects of the pursuit of wealth and power: toil, anxiety, and mortification; the loss of liberty, leisure, ease, and "careless security" (*TMS* I.iii.2.1). It looks like a clean opposition between the spirited and the appetitive faculties. First, the appetitive faculty, whose function is "to provide for the support and necessities of the body," clearly drives the pursuit of necessities. Second, the pursuit of conveniences and amusements comes at the expense of the "ease and security" sought by the appetitive faculty. Third, the spirited faculty is explicitly identified with ambition and pride (VII.ii.1.5). But the vanity that stimulates the desire to better one's condition differs from the spirited faculty as Smith describes it. Vanity seeks "fellow-feeling," "sympathy," and "approbation," whereas *thymos* is characterized by "animosity," "victory," and "revenge" (VII.ii.1.4).[6]

Smith's innovation is to turn the longing for honor and superiority into the longing for fellow feeling and love. As John Danford has argued, egalitarianism partly underlies Smith's elevation of the quest for sympathy at the expense of the quest for independence, glory, or honor (pp. 691, 695). On Smith's presentation, people conceal poverty because it would deprive them of sympathy, not because their pride would suffer if their lack of independence were displayed. The rich man "glories in his riches," as Smith puts it, because they make the world "disposed to *go along with him* in all those agreeable emotions with which the advantages of his situation so readily inspire him" (*TMS* I.iii.2.1), not because they render him independent and self-sufficient. Unlike Hobbes and Rousseau, Smith identifies vanity with peace rather than war; Mandeville did likewise, but at the expense of the distinction between noble and base, which Smith strives to salvage. The desire for esteem and approbation that defines human psychology according to Smith's books is a blend of the concupiscible ends—"ease and security," the bodily appetites—and the thymotic longings for mastery and domination, what Smith calls "natural insolence" (WN V.i.g.19).

Both of Smith's books acknowledge the centrality of the harder side of *thymos* in the human psyche. Early in *The Wealth of Nations*, Smith stresses that an African king, although "the absolute master of the lives and liberties of ten thousand naked savages," is likely to be far poorer than a European peasant (I.i.11). But the longing for mastery periodically bubbles through the calm economic sea. Smith treats envy, malice, and resentment as nearly universal (though usually episodic) human passions (V.i.b.2). In addition, Smith admits that the longing for independence and self-sufficiency may counterbalance the desire for wealth (I.viii.48, III.i.5). Smith's analysis of the factors determining wage levels likewise incorporates our "romantick hopes for honour and distinction" as well as our longings for admiration, adventure, and the conquest of "hardship and danger."[7] Perhaps even more striking is Smith's occasional praise of courage and war.[8]

In *The Theory of Moral Sentiments*, surprisingly, the military virtues are portrayed even more sympathetically in the final edition. "Good soldiers, who both love and trust their general" often proceed more joyously on a hopeless mission than on an easy one because they "feel that they are making the noblest exertion which it is possible for man to make" (TMS VI.ii.3.4). The "habitual contempt of danger and death . . . ennobles the profession of a soldier" and causes it to be regarded as having "a rank and dignity superior to that of any other profession"; indeed, "no character is more contemptible than that of a coward" (VI.iii.7,17). The de-emphasis of self-preservation necessary to sustain this defense of courage and war is most evident in Smith's argument that "a brave man ought to die rather than make a promise which he can neither keep without folly nor violate without ignominy" (VII.iv.13).

The passage referred to by Forbes sheds special light on the interrelation of political and economic impulses:

> The pride of man makes him love to domineer, and nothing mortifies him so much as to be obliged to condescend to persuade his inferiors. Wherever the law allows it, and the nature of the work can afford it, therefore, he will generally prefer the service of slaves to that of freemen. (WN III.ii.10)

This formulation closely parallels a later remark that our "natural insolence" is such that we almost always prefer to govern by violence rather than by "management and persuasion" (V.i.g.19). Pride and insolence make us want to "domineer" rather than "persuade," and Smith does little to combat them directly. Just as his moral philosophy tries to sublimate the thymotic propensity to dominate into the pursuit of esteem, his economic science tries to sublimate it into the persuasion entailed by "exchange."

Persuasion, Compulsion, and Commercial Society

Smith's investigation of the division of labor discloses a counterweight in "human nature" to insolence or the desire to domineer: "the propensity to truck, barter, and exchange" (*WN* I.ii.1), which is indeed "the Principle which gives occasion to the Division of Labour" (I.ii). Smith elaborates this propensity by developing the contrast between human beings and animals. The propensity is "common to all men" but characterizes no other animal. Animals do not engage in contracts or exchange; no animal claims "this is mine, that yours." The only means of "persuasion" available to an animal is "to gain the favour of those whose service it requires," as when a hungry spaniel "endeavours by a thousand attractions to engage the attention of its master" (I.ii.2). Although the human individual occasionally resorts to "servile and fawning attention" to obtain the good will of his fellows, he lacks the time to do so generally: "In civilized society he stands at all times in need of the cooperation and assistance of great multitudes, while his whole life is scarce sufficient to gain the friendship of a few persons" (I.ii.2). Human beings thus differ from animals not only because they distinguish mine and thine and engage in exchange rather than fawning, but because they need more from each other, especially in a civilized society; Smith illustrates this beautifully in the last paragraph of the first chapter by demonstrating that the number of people involved in procuring "the accommodation of the most common artificer or day labourer in a civilized and thriving country . . . exceeds all computation" (I.i.11).[9]

In almost every race of animals, on the other hand, the mature "individual" is totally independent. Smith proceeds with his famous statement on self-love and benevolence:

> But man has almost constant occasion for the help of his brethren, and it is in vain for him to expect it from their benevolence only. He will be more likely to prevail if he can interest their self-love in his favour, and shew them that it is for their own advantage to do for him what he requires of them. Whoever offers to another a bargain of any kind, proposes to do this. . . . It is not from the benevolence of the butcher, the brewer, or the

baker, that we expect our dinner, but from their regard to their own interest. We address ourselves, not to their humanity, but to their self-love, and
never talk to them of our own necessities but of their advantages. (*WN*
I.ii.2)

The relationship of human individuals to one another is thus characterized by a blend of separateness and unity. We distinguish mine and thine;
we need "cooperation and assistance," but we can generally obtain them
only by offering something in return, by exchange.[10] One may infer that
neither benevolence nor belligerence can be relied upon in the long run.
Smith proceeds to explain how the trucking disposition creates a division of labor, as individuals find it in their "interest" to specialize in
certain tasks (I.ii.3).

Division of Labor, Equality, and Philosophy

In contrast to Plato, Smith presents the division of labor in a thoroughly egalitarian light. The best city of the *Republic* relies on the
division of labor, in part because different "natures" are suited to different jobs (370b).[11] Smith, however, argues that the division of labor is
more a cause than an effect of differing talents: "The difference between
the most dissimilar characters, between a philosopher and a common
street porter, for example, seems to arise not so much from nature, as
from habit, custom, and education," although the philosopher's "vanity"
makes him skeptical. Smith explains this to vindicate the more general
proposition that the "difference of natural talents in different men is, in
reality, much less than we are aware of" (*WN* I.ii.4). This is as strong an
argument for natural equality as appears in *The Wealth of Nations*.[12]
Despite the importance and the complexity of the division of labor in a
modern society, Smith emphasizes that it neither reflects nor justifies
any profound cleavages, for example, between master and slave or between wise and ignorant. Within many animal species, the members

derive from nature a much more remarkable distinction of genius, than
what, antecedent to custom and education, appears to take place among
men. By nature a philosopher is not in genius and disposition half so
different from a street porter, as a mastiff is from a greyhound, or a greyhound from a spaniel, or this last from a shepherd's dog. (*WN* I.ii.5)

Lacking the "power or disposition to barter and exchange," however, the
"different geniuses and talents" of the animals "cannot be brought into a
common stock, and do not in the least contribute to the better accommodation and conveniency of the species," whereas the trucking disposition brings products "as it were, into a common stock, where every man

may purchase whatever part of the produce of other men's talents he has occasion for" (I.ii.5).[13] By articulating a version of equality compatible with the apparent differences between people, Smith remains within the ambit of liberalism.

In singling out the philosopher and the porter as "the most dissimilar characters" who nevertheless differ less than greyhound and spaniel, Smith explicitly combats the philosopher's "vanity." Social scientists today are no longer burdened with such combat, and they would not contrast a porter and a philosopher as "the most dissimilar characters." The combat waged by Smith and other modern philosophers against the philosopher's vanity has perhaps succeeded. Compared with Hobbes and Marx, however, Smith concedes a great deal to this vanity. *The Wealth of Nations*, especially the first few chapters, delicately weaves together ancient and modern notions of philosophy to delineate an agenda that harmonizes the interests of philosophy and society.[14]

Exchange Value

The mix of persuasion and compulsion that characterizes the trucking disposition is reflected in the basic concept of Smith's economic science, exchange value. At the beginning of the fourth chapter of *The Wealth of Nations*, "Of the Origin and Use of Money," Smith identifies "commercial society" with the existence of a thoroughly established division of labor: "Every man thus lives by exchanging, or becomes in some measure a merchant, and the society itself grows to be what is properly a commercial society." At the end of the chapter, Smith sketches the economic science that he will present in the remainder of Book I to uncover "the rules which men naturally observe" in exchanging commodities. The investigation will concern not the "value in use" or utility of an object, but "the power of purchasing other goods which the possession of that object conveys," that is, its "value in exchange," or price (I.iv.1,12–13). It is no accident that Smith's political economy and subsequent economics consistently refrain from evaluating the actual usefulness, much less the goodness or rightness, of human possessions and activities; in contemporary parlance, these are "non-economic questions."[15] Smith's political economy, however, is more frank than that of his neoclassical successors in admitting the political dimension of exchange value. The value of a commodity for the person who wishes to exchange it is "the quantity of labour which it enables him to purchase or command" (I.v.1). What "command" is to politics, we might venture, "purchase" is to economics; exchange value represents an authoritative claim on the products of labor. The political dimension is still more prominent in Smith's later identification of the "real value" of the land-lord's rent with his "real power and authority, his command of the necessaries and conveniencies of life with which the labour of other people could supply him" (I.xi.b.36).

Smith wishes nevertheless to maintain a firm line between these political and economic dimensions:

> Wealth, as Mr. Hobbes says, is power. But the person who either acquires, or succeeds to a great fortune, does not necessarily acquire or succeed to any political power, either civil or military. His fortune may, perhaps, afford him the means of acquiring both, but the mere possession of that fortune does not necessarily convey to him either. The power which that posses-sion immediately and directly conveys to him, is the power of purchasing; a certain command over all the labour, or over all the produce of labour which is then in the market. (WN I.v.3)

Smith here alludes to a passage from the tenth chapter of *Leviathan*: "Riches joyned with liberality, is Power; because it procureth friends, and servants; without liberality, not so; because in this case they defend not; but expose men to Envy, as a prey." Soon after this passage follows Hobbes's notorious definition of a man's "value" or "worth" as "his Price . . . so much as would be given for the use of his Power." Hobbes thus substitutes an economic perspective for a moral perspective on human "worth," anticipating the consumer sovereignty embedded in Smith's moral philosophy as well as his economics. In Daniel Bell's words, a market economy is defined by consumer sovereignty because "what is to be produced is determined by the aggregate decision of individuals or households, as consumers, in accordance with their taste."[16] That is, people with money can purchase what they want irrespective of its moral character; the remuneration of your labor will reflect the "de-mand" freely expressed by your fellows for what you are able to produce or provide. According to *The Theory of Moral Sentiments*, insofar as a person's worth is determined by the impartial spectator, it is determined by the valuation of ordinary humanity as expressed through what could be dubbed the bargaining of the sympathy market.[17]

Leo Strauss stresses the contrast between Hobbes's "power" and Ma-chiavelli's "glory" as an "amoral substitute for morality": power is "infi-nitely more businesslike than glory. Far from being the goal of a lofty or demonic longing, it is required by, or the expression of, a cold objective necessity."[18] One might say that Smith, in his sole mention of Hobbes in *The Wealth of Nations*, takes the wealth/power connection alleged by a political philosopher and adds precision to it through political economy: Smithian exchange value is more businesslike and less political than

Hobbesian power. It is likewise more calculable (and more susceptible of systematic treatment), just as power is more calculable than glory.[19]

In the chapter cited by Smith, Hobbes defines a man's power as "his present means, to obtain some future apparent Good." Hobbes's approach in a way culminates in his famous defense of preemptive attacks in the state of nature: it is "reasonable" for a man "to master the powers of all men he can . . . until he see no other power great enough to endanger him."[20] Unlike Hobbesian power, Smithian exchange value (in conjunction with money) is a peaceful "present means" to obtain "future apparent goods."[21] As the primary measure of value and means of exchange, money is a social artifact that overcomes qualitative differences to establish a precise quantitative relationship between a breathtaking variety of entities.[22]

The violent character of Hobbes's state of nature derives in part from the connection between foresight and fear. Invoking Prometheus's punishment, Hobbes argues that the man who "looks too far before him, in the care of future time, hath his heart all the day long, gnawed on by feare of death, poverty, or other calamity; and has no repose, nor pause of his anxiety, but in sleep" (*Leviathan*, ch.XII). Smith tempers the fear associated with foresight by substituting the steady but milder anxiety about gradually improving one's situation. This anxiety helps obviate the need for the absolute monarch extolled by Hobbes, not to mention the Machiavellian remedy for "corruption": cruel executions to keep people in line by reminding them of the primal fear.[23] In Robert Lane's words, "It is the genius of the market to stimulate wants without at the same time stimulating a sense of deserving more than one gets" (p. 384). But the obsession of contemporary Western democracies with economic growth, what Bell calls "the secular religion of advancing industrial societies" (p. 237), perhaps vindicates Machiavelli's implicit thesis that people are not grateful for justice. A salary cut is a more personal injury than inflation.

Smith implies that Hobbes simply identified wealth and power (*WN* I.v.3). Hobbes's statement about "riches" and power, however, is surrounded by illustrations of other kinds of power, and it attributes power only to wealth joined with "liberality," which procures "friends and servants." Smith elsewhere acknowledges the power produced by wealth conjoined with liberality, but stresses its deleterious effects. According to Smith, the vast throng of dependents and retainers in the feudal manor, being dependent for sustenance on the lord's "bounty" and "good pleasure," were obliged to obey him; without commerce and manufacturing, the great proprietors could consume their surplus produce only by means of "rustick hospitality" (*WN* III.iv.5–7). In modern, commercial society, riches are no longer conjoined with liberality and therefore do not bring despotic authority in their train. A rich man still maintains a large number of people—the various individuals involved in producing the things he purchases—but he does so indirectly. "Though he contributes, therefore, to the maintenance of them all, they are more or less independent of him, because generally they can all be maintained without him" (III.iv.11). The contrast emerges likewise from the point of view of the "tradesman or artificer," who

> derives his subsistence from the employment, not of one, but of a hundred or a thousand different customers. Though in some measure obliged to them all, therefore, he is not absolutely dependent upon any one of them. (III.iv.12)

The same contrast is incorporated into the four-stages theory. Whereas the shepherd chief, like the feudal baron, derives despotic authority from his wealth, a man in an "opulent and civilized society" may be even wealthier "and yet not be able to command a dozen": he gives things to others "in exchange for an equivalent" (V.i.b.7). Exchange puts everyone on the more or less equal footing of self-interest, and Smith only sporadically laments the corresponding loss of liberality.[24] In hunting society, there is little dependence, little authority, and little wealth for anyone. In shepherd society, there is great wealth for a few and therewith dependence and despotic authority. In commercial society, wealth for many is accompanied by dependence on many and therefore by the diffused and non-despotic "command" associated with exchange value. The great extension of the division of labor, however, by compromising the "intellectual, social, and martial virtues" of "the great body of the people" (V.i.f.50), compromises self-sufficiency. Although the exchange relationship fundamental to commercial society protects people from the despotism and the slavery that express undiluted pride and insolence, it may subject them to the despotism of "capital." Marx nevertheless endorses most of Smith's description of the contrast between feudal and modern society.[25]

Leading and Directing

When we turn to *The Theory of Moral Sentiments*, however, we see that the trucking disposition is still more subtly interwoven with the human desire to rule. In *The Wealth of Nations*, Smith puts aside the question of whether "the propensity to truck, barter, and exchange" is "one of those original principles in human nature, of which no further account can be given." But he briefly indicates an answer: it "seems more probable" that this disposition is "the necessary consequence of the faculties of reason and speech" (WN I.ii.2–3). Smith added, in the 1790 edition of *The Theory of Moral Sentiments*, a few pages discussing the nature of human belief, suggesting that "speech" is itself rooted in ambition:

> The man whom we believe is necessarily, in the things concerning which we believe him, our leader and director, and we look up to him with a certain degree of esteem and respect. But as from admiring people we come to wish to be admired ourselves, so, from being led and directed by other people, we learn to wish to become ourselves leaders and directors. . . . The desire of being believed, the desire of persuading, of leading and directing other people, seems to be one of the strongest of all our natural desires. *It is perhaps the instinct upon which is founded the faculty of speech*, the characteristical faculty of human nature. . . . *Great ambition, the desire of real superiority, of leading and directing, seems to be altogether peculiar to man, and speech is the great instrument of ambition*, of real superiority, of leading and directing the judgments and conduct of other people. (*TMS* VII.iv.24–25)

There is, of course, a certain tentativeness to this linkage of the commercial "propensity" and ambition: it is "probable" that the propensity is "the necessary consequence" of reason and speech (WN I); the desire of "leading and directing other people" is "perhaps" the foundation of the speech faculty (*TMS* VII).[26] The implications for Smith's juggling of politics and economics are nevertheless enormous, for it seems that a political impulse—ambition, the desire for "superiority," for "leading and directing"—underlies the impulse to exchange. Perhaps one should distinguish the economic/exchanging version of ambition that relies on persuasion from the political/enslaving version that relies on violence. In the lectures, Smith further elaborates the relationship between ambition and the commercial propensity:

> If we should enquire into the principle in the human mind on which this disposition of trucking is founded, it is clearly the naturall inclination every one has to persuade. The offering of a shilling . . . is in reality offering an argument to persuade one to do so and so as it is for his interest. Men always endeavour to persuade others to be of their opinion even when the matter is of no consequence to them. . . . Every one is practising oratory on others thro the whole of his life. (*LJA* vi.56)

Robert Heilbroner, in a review of Donald McCloskey's *The Rhetoric of Economics*, correctly observes that the account of the trucking disposition in *The Wealth of Nations* is more cautious than in the lectures, but he overlooks the relevance of the above passage from *The Theory of Moral Sentiments*.[27] On the whole, Smith's lectures are indeed more blunt than his writings. McCloskey, however, proceeds without any reference to Smith's rhetoric; he mentions Smith only thrice (pp. 15, 27, 77), and for trivial purposes. It seems that Smith's rhetoric tends to mute the place of rhetoric in his "sciences," if not the place of ambition in the human soul; it seems that Smith was uncertain about the extent to which the connection between exchange and ambition should be broadcast. Whatever his concerns about "leading and directing," Smith refrains from directly and comprehensively evaluating the fitness of different groups or types to lead and direct their fellows. He seems to prefer that people be led by less visible hands.

Bourgeois Virtue and Its Alternatives

The Hirschman Thesis

According to Albert Hirschman, Smith, like earlier modern theorists, tried to restrain the "destructive passions" without relying on "moralizing philosophy and religious precept," but innovated by liberating self-interest for "economic" reasons (i.e., for the sake of public opulence).[28] The earlier thinkers pursued several strategies: using the passions centered on avarice to temper other passions, for example, ambition and lust; relying on the calm and calculating features of "interest" to counteract passion generally. Hirschman is especially interested in the *doux commerce* thesis, associated especially with Montesquieu: that commerce produces a general softening of manners and serves to restrain the arbitrary violence of political rulers.[29] Hirschman acknowledges only one vestige of the *doux commerce* thesis in *The Wealth of Nations*: the contribution of commerce to breaking the power of the feudal lords and thereby liberating the countryside from violence and chaos (pp. 100–101). He thus overlooks the general contrast Smith draws between the despotism characteristic of shepherd society and the persuasion/exchange characteristic of commercial society.

I nevertheless agree with Hirschman's account of Smith's legacy: that "scholarly and policy debate" focused on Smith's proposition that laissez-faire is the best means to augment the wealth of nations, a focus that "represented a considerable narrowing of the field of inquiry over which social thought had ranged freely up to then" (p. 112). The complexities of Smith's thought about non-economic subjects (especially religion) have indeed been underappreciated.[30] Even Hirschman, however, is guilty of oversimplifying Smith's account of human psychology. As presented in *The Wealth of Nations*, according to Hirschman, people are "actuated entirely" by the desire to better their condition, and there seems to be no place for "the richer concept of human nature in which men are driven by, and often torn between, diverse passions of which 'avarice' was only one."[31] In fact, Smith portrays the desire to better one's material condition as clashing with a variety of competing human motivations. We have already explored the contribution of the appetitive and the spirited faculties to bettering one's condition and the penetration of exchange value by ambition; we have touched on the tension between opulence and insolence. Hirschman's errors support my suggestion that the dominant messages of *The Wealth of Nations* usually make more of an impression than the complications, including the vestiges of older views. The complexity of Smith's portrayal of human character approaches unintelligibility.[32]

Bourgeois Virtue

The closest approximation to *homo economicus* in Smith's corpus is the individual characterized by what might be called "bourgeois virtue"—commitment to a long and steady course of industry and frugality, within the bounds of justice or law, for the sake of material betterment. This character reflects the economist's assumption that scarcity is permanent; the necessity to acquire is potentially limitless because we never have enough. This character is likewise the embodiment of Weber's "spirit of capitalism." Capitalism, according to Weber, is the pursuit of "forever renewed profit, by means of continuous, rational, capitalistic enterprise." The corresponding individual is "the sober, middle class, self-made man."[33]

The endorsement of bourgeois virtue appears in both of Smith's books. The desire of bettering our condition generates the "frugality," "parsimony," and disposition to save that cause capital accumulation and therewith the progress of opulence.[34] The contrary "passion for present enjoyment"—which prompts spending rather than saving—is "sometimes violent and very difficult to be restrained," although "in general only momentary and occasional." The desire to better one's condition, on the other hand, is "generally calm and dispassionate," though it accompanies us from womb to tomb (*WN* II.iii.28). Elsewhere in *The Wealth of Nations*, we learn that great fortunes are seldom acquired without "a long life of industry, frugality, and attention" (I.x.b.38). Other key components of bourgeois virtue are the "habits . . . of order, oeconomy, and attention" (III.iv.3) and the ability to pay "exact attention to small savings and small gains" (III.ii.7). Needless to say, Smith thinks that "the prejudices of some political writers against shopkeepers and tradesmen, are altogether without foundation" (II.v.7).

The Theory of Moral Sentiments yields similar impressions. The most detailed discussion of bourgeois virtue occurs in Part VI, which was added for the 1790 edition, in a section entitled "Of the Character of the Individual, So Far As It Affects His own Happiness; Or of Prudence." The emphasis here on the virtues of self-interest is indeed stronger, or at least more detailed, than in the earlier editions of the work. The "first and principal object of prudence" is security; prudence is "rather cautious than enterprising" and therefore recommends "real knowledge and skill in our trade or profession, assiduity and industry in the exercise of it, frugality, and even some degree of parsimony, in all our expenses" (*TMS* VI.i.6). In remarks that call to mind the discussion in *The Wealth of Nations* of saving and spending, Smith identifies the "industry and frugality" of the prudent man with his "steadily sacrificing the ease and enjoyment of the present moment." The "situation" of such a man grows "better and better every day" (VI.i.11–12).[35]

In addition to emphasizing the economic virtues possessed by the prudent man, Smith emphasizes his apolitical character. The prudent man "has no taste for that foolish importance which many people wish to derive from appearing to have some influence in the management" of other people's affairs.[36] He would prefer "that the public business were well managed by some other person," leaving him to "the undisturbed enjoyment of secure tranquillity" (VI.i.13). Smith's prudent man, unlike Machiavelli's, shows more interest in maintaining than in acquiring and has his sights set on wealth, not on gaining a principality.

This vision of the prudent man is articulated, however, even in the earlier editions of *The Theory of Moral Sentiments*. First, Smith argues that rising "gradually to greatness" is preferable to a "sudden revolution of fortune" because it produces less envy (I.ii.5.1, III.3.31). Second, bourgeois virtue is identified especially with the lower classes. The "man of inferior rank," the "private man," should attempt to distinguish himself by "the labour of his body and the activity of his mind," by "superior knowledge in his profession, and superior industry in the exercise of it" (I.iii.2.5);[37] the virtues of "the inferior ranks" include "parsimonious frugality" and "painful industry" (V.2.3). In a chapter added for the final edition, Smith points out that "in all the middling and inferior professions, real and solid professional abilities, joined to prudent, just, firm, and temperate conduct, can very seldom fail of success" (I.iii.3.5).[38]

The treatment in Part VII of previous moral philosophers further clarifies Smith's appraisal of bourgeois virtue. Hutcheson's system, which defined virtue as benevolence, fails to explain "our approbation of the inferior virtues of prudence, vigilance, circumspection, temperance, constancy, firmness" (VII.ii.3.15). In the midst of an otherwise accurate presentation of previous thinkers, Smith identifies the Aristotelian virtue that is a mean between "avarice and profusion" as "frugality" (*TMS* VII.ii.1.12) rather than liberality, *eleutheriotes*. The gravity of the substitution is driven home by Smith's definition of frugality as "eager to be rich" (*WN* IV.i.1): Aristotle's liberal man is not acquisitive and rapacious, unlike Machiavelli's.[39] Indeed, Smith adapts Machiavelli (not to mention Mandeville) in arguing that the man of "base and selfish disposition" (who acquires durable objects for himself) may contribute more to public opulence than the man of "liberal or generous spirit" whose wealth is consumed in hospitality (*WN* II.iii.39–42).

Present Enjoyment

To understand fully Smith's promulgation of bourgeois virtue, one must tease from his writings an awareness of those human longings that may compete with it. The most obvious competitor is the "passion for present enjoyment," which Smith explicitly juxtaposes with the desire of bettering one's condition. This passion would lead us to consume rather than produce, and to prefer ease to labor. It seems to be a pure expression of the concupiscible love of "ease and security" (*TMS* VII.ii.1.4), and Smith explicitly acknowledges its power. Forgoing present pleasure for the sake of pleasure "which we are to enjoy ten years hence" requires the "sense of propriety" (i.e., the "consciousness of . . . merited approbation") and thus yields "that eminent esteem with which all men naturally regard a steady perseverance in the practice of frugality, industry, and application, though directed to no other purpose than the acquisition of fortune" (IV.2.8). Indeed, the labor theory of value that provides the foundation for Smith's economic analysis supposes that labor is "toil and trouble" (*WN* I.v.2), a sacrifice of "ease," "liberty," and "happiness" (I.v.7); this is why exchange value—command over others' labor—is valuable. Smith identifies not labor but the "relaxation" that follows it as "the call of nature" (I.viii.44). One could even say that labor is opposed to interest, for Smith asserts that "it is the interest of every man to live as much at his ease as he can" (V.i.f.7). Government itself is chiefly necessary to prevent the invasion of property, which is engaged in by the poor out of "hatred of labour and the love of present ease and enjoyment" (V.i.b.2). When Smith refers to the Blessed Isles depicted by the poets, a "life of friendship, liberty, and repose; free from labour, and from care" (*TMS* I.ii.2.2), one wonders whether the premise of a deep-seated human aversion to labor requires that happiness lie in an impoverished but easy life.[40] As Smith puts it later in a famous passage, "The beggar, who suns himself by the side of the highway, possesses that security which kings are fighting for" (*TMS* IV.1.10).

Grasping Ambition

As we have seen, Smith is reasonably explicit about the potential tension between human insolence and economic progress. A similar contrast may be drawn regarding bourgeois virtue. First, one may contrast slow, steady acquisition with the more violent thrust for rapid gain: Smith warns us that "avarice and injustice are always shortsighted" (WN III.ii.16). Various thinkers, the most illustrious being J. B. Say and Joseph Schumpeter, have argued that Smith's emphasis on gradual advancement, on caution over enterprise, comes at the expense of aggression, creativity, adventure, and risk even in a purely economic setting.[41] Although Smith acknowledges the contribution of speculation to innovation (I.x.b.43), he recommends that the law set a maximum interest rate, not too far above the lowest market rate, in order to discourage the "prodigals and projectors" who would tend to be the sole borrowers if the rate were very high; he even warns banks about lending large sums for capital investment (II.iv.15, II.ii.64). Second, Smith's books are permeated by his attempts to deflate human intoxication with various forms of "dazzling" acquisition.[42] In his one discussion of Machiavelli in *The Theory of Moral Sentiments*, Smith tries to explain why "the violence and injustice of great conquerors are often regarded with foolish wonder and admiration" (VI.i.16). Smith implicitly combats such wonder and admiration by drawing attention to the "sober lustre" that accompanies industry and frugality, virtues "much less dazzling" than "the more splendid actions of the hero, the statesman, or the legislator" (VI.iii.13).

Love and Benevolence

Smith's sympathy for the "benevolent" alternative to bourgeois virtue has been thoroughly noted by scholars. In our detailed examination of love, benevolence, and Christianity, we will see that Smith in *The Theory of Moral Sentiments* cannot say enough on behalf of the kind of love akin to "esteem" and "approbation." But Smith is equally concerned to disparage and constrict the influence of romantic or erotic love and the corresponding "passion for enjoyment." The dangers posed by eros and political ambition partly overlap: kings and lovers are the most interesting subjects for dramatic representation because "the prejudices of the imagination attach to these two states a happiness superior to any other" (TMS I.iii.2.2). In *The Wealth of Nations*, the word "love" appears, if I am not mistaken, only as the "love of present ease and enjoyment" (WN V.i.b.2) and the "love to domineer" (III.ii.10). About sexual attraction, Smith offers only the following: "Luxury in the fair sex, while it enflames perhaps the passion for enjoyment, seems always to weaken . . .

the powers of generation" (I.viii.37). Smith, moreover, includes neither sex nor love among our "great wants" (I.xi.c.2). *The Theory of Moral Sentiments* is similarly critical of erotic love. The "passion by which nature unites the two sexes" is "naturally the most furious of all the passions," but "all strong expressions of it are upon every occasion indecent" (*TMS* I.ii.1.2). For women, "it necessarily leads to the last ruin and infamy"; for men, "it is almost always attended with an incapacity for labour, a neglect of duty, a contempt of fame, and even of common reputation" (I.ii.2.5). In his letter to the *Edinburgh Review*, Smith faults the *Encyclopedia* for including an article on *"amour"* (Letter 7).

Although Smith's words deprecate the joy of sex, his economic doctrines reflect its subterranean urgency. "The demand for men, like that for any other commodity, necessarily regulates the production of men" (*WN* I.viii.39–40) because "men, like all other animals, naturally multiply in proportion to the means of their subsistence" (I.xi.b.1). These considerations underlie Smith's accounts of wages, profit, rent, and economic growth, and have had an illustrious history in the subsequent development of "the dismal science."[43]

The Contemplative Ideal

The non-erotic quality of Smith's prose—its dry, technical, precise, and systematic character—stands in stark contrast to the style of Plato, Rousseau, or Nietzsche, and reflects his elevation of bourgeois virtue at the expense of the philosophic or contemplative life.[44] Smith's evaluation of philosophy as an activity parallels his transformation of political philosophy into political economy. Just as Smith's political economy contains provocative traces of political philosophy while pointing toward its disappearance, his account of philosophy incorporates provocative traces of the ancient view within a framework whose overriding impetus is modern. Whereas the ancients exalted the theoretical or philosophic life as an end in itself, the moderns generally treat philosophy as a means to conquer nature. Among the many scholars who have noted Smith's rejection of the contemplative ideal, Cropsey stresses it most, citing Smith's claim (*TMS* VI.ii.3.6) that "the most sublime speculation of the contemplative philosopher can scarce compensate the neglect of the smallest active duty" (*Polity*, pp. 7–8). But Cropsey does not explore Smith's subtle weaving of ancient and modern strands. *The Theory of Moral Sentiments* also conveys ancient notions of the exclusivity or superiority of philosophy: "A philosopher is company to a philosopher only" (I.ii.2.6). Moreover, Smith identifies "wisdom and real philosophy" as making someone "very much above . . . the ordinary standard of human nature" (I.iii.2.8). Examination of the full context of this claim, however, reveals a blending of ancient and modern notions. The man in question is above human nature, not because of the divine character of his wisdom (or quest for wisdom), but because his confidence in the "propriety of his conduct" renders him indifferent to actual approbation. His attachment to moral virtue thus enables him to despise "rank, distinction, pre-eminence" (I.iii.2.8).[45] The priority of moral over intellectual virtue is a modern notion; the notion of philosophy as "above" human nature is an ancient one. Smith's account also follows the ancients in rendering the philosopher more self-sufficient than other people and less desirous of wealth and power. In the essays, Smith traces the origin of philosophy to "wonder" rather than the quest for "advantage" (Astronomy III.3).

Even in *The Wealth of Nations*, the philosophic life is presented as a possible alternative to bourgeois virtue, and Smith's depiction of it again combines ancient and modern elements.[46] In the key paragraph on bettering one's condition, the fundamental premise is that "there is scarce perhaps a single instant in which any man is so perfectly and completely satisfied with his situation, as to be without any wish of alteration or improvement, of any kind" (II.iii.28).[47] Although, as we have seen, the "improvement" sought is usually increased wealth, the lack of satisfaction could also take a Socratic form: human ignorance as the spur to the lifelong pursuit of wisdom. Socratic philosophy, like bourgeois virtue, supposes that the absence of a fully adequate resting condition requires a life of continual motion, though directed at knowledge rather than wealth. Socratic philosophy was criticized by modern thinkers for its passive side—the notion of disinterested "contemplation" of unchanging essences as a condition superior to the enjoyment of wealth, power, or sensual pleasure—but Smith has a place even for this contemplative vision. Smith indicates that *The Wealth of Nations* is a "speculative work" (V.iii.68) that "may come into the hands of many people who are not men of business" (II.ii.66), including, one presumes, some "men of learning" (Intro.8) along with princes, nobles, "country gentlemen," and members of parliaments (IV.i.10). In the work's first reference to philosophy, Smith identifies "philosophers or men of speculation" as those "whose trade it is not to do anything, but to observe everything." The context, however, is thoroughly modern: the philosophers are introduced as one group responsible for "improvements in machinery"; their ability to observe everything explains why they are "often capable of combining together the powers of the most distant and dissimilar objects" (I.i.9).[48] Later in *The Wealth of Nations*, Smith again seems sympathetic to the contemplative ideal. In a "civilized" society, it is possible for a few individuals to develop an "improved and refined understanding"; the huge array of occupations "present[s] an almost infinite variety of objects to the contemplation of those few, who, being attached to no particular occupation themselves, have leisure and inclination to examine the occupations of other people," which "renders their understandings, in an extraordinary degree, both acute and comprehensive" (V.i.f.51). Like the ancients, Smith accords a high priority to the development of the intellect, and links contemplation with "leisure" and "the few." But Smith replaces the "vertical" contemplation extolled by the ancients— philosophy as an ascent to the contemplation of Plato's "ideas" or Aristotle's "unmoved mover"—with contemplation of occupations.

Philosophy, of course, is not the only vehicle for contemplation, and Smith is highly attuned to the threat posed to bourgeois virtue by religious contemplation as well. Smith identifies "the devout and contemplative virtues" with the spirit of "monks and friars" (*TMS* III.2.35). The contrasting ideal, surprisingly, includes poets and philosophers along with heroes, statesmen, and lawgivers, and Smith describes their accomplishments in economic terms: they "have invented, improved, or excelled in the arts which contribute to the subsistence, to the conveniency, or to the ornament of human life." Smith even likens these activities to the "ennobling hardships and hazards of war" (III.2.35). It would seem that philosophy—especially in its modern, technological form—stands with war, nobility, and economics against monasticism.[49] Can *thymos* be turned toward mastering nature rather than human beings?

The critique of "penance and mortifications . . . austerities and abasement" is equally pronounced in *The Wealth of Nations* (V.i.f.30). The harshness of the criticism is striking in light of the partial kinship between monastic austerity and bourgeois "frugality," "temperance," and "chastity" (*TMS* VI.iii.13). Like bourgeois virtue, such austerity must counteract the longings for present ease and enjoyment, erotic gratification, violent conquest, and dazzling economic acquisitions. Bourgeois virtue requires the sacrifice of present enjoyment for the sake of future reward, but, unlike monasticism, it is oriented completely to this world.[50] Smith even criticizes monasticism with reference to "the liberal, generous, and spirited conduct of a man" (*WN* V.i.f.30)—a standard that would also serve to challenge *homo economicus* and bourgeois virtue.

Careful examination of Smith's bourgeois virtue has revealed its grounding in a mixture of appetitive and thymotic longings. The connection between wealth and esteem, although quietly acknowledged in *The*

Wealth of Nations, is trumpeted in *The Theory of Moral Sentiments*: the former book's account of the longing to better one's condition by means of wealth, although not incompatible with the notion that wealth itself is desirable for the sake of esteem, mutes the connection between them, leaving wealth to fill the soul without distraction from esteem and ambition. There are, however, less obvious inconsistencies in Smith's account of human psychology. In *The Theory of Moral Sentiments*, esteem is used as a counter to ambition—"Humanity does not desire to be great, but to be beloved" (III.5.8)—at the same time that ambition is explained as seeking esteem. Whereas the place of esteem is minimized in *The Wealth of Nations*, insolence (the desire to domineer) is explicitly presented as an antagonist of "persuasion" and "interest" and as an obstacle to opulence. Smith articulates three broad objects pursued for the sake of esteem—wealth and greatness, virtue, leading and directing—but does not definitively indicate their respective power as motivating forces. The attention given in *The Wealth of Nations* to wealth, in any case, clashes with the view that wealth is desired as a means to esteem, and invites construction of "economic man."

Epicureanism and Stoicism

Epicurus

Smith's delicate mixing of the psychological faculties is also illustrated by his treatment in *The Theory of Moral Sentiments* of Epicurus and the Stoics. The system of Epicurus, as Smith expounds it, conveys an appetitive model of human character. Epicurus is discussed in a chapter entitled "Of those Systems which make Virtue consist in Prudence." According to Epicurus, the "sole object" of the virtues is to procure the individual's happiness, defined as "ease of body" and "security or tranquillity of mind" (*TMS* VII.ii.2.7). This definition of happiness is a consequence (according to Smith) of Epicurus's view that pleasure and pain are "the sole ultimate objects of natural desire and aversion" (VII.ii.2.2). Although Smith in general tries to portray his moral philosophy in a nobler light, he at once point concedes the centrality of pleasure and pain, identifying them as "the great objects of desire and aversion" (VII.iii.2.8). And in the paragraph on the invisible hand, Smith adopts the Epicurean standard ("ease of body, and peace of mind") in arguing that the "different ranks of life are nearly upon a level" (IV.1.10).

In a later summary of the Epicurean position, Smith says that it shows how virtue is "conducive to our own interest," understood as "ease," "safety," and "quiet" (*TMS* VII.ii.4.5). The system thus corresponds to the appetitive faculty's concern with "ease," "security," and bodily "appetites" (VII.ii.1.4). Smith's presentation of the Epicurean system, however, incorporates additional elements. Although the pleasures and pains of the mind, according to Epicurus, are "ultimately derived from those of the body," they are "vastly greater than their originals" because the body knows only "the sensation of the present instant" (VII.ii.2.4). The latter corresponds to "the passion for present enjoyment" at odds with the desire of bettering one's condition. This Epicurean elevation of mind over body has a further consequence distinguishing it from Smith's teaching. For Epicurus, the good ordering of our "thoughts and opinions" renders the actual disposition of the body "of little importance" (VII.ii.2.5). Smith's writings, by contrast, appear to minimize the place of opinion, although it is surely opinion that Smith wishes to influence.

One of the most important opinions promoted by the Epicurean system is that death "could not be regarded as an evil" (*TMS* VII.ii.2.5).[51] The Epicurean's indifference to death implies a degree of tranquillity or resignation that would nullify bourgeois virtue. In an earlier section, Smith refers to the "peaceful and indolent" Epicureans (VII.ii.1.28), whereas his ideal seems closer to "peaceful and active." In *The Theory of Moral Sentiments*, Smith draws on other ancient philosophers—Plato, Aristotle, and the Stoics—to promote an "active" ideal of virtue against Epicurus; Smith concludes the section on Epicurus by observing that, according to these non-Epicureans, man is "born for action" and his happiness therefore consists not merely in "passive sensations" but in "the propriety of his active exertions" (VII.ii.2.17).[52] The great activity of *The Wealth of Nations* is the lifelong enterprise of bettering one's condition, which might be negated by the Epicurean's detachment of pain from the body and his consequent orientation toward the present. Proper thoughts and opinions might thus tame acquisitiveness. The bane of the mind, according to Epicurus, moreover, was "fear and anxiety" (*TMS* VII.ii.2.6). Although Smith, like Hobbes, wishes to mollify rather than aggravate our fears of "powers invisible," bourgeois virtue seems to presuppose a sustained, low-level anxiety incompatible with Epicurean tranquillity and asceticism.[53]

Perhaps the most pronounced kinship between the appetitive faculty and the Epicurean ideal concerns the evaluation of esteem. Epicureanism errs, according to Smith, in failing to realize that deserving and receiving esteem are more highly valued by "every well-disposed mind" than any "ease and security" esteem may bring (VII.ii.2.12). Both Smith and Epicurus view esteem/love and resentment as prime levers for inducing virtuous behavior. For Epicurus, however, the ultimate beneficiary is the appetitive faculty,[54] whereas Smith's whole moral system turns on esteem being more cherished than ease and security. Because of his apotheosizing of esteem, Smith can account for phenomena like patriotism and courage more convincingly than Epicurus (VII.ii.2.10, VI.ii.2.2), not to mention Hobbes.

There is nevertheless a profound kinship between Epicurus and bourgeois virtue.[55] In the earlier section on prudence, Smith identifies the Epicurean sage with an "inferior prudence" whose concern is with "the health, the fortune, the rank, and reputation of the individual," in contrast to the "superior" prudence of "the Academical or Peripatetic sage," displayed by the outstanding general, statesman, or legislator concerned with "greater and nobler purposes" (VI.i.15). The inferior prudence indeed defines the "temperance," "industry," and "frugality" of bourgeois virtue (VI.i.9,11). Smith sings glowing praise for superior prudence, which supposes "the utmost perfection of all the intellectual and of all the moral virtues" (VI.i.15), but he ultimately employs the bourgeois ideal in a way that eclipses the noble projects of great individuals; inferior or bourgeois prudence is a virtue that can be exercised by many. The linking of ease, comfort, health, and wealth with rank and reputation reveals the fusion of the appetitive desire for present physical comfort with the thymotic desire for superiority and demonstrates the ambiguous nature of the desire for esteem.

Smith's delicately mixed, that is, partially rhetorical, evaluation of Epicurus is matched by his explicit concern with the rhetorical dimensions of Epicureanism. We explored a similar phenomenon in Smith's treatment of Mandeville and Rousseau. Whereas Mandeville, according to The Theory of Moral Sentiments, is the sole author of "licentious systems," Epicureanism is "undoubtedly the most imperfect" of the remaining systems. Smith's official, critical appraisal of the two authors is called into question by the profound implicit (and often explicit) kinship between his doctrines (especially in The Wealth of Nations) and theirs. Regarding Epicurus, Smith's attention to rhetorical considerations goes back to the essay on astronomy. Smith there identifies Epicurus as a reviver of the ancient school of Leucippus, Democritus, and Protagoras, a school that Plato "seems to have bent the whole force of his reason to discredit and expose"; this school, apparently having been discredited by Plato's "eloquence," lay dormant until more successfully promulgated by Epicurus.[56] The Epicurean system has enormous rhetorical advantages for those seeking "to persuade others to regularity of conduct":

> When men by their practice, and perhaps too by their maxims, manifestly shew that the natural beauty of virtue is not like[ly] to have much effect

upon them, how is it possible to move them but by representing the folly of their conduct, and how much they themselves are in the end likely to suffer by it? (*TMS* VII.ii.2.13)

Because he emphasized the "outward prosperity and safety" virtue brings (in addition to "inward tranquillity and peace of mind"), Epicurus was studied by "different philosophical parties" and drawn on even by Stoic opponents of Epicureanism (VII.ii.4.5). Smith faults the Epicurean system because it seems to degrade both the "amiable" virtues of humanity and benevolence and the "respectable" virtues (central to the other ancient schools) of self-command, fortitude, and magnanimity (VII.ii.4.2–4). Smith's final statement comparing Epicureanism with the moral philosophies emphasizing the two nobler sets of virtue suggests, in a characteristically subtle way, Epicureanism's rhetorical advantages. "If it were possible, by precept or exhortation, to inspire" the nobler virtues, the corresponding systems "would seem sufficient" or "might seem capable" of doing so. But Smith simply asserts the Epicurean doctrine that the practice of the virtues promotes one's interest, ease, and safety (VII.ii.4.5). Smith's implicit concessions to the Epicurean view might likewise reflect his wish to be useful to "different philosophical parties,"[57] if not his fear that his contemporaries were only marginally moved by "the natural beauty of virtue."

The Stoics

In *The Theory of Moral Sentiments*, Smith examines the Stoics and Epicurus more thoroughly than he examines Plato and Aristotle. Stoicism receives far greater attention, both in Part VII and in the remainder of the book, than any other philosophical doctrine. On a rhetorical level, the Stoics receive the opposite treatment from Mandeville and Epicurus. Whereas Smith's harsh explicit appraisals of Mandeville and Epicurus mask broad areas of underlying agreement, Smith's criticisms of the Stoics are muted in light of his ultimate divergence from them: we may infer that the Stoics provide a noble rhetoric that does not withstand philosophical scrutiny.

Although the Stoics were "the sect most opposite to that of Epicurus" (*TMS* VII.ii.4.5), both doctrines explicitly mesh as well as clash with the ideal of bourgeois virtue. Smith's whole theory of "propriety" and the impartial spectator is drawn from the Stoics; his recounting of Stoic doctrine incorporates both notions as central Stoic concepts (VII.ii.1.20–21). By relying on propriety (and bourgeois virtue) to temper the pursuit of substantive goods, Smith adapts the Stoic notion that life is a "game of great skill" with "a mere two-penny stake" (VII.ii.1.24)—the goal is playing well, not winning. Smith's bourgeois virtue implies a similar, though less radical, detachment from life's substantive ends. As we have seen, bourgeois virtue entails a long course of prudence, frugality, and industry, and is sustained largely by the sense of propriety. Stoicism is especially useful as a counter to the Machiavellian longing for a sudden, bold, and violent stroke to change one's fortune.

This Stoic detachment also anticipates Smith's effort to make virtue, by means of the desire for esteem and honor, prevail against self-interest and even self-preservation. Smith extols

> that great stoical maxim, that for one man to deprive another unjustly of any thing, or unjustly to promote his own advantage by the loss or disadvantage of another, is more contrary to nature, than death, than poverty, than pain, than all the misfortunes which can affect him, either in his body, or in his external circumstances. (*TMS* III.3.6)

Smith invokes this Stoic maxim to bolster his claim that "the man within" will not condone the poor stealing from the rich. Smith in his own name later argues that the "wise and virtuous man is at all times willing that his own private interest should be sacrificed to the public interest" (VI.ii.3.3). This Stoic detachment, however, does not require the annihilation of self-interest: "Every man, as the Stoics used to say, is first and principally recommended to his own care" (VI.ii.1.1). Thus presented, Stoicism blends with Smith's political economy while serving as a foil to Christian benevolence and enthusiasm.[58]

Stoicism, as interpreted by Smith, nevertheless goes too far in attempting to moderate human attachment to substantive ends. In particular, Stoicism does not concede enough to human individuality. A "wise man," according to the Stoics, "does not look upon himself as a whole, separated and detached from every other part of nature, to be taken care of by itself and for itself"; he considers himself as "an atom, a particle, of an immense and infinite system, which must and ought to be disposed of according to the conveniency of the whole" (*TMS* VII.ii.1.20).[59] Although "stoical apathy and indifference" is usually an appropriate posture toward one's own concerns (III.3.16), the Stoics err in denying the propriety of giving special consideration to family and friends and in extending "citizenship" to "the vast commonwealth of nature" (III.3.11,13). Stoicism also has inegalitarian tendencies that would clash with bourgeois virtue: Smith ridicules the Stoic doctrine that even the smallest departure from the "perfection" attained by the wise will produce misery (VII.ii.1.40–41).

Smith's thematic analysis of Stoicism concludes with a strong criticism: "The plan and system which Nature has sketched out for our conduct, seems to be altogether different from that of the Stoical philoso-phy" (VII.ii.1.43). Nature has *not* prescribed the "sublime contempla-tion" of "that benevolent wisdom which directs all the events of human life" as "the great business and occupation of our lives"; such contempla-tion should be employed only as "the consolation of our misfortunes." Stoicism tries "to eradicate all our private, partial, and selfish affec-tions," not simply to moderate them by means of the impartial spectator (VII.ii.1.45–46). Despite these criticisms, *The Theory of Moral Senti-ments* is permeated by quasi-Stoic statements about the "benevolent wisdom" of the whole.[60] Indeed, the book draws on both Stoicism and Epicureanism to promote a vision of tranquillity and resignation missing from *The Wealth of Nations*. Because of his "perfect confidence in that benevolent wisdom which governs the universe," the Stoic sage is "in great measure indifferent" to "all the events of human life" (VII.ii.1.21). Smith's model for the ebullient side of Stoicism is Marcus Aurelius, who "delights in expressing his contentment with the ordinary course of things."[61]

Spiritedness, Tranquillity, and Bourgeois Virtue

In a posthumously published essay, Smith defines "the natural state of the mind" as "the state in which we are neither elated nor dejected, the state of sedateness, tranquillity, and composure" (Imitative Arts II.20); he extols resignation and tranquillity throughout *The Theory of Moral Sentiments*.[62] The Stoic notion that there is no "essential difference" between one permanent situation and another derives its plausibility from the "certainty with which all men, sooner or later, accommodate themselves to whatever becomes their permanent situation." Happiness consists in "tranquillity and enjoyment," and where there is no "expecta-tion of change," the mind eventually "returns to its natural and usual state of tranquillity" (*TMS* III.3.30). These passages accentuate the im-portance of opinion, and Smith's writings are surely intended to influ-ence our views about the possibilities for change.

The spirited passions are a special threat to Stoical contentment: ha-tred and anger, because they destroy the mind's "composure and tran-quillity," are "the greatest poison to the happiness of a good mind" (I.ii.3.7); there is "no greater tormentor of the human breast than vio-lent resentment which cannot be gratified" (III.2.11). Smith neverthe-less wants to retain a substantial element of indignation in the human soul. Someone who "tamely sits still and submits to insults" is "mean-spirited" and thus contemptible. Although resentment is the passion about whose indulgence people should be most assiduous in consulting the impartial spectator, it may be "generous and noble" when properly restrained and directed (I.ii.3.3,8). We even possess a residual "malice . . . which not only prevents all sympathy with little uneasinesses, but renders them in some measure diverting" (I.ii.5.3).

Smith identifies "avarice," "ambition," and "vainglory" as the "great source[s]" of human "misery and disorders" because they overrate "the differences between one permanent situation and another." A "well-disposed mind" consequently "may be equally calm, equally cheerful, and equally contented" in "all the ordinary situations of human life" (III.3.31). Such claims are surprising in light of the centrality of avarice, ambition, and even vainglory to Smith's moral philosophy and political economy. Smith sums up this exposition with a remarkable assertion:

> In the most glittering and exalted situation that our idle fancy can hold out to us, the pleasures from which we propose to derive our real happiness, are almost always the same with those which, in our actual, though humble station, we have at all times at hand, and in our power. (*TMS* III.3.31)

These passages would surely rule out pursuit of human longings beyond the bourgeois ideal of bettering one's condition by a gradual increase of material wealth. We may infer that devotion to gradual enrichment is defensible because some of the "ordinary situations" are indeed preferable to others. "Passionate ardour," however, must not lead us "to violate the rules of either prudence or justice," for outside of these bounds, "the attempt to change our situation" is "the most unequal of all games of hazard."[63] That military adventure is an especially poor means to alter one's "situation" is suggested by the tale Smith proceeds immediately to recount of the king of Epirus (III.3.31), winner of the original "Pyrrhic victory." All these passages help explain Smith's rejection and disparagement of the gambling grab.

Even in *The Theory of Moral Sentiments*, there are qualifications to this rosy assessment of the availability of happiness, but the portrayal is transformed in *The Wealth of Nations*. Smith there says very little about tranquillity and happiness, and he says nothing to suggest that they are easy to obtain. Smith admits that the "beauty," "pleasures," and "tranquillity of mind" afforded by country life are "charms that more or less attract every body" (III.i.3), but this way of life is not constitutive of a commercial society. In place of the frequent pleas for resignation, the reader encounters the desire of bettering one's condition and the premise that no one is ever "completely satisfied with his situation" (II.iii.28).[64] But there remains enough tranquillity and resignation to obviate the need for large-scale ambition, not to say religious longing or proletarian revolution. The strictures set forth in *The Theory of Moral Sentiments* about remaining within the bounds of prudence and justice (III.3.31), moreover, apply perfectly to *The Wealth of Nations*. Smith's system of natural liberty leaves each individual "free to pursue his own interest his own way" as long as "the laws of justice" are not violated (*WN* IV.ix.51). The strictures regarding prudence also blend easily with the disparagement in *The Wealth of Nations* of the "dazzling objects of giddy ambition." Among the most dazzling of such objects are conquest and empire. We proceed next to examine Smith's juggling of politics and economics in his treatment of international relations.

CHAPTER FIVE

International Relations

The Parallel Between Individual and Nation

Smith's balancing of competing drives within the soul corresponds to his evaluation of the competition between politics/war and economics/trade in relations among states. The tension between the two spheres is even more pronounced in international relations: material opulence competes with pride, conquest, and self-sufficiency, if not self-defense.

Smith explicitly formulates the parallel between individual and nation. A crucial step in the argument for free international trade, specifically for eliminating the domestic monopolies created by prohibitions on foreign imports, is the proposition that "what is prudence in the conduct of every private family, can scarce be folly in that of a great kingdom." That is, one should not attempt to produce things that can be purchased more cheaply abroad (*WN* IV.ii.11–12). Smith says nothing about the obvious objection that only the private family, existing within a framework of domestic order and law, can be confident about purchasing the things it needs from others. Just as the division of labor renders individuals dependent upon "the assistance and cooperation of many thousands" (I.i.11), its global development diminishes the self-sufficiency of nations. Nations, like families and individuals, should not aspire to be self-sufficient wholes.

Smith, like Plato and Aristotle, uses the parallel between individual and society to establish the primacy of peace over war. For these ancient thinkers, however, the critique of war was linked with the primacy of the theoretical or contemplative life: the superiority of leisure and thinking to making or doing.[1] As we saw earlier, Smith's "peaceful and active" individuals of bourgeois virtue are modifications of the "peaceful and indolent" Epicureans. The primacy of the critique of war to Smith's political economy is driven home by his choice to end *The Wealth of Nations* with a long discussion of the public debt. This discussion criticizes existing funding mechanisms, because, among other things, they make war too palatable, and culminates in a call for Great Britain to disgorge its colonial empire for financial reasons.

Smith's juggling of politics and economics on an international level parallels his juggling of them on a domestic level. Smith grants numerous concessions to the traditional primacy of politics and war, but the impetus of his approach is to subordinate them to economics, to interdependence and opulence.[2]

Vestiges of Tradition

It is not difficult to assemble a set of passages from *The Wealth of Nations* that suggest the traditional primacy of war and politics over economics.[3] The art of war is "certainly the noblest of all arts" (V.i.a.14). National defense is "the first duty of the sovereign" (V.i.a.1) and constitutes "the most important part of the expence of government" (IV.vii.b.20); Smith even asserts that defense "is of much more importance than opulence" (IV.ii.30). Smith consequently admits as exceptions, to his general proscriptions against supporting a particular domestic industry by taxing imports (or paying bounties for exports), those industries necessary to national defense.[4] Smith likewise recommends that a "prince, anxious to maintain his dominions at all times in the state in which he can most easily defend them" should tightly restrict the usage of paper currency (II.ii.87). Martial spirit in the citizenry, finally, is treated by Smith not only as useful to national defense and security, but as intrinsically worthy of governmental cultivation—to prevent the "mental mutilation, deformity and wretchedness" entailed by cowardice (V.i.f.59–60).[5]

The assertion that war is the noblest art seems strange in *The Wealth of Nations*, which says little or nothing to encourage war and devotes more attention to arts such as banking, sheep raising, and pin making. But Smith makes it clear that war is a permanent feature of human life: "The violence and injustice of the rulers of mankind is an ancient evil, for which, I am afraid, the nature of human affairs can scarce admit of a remedy" (IV.iii.c.9). The pacifying effects of commerce, according to

Smith, are mediated through the hard realities of power politics. Extensive worldwide commerce "naturally" will spread knowledge and "improvements" and is therefore the most likely source for increasing "equality of courage and force." This equality, "by inspiring mutual fear, can *alone* overawe the injustice of independent nations into some sort of respect for the rights of one another" (IV.vii.c.80). The prevention of war is thus a function of deterrence, not moral enlightenment or even economic interdependence. Smith's pessimism about perpetual peace is less surprising in light of his hints about the precariousness even of domestic peace and unity.[6]

Whatever Smith prescribes, he *describes* a world in which war's necessities occasionally take precedence over economic considerations. Holland, the great mercantile republic for which *The Wealth of Nations* generally sings such high praise, was forced, despite its "wisdom" and great frugality, to tax basic necessities in order to acquire and maintain its independence by military means (V.ii.k.80). Even a highly taxed people will submit (because of "animosity of national vengeance" or "anxiety for national security") to new taxes when faced with the exigencies of a new war (V.iii.40).

Smith also provides, however, empirical observations that illustrate the growing power of commercial considerations in the international realm. Smith observes wryly that the expectation of a break in England's trade with its colonies "has struck the people of Great Britain with more terror than they ever felt for a Spanish armada, or a French invasion" (IV.vii.c.43). More revealing is Smith's recognition of the inherently trans-political character of the merchant: "A merchant, it has been said very properly, is not necessarily the citizen of any particular country" (III.iv.24); whereas the proprietor of land is "necessarily a citizen of the particular country in which his estate lies," the owner of stock is "properly a citizen of the world" (V.ii.f.6).[7] In pushing humanity along the "natural course" to commercial society, Smithian nature thus constricts the sphere of citizenship, of the political.

There are further qualifications to Smith's concessions on behalf of war and politics. The claim that defense is the "first duty of the sovereign" may reflect a Hobbesian commitment to preventing violent death, a commitment hostile to the cultivation and the exercise of a martial spirit. Smith claims that defense is "the most important part of the expence of government," but perhaps this just means that "the expence of fleets and armies is out of all proportion greater than the necessary expence of civil government" (IV.vii.b.20).[8] Smith reveals later that the disproportionate size of this expense characterizes "modern times" rather than the ancient republics of Greece and Italy, where state costs were minimal because each citizen was a soldier (V.ii.a.14). In other words, the demilitarization of society—the split between citizenship and soldiering—is itself a cause of the mushrooming cost of defense to society as a whole.

The primacy and the permanence of national pride as a root of imperialistic expansion are simultaneously asserted and questioned by Smith. Smith concludes his elaboration of the financial losses incurred by Britain's maintenance of its colonial dominion with the sobering reflection that the logical remedy, a voluntary abandonment of dominion, is "such a measure as never was, and never will be adopted, by any nation in the world." Although such sacrifices are often in a nation's "interest," they

> are always mortifying to the pride of every nation, and what is perhaps of still greater consequence, they are always contrary to the private interest of the governing part of it, who would thereby be deprived of the disposal of many places of trust and profit, of many opportunities of acquiring wealth and distinction. (*WN* IV.vii.c.66)

Smith thus leaves it open whether national pride or the rulers' "interest" is the more decisive obstacle to colonial abdication. He does, however, spell out the content of the rulers' interest with some specificity: disposal of "places," opportunities for "wealth and distinction." We again confront an apparently equal balance between wealth and greatness, the twin aims of political economy. Although Smith goes on to assert that "the most visionary enthusiast would scarce be capable of proposing such a measure [abdication], with any serious hopes at least of its ever being adopted," he continues by elaborating the additional advantages that would follow (IV.vii.c.66). The final theme taken up in *The Wealth of Nations* is indeed Smith's proposal, admitted to be utopian, that the colonies be incorporated into the British Constitution (V.iii.68); the discussion concludes with a call for Britain to awaken from its "golden dream" of empire (V.iii.92). We are left uncertain about the degree to which national pride can be tamed.

Economics Triumphant: Methodology

The very form taken by Smith's investigation of political economy suggests an eclipse of politics by economics. The book's title, by promising an inquiry into the wealth of *nations*, defers to the political units that divide mankind even as they unite the citizens of particular nations. The title also implies, however, that Smith seeks to share his knowledge of enrichment with all nations—not with a particular nation, alliance, or type of nation. In this regard, Smith resembles Machiavelli rather than

Aristotle. For Aristotle, the political philosopher, by finding flaws in all existing regimes, is indeed beyond simple partisanship. But Aristotle's political science only transcends partisanship by taking seriously the claims made on behalf of the different regimes and by appraising them in light of a best regime that is not extant. With respect to systems of political economy, however, Smith's procedure resembles Aristotle's: the ultimate standard, though very difficult to actualize, is the single system of "nature" itself, the system of natural liberty. Like Aristotle, furthermore, Smith carefully and dispassionately examines the defective systems, both actual (mercantilism) and theoretical (Physiocracy). Smith's schema is of course less complex than Aristotle's schema of regimes, at least in part because all systems of political economy take the ends of political economy for granted. With regard to political regimes, however, Smith resembles Machiavelli, who generously advises tyrants as well as princes and republics. Smith's analyses and recommendations are of use to any country seeking to increase its wealth and greatness. Unlike Machiavelli's, Smith's impartiality carries him in the direction of internationalism: Smith's perspective is itself global, chronicling as well as promoting the development of a world economy.[9] This procedure is anticipated in *The Theory of Moral Sentiments* by the universality of the impartial spectator, by the underlying metaphysics that views nature or God as concerned with the welfare of the whole human species, and by the concluding call for a science of natural jurisprudence applicable to all regimes.

The desirability of globalization reflects a fundamental economic truth. The great cause of the increase of labor's productivity, according to Smith, is the division of labor, and the title of the third chapter of *The Wealth of Nations* reveals that what limits the division of labor is the extent of the market. As Michael Ignatieff pithily observes, "The domain of polity is the nation; the domain of economy, the world" (p. 22). Whereas Locke flirts with viewing mankind as "one great and natural community," "one fellowship and society," Aristotle and Rousseau argue that only a small society can have a virtuous citizenry.[10] For Smith, a populous society is a "great society" because it facilitates the division of labor and technological progress (*WN* I.viii.57). Although Aristotle is on several occasions mentioned in passing, the most extended discussion of him in *The Wealth of Nations* concerns his critical allusion to the huge territory that would be required in "the ideal republick" of Plato's *Laws* to support its five thousand warrior-citizens (III.ii.9). One wonders how Aristotle would have appraised the British Empire.

Smith's cosmopolitanism and his endorsement of globalization thus represent a constriction of the political realm—citizenship, human identification with a contained and distinct community—by the economic realm of trade and travel. The single reference in *The Wealth of Nations* to "natural justice" reiterates this message:

> The smuggler . . . though no doubt highly blameable for violating the laws of his country, is frequently incapable of violating those of natural justice, and would have been, in every respect, an excellent citizen, had not the laws of his country made that a crime which nature never meant to be so. (*WN* V.ii.k.64)

This passage pairs an exalted vision of nature's support for free trade and an impoverished vision of the "excellent citizen."

Universalism is a tacit theme of the work's Book IV, "Of Systems of political Oeconomy," which is the only book whose subject matter is "systems." A system is a whole. The longest chapter in Book IV examines colonies, the seeds by which a city or country spreads itself to distant turf. Smith argues for a union between Britain and its colonies, articulating the conditions necessary for good government of "the whole empire"; because the "idea of representation" is now known, union would not be the bane to Britain that it was to the Roman Republic (IV.vii.c.70,77).[11] Representation would be in proportion to tax revenues. As a result, if America's economic progress ultimately boosted its contribution above Britain's, the "seat of the empire would then naturally remove itself" to America (IV.vii.c.78–79). The capital would "remove itself," one presumes, because the British might balk at becoming a province of America. In a Smithian world, financial considerations "naturally" overcome the parochial sphere of national identity.

Smith's discussion of colonies reveals other manifestations of internationalization. Smith explicitly sets out to assess the advantages accruing to "Europe, considered as one great country" from its discoveries in both the West and the East (IV.vii.c.3). This investigation occurs in the longest of the chapter's three parts, whose title is "Of the Advantages which Europe has derived from the Discovery of America, and from that of a Passage to the East Indies by the Cape of Good Hope." The discussion of the benefits accruing to Europe "considered as one great country" is in fact dwarfed in length by the subsequent analysis of the "particular advantages" certain countries have gained from the control they exercise over their own colonies (IV.vii.c.3); Smith thus quietly acknowledges the tenacity of national divisions. On another occasion in Book IV, Smith's perspective likewise threatens to overcome national differentiations. "Were all nations to follow the liberal system of free exportation and free importation," Smith writes, "the different states into which a great continent was divided would so far resemble the different provinces of a great empire" (IV.v.b.39).[12] We may infer that free trade policies make states (at least within a continent) like provinces, despite differences of language and regime.

Smith's sober, explicit evaluation of the benefits gained by particular countries because of their colonies is perhaps overshadowed by the majesty of the picture of world unification that unfolds. The two discoveries are no less than "the two greatest and most important events recorded in the history of mankind." Their greatness and importance on the positive side are a result of their "uniting, in some measure, the most distant parts of the world, by enabling them to relieve one another's wants, to increase one another's enjoyments, and to encourage one another's industry" (IV.vii.c.80). The unity brought by economics is thus defined by "wants," "enjoyments," and "industry." Earlier in Book IV, Smith described the "essential change in the state of Europe" triggered by the discovery of America: trade introduced new commodities to each partner, and the vast new markets "gave occasion to new divisions of labour and improvements of art, which, in the narrow circle of the antient commerce, could never have taken place" (IV.i.32).[13]

The greatness of the two discoveries, in Smith's account, reflects their pernicious as well as their beneficial effects. In the Americas, "the savage injustice of the Europeans rendered an event, which ought to have been beneficial to all, ruinous and destructive to several of those unfortunate countries" (IV.i.32). The "commercial benefits" enjoyed by the Europeans are, for the natives both East and West, "sunk and lost in the dreadful misfortunes which they have occasioned" (IV.vii.c.80). In both these passages, however, Smith is careful to suggest that the ill effects be attributed to accident rather than nature. Here again we see nature siding with economics against politics.

Despite his enthusiasm for economic liberty and the division of labor, Smith acknowledges the possible need for political centralization to match the growing economic interdependence. Smith criticizes a proposal that the American colonial assemblies be left with the task of raising the appropriate contributions to the revenue of the empire, in part because these assemblies "cannot be supposed to be proper judges of what is necessary for the defence and support of the whole empire." Although an assembly "may judge very properly concerning the affairs of its own particular district," the revenue structure of the whole "can be judged of only by that assembly which inspects and superintends the affairs of the whole empire" (IV.vii.c.70). Characteristically, Smith's only discussion of the bearing of wholes and parts on political institutions concerns the question of revenue.

The conclusion of *The Wealth of Nations*—where Smith elaborates the advantages of union between Britain and its colonies—further illustrates how his enthusiasm for unification suggests the eclipse of politics by economics. Such a union would free Ireland from an "oppressive aristocracy" founded on "religious and political prejudices" that render a nation's inhabitants "more hostile to one another" than inhabitants even of different nations (V.iii.89). The American colonies, on the other hand, would be saved "from those rancorous and virulent factions which are inseparable from small democracies" (90). This prepares for the sole mention in *The Wealth of Nations* of "impartial spectator": remote provinces suffer less from "the spirit of party" because distance insulates them from the partisanship that prevails in the capital; the provinces thus become "more indifferent and impartial spectators of the conduct of all" (90). The political equivalent of the impartial spectator is thus the geographical transcendence of partisanship. Though Britain is apparently blessed by being neither a "small democracy" nor an "oppressive aristocracy," Smith seems to be hinting that the colonies would bring a certain impartiality of perspective into British politics; his remarks about the financial gains that would accrue to Britain are of course more prominent and straightforward (V.iii.92). The colonies, in any case, would benefit from union by being distanced from the center of "the great scramble of faction and ambition" that is such a bane to small democracies.[14] We may infer that government from afar, by removing the display of tempting political prizes, allows people on the periphery to be occupied with the peaceful bettering of their condition.

Economics Triumphant: War and Acquisition

One might suppose that the ends of political economy, wealth and greatness, are best procured by war. Smith tries to discourage this supposition without confronting it. Locke's famous chapter on property is similarly flirtatious. When Locke says that "the increase of lands and the right employing of them is the great art of government," the reader might suppose that government should conquer and then farm. But Locke finishes the sentence as follows:

> That prince who shall be so wise and godlike as by established laws of liberty to secure protection and encouragement to the honest industry of mankind, against the oppression of power and narrowness of party, will quickly be too hard for his neighbors. (*Second Treatise*, sec. 42)

The sentence beginning with the prospect of imperialism thus ends with that of Smith's natural liberty: the "wise and godlike prince" promotes prosperity not by directing the economy but by establishing "laws of liberty" to protect honest industry against the political ills of "power" and "party."[15] Locke's sentence is preceded by the anti-imperialist observation that a large population is preferable (because of the great value of labor compared with land) to "largeness of dominions"; but his conclusion—that the godlike prince will quickly become "too hard for his neighbors"—raises the specter, partially exorcised by Smith, that the wealth of a neighboring nation is dangerous.

Smith's initial salvo against the view that war is a means to the ends of political economy is his account of productive and unproductive labor. The army and navy are counted (along with priests, servants, lawyers, and doctors) as unproductive because "their service, how honourable, how useful, or how necessary soever, produces nothing for which an equal quantity of service can afterwards be procured" (*WN* II.iii.2).[16] A crucial premise of this classification of the military is spelled out only later: even in wartime, fleets and armies "acquire nothing which can compensate the expence of maintaining them, even while the war lasts" (II.iii.30). Still later, in his first detailed discussion of foreign trade, Smith states that "war and conquest excepted, foreign goods can never be acquired, but in exchange for something that has been produced at home" (II.v.28). *The Wealth of Nations* as a whole overlooks, that is, tries to discourage, the use of war and conquest to acquire foreign goods. Smith admits that a nation "should . . . regard the riches of its neighbours, as a probable cause and occasion for itself to acquire riches," but he has trade in mind as the means of acquisition (IV.iii.c.11).[17] The claim that an army cannot, even during a war, acquire enough to maintain itself is the political economist's weightiest objection to regarding conquest as a means to wealth. The more challenging project of reducing the appeal of war as a means to "greatness" and "power" is approached by Smith less straightforwardly. The title of the work does not mention greatness or power, and the subsequent linkage of wealth and greatness, of riches and power, coupled with the emphasis on wealth and riches, would likewise tend to discourage conquest.[18]

The Wealth of Nations implicitly assumes and therefore encourages the supposition that war and crime are not among the causes of the wealth of nations. Commerce, we recall, "ought naturally to be, among nations, as among individuals, a bond of union and friendship" (IV.iii.c.9). Smith thus rejects the account given in Plato's *Republic*, according to which the city's unlimited acquisition of money, overstepping the bounds of the necessary, results in war (373d–e). As we have seen, commercial society is defined by the pursuit of riches in the full sense—"conveniencies and amusements" beyond necessities—but this can be done peacefully.

Leo Strauss, who claims that "economism" is Machiavellianism come of age, argues that Machiavelli saw "acquisitiveness or competition" as "the fundamental human fact."[19] For Smith, acquisition is almost wholly stripped of its military dimension.[20] The void caused by the removal of conquest is more than filled by the exaltation of competition, which, in its economic sense, is both peaceful and productive. Even a pro-capitalist thinker like Nathan Rosenberg, however, concedes that "a genuinely competitive marketplace is an intensely coercive institution" ("Smith and Laissez-Faire," p. 24).

Economics Triumphant: Mercantilism and Empire

Perhaps the single most important battle Smith wages on behalf of economics against war is his demystification of empire and conquest. One stage in Smith's critique of war is the separation of war and acquisition. Another obvious but crucial stage is pointing out the damage war does to a nation's economy (*WN* II.iii.35, III.iv.24). Because political economy aims at greatness as well as wealth, war and empire may always threaten to eclipse the more pedestrian sphere of economic advancement. Indeed, Smith's predecessor, Sir James Steuart, argued that Lycurgus's Sparta followed "the most perfect plan of political oeconomy."[21]

The deflation of the "dazzle" or "splendour" of war, empire, and perhaps even politics in general pervades the last two Books of *The Wealth of Nations*. With respect to politics, the most comprehensive statement has already been noted: Smith's contrast between the "little prizes" of "the paltry raffle of colony faction" and the more tempting gems of "the wheel of the great state lottery of British politicks" (IV.vii.c.75). Smith's tone here is blatantly sarcastic. With respect to the temptations of war and empire, Smith is perhaps even more condescending. A British monopoly of trade with America initially strikes people as "a very dazzling object" amid "the confused scramble of politicks and war" (IV.vii.c.85). Citizens not directly affected by their country's war are excited by "a thousand visionary hopes of conquest and national glory" (V.iii.37). A proper funding system would hinder the people from "wantonly" calling for war "when there was no real or solid interest to fight for" (V.iii.50); we may infer that war is justifiable only where a "solid interest" is at stake— certainly not for glory or to save souls. Britain's present colonies in America and Ireland, finally, are the "splendid and showy equipage" of an empire that is in fact a "golden dream." Smith's critique of this "project of an empire" is, not surprisingly, pecuniary: it incurs "immense expence" but brings no profit (V.iii.92). Britain would be better off with the Americans as allies rather than subjects (IV.vii.c.66).

The splendor of empire is linked in a peculiar way with the mercantilist political economy Smith combats. Mercantilism is more political than the system of natural liberty because it treats international trade as an inherently competitive process, in which one nation's gain is another's loss, and because it lauds (as an economic bonanza) the acquisition of colonies whose trade the mother country can monopolize.[22] The discovery of America and the discovery of a sea passage to the East had indeed raised "the mercantile system to a degree of splendour and glory which it could never otherwise have attained to" (IV.vii.c.81). Smith combats this mystification primarily by invoking economic considerations. First, he suggests that the advantage obtained by monopolizing colony trade is "relative" rather than "absolute": compared with free trade, the monopoly retards other countries' progress but does not enhance that of the mother country (IV.vii.c.16). Smith's conclusion is still less tentative:

> After all the unjust attempts, therefore, of every country in Europe to engross to itself the whole advantage of the trade of its own colonies, no country has yet been able to engross to itself any thing but the expence of supporting in time of peace and of defending in time of war the oppressive authority which it assumes over them. The inconveniences resulting from the possession of its colonies, every country has engrossed to itself completely. The advantages resulting from their trade it has been obliged to share with many other countries. (*WN* IV.vii.c.84)

Mercantilism derives some of its splendor from its concern with gold and silver, objects Smith also tries to demystify. The "principle" of the mercantile system is derived from the "popular notion" that "wealth consists in money, or in gold and silver," a notion enhanced by the perceived need of gold and silver for carrying on foreign war (IV.i.1,4).[23] Nations therefore strove to accumulate these metals and prohibited their export (IV.i.5); the quest for mines spurred the colonization of the Americas (IV.vii.b.59). As nations "became commercial," merchants, whose businesses suffered because of the export prohibition, persuaded rulers that a favorable balance of trade would suffice to produce a net importation of gold and silver and would thereby augment national wealth. The result was the various mercantilist devices for restraining imports and encouraging exports (IV.i.6–10,35). Smith's demystification of gold and silver includes his labeling them "glittering baubles" (I.xi.c.36) and his definition of wealth as the "necessaries and conveniencies of life" supplied by a nation's annual labor (Intro.1). A nation need pay no more attention to its gold and silver than it does to wine or "pots and pans" (IV.i.11,19). Unlike "annual labor," however, the precious metals can be both stolen and hoarded. To the extent that they are exalted but scarce commodities, the struggle to acquire them will be inherently competitive.

Gold and silver represent Smith's weaving of politics and economics in yet another respect. Because of their scarcity and their beauty, they are desired especially by the rich (I.xi.c.31, g.28). They provide the occasion for Smith's remark that for "the greater part of rich people, the chief enjoyment of riches consists in the parade of riches"; this remark is the major reminder in *The Wealth of Nations* of the wealth/esteem connection dwelt on in *The Theory of Moral Sentiments*. The overthrow of feudalism was indeed partly a consequence of the vanity of the wealthy lords, who squandered their "weight and authority" to acquire "trinkets and baubles" (*WN* III.iii.15, III.iv.10,15). The obsession with gold (and with baubles generally) tends toward a zero-sum game domestically as well as internationally, in part because it involves pride and vanity.

Smith's account of the evolution of mercantilism, one of the more neglected aspects of his thought, suffices to dispel any crude notion that he was an apologist or an ideologist for the capitalist classes. Smith identifies mercantilism, the chief antagonist of the system of natural liberty, with the advent of "commercial society"—the post-feudal order characterized by a complex division of labor (which requires everyone to become "in some measure a merchant") and the development of the economy beyond agriculture and "crude household" manufacturing to "improved" manufacturing and extended foreign commerce (*WN* I.iv.1, V.i.f.51). Because Smith's project seems to be so intimately linked with a defense of commercial society, the kinship he indicates between this society and mercantilism is easy to overlook. The kinship is nevertheless explicit and unambiguous. Mercantilism is "the system of commerce," the "modern system . . . best understood in our own country and in our own times," as opposed to the agricultural system (IV.Intro.2); the first chapter of Book IV identifies "mercantile" with "commercial."

There are two key issues, on Smith's presentation, that divide mercantile and agricultural political economy: the respective merits of commerce and agriculture (town and country); and the proper degree of governmental intervention. Regarding the latter, Smith stands with the Physiocrats (originators of the phrase "laissez-faire," which Smith does not employ), who advocate "perfect liberty" (IV.ix.38), rather than with the mercantile system, whose essence is "restraint and regulation" (IV.ix.3).[24] Smith breaks, however, with the Physiocrats' view of artificers, merchants, and manufacturers as "altogether barren and unproductive" (IV.ix.29). The whole structure of *The Wealth of Nations* is never-theless dominated by Smith's attempt to counteract mercantilist dis-paragement and neglect of agriculture.[25]

In Smith's account, the notion that wealth consists in gold and silver, and the consequent public emphasis on importing them, predated both mercantilism and commercial society. Theories about the balance of trade were articulated by the merchants to enable them to continue their trade abroad; the resulting policies of import restriction and export encouragement propelled the formation of domestic monopolies. Not surprisingly, the various mercantile devices served the "interests" of the protected industries, who were in competition with foreign merchants and manufacturers. Restrictions on imports of particular goods that could be produced at home were simple expressions of mercantile inter-est (IV.ii). But generalized restrictions on imports from certain coun-tries—those with respect to which there was concern about the overall balance of trade—were fueled likewise by a political phenomenon: a nation's feeling of competition with its rich and powerful neighbors. Smith indicates that the principles discussed in the first chapter of Book IV were motivated simply by "private interest," but that the principles of the second chapter reflected a complex fusing of mercantile interest with "national prejudice and animosity" (IV.iii.a.1,4). Smith's presentation long obscures which factor is primary.[26] His final formulation suggests a certain parity: "Mercantile jealousy is excited, and both inflames, and is itself inflamed, by the violence of national animosity" (IV.iii.c.13). The mercantile restrictions brought economic benefits to the protected sec-tors at the expense of the rest of society, not to mention foreigners.[27]

Mercantilism constituted a powerful and independent force in the realm of opinion:

> By such maxims . . . nations have been taught that their interest consisted in beggaring all their neighbours. Each nation has been made to look with an invidious eye upon the prosperity of all the nations with which it trades, and to consider their gain as its own loss. (IV.iii.c.9)

The "beggar thy neighbor" doctrine depicts international trade as a zero-sum game; according to Smith, the doctrine is not a natural phenomenon but something nations have been "taught." Smith continues his discus-sion with some justly famous prose:

> Commerce, which ought naturally to be, among nations, as among individ-uals, a bond of union and friendship, has become the most fertile source of discord and animosity. The capricious ambition of kings and ministers has not, during the present and the preceding century, been more fatal to the repose of Europe, than the impertinent jealousy of merchants and manufac-

turers. The violence and injustice of the rulers of mankind is an ancient evil, for which, I am afraid, the nature of human affairs can scarce admit of a remedy. But the mean rapacity, the monopolizing spirit of merchants and manufacturers, who neither are, nor ought to be the rulers of mankind, though it cannot perhaps be corrected, may very easily be prevented from disturbing the tranquillity of any body but themselves. (IV.iii.c.9)

Commerce's "natural" connection to "union and friendship" has thus been distorted by mercantile jealousy and rapacity to the point that it has caused more strife than the irremediable strife caused by politics, "the violence and injustice of the rulers of mankind." Free trade, by contrast, expresses and channels the benevolence of nature: "that trade which, without force or constraint, is naturally and regularly carried on between any two places, is always advantageous, though not always equally so, to both" (IV.iii.c.2). The admission that benefit is not necessarily equal is a concession to mercantilism.[28]

Not long after condemning mercantilism for having outdone "the violence and injustice of the rulers of mankind," Smith makes further concessions to mercantilism, the primacy of politics, and the zero-sum perspective on international relations. "The wealth of a neighbouring nation, however, though dangerous in war and politicks, is certainly advantageous in trade." During a "state of peace and commerce," a rich neighbor will make us richer; during "hostility," however, our neighbor's riches may enable it to deploy superior fleets and armies (IV.iii.c.11).[29] Smith is even more blunt in describing the relationship between France and England:

> Being neighbours, they are necessarily enemies, and the wealth and power of each becomes, upon that account, more formidable to the other; and what would increase the advantage of national friendship, serves only to inflame the violence of national animosity. (*WN* IV.iii.c.13)

In the preceding paragraph, however, Smith suggested that the "real interest" of France and England, as opposed to "mercantile jealousy or national animosity," would dictate extensive trade (IV.iii.c.12). This claim seems to vindicate the perspective of "trade," according to which a neighbor's wealth is advantageous, rather than the perspective of "war and politicks," according to which a neighbor's wealth is dangerous (c.11). What kind of necessity, therefore, makes neighbors enemies? Wealth and power, the things that neighboring enemies dread in one another, are the aims of political economy. Smith offers the natural system of political economy to the world as a whole—to all "nations." This science claims to be anything but a tool for the use of a particular nation, or kind of nation, or alliance, to promote itself at the expense of others. Smith both argues and assumes that there is an international common good attainable through efficient national pursuit of wealth and greatness, but he does not quite expunge the mercantilist specter. The ideology of free international trade has been controversial since its inception.

The puzzles arising from the mercantilist fusion of politics and economics in the international sphere are anticipated in *The Theory of Moral Sentiments*. Smith there uses the impartial spectator to explain why the "laws of justice" are seldom observed in "war and negotiation." Only neutral nations can be the "indifferent and impartial spectators" of interstate relations because citizens within a contending nation look only to each other for approval (*TMS* III.3.42). One may infer that human moral sentiments express a disproportion between public and private virtue. The "just man who disdains either to take or give any advantage" is "regarded as a fool and an idiot" in public (especially international) transactions (III.3.42).

In the section of *The Theory of Moral Sentiments* added after the publication of *The Wealth of Nations*, needless to say, Smith touches more directly on mercantilist themes. As in the passage above, Smith reveals a cynical or realistic view about international justice (*TMS* VI.ii.2.2). Without mentioning mercantilism, furthermore, Smith suggests that it is a most natural phenomenon:

> The love of our own nation often disposes us to view, with the most malignant jealousy and envy, the prosperity and aggrandizement of any other neighbouring nation. . . . Each nation foresees, or imagines it foresees, its own subjugation in the increasing power and aggrandizement of any of its neighbours; and the mean principle of national prejudice is often founded upon the noble one of the love of our own country. (*TMS* VI.ii.2.3)

Smith does not explicitly resolve the question of whether the connection between a neighbor's power and one's own subjugation is foreseen or merely imagined, perhaps because "national prejudice" cannot be eliminated without eliminating patriotism ("the love of our own country"). Smith proceeds immediately to a formally neutral juxtaposition of Cato, who continuously exhorted Rome to destroy Carthage, and Scipio Nasica, who continuously counseled against this; it is nevertheless clear that Smith prefers the "liberal" and "enlightened" Scipio to the "savage" and "coarse" Cato. The dilemma in the eighteenth century, of course, was not Rome and Carthage, but France and England. Smith continues by alleging that they "may each of them have some reason to dread the increase of the naval and military power of the other," but not "internal happiness and prosperity": ports and harbors, cultivated land, and the advancement of manufacturing, commerce, and "all the liberal arts and sciences." These are the "real improvements of the world we live in," by which "mankind are benefited" and "human nature is ennobled" (VI.ii.2.3). Smith's system of political economy tries to separate economic development from military power, thereby expanding the sphere that benefits the whole of mankind and contracting the arena of international conflict and competition.[30] The stakes of this deflection are high indeed, for "the liberal arts and sciences" have yielded deadly military technologies.

Progress, War, and the Survival of Civilization

The Smithian "nature" that supports free trade shows itself also in history, in "the natural progress of opulence" and the evolution of society from hunting to commerce. The progress or "improvement" that characterizes the later of the four stages entails a widening conquest of nature: hunters live directly from nature's provision, shepherds mobilize and propagate their flocks, and farmers systematically harness natural processes. Manufacturing and commerce, however, represent a quantum leap in human mastery over nature.[31] Even the penultimate stage, agriculture, is characterized more by "subsistence" than by "conveniency and luxury" (*WN* III.i.2, III.iii.12); with agriculture, "nature labours along with man"; whereas in manufacturing, "nature does nothing; man does all" (II.v.12). Smith's thematic discussion of the sovereign's duties for defense bridges his investigations of war and economic progress: dominating the section on defense is the question of how the fate of "civilization" is determined by the interplay between economic development and military organization.[32]

Despite the general trustworthiness of nature's promptings to trade and commerce, nature ill provides for the ongoing commercialization of society in at least one crucial respect. The wealth possessed by a commercial people "provokes the invasion of all their neighbours," but their "natural habits . . . render them altogether incapable of defending themselves" (V.i.a.15). This incapacity has two causes: unlike more primitive peoples, they lack the "leisure" to undertake military exercises, and their ordinary activities do not prepare them for war.[33] In other words, success in the war against nature, by triggering wars of aggrandizement between societies, creates the seeds of its own negation. This is one of the few serious problems discussed in *The Wealth of Nations* for which the remedy is not nature, the invisible hand, or liberated individual self-interest, but "the *wisdom* of the state." Only this wisdom—not "the prudence of individuals" by which the division of labor is "naturally introduced" into the other arts—can "render the trade of a soldier a particular trade separate and distinct from all others" (V.i.a.14); "it is only by means of a standing army . . . that the civilization of any country can be perpetuated, or even preserved for any considerable time" (a.39). The absorption of the whole of society in the conquest of nature thus necessitates that government create a military sector, despite the threats it may pose to the people it is supposed to protect.[34] The "expence of defence" (and therewith the "unproductive" consumption of resources) increases with progress toward civilization because, among other reasons, the citizenry's time and energy are increasingly devoted to economic pursuits.[35]

In the ancient world, nature seemed to stand with the barbarians: the militia of a shepherd nation has an "irresistible" and "natural superiority" over a civilized nation of "husbandmen, artificers, and manufacturers." The only recourse for civilization is a standing army, which, when well organized, is "superior to every militia"; an "opulent and civilized nation" is indeed best situated to maintain such a standing army (V.i.a.36,39). A standing army is superior to a militia because it is dominated by the "military character" rather than by the "civil" character of the "labourer, artificer or tradesman"; the troops are more skillful with their weapons and more disciplined (V.i.a.19,24–25,36). The members of a civilized militia are generally at "liberty to manage their own affairs their own way" and therefore lack the "awe" and "disposition to ready obedience" of full-time soldiers "whose whole life and conduct are every day directed" by their officers (a.25).[36] This liberty to manage one's own affairs entails the liberty to pursue one's *"own interest"* (IV.vii.b.4–5, IV.ix.51). Smith's exaltation of individual liberty and self-interest for the sake of economic progress thus clashes with the military ethic—hierarchy and self-sacrifice—necessary to protect that progress.[37]

The first three "great revolution[s] in the affairs of mankind of which history has preserved any distinct or circumstantial account" illustrate the superiority of standing armies over militias and of barbarous over civilized militias. The Greek republics and their "gallant and well-exercised militias" were overcome by Philip of Macedon's standing army; Rome defeated Carthage; the Roman Empire ultimately fell to barbarian militias as its standing armies "gradually degenerated into a corrupt, neglected, and undisciplined militia." Smith's explanation of Rome's decline highlights the dialectical interplay of politics and economics that dominates his discussion of military matters. Because of the dangers posed to the emperor by some of Rome's standing armies, legions were withdrawn from the frontier and dispersed in "trading and manufacturing towns"; the "military character" of the troops was consequently eclipsed by their "civil" character (V.i.a.29,35−36).

Smith's final discussion of the militia question as it relates to the ancient-modern contrast occurs at the conclusion of the section on education. The ancient militias did a far better job of maintaining "martial spirit" (V.i.f.60). In a civilized society, a militia can be established only "by means of a very rigorous police, and in spite of the whole bent of the interest, genius and inclinations of the people" (V.i.a.17); a militia cannot so readily define the character of a whole nation. Smith's evaluation of ancient versus modern civilization on the question of martial spirit is quite complex. To the extent that he sees ancient "civilization" as less commercial than modern civilization, the four-stages framework is inadequate. Polity dominated economy in Greece and Rome, it would seem, insofar as the sphere of citizenship, martial virtue, and war was insulated from commercial activity.[38] Smith flirts with the view that their decline was inevitable.[39]

The military superiority of civilization over barbarism, and therewith civilization's "permanency and extension," was secured by the invention of firearms. Smith closes the section on defense with a provocative observation:

> In antient times the opulent and civilized found it difficult to defend themselves against the poor and barbarous nations. In modern times the poor and barbarous find it difficult to defend themselves against the opulent and civilized. The invention of firearms, an invention which at first sight appears to be so pernicious, is certainly favourable both to the permanency and to the extension of civilization. (*WN* V.i.a.44)

The decisive military shift in favor of civilization renders obsolete the ancients' fear that those engaged in commerce and manufacturing would lose their martial virtue (IV.ix.47), although Smith laments the decay of martial virtue even apart from its consequences (V.i.f.60). Smith concedes, however, that the invention of firearms "appears" to be pernicious. Standing armies and modern weapons are expensive (V.i.a.39,42−44), but there are other costs. Smith elsewhere describes the "savage injustice" and "dreadful misfortunes" inflicted by the "opulent and civilized" Europeans on many inhabitants of India, the Americas, and Africa.[40] Smith discloses the economic goals (markets and precious metals) of this imperialism, which strangely inverted the ancient pattern—shepherds plundering the civilized. But Smith quietly reveals that even the ancient civilizations were led by economic considerations to practice colonialism. Population pressures and the land-hunger of poor freemen made colonization a matter of "interest," "irresistible necessity," and "evident utility," in contrast to the "folly," "injustice," and hypocritical "piety" that spurred the modern Europeans.[41]

The pernicious character of firearms is more explicitly portrayed in Smith's account of ancient and modern battle. Before firearms, military superiority was determined by the skill, strength, and agility of the individual; with firearms, the key factors are "regularity, order, and prompt obedience to command," which can only be acquired by troops "exercised in great bodies" (V.i.a.21–22). Individuality is thus sacrificed in the modern army as well as in the modern factory. Smith continues with one of the most tragic passages of his corpus, invoking "the noise of fire arms, the smoke, and the invisible death to which every man feels himself exposed" in a modern battle. Ancient battle, however, had a different character:

> There was no noise but what arose from the human voice; there was no smoke, there was no invisible cause of wounds or death. Every man, till some mortal weapon actually did approach him, saw clearly that no such weapon was near him. (*WN* V.i.a.22)[42]

"Progress" is not simply gentle (*doux*), and the invisible hand is tinged with "invisible" death that makes war more horrifying but less noble.[43]

Book III of *The Wealth of Nations* ends with a melancholy assessment of feudal Europe's distorted pattern of economic development (commercial development preceded agricultural):

> The ordinary revolutions of war and government easily dry up the sources of that wealth which arises from commerce only. That which arises from the more solid improvements of agriculture, is much more durable, and cannot be destroyed but by those more violent convulsions occasioned by the depredations of hostile and barbarous nations continued for a century or two together; such as those that happened for some time before and after the fall of the Roman empire in the western provinces of Europe. (*WN* III.iv.24)

These "violent convulsions" that destroyed Rome, so nonchalantly referred to here, not only occasioned the feudal disorder that is the theme of Book III, but represent the military vulnerability of premodern civilization. As we have seen, Smith concedes the intractability of the ancient evil caused by rulers' "violence and injustice" (IV.iii.c.9), offering a remedy (natural liberty) only to the "mean rapacity" and "monopolizing spirit of merchants and manufacturers." His political economy is likewise a vaccine against only "the ordinary revolutions of war and government" (III.iv.24). By securing the "permanency . . . of civilization" (V.i.a.44), firearms, in conjunction with technologies protecting us from natural disasters, might render obsolete the ancient view that civilizations are periodically destroyed and reconstituted.[44] The invention of gunpowder, which precipitated the permeation of war by "invisible death," was indeed a "mere accident" (V.i.a.43). But technological innovation, though never predictable, is no accident in modern societies organized for systematic economic and scientific progress.

Smith barely acknowledges this distinguishing feature of *modern* civilization, and there is dispute about his awareness of the dawning Industrial Revolution. Marx identifies Smith with the era of "manufacture" that has been superseded by the era of "machinery and large-scale industry."[45] Smith certainly did not trumpet the prospects for an industrial revolution the way he trumpeted the Newtonian revolution. Smith did, however, help his friend James Watt, the inventor of the modern steam engine, open a workshop within the precincts of Glasgow University, and praised (in his lectures) the contribution of the "ingenious philosopher" to such developments (*LJA* vi.42).[46] Smith also recommends that the universities promote scientific "experiment and observation" (*WN* V.i.f.28,34–35, V.i.g.14), that the youth all be instructed in geometry and mechanics (V.i.f.55), and that patents be granted to the inventors of new machines (V.i.e.30). In explaining the contribution of machinery to increasing productivity, finally, Smith credits not only inventors but the division of labor among philosophers that helps them combine "the powers of the most distant and dissimilar objects" (I.i.9).[47] It is not difficult to imagine that Smith anticipated and welcomed the prospect of technological and industrial leaps.

The development of chemical, biological, and nuclear weapons, along with airplanes and missiles, means that "civilization" (if not the human race) is exposed to rapid, invisible death. Haakonssen correctly points out that technological development eliminated the dangers to Europe from barbarian depredations (p. 179), but he overlooks Smith's remark that the destruction of Roman civilization required "a century or two" (*WN* III.iv.24). The conquest of nature for the sake of "civilization"— human preservation, propagation, and prosperity—is now a threat to life on earth. Is this where we have been led by the invisible hand?

CHAPTER SIX

The Invisible Hand

> All who govern find themselves subject to a greater power.
> They do more or less than they intend. . . . Neither are they
> masters of the dispositions which past ages have given affairs,
> nor can they foresee what course futurity will take. . . . In a
> word, there is no human power that does not minister,
> whether it will or no, to other designs than its own.
> —Bossuet, *Discours sur l'histoire universelle*

THE CONCEPT OF THE INVISIBLE hand was perhaps Adam Smith's greatest legacy. Despite its fame, however, the phrase is only used once in *The Wealth of Nations*, a very long book: it is almost invisible. The phrase also appears once in *The Theory of Moral Sentiments*, and once in Smith's posthumously published philosophical essays,[1] creating another set of questions and paradoxes about the interrelation of Smith's works. The invisible hand is portrayed in a different theological context in each of its three appearances. In the essays, it is the hand of Jupiter imagined by primitive human beings as determining the "irregular" phenomena of nature; in *The Theory of Moral Sentiments*, it is the hand of a deistic "Providence" ensuring that the lowly are fed despite the greed of the rich; in *The Wealth of Nations*, it is a metaphor for the utterly impersonal workings of a godless nature to harmonize individual avarice and public opulence. These differences are signposts for the "Adam Smith Problem." Scholars have neglected the subtle development of the invisible hand, just as they have neglected the glaring contrasts between *The Theory of Moral Sentiments* and *The Wealth of Nations* regarding religion generally.[2] The whole of Smith's work is clearly greater than the sum of its parts.

There is a popular impression that the invisible hand reveals Smith's faith that God works behind the scenes to bolster the free market: most references to the invisible hand by scholars, journalists, and politicians are intended to mock such faith.[3] The popular impression is ironic given the atheism of *The Wealth of Nations*, but it is not surprising given the theological nature of the phrase—a hand is a part, an agent, but of what or whom? As employed in the two published works, the invisible hand is the bridge between theology and political economy, and addresses the central question of Smith's thought: the relation of the individual to the whole (both social and cosmic).

In Smith's answers to this question, economics rises in various ways at the expense of politics and religion. On a practical level, the invisible hand represents the liberation of individual self-interest and a concomitant restraining of the political impulse to supervise society as a whole. Smith is famous for this attempt to harmonize the interests of individual and society, but his quiet exploration of the religious and metaphysical versions of this project have been insufficiently addressed. Toward what does the invisible hand point or lead? What status does the invisible hand—and the larger natural order to which it belongs—assign to the human individual?[4] Life teaches each human being that he or she is not the center of the universe. Smith powerfully reiterates this lesson and even documents the means by which it is generally taught. But he removes many tonics that were previously relied upon to sweeten the message: intergenerational attachment to family, church, and country; eros or romantic love; love of Heaven, God, Jesus, or the Platonic ideas that do not come into being and decay. In their place, Smith offers the individual the liberty "to pursue his own interest his own way." Smith also incorporates elements of Popean, Epicurean, and Stoic rhetoric to reconcile us to a world whose highest purposes are the propagation of species and the progress of opulence.[5]

The Philosophical Essays

"Astronomy" and Jupiter

The "invisible hand of Jupiter" is mentioned by Smith in his long essay on the history of astronomy, whose purpose is to illustrate the "Principles which lead and direct philosophical enquiries." The essay implies that the directing "principles" are a trio of passions: wonder, surprise, and admiration.[6] Although God is depicted in *The Theory of Moral Sentiments* as "the great director" and by similar designations, the analysis (in the essays) of the directing passions serves to explain away God. Taken together, the essays and *The Theory of Moral Sentiments* provide a comprehensive history, sociology, and psychology of religion. Although Smith was unable to complete his philosophical project by providing a "theory of jurisprudence," he lived long enough to provide something more fundamental: a theory of religion.

In section III of the astronomy essay, "Of the Origin of Philosophy," Smith describes the origin, among savages, of polytheism and the "vulgar superstition which ascribes all the irregular events of nature to the favour or displeasure of intelligent, though invisible beings, to gods, daemons, witches, genii, fairies" (Astronomy III.2). In the absence of law, order, and security, people have no delicate interest in nature's "hidden chains," but cannot help being awed by more "magnificent" irregularities, such as lightning, thunder, and comets. These phenomena produce "amazement," "fear," and "reverence." And because "our passions . . . suggest to us opinions which justify them,"[7] the irregularities are attributed to "intelligent, though invisible causes," reinforcing our consciousness of our weakness; we are "exposed, defenceless" (III.1). In Smith's account, such is the origin of our perception of intelligent but invisible causes and therewith the origin of religiosity.[8]

Smith introduces the invisible hand to explain why people responded differently to regular and irregular phenomena:

> It is the irregular events of nature only that are ascribed to the agency and power of their gods. Fire burns, and water refreshes; heavy bodies descend, and lighter substances fly upwards, by the necessity of their own nature; nor was the *invisible hand* of Jupiter ever apprehended to be employed in those matters. (III.2)

Smith proceeds to elaborate why the gods' activity was perceived only in irregular events. Man was the only "designing power" with which people were acquainted, and man "never acts but either to stop, or to alter the course, which natural events would take, if left to themselves"; the "ordinary course of things . . . went on of its own accord."[9] Such perception of the gods is not philosophy but "the lowest and most pusillanimous superstition" (III.2).

This discussion reverberates through *The Wealth of Nations* and *The Theory of Moral Sentiments*. Because Smith frequently identifies nature with the way things operate of their "own accord," it is clear (from the above passages) that even the superstitious savage perceives some of the necessity and regularity present in the world as *nature*. The savage only perceives a divine invisible hand behind "irregular" phenomena. The divine being's activity is understood on the analogy with a more familiar "designing power," human agency. Nature is characterized by necessity, man by the capability to design. There are invisible causes, but they are intelligent: people perceive gods rather than an arbitrary, impersonal, and unfathomable fate. Smith's argument for the system of natural liberty, needless to say, is intended to promote trust in the "natural course of things" and to limit the scope of human designing. The invisible hand metaphor in *The Wealth of Nations* serves precisely to constrict the sphere of human "intention" and foresight (*WN* IV.ii.9).[10] In *The Theory of Moral Sentiments* and *The Wealth of Nations*, Smith attributes so much to nature that he has difficulty accounting for both the necessity and the possibility of his freely undertaken and spontaneously conceived philosophic enterprises on behalf of nature. To preempt rebellion by the human spirit against nature, Smith must reconcile us to the purposes or intentions of nature—which may or may not involve will and intelligence.[11] Paradoxically, Smith expounds the natural order, i.e., the invisible "chains" of nature as explained by his inquiry into wealth's nature and causes, on behalf of "natural liberty." The latter liberates economic or micro-liberty—the individual's liberty "to pursue his own interest his own way," to allocate his labor and capital as he sees fit—at the expense of macro-liberty that is political and spiritual.[12]

As we have seen, primitive superstition projects the "designing" capacity onto the gods, extrapolating from our experience of human agency. According to *The Wealth of Nations*, superstition first attempts to explain the "great phenomena of nature" in terms of the "agency of the gods"; philosophy later attempts to invoke more "familiar" causes (V.i.f.24); Smith subsequently describes science/philosophy as "the great antidote to the poison of enthusiasm and superstition" (V.i.g.14). One could conclude that belief in the invisible and unfamiliar pagan gods is pure superstition. But philosophy too is concerned with the invisible: its goal is to represent or to "lay open" the "invisible chains which bind together" the natural world, especially where that world initially appears "disjoined" and "discordant" (Astronomy II.12, III.3). When a habitually observed "succession of objects" is interrupted, people naturally seek to determine a "chain of intermediate, though invisible, events" to fill the interval (II.5,8). We may infer that philosophy struggles with superstition to characterize invisible things.[13] Because *The Wealth of Nations* is a work of science/philosophy, Smith is obliged to acquaint his readers with the operation of a hand that though equally invisible is more "familiar" than Jupiter's.

In the paragraph following the reference to the invisible hand in the astronomy essay, Smith proceeds to the theme of the section, the "origin of philosophy." Philosophy emerges with "civilized" society: one where "law has established order and security, and subsistence ceases to be precarious" (III.3). Civilized society, Smith adds, is conducive to a certain cheerfulness; because people are more "conscious of their strength and security" than were their "rude forefathers," they do not rely on invisible beings to explain nature's "seemingly disjointed phaenomena" (III.3)— being less afraid in general, they are less inclined to form terrifying "opinions" (III.1). In *The Wealth of Nations*, Smith identifies the "melancholy and gloomy humour" as "the nurse of popular superstition and enthusiasm" (V.i.g.15). Primitive living, from Smith's point of view, is clearly rife with the psychic roots of superstition: fear, gloom, melancholy, and the consciousness of weakness.[14] Civilized life is less precarious, fearful, and chaotic; as order and regularity within society increase, as our strength vis-à-vis nature increases, we perceive the universe as more orderly and regular. Progress in the realm of opinion, the development from superstition to science, derives from progress in the realm of passion—the replacement of melancholy and fear by security and cheer—which derives from socioeconomic progress.

Amazement, fear, and reverence, however, are not the only passions triggered in the savage by nature's irregularities: the more "beautiful and agreeable" irregularities are beheld with "gratitude" (Astronomy III.1–2). The combination of gratitude, fear, and reverence calls to mind the human response to the biblical God, the God depicted in the Old and New Testaments. The philosophical essays (like *The Wealth of Nations*) are silent about the biblical God. The silence proves to be a mask for Smith's dismissal of the biblical God, as we will see by juxtaposing the account of polytheism in the astronomy essay with the account of monotheism in the essay on the history of physics—the second of Smith's three essays illustrating the "Principles which lead and direct Philosophical Enquiries."[15]

"Physics" and Theism

Physics or natural philosophy endeavored to explain "the inferior parts of nature," by deducing their "qualities, operations, and laws of succession" from those of some "particular things" with which the mind was "perfectly acquainted and familiar" (Physics 1–2). Like superstition, philosophy/science projects the familiar onto the unfamiliar. The crucial difference is that philosophy projects necessity—"order," "regularity," and "chains"—and superstition projects freedom: "will," "design," and foresight. These two sets of qualities, however, are united in theism.

As he did in the astronomy essay, Smith labels as "pusillanimous superstition" the attribution of an unexpected event "to the arbitrary will of some designing, though invisible beings, who produced it for some private and particular purposes" and indicates that superstition emerges naturally as a response to nature's "seeming incoherence" (Physics 9). The physics essay, however, proceeds to fault superstition for lacking the "idea of an universal mind, of a God of all, who originally formed the whole, and who governs the whole by general laws, directed to the conservation and prosperity of the whole, without regard to that of any private individual"; the world was thought to predate the gods, who acted by interposing. As nature's binding "chain" became more and more palpable, the universe took on the appearance of "a complete machine . . . a coherent system, governed by general laws, and directed to general ends, viz., its own preservation and prosperity." As such, it resembled the "machines . . . produced by human art," suggesting that some superior art had been involved in its creation.[16] Smith concludes with a flourish. The unity of the system suggested the unity of the "principle" forming it: "And thus, as ignorance begot superstition, science gave birth to the first theism that arose among those nations, who were not enlightened by divine Revelation." As examples of such theism, Smith seems to designate Timaeus and Plato (Physics 9).

This is the only reference in any of Smith's writings to "divine revelation." Smith here links theism and revelation against superstition while explaining how theism arose naturally, independent of revelation; he appears to exclude the doctrines of revelation, i.e., the Bible, from his naturalistic explanation of the origin of religion. Pagan theism and the Bible clearly agree that the world is the product of a unitary creator. Theism results from a two-stage projection: the perception of order and regularity in nature suggests that nature is a "system"; human *technē* suggests divine creation. The crucial differences between biblical theism and Smith's version of pagan theism, apart from the manner in which the views arose, concern interposing and particular Providence. The pagan god apparently does not "interpose" to disrupt the workings of nature and is limited in its concern for particular beings: Smith faults superstition for not conceiving "a God of all" who governs the cosmos by "general laws" that promote the well-being of "the whole" rather than of "any particular individual."[17] Smith does specify that the "preservation and prosperity" of the universe include the preservation and prosperity of every species (Physics 9).

The biblical God, on Smith's framework, would be a cross between polytheistic superstition and pagan theism. Like the pagan god, He is the unitary creator of the whole, but the created universe is not a "machine . . . a coherent system" governed by general laws without regard to "particular" individuals.[18] The biblical God intervenes miraculously, like Jupiter, to disrupt the ordinary workings of nature; He expresses anger and jealousy; He singles out particular individuals (not to mention the "chosen people") for covenants, revelation, rewards, and punishments; according to the New Testament, He sends His son to redeem mankind. Unlike the god of pagan theism, Jehovah and Jupiter have names; they speak; they call forth "gratitude" and "reverence," not to mention prayer and sacrifice.[19] From Smith's point of view, the biblical God represents theistic superstition, and one suspects the bad news (superstition) outweighs the good news (monotheism). The biblical God would seem to be a historical anomaly—Smith does not explain how the superstitious aspects of Jupiter, spawned in primitive and fearful times, became fused with the idea of a unitary creator that emerges with civilization and order. Or is biblical religion an intermediary stage? In pagan theism, the free and willful divine activity that escapes the confines of natural necessity is relegated to the distant past and dissociated from the "private and particular purposes" of the local gods. By virtue of His unity and His relatively infrequent disruptions of the natural order, the biblical God displays less freedom and individuality than the bustling superstitious pantheon, but still too much; and He interacts too much with *human* individuals. In his only reference to "inspired writers," Smith notes their emphasis on "the wrath and anger of God" (*TMS* II.i.5.9), and he nowhere suggests that the God portrayed by inspired Christian writers is more gentle or less intrusive than the God portrayed by inspired Jewish writers.[20] Although in some versions eminently natural, religion, for Smith, may also be nature's most formidable enemy: as we shall explore in the chapters that follow, religion's projections of will, consciousness, and individuality onto the universe can deflect willing, conscious individuals from the natural system of political economy and corrupt their natural moral sentiments.

Smith, in treating society and the universe as machines/systems, might seem to shortchange the human individual. He replaces the organic metaphor of the state—the body politic—with a mechanical metaphor of the state and the universe. A system or machine combines the two qualities human beings perceive in nature by extrapolating from their own experiences: order and design. With respect to moral sentiments and the wealth of nations, Smith strives to display both order and design. Smith's version of order is incompatible with the biblical God; his removal of this God, however, removes one source of a wise and benevolent design. Smith's science/philosophy must therefore demonstrate the design or purpose as well as the order of things; not surprisingly, Smith tends to extrapolate the purpose from the order. Aristotle, according to Smith, saw a "Divine Intelligence" at work in the heavens, but not in "things below," which were characterized by "disorder and confusion." In his only mention of atheism, Smith notes that this opinion of Aristotle's "saps the foundations of human worship, and must have the same effects upon society as Atheism itself" (Physics 10). Smith says nothing to specify these effects, but one suspects he is concerned with atheism's potential to demoralize people: while Smith offers no substitute for the attention to individuals displayed by Jupiter or Jehovah, Smith devotes his entire corpus to showing that "things below," including economy, government, and law, are not pervaded by "disorder and confusion."

Smith's specification of the cosmic design or purpose will help determine the answers to crucial questions. How content will people be as parts of the great machine or system articulated by Smith? Will they be "good soldiers, who . . . cheerfully sacrifice their own little systems to the prosperity of a greater system" (*TMS* VI.ii.3.4)? Will the well-being of the whole compensate them for the finitude of all the particulars they know and love?[21] Smith criticizes the political fanatic who, thinking he can rearrange society as easily as one moves chess pieces, has forgotten that on the "great chess-board of human society, every single piece has a principle of motion of its own" (*TMS* VI.ii.2.17). Smith offers the individual protection against the reformer's arrogance, but in the name of a pawn-like "principle of motion" rather than the soul.

The Theory of Moral Sentiments

The invisible hand in the astronomy essay was the invisible hand of Jupiter acting willfully to create the "irregular" phenomena of nature. This superstitious, polytheistic outlook was replaced, as civilization developed, with a pagan theism in which the natural order apprehended by philosophy was attributed to a unitary creator. The invisible hand in *The Theory of Moral Sentiments* is closer to the theistic perspective: it is part of the "regular" workings of nature and reflects a certain providential care for the whole. Like the invisible hand in *The Wealth of Nations*, it shows how social benefit emerges as the unintended outcome of selfish activity; it appears in a chapter revealing the core of the "Adam Smith Problem," in the central Part of *The Theory of Moral Sentiments*.

Part IV of *The Theory of Moral Sentiments* is entitled "Of the Effect of Utility Upon the Sentiment of Approbation."[22] The invisible hand is mentioned in the first of this Part's two chapters: "Of the Beauty which the Appearance of Utility bestows upon all the Productions of Art, and of the extensive Influence of this Species of Beauty." This is the only mention of "Art" in any of the Part, section, or chapter headings of the book. Art is a central theme of the chapter; the paragraph containing the invisible hand begins with praise of "the sciences and arts, which ennoble and embellish human life" and are integral to the development of civilization.

In the first paragraph of the chapter, Smith articulates what he claims is a universally acknowledged fact: utility, or "the fitness of any system or machine to produce the end for which it is intended," is the source of "a certain propriety and beauty." Smith claims originality, however, for his subsequent observation that this fitness or "happy contrivance" of the means often comes to be valued more than the end it produces (IV.1.3). He gives as an example people who "ruin themselves" by squandering their money on "trinkets of frivolous utility": toys and baubles (6). More important than these toys and baubles, however, are two other trinkets of frivolous utility, "wealth and greatness," the pursuit of which is likewise motivated by human infatuation with the contrivance of "means" (8). This brings us face-to-face with the "Adam Smith Problem," because the science of political economy elaborated in *The Wealth of Nations* takes as its aim the promotion of a nation's "riches and power," or "wealth and greatness" (*WN* II.v.31, IV.ix.50). Do pursuers of these trinkets likewise "ruin themselves"?

Smith goes on to provide his most detailed account of the ambivalences surrounding wealth and greatness. Smith describes two different perspectives for evaluating wealth and greatness. From one perspective, they are no more conducive to "ease of body or tranquillity of mind" than tweezers cases, and the restless pursuit of them comes at the expense of "humble security and contentment." This unfavorable perspective is a "splenetic" philosophy that views things in an "abstract and philosophical light"; it is natural to the "languor of disease and the weariness of old age," which require a man "to observe with attention his own situation" (*TMS* IV.1.8–9).[23]

There is, however, a more "complex" perspective favorable to the pursuit of wealth and greatness. In times of ease and prosperity, the imagination "expands" and confounds the satisfaction truly available from wealth and greatness with the order and regularity of "the system, the machine or oeconomy." In this light, Smith asserts, the "pleasures of wealth and greatness" appear "grand," "beautiful," and "noble" (9). Does this explain why Smith developed a mammoth intellectual "system" to augment "trinkets of frivolous utility," or only his strategy for co-opting the readers of *The Wealth of Nations*?[24]

There is a crucial difference between the two kinds of frivolous trinkets—wealth/greatness and toys/baubles (including tweezers cases)—that reveals much about the relationship of politics and economics. Wealth and greatness are more "observable" and therefore appeal to human vanity and "love of distinction"; what "the spectator" admires about the possessions of the rich and great, of course, is primarily their happy "contrivance" for promoting "ease or pleasure" (*TMS* IV.1.8). The quest for admiration is more political than the quest simply to accumulate material possessions. As we have seen, whereas *The Theory of Moral*

Sentiments emphasizes that wealth is pursued for the sake of esteem, *The Wealth of Nations* tends to present wealth as an end in itself. The esteem that motivates the pursuit of wealth partakes of *thymos* (but not the hard *thymos* of domination and violence) because it involves vanity. In the discussion of the invisible hand, this vanity is revealed to incorporate another kind of *thymos*: the "love of system," our intoxication with the very fitness of "means," which is an intoxication with "order," "regularity," "art," and "contrivance"—with power more than comfort.

In this key paragraph (*TMS* IV.1.8), the longest paragraph in the whole work, Smith also develops the links between political economy and history. In *Essays on Philosophical Subjects*, Smith argues that vulgar superstition evolved into theism with the development of civilization. In *The Theory of Moral Sentiments*, Smith argues that "power and riches" (i.e., greatness and wealth), despite their initial appeal, are no more than

> enormous and operose machines contrived to produce a few trifling conveniencies to the body, consisting of springs the most nice and delicate, which must be kept in order with the most anxious attention, and which in spite of all our care are ready every moment to burst into pieces, and to crush in their ruins their unfortunate possessor. . . . They keep off the summer shower, not the winter storm, but leave him always as much, and sometimes more, exposed than before, to anxiety, to fear, and to sorrow; to diseases, to danger, and to death. (*TMS* IV.1.8)

This poignant passage suggests that humankind's attempt to escape the ills of its beginnings is futile. Vulnerability and mortality cannot be overcome even by technology; the "splenetic" and "philosophical" perspective critical of wealth and greatness is vindicated.[25] As was discussed in the previous chapter, there are traces of this dilemma in Smith's account of civilization's vulnerability to sustained aggression by barbarians. *The Wealth of Nations* otherwise assumes, without the plaintive questioning of *The Theory of Moral Sentiments*, the ultimate desirability of "progress" and "improvement." The latter book, however, also expresses much more optimism and encouragement, as if to vanquish the deep doubts raised by the questioning.

Smith invokes the invisible hand in arguing that the earth's increasing fertility benefits humanity as a whole, despite inequality and the monopolization of landownership by a few. The landlord can only eat a tiny portion of his land's produce, the rest of which feeds the people who provide his luxuries (*TMS* IV.1.10).[26] The rich, despite their "natural selfishness and rapacity," are thus

> led by an *invisible hand* to make nearly the same distribution of the necessities of life which would have been made had the earth been divided

into equal portions among all its inhabitants; and thus without intending it, without knowing it, advance the interest of society, and afford means to the multiplication of the species. (*TMS* IV.1.10)

The rich man, motivated by "luxury and caprice" rather than "humanity" or "justice" (IV.1.10), thus promotes a salutary "end which was no part of his intention" (*WN* IV.ii.9). The demise of feudalism, as depicted in *The Wealth of Nations*, was likewise an unintended and unforeseen but very beneficial "revolution," triggered by the commercial progress that caused vain and selfish lords to squander their resources on "frivolous" and "useless" objects, i.e., "trinkets and baubles."[27]

In the sentence following the mention of the invisible hand in *The Theory of Moral Sentiments*, Smith links it with Providence:

When Providence divided the earth among a few lordly masters, it neither forgot nor abandoned those who seemed to have been left out in the partition. . . . In what constitutes the real happiness of human life, they are in no respect inferior to those who would seem so much above them. In ease of body and peace of mind, all the different ranks are nearly upon a level, and the beggar, who suns himself by the side of the highway, possesses that security which kings are fighting for. (*TMS* IV.1.10)

Consistent with the book's more cynical tone, *The Wealth of Nations* abandons the pretense that Providence was responsible for the division of land (*WN* III.ii.1) and emphasizes the economic benefits of subdividing land.[28] Parts IV and V of *The Theory of Moral Sentiments* are the only Parts of the book in which "God" does not appear, despite the prominence of the term and its various equivalents in the rest of the work, and they therefore anticipate the godlessness of *The Wealth of Nations*. In Part V, the closest approximation to God is "Fortune." In Part IV, the closest approximation is "Providence," whose care for humanity is illustrated by the invisible hand.

What are the aims or ends of Providence as presented in *The Theory of Moral Sentiments*? Throughout the book, the emphasis is on God's systematic achievements; He is responsible for designing a general system of order and regularity. The terms Smith freely substitutes for God—the "Author of Nature," the universe's "Director," "Conductor," or "administrator"—clearly indicate the deistic drift. The activities of Providence as described in conjunction with the invisible hand, however, call to mind the savage's belief that the gods take a more particular or personal interest in human affairs. Smith accentuates the concern of Providence for the lowly, "those who seemed to have been left out in the partition" of the earth. Smith proceeds to argue that those who provide and maintain "all the different baubles and trinkets which are employed in the oeconomy of greatness" are not shortchanged of "real happiness"; the beggar and the king are on a par (*TMS* IV.1.10).[29]

As portrayed in Part IV.1, however, Providence's presence is not altogether benign. The paragraph arguing that wealth and greatness are "mere trinkets of frivolous utility" begins by considering the "poor man's son, whom heaven in its anger has visited with ambition." It is he who sacrifices "humble security and contentment" for the spurious pursuit of wealth and greatness (IV.1.8).[30] Smith says no more about heaven or its anger, but he begins the invisible hand paragraph by revealing that our intoxication with wealth and greatness is a quasi-benevolent "deception" perpetrated by nature:

> And it is well that nature imposes upon us in this manner. It is this deception which rouses and keeps in continual motion the industry of mankind. It is this which first prompted them to cultivate the ground, to build houses, to found cities and commonwealths, and to invent and improve all the sciences and arts, which ennoble and embellish human life; which have entirely changed the whole face of the globe, have turned the rude forests of nature into agreeable and fertile plains, and made the trackless and barren ocean a new fund of subsistence, and the great high road of communication to the different nations of the earth. The earth by these labours of mankind has been obliged to redouble her natural fertility, and to maintain a greater multitude of inhabitants. (*TMS* IV.1.10)

The deception, speaking precisely, is the common supposition that wealth and greatness, whose pursuit is fueled by our intoxication with the systems that procure them, are "worth all the toil and anxiety" they generate. The deception is responsible for civilization—the development of human society from hunting and shepherding to agriculture and commerce—and it serves as Smith's substitute for original sin, which condemned man to earn his bread by the sweat of his brow.[31] Smith's political economy presupposes the desirability of civilization, and the language above seems favorable to it: sciences and arts that "ennoble and embellish human life"; "agreeable and fertile plains"; "the trackless and barren" ocean transformed into "a new fund of subsistence, and the great high road of communication." But why is it "well" that nature has deceived mankind into ceaseless "industry"?[32] Doesn't the beggar enjoy "ease of body and peace of mind" (IV.1.10)? Don't "power and riches" leave their possessor as much if not "more exposed" to fear, sorrow, danger, and death (IV.1.8)?

In addressing these questions, we must first note that Smith's defense of civilization is made with less qualification than his defense of the individual's pursuit of wealth and greatness. A whole society cannot subsist by begging. The ambition of the poor man's son may be a curse, but the delusion that motivates the son is beneficial when it acts on whole societies, if not the human race.[33] Smith is silent, however, about whether a society advancing to wealth and greatness will leave behind the "humble security and contentment" always available to the poor. Indeed, Smith generally portrays primitive society as harsh and miserable. There does not seem to be a resting point—for example, an Aristotelian polis that pursues the amount of wealth necessary for the "good life"—between the necessitousness of hunting societies and the frenetic motion of capitalist societies.[34]

The passage defending nature's deception, because it culminates in a reference to the "greater multitude of inhabitants" that the earth thereby maintains (*TMS* IV.1.10), may help resolve an ambiguity that pervades *The Theory of Moral Sentiments*: does nature provide vigorous support for human virtue, nobility, and happiness, or only for preservation and propagation? This ambiguity is especially prominent in the discussion, later in the same paragraph, of the invisible hand and Providence. Does Providence guarantee that "real happiness" is available to all or only that no one is shortchanged of the "necessaries of life"—food? Smith mentions two ends that the rich are unwittingly led by the invisible hand to advance: "the interest of the society" and "the multiplication of the species" (IV.1.10). The two ends are generally conflated in *the* end of Smith's political economy—the wealth of nations. Smith argues that the accumulation of capital and the increase of national wealth help "the great body of the people" to "thrive," and that population growth is "the most decisive mark of prosperity" (*WN* I.viii.21–23,43).[35]

Smith indicates, however, that there are limits to nature's support for even the modest ends of preservation, propagation, and prosperity. In explaining that the "demand for men" causes an increase in "the production of men," Smith presents the law of supply and demand as the law of Darwinian nature: "Every species of animals naturally multiplies in proportion to the means of their subsistence" (*WN* I.viii.39–40). The increase of wages that occurs in the "progressive" state of society, which Smith characterizes as "cheerful" and "hearty" (I.viii.21–22,43), causes a drop in childhood mortality, which ultimately increases competition among the workers and decreases wages. In a stagnant economy, "the great body of the people" merely subsist; in a decaying economy, their ranks are thinned by premature deaths.[36] It is not difficult to suggest circumstances that might, from Smith's point of view, extend the "progressive" state and its attendant prosperity: adoption of the system of natural liberty, the use of birth control by workers, or perhaps an expansion of the concept of "necessity" that would raise the "subsistence" wage.[37] Smith speaks of the "full complement of riches" "allowed" to a society by the "nature" of its soil, climate, and international situation (I.ix.14), but also of the riches "permitted" by its "laws and institutions" (I.viii.24). He thus assigns the ultimate limits equally to nature and convention. Smith recounts the circumstances that have "maintained the progress of England towards opulence and improvement in almost all former times, and which, it is to be hoped, will do so in all future times" (II.iii.36), but he also states that two hundred years is "as long as the course of human prosperity usually endures" (III.iv.20). His predictions for the future seem deliberately hazy.

The religious question reemerges as one dwells on the paradoxical account in *The Theory of Moral Sentiments* of the desirability of civilization. As we saw, Smith distinguishes two perspectives for evaluating the pursuit of wealth and greatness: the "splenetic" perspective of disease and old age, in which a man "observe[s] with attention his own situation," and the "complex" perspective in which "ease and prosperity" cause our imaginations to expand "to everything around us" (*TMS* IV.1.8–9). The first dwells on what is particular, finite, and mortal; can the second uncover something general and eternal? The first view calls to mind the "melancholy and gloomy humour" Smith describes as "the nurse of popular superstition and enthusiasm" (*WN* V.i.g.15); Smith here follows Hume's argument that superstition is rooted in the "gloomy and melancholy disposition."[38] As we will see, Smith is concerned to remedy superstition and the humors that breed it, though *The Wealth of Nations* has its gloomy or "splenetic" side. *The Theory of Moral Sentiments* conveys rather the mood of "ease and prosperity" that causes the mind to expand. Unlike Smith, however, Hume also warns about the danger of this mood: "enthusiasm," in which "the imagination swells with great, but confused conceptions" and "every thing mortal and perishable vanishes as unworthy of attention."[39] Smith tries to accommodate both moods while stripping them of their tendency to produce religious excesses; he strives to temper the extremes of both melancholy and bliss. In *The Wealth of Nations*, the splenetic humor is converted into economic progress via bourgeois virtue in the long and taxing struggle to better one's condition. In *The Theory of Moral Sentiments*, the expansive humor is converted into economic progress by being deflected, via the charm of system, to the march of civilization.

The view favorable to wealth and greatness, applied to society as a whole, would be favorable to civilization. With civilization comes perception of order and consciousness of strength; the development of civilization is the development of our strength vis-à-vis nature. But what does this continued development achieve? Doesn't the inevitability of death vindicate the splenetic perspective? The fear of death is a major theme of *The Theory of Moral Sentiments*, but Smith provides diverging answers to the question of whether death is truly fearful.[40] Death does not apply with the same necessity to the society or the species as it does to the individual,[41] however, and this may be the key to the paradox of wealth and greatness. During good times, an individual can be emotionally sustained by the accumulation of trinkets and the infatuation with contrivance. The very endlessness of this quest may indeed distract us from the inevitability of "the winter storm." But when the reality of death becomes palpable, one can (in the Smithian universe) focus more happily only on civilization and the propagation of the species, both of which might continue indefinitely.[42] Hobbesian self-preservation yields, in Smith's thought, to species-preservation. But Locke got there first, identifying "the main intention of nature" as "the increase of mankind, and the continuation of the species"; the "law of nature . . . willeth the peace and preservation of all mankind."[43] One should hesitate before accusing classical liberalism of elevating the individual at the expense of the species.[44]

Smith concludes the invisible hand chapter with a long paragraph detailing the political consequences of the "spirit of system"—human infatuation with the fitness of means or contrivance. Just as the love of system makes wealth and greatness appear grand, beautiful, and noble, the "regard to the beauty of order, of art and contrivance" often recommends "those institutions which tend to promote the public welfare"; police, trade, and manufacturing become "noble and magnificent objects" whose "contemplation . . . pleases us" and makes us "interested" in their promotion (*TMS* IV.1.9,11).[45] As with wealth and greatness, our infatuation with the means of government may eclipse our concern with the ends it serves. Smith here gives his most detailed recommendations for the promotion of public spirit—how to "rouse" people "to seek out the means of promoting the happiness of the society." The key is the "study of politics"—suitable disquisitions about "systems of civil government," constitutions, foreign policy, and so on (IV.1.11). The elaborate structure of Smith's science of political economy might itself open up a new means, characteristically indirect, of promoting concern for the common good. The spirit of system is not an unmixed blessing, however. In a later section of *The Theory of Moral Sentiments*, Smith argues that system can be a source of "fanaticism"; intoxicated by the "imaginary beauty" of their "ideal system," reformers may pursue utopian hopes with great violence (VI.ii.2.15).[46]

In *Essays on Philosophical Subjects*, Smith describes the awe or admiration with which people regard nature or gods. In the central Part of *The Theory of Moral Sentiments*, there is no mention of God, and the focus shifts to human contrivances—"the Productions of Art"—which include "systems of police," trinkets and baubles, and all the sciences and crafts employed in the conquest of nature. With the progress toward civilization, humanity grows more conscious of its strength, nature takes on the appearance of a system or machine, and superstitious polytheism is replaced by theism. One may infer that there is less need for a divine presence as humanly created machines and systems proliferate and develop in complexity. *The Wealth of Nations* presupposes and encourages the technological revolutions of modernity and adds a new kind of system to civilization: the mammoth intellectual edifice of social science. In *The Theory of Moral Sentiments*, Smith freely builds on the great systematic achievements of his predecessors in the field of moral philosophy, from Plato, Aristotle, and Cicero to Mandeville, Hutcheson, and Hume. Only Quesnay plays a comparable role in *The Wealth of Nations*, which launches the new science of economics and modern social science as a whole. Only when presented in the godless landscape of political economy, to which we now turn, did Smith's invisible hand capture the human imagination and leave its mark on history.

The Wealth of Nations

Unlike Smith's other works, *The Wealth of Nations* completely severs the invisible hand from the divine. Although mentioned only once in a large book, the invisible hand pervades the whole work.

The invisible hand is mentioned early in the fourth of the five Books of *The Wealth of Nations*, in the middle pages of the work. The context is more pedestrian than in *The Theory of Moral Sentiments*. The invisible hand is invoked to bolster Smith's argument for free trade, especially free international trade. Because Book IV as a whole both portrays and encourages the extension of global economic interdependence, rejecting self-sufficiency as a goal for nations as well as for families and individuals, the invisible hand again serves to elevate the species at the expense of smaller human aggregations.

The immediate point Smith illustrates by means of the invisible hand is that people engaged in foreign trade promote society's interest merely by effectively pursuing their own "advantage" (*WN* IV.ii.4). Government attempts to restrict imports, thereby encouraging domestic monopoly, are unnecessary and unproductive:

> Every individual necessarily labours to render the annual revenue of the society as great as he can. He generally, indeed, neither intends to promote

the publick interest, nor knows how much he is promoting it. By preferring the support of domestic to that of foreign industry, he intends only his own security; and by directing that industry in such a manner as its produce may be of the greatest value, he intends only his own gain, and he is in this, as in many other cases, led by an *invisible hand* to promote an end which was no part of his intention. Nor is it always the worse for the society that it was no part of it. By pursuing his own interest he frequently promotes that of the society more effectually than when he really intends to promote it. (*WN* IV.ii.9)

The case for laissez-faire is completed in the next paragraph when Smith argues that the individual "in his local situation" can determine the productive uses of his capital "much better than any statesman or lawgiver can do for him" (IV.ii.10).[47]

The individual who thus promotes the common good is in a sense not acting on his own: he is "led" by the invisible hand. In *The Theory of Moral Sentiments*, similarly, the rich are "led by an invisible hand" to promote the common good "without intending it, without knowing it" (IV.1.10). But to whom does the hand belong, and where does it point? In the primitive consciousness sketched in *Essays on Philosophical Subjects*, the irregular phenomena of nature are thought to be the work of Jupiter's invisible hand acting intentionally for particular purposes. This invisible hand is perceived or imagined by people generally; it is not something they hear about, for example, via prophetic tradition. In *The Theory of Moral Sentiments*, the leading is done by a hand doing the work of Providence, but the hand operates through a general system, not as an instrument of Providence acting spontaneously in particular cases. This invisible hand is *not* immediately perceived by the people on whom it operates; its presence is revealed by Smith, to assure his readers that the few rich unintentionally provide for the many poor. In *The Wealth of Nations*, the invisible hand is likewise a metaphor created by Smith to assure his readers that public opulence is advanced by individuals who intend only their own enrichment. Smith thus retains the systematic and philosophic drift of *The Theory of Moral Sentiments*, but removes God or Providence altogether. We are led simply by nature.

Scholars universally acknowledge the importance of unintended consequences in *The Wealth of Nations*. The division of labor, the great cause of the increasing productivity of labor, "is not originally the effect of any human wisdom, which foresees and intends that general opulence to which it gives occasion" (I.ii.1); feudalism fell because of the "silent and insensible operation of foreign commerce and manufactures" rather than institutional "violence" (III.iv.10); the people responsible for this "great revolution" lacked either "knowledge or foresight" of the larger impact of their actions (III.iv.17); the discovery of huge gold and silver deposits in the New World was the result of "accidents, which no human wisdom could foresee" (IV.vii.a.21); "no human wisdom can foresee" the benefits and misfortunes that will result from the emerging global economy (IV.vii.c.80); political authority and the administration of justice emerge spontaneously with the progress of society toward civilization.[48] Not all of these unintended consequences, however, can be likened to the operation of an invisible hand promoting the common good by means of individual selfishness.

Of all the limitations on human intention, foresight, and wisdom adduced by Smith in *The Wealth of Nations*, one stands out. Smith's case for his system of natural liberty hinges on the proposition that "no human wisdom or knowledge could ever be sufficient" to provide the sovereign the capability of "superintending the industry of private people" and "directing it towards the employments most suitable to the interest of the society." The alternative is to leave each individual free "to pursue his own interest his own way" within "the laws of justice" (IV.ix.51). Smith radically denigrates the possibilities for human choice acting at a macro-level: the great "revolutions" in history have not been plans and projects, the product of human intention and foresight. As we have seen, this denigration is coupled with Smith's redirection of philosophy so as to efface the kind of inquiry that would serve to guide such choices—political philosophy, the quest for the best regime, and even a prescriptive moral philosophy answering the question "How should I live?" This constriction of macro-choice, however, is accompanied by a huge expansion of micro-choice: above all, the freedom to pursue one's livelihood as one sees fit, to pursue "interest" in this world relatively unfettered by traditional political, religious, and moral constraints. This expansion of micro-liberty is the powerful strand of individualism that counterbalances the various strands of anti-individualism we have explored in this chapter. The individual liberty that defines the system of natural liberty requires that government be limited, but "natural liberty" is not anarchy; in "securing to every man the fruits of his own industry" (*WN* IV.vii.c.54), government is the servant of individualism. The paramount function of Smith's science of political economy is to elaborate the "natural" order that emerges when conscious interference is minimized. This is why Adam Smith is so renowned as a libertarian, despite his indifference to freedom as an end in itself or as a moral imperative.[49]

The Wealth of Nations never invokes a divine wisdom that transcends the limitations of human wisdom, even though Smith's attack on human meddling would be more powerful if he could portray such meddling as treading in God's department.[50] If the economy is a "machine" (*TMS*

IV.1.9) without an apparent inventor or mechanic, why resist the temptation to tinker with it?[51] Phyllis Deane errs seriously in attributing to Smith the view that economic liberty is part of "the Divine Plan": that no one should tamper with the socioeconomic machine because it is the work of a "great architect," a "benevolent deity" identified with God and the invisible hand (pp. 7–8, 13). Nature indeed bears a great burden as Smith counsels deference to the "natural course of things."

The eclipse of God by nature in *The Wealth of Nations* is most palpably conveyed by Smith's discussion of "the Deity" in the Article on education; the book never mentions "God." Smith endorses the ancient Greeks' tripartite division of philosophy into physics (natural philosophy), moral philosophy, and logic. Under this division, investigation into the human mind and "the Deity" was subsumed under physics, which investigates "the origin and revolutions of the great system of the universe." The human mind and the Deity "in whatever their essence might be supposed to consist, were parts of the great system of the universe" (V.i.f.28). That is, the Deity does not stand above the universe as Creator; it is one among many parts of the system and is therefore bound by the laws of that system. Smith here praises the division of philosophy that thus bounds the Deity, without alleging that there is a Deity.

The "great system" of *The Wealth of Nations*, unlike that of *The Theory of Moral Sentiments*, operates without an "administrator," "Director," or "Author." The relatively godless landscape of *The Theory of Moral Sentiments*, Part IV, in which the invisible hand appears, prepares the completely godless landscape of *The Wealth of Nations*. The change of the invisible hand's theological context in its three presentations mirrors the path (suggested by *Essays on Philosophical Subjects*) from biblical religion to deism to atheism. Smith's political economy transcends his moral philosophy by offering a picture of order without design. In *The Theory of Moral Sentiments*, Smith provides an account of society and the cosmos that demonstrates their order and beneficent purpose, despite the substitution of the deist God for the biblical God whose "irregular" interferences thereby disappear. In *The Wealth of Nations*, Smith provides an account of society and the cosmos in which the order that promotes nature's purposes is demonstrated so thoroughly that the operations of the invisible hand are intelligible without recourse to Providence or God. The removal of God parallels (if it does not necessitate) the contradictions between the two books that called forth the "Adam Smith Problem"; these contradictions generally reflect the pessimism and the lowered horizons of *The Wealth of Nations*.

As Irving Kristol observes (awkwardly but accurately): "Smith's original insight that commercial relations are such that, as in the cosmos itself, the seemingly inchoate flux of phenomena and events can be explained in terms of an orderly disorder (so to speak)—that is the rock upon which economics is built." Kristol goes astray, however, in contrasting the "expansive spirit" of *The Wealth of Nations* with the dismal science of Malthus and Ricardo that presented a "Newtonian universe without God as creator, sustainer, or redeemer."[52] Smith acknowledges that Newtonianism may not be the last word on the cosmos, but God in every capacity is absent from *The Wealth of Nations*. Pocock wonders how Smith's "complex synthesis of 'moral sentiment' with 'the wealth of nations'" could "evolve or degenerate into the science of classical economics"; to solve this puzzle, "we must write or rewrite the whole ideological and philosophical history of the half-century of counter-revolution, industrial revolution and war that separate the time of Smith from that of Ricardo."[53] As we have seen in previous chapters, *The Wealth of Nations* is sprinkled not only with digressions but with danglers: provocative and paradoxical vestiges of traditional perspectives that clash with the book's overall thrust. If *The Wealth of Nations* shorn of danglers and digressions is classical economics, Pocock's call may be disregarded; Smith's two books are not easily synthesized, and there is not a single word in *The Wealth of Nations* that would lead the reader to *The Theory of Moral Sentiments*. The Advertisement in the 1790 edition of the latter refers to *The Wealth of Nations*; the title page of *The Wealth of Nations*, however, is silent about Smith's other writings, though it does invoke his former status as Professor of Moral Philosophy at Glasgow. The popularity of *The Theory of Moral Sentiments* in 1776 might have helped *The Wealth of Nations* gain a hearing; its deism and its "warmth in the cause of virtue" might have helped shield the later book against accusations of Humean atheism or Mandevillean "licentiousness." Smith, however, may have anticipated that *The Wealth of Nations*, in the long run, would prosper on its own.

Malthus and Ricardo are more rigidly deterministic than Smith.[54] By tightening the "invisible chains" that "connect" the phenomena of the economic world, however, they promote a Smithian agenda. If they insufficiently considered the possibility that philosophy creates rather than discovers the chains,[55] Smith is partly responsible, for the chains are presented in *The Wealth of Nations* as products of nature rather than of the author's mind.

If Smith's account of society and the cosmos were both irrefutable and easily understood, there would be no need for a perplexing metaphor like that of the invisible hand. It seems as if the philosophic attempt to render nature a "coherent spectacle" by displaying its "connecting chains" is a process that is never completed. Raphael (p. 112) indicates that Smith "would say" of his economic doctrines what he does say of Newtonian astronomy: they are "all products of the imagination which help us to connect observable facts but are not themselves facts or realities that might be observable or otherwise knowable." Raphael fails to stress, however, that Smith *did not* say this of his economic doctrines, and that he left the relevant epistemological reflections buried in a ponderously titled unpublished essay, "The Principles which lead and direct Philosophical Enquiries; illustrated by the History of Astronomy." Nature's connecting chains, as presented in *The Wealth of Nations*, can ensnare the unwary reader.

In Smith's account, the notion of an invisible hand entered the universe as a superstitious response to phenomena that people could neither understand nor control. Smith's employment of this metaphor to convey the core of his teaching may entail several things: that Smith has not yet succeeded in providing a compelling account of the whole, that the universe remains uncontrollable if not unfathomable; that philosophy continually moves toward such an account but never arrives at it; that simplifying metaphors have to be employed to convey the account to others.[56] The very "novelty" or "unexpectedness" of the metaphor may have rhetorical advantages:

> Though it is the end of Philosophy, to allay that wonder, which either the unusual or seemingly disjointed appearances of nature excite, yet she never triumphs so much, as when, in order to connect together a few ... objects, she has, if I may say so, created another constitution of things, more natural indeed, and such as the imagination can more easily attend to, but more new, more contrary to common opinion and expectation, than any of those appearances themselves. (Astronomy IV.33)

Although certain people might support Smith's system of natural liberty because of the divine agency they associate with an invisible hand, others, especially those with the time and the inclination to study the whole of Smith's corpus, might be led by "the invisible hand" to appreciate the metaphorical aspects of "the natural order." The invisible hand may also be a warning that religion will always be able to exploit the mysteries, fears, and feelings of impotence that cannot be expunged by "progress."

The invisible hand chapter in *The Wealth of Nations*, unlike the chapter in *The Theory of Moral Sentiments*, ends on a pessimistic note. Smith laments that expecting full restoration of free trade in Great Britain would be as absurd as expecting a "Utopia," because of the obstacles posed by public prejudice and private interests (*WN* IV.ii.43). He continues by suggesting that the "legislature, were it possible that its

deliberations could be always directed, not by the clamorous impor-
tunity of partial interests, but by *an extensive view of the general good"*
should avoid establishing domestic monopolies (IV.ii.44). These passages
call to mind the concluding paragraph of the invisible hand chapter in
The Theory of Moral Sentiments, where Smith showed how the spirit of
system could be converted into public spirit. Here, too, direct "fellow-
feeling" for the happiness of other citizens is disparaged as a spur to
public-spiritedness; the more effective spur is intoxication with the
nobility, beauty, and order of "the great system" of government (*TMS*
IV.1.11).

The "system of moral philosophy" articulated in *The Theory of Moral
Sentiments* possesses its own intoxicating grandeur, intertwined with
the elaborate deistic teleology that pervades the book. In Part IV.1, however, we are led to admire not God, the "author of nature," but human
beings, the conquerors of nature: the chapter reaches its climax with
praise of "the sciences and arts, which ennoble and embellish human
life" (*TMS* IV.1.10). Hence the prospect that intoxication with the means
of preservation will eclipse preservation itself (obviously futile as a long-
term goal for the individual). In this respect, Smith's teaching lies at a
crucial nexus of modern philosophy. The principle of self-interest, fundamental to philosophers such as Machiavelli, Hobbes, Spinoza, Locke,
Mandeville, and Montesquieu, now informs a new science—economics.
The twin engines of commerce and natural science build on one another
in the ongoing conquest of nature.[57] Social science (especially economics) reveals and facilitates the complex processes of society at work
perfecting the technology to control nature for the sake of human comfort, longevity, and even freedom.[58]

When we compare Smith's account in *The Wealth of Nations* of the
three great societal classes with the account of the invisible hand in *The
Theory of Moral Sentiments*, a paradox emerges—still another facet of
the "Adam Smith Problem" that has escaped scholarly notice. According
to *The Theory of Moral Sentiments*, people become intoxicated with
wealth and greatness in times of "ease and prosperity," when their imaginations expand. In the section of *The Wealth of Nations* that describes
the fundamental social orders, the landlords' intellectual deficiencies are
attributed to the "indolence" produced by their "ease and security": their
revenue comes to them "independent of any plan or project of their own"
(*WN* I.xi.p.8). The movers of society are rather those who "live by profit":
because "during their whole lives they are engaged in plans and projects,
they have frequently more acuteness of understanding than the greater
part of country gentlemen" (I.xi.p.10).

The two books thus seem to disagree about whether prosperity or penury is the spur to industry. Perhaps the accounts can be rendered consistent by the following supposition: although the material advancement of civilization is motivated partly by real necessities, it becomes an all-consuming quest only when people perceive enough ease and prosperity to suggest the possibility of guaranteed protection against the "winter storm," against pain, sorrow, sickness, and, ultimately, death. This is nature's benevolent "deception," discussed above. Too much ease, or ease achieved without manifest effort, produces indolence. The continuing transformation of conveniences into necessities keeps the original hunger alive, as does the contribution of vanity (because vanity requires one to have *more* than another). Hopelessness, on the other hand, is as enervating as the landlord's ease.[59] Individuals consumed by the effort to better their condition are on the way up but they never arrive; is the same not true of the social progress toward opulence, the march of civilization? Smith says that agriculture (the third stage) "was the original destination of man" (*WN* III.i.3). The fourth and final stage, commerce, is an endless journey.

There is a second way to address the paradox. Smith suggests that progress may blur class differentiations. In a commercial society, everyone "becomes in some measure a merchant" (I.iv.1); in a society that has "acquired its full complement of riches"—a situation approximated by Holland—it "would be necessary that almost every man should be a man of business" (I.ix.20). This would reduce the "ease and security" that breed indolence and ignorance in the landlords, leaving the bulk of society on the front lines of the war against nature.[60]

This second prospect meshes neatly with Smith's account of how nature's "wisdom" mobilizes human energies. In *The Theory of Moral Sentiments*, Smith pays frequent homage to the wisdom of nature and God, despite the ambiguities in his account of their ultimate purposes. These ambiguities seem to be resolved in *The Wealth of Nations*, where God is absent and the sole reference to the "wisdom of nature" identifies it with preservation.[61] Smith is criticizing Quesnay's thesis that the "political body" requires "an exact regimen of perfect liberty and justice." Smith responds that the human body, because it contains "some unknown principle of preservation," can be healthy under imperfect regimens. The same is true of the political body: thus "the wisdom of nature" remedies "many of the bad effects of the folly and injustice of man." Quesnay failed to grasp the importance of "the natural effort which every man is continually making to better his own condition" as a "principle of preservation" that corrects an imperfect political economy and maintains "the natural progress of a nation towards wealth and prosperity" (IV.ix.28).

By describing the effort to better one's condition, the motivational linchpin of the psychology and the policy of *The Wealth of Nations*, as a "principle of preservation," Smith suggests how he has appropriated and modified the "self-preservation" extolled by Hobbes and Locke. Smith stresses the power this natural "principle" possesses—especially where individual "freedom and security" prevail (IV.v.b.43)—to maintain economic progress despite the "errors," "folly," "extravagance," "oppression," "injustice," "profusion," "presumption," and "impertinent obstructions" of government (II.iii.31,36, IV.ix.28). By leaving "every man . . . perfectly free to pursue his own interest his own way" and by "securing to every man the fruits of his own industry,"[62] natural liberty would perfect the translation of the individual's drive to better his condition into the wealth of nations—"the natural progress of things towards improvement" (II.iii.31). Nature's power is manifested first or primarily in the individual "body," secondarily in the "political body," and ultimately in the preservation, propagation, and prosperity of the species.[63]

Hobbes's Leviathan is created by and for the people, as a remedy for the state of nature; one might say that Hobbes has thus democratized Machiavelli's teaching that human beings are essentially unprotected and needy. Hunting society, the Smithian equivalent of the state of nature, is ravaged not by war but by the poverty that reflects the scantiness of our natural inheritance;[64] Smith's system of natural liberty enables and compels *each* individual to labor toward a remedy for nature's stinginess.[65] One could say that the violent "acquisition" or aggrandizement of Machiavellian princes has been replaced by "the natural progress of a nation towards wealth and prosperity."[66]

For Smith, "monopolies" are perhaps the greatest obstacle to this translation of avarice into public opulence. "Good management" cannot prevail universally without "that free and universal competition which forces *every body* to have recourse to it for the sake of self-defence," and monopoly is "a great enemy to good management" (*WN* I.xi.b.5). The division of labor, by contrast, helps elicit effort and increase output; its debilitating effects are the price paid, in the harsh accounting of Darwinian nature, by the mass of individuals for the progress of the species.

Smith's invisible hand, finally, is an echo of Machiavelli's "invisible government" (*Discourses*, II:21). Its rule is impersonal and apolitical, like the "command" involved in Smithian exchange value. Although the system of natural liberty frees individuals to pursue their own aims, rather than those of kings, priests, aristocrats, or mercantilists, the invisible hand reminds the individual that human power continues to serve "other designs than its own."[67] Marx argues that "natural liberty" is really slavery to the designs of *capital*, combats the identification of the invisible hand with the natural order, and tries to reveal the "hands" of the bourgeois ideologists (including Smith) who have promoted these illusions. Leo Strauss, however, implies that Smith and Marx were both lieutenants in a campaign initiated by the unseen Machiavelli; if so, they have helped render their prince's hand invisible.

The invisible hand for Smith is the perfect symbol of the individual's paradoxical relation to both the social whole and the cosmic whole. The invisible hand obviously symbolizes the somewhat mysterious translation of individual interest into social progress, but it also symbolizes a more fundamental mystery. Human beings experience themselves as conscious, intelligent, and purposive, but wonder about the place of consciousness, intelligence, and purpose in their origin and destiny. The ongoing development of commercial society, by virtue of which we collectively mold nature to our purposes, may reconcile the individual to the cosmic and the social whole, but never perfectly.[68] We seek and perhaps intuit a guiding hand, but we never see it.

CHAPTER SEVEN

The Atheistic Science of Political Economy

> We must understand this respectable author . . . as we do
> Scripture, by comparing one passage with another, and taking
> the general scope of the whole.
> —Alexander Carlyle, letter to the Duke of Buccleuch (1778)

IAN BARBOUR CONTRASTS THE goal of modern science—the "description, prediction, and control of a limited phenomenon"—with that of Greek and medieval science: "the understanding and contemplation of the meaning of the part in relation to the whole and, above all, to God." According to Aquinas, for example, although natural processes can be explained (via "secondary causes") in "relative independence of any direct acts of God," their "functioning depends on power not inherent in them, but provided by God's sustaining activity" as the "prime cause" of every event.[1] Speculation about society and morality, of course, labored even longer than natural science under the watchful eye of theologians, a phenomenon of great concern to the philosophers who laid the groundwork for modern social science. The emergence of sociology and economics as independent sciences also implied the liberation of certain "parts" of society—the market, the mode of production, the household—from the political "whole," from the prophets, philosophers, legislators, and statesmen who seek to create and sustain a particular form of life.

The Wealth of Nations is an atheistic and anti-Christian work. The works of Smith's two most illustrious successors in the field of political economy, David Ricardo and Karl Marx, are as irreligious as The Wealth of Nations is. Contemporary social science is irreligious from habit more than from reflection; it is certainly not challenged by any powerful Christian orthodoxy. In the political philosophy of the present day (undergoing a revival spearheaded by Rawls and Nozick), economics is central but religion is peripheral. For example, God is not mentioned in *Anarchy, State, and Utopia* and is quickly disposed of in *A Theory of Justice*.[2]

Adam Smith helped prepare these developments by removing theology from political economy. Sir James Steuart, by contrast, explicitly defers to religion on several points where it clashes with political economy;[3] even Physiocratic economics had a theological foundation.[4] The subsequent liberation of economics from political economy required the abandonment of *other* features of *The Wealth of Nations*, especially its comprehensive and systematic investigation of the "duties" of government (V.i), its lengthy historical discussions (both theoretical and concrete), its ubiquitous quasi-philosophic terminology ("nature," "natural," "naturally"), and its various "danglers." Some scholars mistakenly impute religious doctrines to *The Wealth of Nations*,[5] but on the whole the question has been treated perfunctorily. The only inexcusable failure in this regard is the abundance of recent denials of the "Adam Smith Problem," despite the glaring contrasts between *The Theory of Moral Sentiments* and *The Wealth of Nations* on religious matters. Some who notice the discrepancies attribute them to a change in Smith's religious "views," but this response is inadequate.[6]

Our explorations of Smith's contribution to the eclipse of politics by economics have confirmed Winch's judgment that Smith was a "master of the art of equipoise." The posture of *The Wealth of Nations* toward Christianity, though not without its share of puzzles, is far more blatant. The variety, subtlety, and consistency of the book's impieties, moreover, reveal the importance Smith attached to them. On the essential points, the book's teaching is unambiguous, but Smith's subtlety saved him from Hume's reputation. Curiously, Smith only rarely resorts to direct disparagement of religious precepts as obstacles to opulence; by 1776, it seems, the dominant churches lacked the ability if not the motivation to derail Europe's accelerating economic progress.[7] Smith criticizes the prohibition of usury (*WN* I.ix.5), faults the ancient Egyptians for their "superstitious aversion to the sea" (IV.ix.45), and tacitly disparages the religions of India and Egypt for binding sons to their fathers' occupations (I.vii.31). The brunt of his campaign against religion, however, emerges indirectly—from his wholly secular examination of "nature and causes."

I shall begin with a sort of economic analysis of *The Wealth of Nations*—an examination of the "supply" of key Christian concepts—to scrutinize the materials from which Smith's "great system" or machine is constructed. Smith's injunctions on behalf of literary concision (Languages 43,45), conjoined with the great length of *The Wealth of Nations*, amplify the work's silence about God and Jesus. The very indirection of

Smith's account may make it more corrupting. In the words of Michael Ignatieff, "The great enemy of religion is not science, nor the active profession of unbelief, but rather the silent and pervasive plausibility of earthly need as a metaphysics of ordinary life" (p. 77).

Key Christian Concepts

God and His Son

In *The Wealth of Nations*, Smith never mentions God or Providence; in none of Smith's writings (including his correspondence) does "Jesus," "Christ," or "the Son" appear.[8] In the section on education in Book V, Smith does mention "the gods" and "the Deity"; his discussion of them both explains and enhances the absence of God. Smith is arguing the preferability of "antient Greek philosophy"—whose division into natural philosophy, moral philosophy, and logic "seems perfectly agreeable to the nature of things" (V.i.f.23)—to "modern" (i.e., Scholastic) philosophy's five-part curriculum that stresses "metaphysics" and "ontology" (f.27–29). Greek natural philosophy, according to Smith, investigated the "great phenomena of nature":

> As they necessarily excite the wonder, so they naturally call forth the curiosity of mankind to enquire into their causes. Superstition first attempted to satisfy this curiosity by referring all those wonderful appearances to the immediate agency of the gods. Philosophy afterwards endeavoured to account for them, from more familiar causes, or from such as mankind were better acquainted with, than the agency of the gods. (*WN* V.i.f.24)

This is all *The Wealth of Nations* has to say about the gods: they were creatures of superstition later replaced by the "more familiar causes" uncovered by philosophy. As we have seen, a careful examination of *Essays on Philosophical Subjects* suggests that the biblical God, for Smith, is likewise a creature of superstition.

Smith refers to the Deity in describing the modern, five-part division of philosophy. In the ancient scheme, "the Deity" and the human mind, being "parts of the great system of the universe," were investigated by that "science which pretended to give an account of the origin and revolutions of the great system" (V.i.f.28). Thus, in the division of philosophy that "seems perfectly agreeable to the nature of things," the Deity is but a "part" of "the great system of the universe." This is hardly the Deists' watchmaker God, to say nothing of the biblical God associated with miracles, revelation, prophecy, covenants, and creation. Smith seems to mimic Greek philosophy by constructing "systems" that confine or eliminate God.[9] Smith's disparagement of God is accentuated by his not mentioning the Deity in the initial account of ancient physics (f.24). The place of the Deity in the ancient scheme, it seems, is discussed only to explain the "modern" aberrations.

In *The Theory of Moral Sentiments*, Smith provides a veritable bevy of divine designations—nature's "Author," "Director," "Superintendent," and "Architect"—but only a few references to God as creator. Architects and authors, because they operate with preexisting languages and writing implements do not create *ex nihilo*.[10] Smith strives to display the potency of social progress that relies on the gradual advance of the human collectivity (augmented by the division of labor) and is independent of the intentions, power, or intelligence of a superintending being. The scale, speed, and willfulness of the biblical God's creations make Him a poor model for political economy.

Not surprisingly, Smith laments the "modern" incorporation of philosophy by theology, as a result of which the study of mind and Deity mushroomed into "metaphysics or Pneumaticks" and served as the pinnacle of education. In ridiculing such philosophy, Smith draws on the worldly wisdom of economics:

> Speculative systems have in all ages of the world been adopted for reasons too frivolous to have determined the judgment of any man of common sense, in a matter of the smallest pecuniary interest. Gross sophistry has scarce ever had any influence upon the opinions of mankind, except in matters of philosophy and speculation; and in these it has frequently had the greatest. (*WN* V.i.f.26)

Ancient natural philosophy, according to Smith, sought to determine "the Nature and essence" of every "particular species of things" and thus spawned metaphysics/logic to investigate universals and species (Logics 1). Smith confines his investigations, however, to the "nature and causes" of things[11] and portrays the first two branches of Greek philosophy more respectfully than the third (*WN* V.i.f.26). Smith surely expects that his political economy, which gazes downward to the earth (devoting great attention to matters of small "pecuniary interest") rather than upward to heaven, will be closer to common sense than either theology or speculative philosophy. But Smith's lamentations about mercantilist "sophistry" and his use of the "invisible hand" indicate that the disjunction is not total.

The Wealth of Nations does not even allude to Jesus. This silence is accentuated by the thoroughness with which the work touches on other illustrious historical figures (not to mention the parade of authors and philosophers): Alexander the Great, Philip of Macedon, Mithridates,

Cato, the Gracchi, Hannibal, Scipio Africanus, Julius Caesar, Augustus, Constantine, Marcus Aurelius; Genghis Khan, Marco Polo, Montezuma; Walter Raleigh, Pizarro, da Gama, Balboa, Columbus; Lorenzo de' Medici, Peter the Great, Oliver Cromwell, Robert Walpole; Charles V, VI, VII, and VIII; Henry IV and VIII; Edward IV and VI; Queen Elizabeth; Ferdinand and Isabella; James I, Philip I, William III, King John; and Luther, Zwingli, and Calvin. Smith manages a reference even to Mohammed, who, by means of "religious enthusiasm," united the Arabs and thus launched their conquests (V.i.a.5). He is silent about Mohammed's status as a prophet.

The absence of God and Jesus does not establish that Smith rejected all forms of religion. It does suggest, however, that he rejected all forms of Christianity, not just medieval Catholicism. Even the truly latitudinarian Protestants of the eighteenth century did not portray God as a "part" of "the great system of the universe" or erase Jesus from world history. Indeed, by describing Christianity as a "sect" (*TMS* III.6.1), and by freely applying the terms "Christian" and "Christianity" to Catholic phenomena,[12] Smith minimizes the distinctiveness of Christianity's different forms.

The Soul and the Afterlife

In light of Smith's silence about Jesus, it is not surprising that he is silent about resurrection. The prospects for eternal life would therefore rest exclusively on the human soul, which appears in *The Wealth of Nations* in but a single sentence. "Pneumatology, comprehending the doctrine concerning the nature of the human soul and of the Deity" was followed in the modern university curriculum by

> a debased system of moral philosophy, which was considered as immediately connected ... with the immortality of the human soul, and with the rewards and punishments which, from the justice of the Deity, were to be expected in a life to come. (*WN* V.i.f.31)[13]

Recall that Smith praised ancient natural philosophy for investigating both "the human *mind*" and the Deity (f.28). He thus minimizes the kinship between the Greek *psychē* and the otherworldly, immortal soul of the Christians.[14] Not surprisingly, Smith also lambastes the modern curriculum because "the doctrine of spirits, of which so little can be known, came to take up as much room in the system of philosophy as the doctrine of bodies, of which so much can be known" (f.28). In Smith's system of philosophy, needless to say, the fundamentals of Christian doctrine take up little room.

When Smith talks of wealth or riches, his concern is with the goods of the body, not those of the soul. The possible tension between Christianity and political economy on these matters is beautifully intimated in the fifth chapter of Locke's *Second Treatise*, "Of Property." Locke cites the New Testament only twice in the whole of the book, and only once without the Old Testament: "God has given us all things richly" (sec. 31). Locke's departure from the Bible (1 Timothy 6:17) is suggested by his subsequent argument that labor rather than nature—which supplies "only the almost worthless materials" (sec. 43)—is the source of value, and more generally by the clash between the passages considered in their respective contexts. According to Paul, "Love of money is the root of all evil" (1 Timothy 6:10). Timothy should therefore instruct those "rich in this world's goods not to be proud" but to depend on God (who "has given us all things richly") rather than on money, and to grow "rich in noble action," "to give away and to share." According to Paul, presumably, God's generous gifts would include the acorns, water, and skins that Locke belittles in the name of bread, wine, and cloth (secs. 42–43); like Smith, Locke condones the limitless quest for superfluities, "comforts," and "conveniencies."[15] God appears frequently in the property chapter until Locke introduces the labor theory of value, after which we read of the "wise and godlike" prince who proceeds "by established laws of liberty to secure protection and encouragement to the honest industry of mankind." In a sense, the godlike prince is a substitute for the God who "has given us all things richly."[16] Unlike Locke's *Two Treatises of Government*, *The Wealth of Nations* removes every trace of the medieval conception that property is only a temporary stewardship of the gifts God has bestowed upon mankind as a whole.[17] For Smith, furthermore, the system of natural liberty obviates even the need for a godlike prince.

Smith argues that the desire of bettering our condition, which "never leaves us till we go into the grave," is universal and unceasing because no one is ever content with his "situation" (*WN* II.iii.28,31). As we have seen, Smith judges wealth to be a "vulgar" means of betterment, but he does not specify the less vulgar alternatives. It is clear, however, that he rules out piety, holiness, atonement, divine communion, salvation, or any fate after "the grave." A common laborer, when well paid, is spurred to exertion by the "comfortable hope of bettering his condition, and of ending his days perhaps in ease and plenty" (I.viii.44); hope for "ease and plenty" replaces hope for salvation. Smith insists that the individual be left "perfectly free to pursue his own interest his own way" within the limits of justice (IV.ix.51), but seems to deprecate the interests of the soul: "A person who can acquire no property, can have no other interest but to eat as much, and to labour as little as possible" (III.ii.9).[18]

Smith is an archetypical liberal in favoring the separation of church and state:

> Spiritual matters, it is evident enough, are not within the proper department of a temporal sovereign, who, though he may be very well qualified for protecting, is seldom supposed to be so for instructing the people. (*WN* V.i.g.18)

Characteristically, Smith, unlike Locke, does not argue for the exclusion: it is "evident"; the sovereign "is seldom supposed" to be so qualified. Smith, however, does not simply limit government to the protection of life, liberty, and property: government is obliged to tend to the essential parts of "character," at least to prevent gross stupidity and cowardice (V.i.f.60–61). These remarks come on the heels of Smith's praising ancient Greece and Rome for maintaining "martial spirit," and thus call to mind the anti-Christian republicanism of Machiavelli and Rousseau. Smith here makes concessions to Aristotle, but not to Christianity. The teleology conveyed demotes the body but elevates the "mind" and the "martial spirit" rather than the soul or the Holy Spirit.[19]

In *The Wealth of Nations*, Smith unambiguously (though not always directly) rejects the afterlife. Whereas Smith's account of our "essential character" implicitly adopts Aristotelian rather than Christian virtue, the book's most detailed discussion of the afterlife explicitly proffers Greek thought over Christian. The goal of ancient moral philosophy was ascertaining "wherein consisted the happiness and perfection of a man, considered not only as an individual, but as the member of a family, of a state, and of the great society of mankind"; the "duties of human life were treated of as subservient to the happiness and perfection of human life"; virtue could produce "perfect happiness in this life." In modern philosophy, on the other hand, the duties were "subservient to the happiness of a life to come"; virtue was inconsistent with "happiness in this life"; "heaven was to be earned only by penance and mortification, by the austerities and abasement of a monk; not by the liberal, generous, and spirited conduct of a man." Smith may depart from liberalism in praising a moral philosophy oriented toward duties, virtue, happiness, and perfection (V.i.f.30), but he certainly excludes our happiness and perfection as creatures of God with duties to something higher than "human life."

Smith further criticizes the modern university curriculum for not being suitable preparation for "the real business of the world" (V.i.f.35), that is, the real business of this world. He laments that a well-educated gentleman should "come into the world completely ignorant of every thing which is the common subject of conversation among gentlemen and men of the world" (f.46). In *The Theory of Moral Sentiments*, Smith contrasts the "man of the world" with "the religious man" who acts always "as in the presence" of the "Great Superior" (*TMS* III.5.13).[20] However enthusiastically certain Calvinists embraced worldly pursuits, they continued to act "as in the presence," unlike the worldly men of *The Wealth of Nations*.

The above passages on the curriculum occur in the Article entitled "Of the Expence of the Institutions for the Education of Youth." Smith reappraises the afterlife in the sequel, "Of the Expence of the Institutions for the Instruction of People of all Ages." He here examines institutions for "religious instruction," whose "object is not so much to render the people good citizens in this world, as to prepare them for another and a better world in a life to come" (*WN* V.i.g.1). Smith later adds that the authority of an established church depends on the "supposed necessity," "in order to avoid *eternal misery*," of fully and faithfully adopting its doctrine (g.17). This is as close as *The Wealth of Nations* comes to the Christian Hell. The Article on instruction begins by stating that the aim of instruction is preparation for the afterlife, but the only subsequent reference to the afterlife suggests that it is a fiction promulgated on behalf of clerical authority. When Smith, in explaining why religions adopt an "austere" morality, says that "a single week's thoughtlessness and dissipation is often sufficient to undo a poor workman for ever" (g.10), the reference to "for ever" is manifestly ironic. The one other reference to the afterlife in *The Wealth of Nations* occurs in a passage that disparages religion:

> The laws concerning corn may every where be compared to the laws concerning religion. The people feel themselves so much interested in what relates either to their subsistence in this life, or to their happiness in a life to come, that government must yield to their prejudices. . . . It is upon this account, perhaps, that we so seldom find a reasonable system established with regard to either of these two capital objects. (*WN* IV.v.b.40)

The Wealth of Nations is clearly intended to facilitate the acquisition of "subsistence in this life"; the second "capital object" disappears as an end, though the prejudices surrounding it must be tempered to prevent "interest" in the afterlife from compromising interests in this world. Though Smith concedes that "every empire aims at immortality" (V.ii.c.6),[21] he strives to divert attention from the proposition that every individual aims at immortality. Smith's denial of the afterlife, though intransigent, is presupposed rather than argued.

Smith concludes *The Wealth of Nations* by criticizing Great Britain's New World empire as having "existed in imagination only": if unable to realize "this golden dream," Britain must awaken from it and "accommodate her future views and designs to the real mediocrity of her circumstances" (V.iii.92). Smith thought of the Kingdom of God what he said of Britain's empire: it is a "golden dream" that exists "in imagination only." Accommodating ourselves to the godless and heavenless world of *The Wealth of Nations* would likewise be an accommodation to the mediocrity of our circumstances.

The Protestant Ethic

It remains puzzling, however, that Smith criticizes asceticism and otherworldliness in the name of the "liberal, generous, and spirited conduct of a man" (*WN* V.i.f.30), a standard that might also condemn the reliance on self-interest that grounds the system of natural liberty and liberalism generally. This passage is another vestige of classical political philosophy, briefly articulated, that dangles provocatively in a larger system with whose spirit it seems to clash.[22] One might say that the impetus of *The Wealth of Nations* is to abandon the "liberal, generous, and spirited conduct of a man," the "perfection" of character, for the sake of opulence and *homo economicus*. This view about the rhetorical effect of *The Wealth of Nations* is borne out by the subsequent development of philosophy and political economy in the likes of Bentham and Ricardo, and by the subsequent reputation of Smith among all but the most careful scholars.

The presence of this vestige or dangler may be explained in various ways. Perhaps all of the explanations are valid; at least some of them are applicable to the other danglers. First, the dangler may suggest the inadequacy of the dominant drift of Smith's teaching, pointing to a whole that is greater than the parts Smith bequeathed to posterity. Second, the dangler may soften the anti-Aristotelian impact of *The Wealth of Nations*, functioning as a sop to traditionalists or preparing them to appreciate the compelling reasons for the break with tradition. Third, the dangler may accentuate the break with tradition that generally obtains. Fourth, the dangler may point to the costs of developments Smith thinks are irreversible: Smith invokes "essential" character while recommending palliatives for the debilitating consequences of the natural path of societal evolution. Fifth, the "liberal, generous, and spirited conduct of a man" may be a noble goal that cannot be realized by "the great body of the people." Sixth, the dangler may intimate Smith's complex posture toward Christianity and antiquity. The monastic outlook criticized by *The Wealth of Nations* with reference to the "liberal, generous, and spirited conduct" exalted by Greek moral philosophy is criticized in *The Theory of Moral Sentiments* with reference to the nobility that economic progress shares with war, heroism, statesmanship, poetry, and philosophy (*TMS* III.2.35). The Greeks tended to regard commerce as a threat to virtue, nobility, and heroism. In a Christian world, Smith combats monasticism by allying the noble with commerce. His political economy incorporates liberality/generosity, a pagan virtue, but erases *caritas*.[23]

Although bourgeois virtue, like the Greek ideal, is thoroughly worldly, it has perhaps borrowed from Christianity. Monastic austerity, penance, and mortification are borne with a view toward the future, as Smith plainly indicates. Must not Smith's bourgeois virtue—the "long life of industry, frugality and attention" (*WN* I.x.b.38)—likewise oppose the eminently natural "passion for present enjoyment"? Does it not require an individual to practice abstinence in the near, indeed in the foreseeable future, with the hope of "ending his days perhaps in ease and plenty" (I.viii.44)?[24] In the 1790 edition of *The Theory of Moral Sentiments*, it is in fact self-command—defined partly by detaching from the present and taking the long view—that comes to light as the crown of the virtues. Smith's bourgeois virtue is mass virtue; if it is not for everyone, it is at least for the merchants and businessmen who proliferate as commercial society develops (*WN* I.iv.1, I.ix.20). Perhaps it entailed as much "liberal, generous, and spirited conduct"—not to mention "happiness and perfection"—as circumstances allowed.

The all-important discussion of the tension between saving ("bettering one's condition") and spending ("present enjoyment") occurs in a chapter in which the contrast between ephemeral and lasting is a prominent theme. Smith's account of capital accumulation as a key determinant of national wealth is built upon the distinction between productive and unproductive labor. Productive labor "fixes and realizes itself in some particular subject or vendible commodity, which lasts for some time"; it may later "put into motion a quantity of labour equal to that which had originally produced it." Unproductive labor, by contrast, consists of services that "generally perish in the very instant of their performance" (II.iii.1). The labor of armies, governments, doctors, musicians, servants, and "churchmen" may thus be "honourable," "useful," or "necessary," but such labor

> produces nothing which could afterwards purchase or procure an equal quantity of labour. Like the declamation of the actor, the harangue of the orator, or the tune of the musician, the work of all of them perishes in the very instant of its production. (*WN* II.iii.2)[25]

As we have seen, there are no souls whose access to eternity can be facilitated by priestly labor.

In developing the contrast between the parsimony that increases capital and the prodigality that decreases it (II.iii.18), however, Smith employs uncharacteristically religious language. The frugal saver is "like the founder of a publick workhouse" because saving establishes an enduring fund for maintaining workers (II.iii.19). The "prodigal," by contrast, spends beyond his income and therefore reduces his capital.

> Like him who perverts the revenues of some pious fund to profane purposes, he pays the wages of idleness with those funds which the frugality of his forefathers had, as it were, consecrated to the maintenance of industry. (*WN* II.iii.20)[26]

This religious language, though employed to exalt economic concerns, clashes with the usual tone of *The Wealth of Nations*, and would be unthinkable in the economics of Ricardo, J. S. Mill, Keynes, Hayek, or Milton Friedman. Smith has consciously appropriated the Christian language of piety and consecration. His account of capital accumulation establishes a kind of eschatology, subordinating present enjoyment to a destiny linking "forefathers" with the future.

The equivalent in the *Second Treatise* to Smith's eschatology of capital accumulation is Locke's doctrine of inheritance, which seems to emphasize property at the expense of divine covenant and original sin. A man "cannot by any compact whatsoever bind his children or posterity" (sec. 116), and "the miscarriages of the father are no faults of the children" (sec. 182); but "every man is born with ... a right, before any other man, to inherit with his brethren his father's goods" (sec. 190). Because this right to inherit property promotes "the preservation of all mankind" (sec. 182), it supports the law of nature, which "wills the peace and preservation of all mankind" (sec. 7). Property and capital accumulation are legacies that accrue simultaneously to the individual and the group; the economic and technological progress integral to "civilization" may accrue to the whole species—what Smith calls "the great society of mankind."[27]

The abstraction and durability of money make it a special friend to collective progress. For Locke, the imaginary value gold and silver obtain from "fancy or agreement" remedies the short duration of the "really useful" things (sec. 46). For Smith, national wealth can soar higher, albeit less securely, upon "the Daedalian wings of paper money" than upon the "solid ground of gold and silver" (*WN* II.ii.86). The purely conventional character of paper money, inspired by the natural durability of the precious metals, is a collective trust facilitating economic advancement through the centuries.[28] As we will see, Smith promotes "progress" at the expense of the reverence integral to feudal politics and the biblical religions.

Capitalism obviously requires a certain faith in the future, especially faith in one's business associates.[29] Smith attaches more importance to the "faith of contracts" than to religious faith, and stresses the importance of the civil sword in the enforcement of contracts (*WN* I.ix.16, V.iii.7).[30] Smith acknowledges the credibility that the Bank of Amsterdam derives from the oath sworn by its chief officers—Holland being a "sober and religious country" where "oaths are not yet disregarded" (IV.iii.b.15)—but is otherwise silent about the contributions religious faith might make to legal testimony or the fulfillment of contracts.[31] Smith explains the efficacy of Roman oaths in purely sociological terms (V.i.f.44).

Calvinism's contributions to the development of capitalism were facilitated by theology to the extent that Calvinists tended to regard economic activity as a "calling" to display the glory of God, as a means of demonstrating neighborly love, or as a means of demonstrating one's membership in an "elect" of the saved.[32] The bourgeois virtue depicted by Smith, however, operates independently of religion. Smith's discussion of the Reformation, as we will see, focuses on authority and government, not doctrine.

In concluding *The Wealth of Nations*, Smith pessimistically assesses the huge public debts that will "in the long-run probably ruin" Europe (V.iii.10). The core of the problem is that governments do not take sufficient care of the future:

> To relieve the present exigency is always the object which principally interests those immediately concerned in the administration of publick affairs. The future liberation of the public revenue, they leave to the care of posterity. (*WN* V.iii.26)

In France, the problem is aggravated because many of the financiers "desire only to live in splendor during their own time"; generally, unmarried people "have little or no care for posterity."[33] When confronted with circumstances that require extraordinary expense, governments find it easier to misapply the funds designed to pay off the debt than to impose new taxes, for the pain of the latter is immediate (V.iii.36,40). By admitting that civilized societies are incapable of fully balancing the needs of the present with the needs of the future,[34] Smith implicitly acknowledges that political economy cannot entirely fill the void left by the abandonment of more traditional perspectives on time, especially biblical perspectives.

Piety and the Sacred

Given the absence of language about acknowledging and conserving God's gifts, obeying God's law, eschewing luxury for the sake of charity or salvation, glorifying the Creation via labor, or disciplining one's character to atone for sin, Smith's resort to the language of piety to describe prodigality is a challenge to piety as conceived by the biblical religions. The other references to piety in *The Wealth of Nations* consistently disparage it or at least deflate claims to it that might be made by existing churches. Smith implicitly criticizes the pensions and scholarships, created by "the piety of private founders," that supported the education of priests (I.x.c.34): such subsidies cause too many people to enter the profession. Smith apologizes for analyzing such labor in secular terms, but his elaboration redoubles the irreverence:

> It would be indecent, no doubt, to compare either a curate or a chaplain with a journeyman in any common trade. The pay of a curate or chaplain, however, may very properly be considered as of the same nature with the wages of a journeyman. They are, all three, paid for their work according to the contract which they may happen to make with their respective superiors. (*WN* I.x.c.34)

Smith's rhetoric in this passage is typically delicate. Even in his initial concession to the distinctiveness of priestly labor, he does not acknowledge its traditional status as a vocation or a calling rather than a "trade."[35] In arguing that the wages paid are "of the same nature," moreover, Smith implies that the special rewards associated with service to the Lord are inconsequential. We may also infer that the "superiors" with whom the curate establishes a "contract" or covenant are mere human beings.

The other references to piety in *The Wealth of Nations* are unambiguously disparaging of the Catholic church, if not of Christianity. Smith rejects the Church's claimed contribution to the termination of feudal slavery: the papal bull calling for emancipation was more of "a pious exhortation, than a law to which exact obedience was required from the faithful" (III.ii.12).[36] In one of the book's two mentions of Christianity, Smith says the following about the Spanish expansion into the New World: "The pious purpose of converting them [the natives] to Christianity sanctified the injustice of the project. But the hope of finding treasures of gold there, was the sole motive which prompted to undertake it" (*WN* IV.vii.a.15).[37] Smith illustrates the power of "this sacred thirst of gold" (IV.vii.a.17) by describing a Jesuit priest who "expressed with great warmth, and I dare to say, with great sincerity, how happy he should be to carry the light of the gospel to a people who could so well reward the pious labours of their missionary" (IV.vii.a.19). This is Smith's only reference to "the gospel," and it calls to mind the only mention in the book of "sin." The colonies of Spain, France, and Portugal are all

> oppressed with a numerous race of mendicant friars, whose beggary being not only licensed, but consecrated by religion, is a most grievous tax upon the poor people, who are most carefully taught that it is a duty to give, and a very great sin to refuse them their charity. (*WN* IV.vii.b.20)

Christian doctrines of piety and sin, as portrayed in *The Wealth of Nations*, served primarily if not exclusively to "consecrate" oppression. The final mention of piety is Smith's reference to the "mistaken piety" of individuals who had bestowed land on the Church (V.i.g.22).

Smith invokes the "sacred" on six occasions in *The Wealth of Nations*. It is thrice applied to economic rights: the property a person has in his own labor is "the most sacred and inviolable" form of property (I.x.c.12); there are "sacred rights of private property" (I.xi.c.27); restricting economic liberty may violate "the most sacred rights of mankind" (IV.vii.b.44).[38] By appropriating an essentially religious category on behalf of economic advancement, Smith suggests limits to his faith in the calculations of enlightened self-interest.

Of the three other mentions of "sacred," two occur in a religious or, should we say, anti-religious context. First is the Spaniard's "sacred thirst" for gold (IV.vii.a.17). Second, Smith provides a secular explanation of how the sacred emerged and functioned as a perceived characteristic of clerics:

> The hospitality and charity of the clergy too, not only gave them the command of a great temporal force, but increased very much the weight of their spiritual weapons. Those virtues procured them the highest respect and veneration among all the inferior ranks of people, of whom many were constantly, and almost all occasionally, fed by them. Every thing belonging or related to so popular an order, its possessions, its privileges, its doctrines, necessarily appeared sacred in the eyes of the common people, and every violation of them, whether real or pretended, the highest act of sacrilegious wickedness and profaneness. (*WN* V.i.g.22)[39]

This passage prepares Smith's famous assertion that the Church had constituted "the most formidable combination that ever was formed against the authority and security of civil government, as well as against the liberty, reason, and happiness of mankind" (V.i.g.24). The "arms" of the Catholic "spiritual army" were derived from wealth—from the great landed estates bestowed on them out of "mistaken piety." The clergy's power was, like that of the feudal barons, derived from the "hospitality" and "charity" with which they disposed of their surplus wealth (g.21–22). The passage above derives both the "temporal" and the "spiritual" power of the clergy from this wealth. Strictly speaking, the spiritual weapons were enhanced rather than spawned by wealth, but if feeding the people makes the feeders appear sacred, what distinguishes the clergy from the barons? Smith explains the downfall of both elites in economic terms. Human reason might have sufficed to weaken the "delusions of superstition" that supported the Church, but "it could never have dissolved the ties of private interest." The Church's power indeed "must have endured *forever*" if the "natural course of things"— the evolution of commerce and manufacturing—had not dissolved "the ties of interest" by providing the clergy with a selfish outlet for their wealth (V.i.g.24–25). Smith has issued a retrospective declaration of war between nature and the Church.

What, then, was the content of the "spiritual weapons"? Commerce directly undermined the Church's temporal power; but even its "spiritual authority" was

> much weakened when it ceased to be supported by the charity and hospitality of the clergy. The inferior ranks of people no longer looked upon that order, as they had done before, as the comforters of their distress, and the relievers of their indigence. (*WN* V.i.g.25)

Spiritual warfare thus employs two chief weapons: the "delusions of superstition" (g.24), including the afterlife (g.17), and the appearance of sacredness derived from comforting distress and relieving indigence. Human reason, at least with help from philosophy or science (V.i.g.14,24), could overcome superstition but not the "sacred" supported by the clergy's charity and hospitality. Although the "distress" comforted by priests might encompass the spiritual as well as the material, the "indigence" they relieved is clearly a matter of interest, in this case, food. One is reminded of Smith's striking equation of grain and religion: "The people feel themselves so much interested in what relates either to their subsistence in this life, or to their happiness in a life to come, that government must yield to their prejudices" (IV.v.b.40). By ignoring prospects for happiness in the next life and confining the people's "interest" to their "subsistence in this life," Smith reveals his hope that bread will eclipse the Word.[40] The Church was so mighty because it *fused* bread and the Word. Smith directly combats neither, claiming that the "natural course" destroyed the one and philosophy the other. But the latter is conditional— "human reason *might perhaps have been able* to unveil . . . *some* of the delusions of superstition"—and the conflict is not finished: the Church's power "is now likely, in the course of a few centuries more, perhaps, to crumble into ruins altogether" (V.i.g.24). Smith's science of political economy was surely intended to consolidate the victories achieved as of 1776. Smith exalts wealth while he effaces God, Providence, the soul, the sacred, the next world, the Bible, and "the Word made flesh."

The Bible

The treatment of the Bible in *The Wealth of Nations* parallels the treatment of Christianity generally: it is usually ignored, and where it is not ignored it is trivialized or attacked.[41] Smith nowhere acknowledges the books of Augustine and Aquinas, and the only "apostles" he mentions are Marcus Aurelius and Epictetus, the Stoic philosophers (*TMS* VII.ii.1.35).[42]

The Wealth of Nations mentions or alludes to the Bible on only a few occasions. The first mention is manifestly disparaging: Smith's report of a priest's desire "to carry the light of the gospel to a people who could so well reward the pious labours of their missionary" (*WN* IV.vii.a.19). The remaining mentions occur in two paragraphs of the education Article where the Bible is an explicit theme, and that indeed introduce the Article's denunciations of Scholasticism, monasticism, and superstition. Smith here explains how the study of Greek and Latin was incorporated into the curriculum of universities, which were originally "instituted for the education of churchmen" (V.i.f.19); Latin was taught because of its use in church. Smith's larger point seems to be that "the reverence of the people naturally preserves the established forms and ceremonies of religion, long after the circumstances which first introduced and rendered them reasonable are no more" (f.20). Smith negotiates more dangerous territory in explaining how Greek became part of the curriculum. The "infallible decrees of the church had pronounced the Latin translation of the Bible" (the Vulgate), compared to the original Greek and Hebrew texts, "to have been equally dictated by divine inspiration" (f.21). This is the only reference to "divine inspiration" in any of Smith's writings or lectures (and the only acknowledgment of anything resembling revelation in *The Wealth of Nations*), and Smith lightly brushes it aside. The reformers resorted to the original biblical texts in defense of their opinions; the Vulgate, "as might naturally be supposed, had been gradually accommodated to support the doctrines of the catholick Church." After commenting that Greek was incorporated into the curriculum as a result of the biblical disputes (f.21), Smith proceeds to his digression on the tripartite division of Greek philosophy. Just as the reformers reached back and used the Greek language as a weapon against the Church, Smith reaches back to Greek, nay, pre-Socratic philosophy to combat the Christian subordination of philosophy to theology.

The subsequent comparison of ancient and modern philosophy indeed contains the only explicit reference in *The Wealth of Nations* to any part of the Bible. Solomon's Proverbs, along with writings of Aesop, Theognis, Phocylides, and Hesiod, are cited as examples of the following phenomenon:

> In every age and country of the world men must have attended to the characters, designs, and actions of one another, and many reputable rules and maxims for the conduct of human life, must have been laid down and approved of by common consent. As soon as writing came into fashion, wise men, or those who fancied themselves such, would naturally endeavour to increase the number of those established and respected maxims, and to express their own sense of what was either proper or improper conduct. (*WN* V.i.f.25)

As is typical of the historical forays in *The Wealth of Nations* that touch upon events crucial to Jewish or Christian faith, Smith's stance is quietly heretical. Smith here cites the Proverbs as the only non-heathen example of an activity characteristic of "every age and country of the world," implicitly ruling out the spatially and temporally unique contexts of biblical revelation.[43] Moral maxims, in Smith's account, are "approved of by common consent," with no reference to God. The historical context for Solomon, in Smith's account, is not divine revelation but the coming "into fashion" of writing. The "wise men," according to Smith, tried to "express *their own sense* of . . . proper or improper conduct." The biblical Solomon, by contrast, insists that the beginning of wisdom is "fear of the Lord."[44]

Smith's account of how moral *philosophy* emerged from the maxims compiled by wise men seems to replace divine authority with the authority of nature, but even the latter diminishes upon close inspection. Moral philosophy attempted to "arrange" the various maxims in a "distinct or methodical order," and it imitated natural philosophy in attempting to "connect" them by "general principles, from which they were all deducible, like effects from their natural causes" (V.i.f.25). Although this definition of moral philosophy subsumes *The Theory of Moral Sentiments*, it excludes not only theological approaches, which derive duty from God's command or will, but teleological approaches, which derive duty from knowledge of natural ends. Philosophy thus adds "beauty" (*WN* V.i.f.25) rather than authority to morality. Smith's formulation likewise seems to exclude the existence of effects—for example, miracles—not derivable from "natural causes." Knowledge of causes and effects replaces particular Providence along with revelation and teleology.

Apart from the discussion of Solomon, Smith in *The Wealth of Nations* makes three allusions to the Old Testament; there are none to the New Testament. The book refers twice to Old Testament stories. First, "Abraham weighs to Ephron the four hundred shekels of silver which he had agreed to pay for the field of Machpelah." Smith's main point is purely secular: that early "publick stamps" on currency determined the fineness rather than the weight of the metal (I.iv.8). This story, however, had occasionally served as a model for non-usurious economic transactions;[45] Smith may invoke it to intimate his abandonment of the old ethos. Second, the feudal barons, in squandering their surplus wealth, "sold their birth-right, not like Esau for a mess of pottage in time of hunger and necessity, but in the wantonness of plenty, for trinkets and baubles" (III.iv.15). Smith's allusion is innocent enough, though one should recall that Esau was ultimately deprived by Jacob not only of his inheritance but of their father's blessing (Genesis 25). The remaining biblical allusion is the only allusion in *The Wealth of Nations* to a biblical precept or law: "the Mosaical law" on inheritance. This law, according to Smith, is superior to primogeniture (IV.vii.b.19) but inferior to what he earlier dubbed "the natural law of succession" adopted in pagan Rome (III.ii.3). Smith's writings otherwise ignore natural law, despite its prominence in Stoicism, Catholic theology, Protestant theology, and modern political philosophy; his brief resuscitation of "natural law" thus serves to highlight his even deeper quarrel with biblical law. His erasure of "grace" and his complete indifference to the distinction between original nature and fallen nature further accentuate the clash between Christianity and his ubiquitous naturalism.

In the Article of *The Wealth of Nations* devoted to the subject of religion—"Of the Expence of the Institutions for the Instruction of People of all Ages"—the Bible is never mentioned, quoted, or alluded to.[46] The only authors cited in the Article are Hume, Machiavelli, and Voltaire, all notorious in Smith's day and even in our day for their antipathy toward religion in general and Christianity in particular. (Smith was almost expelled from Oxford for possessing a copy of Hume's *Treatise of Human Nature*.) Smith has been spared their reputation, although *The Wealth of Nations* is equally irreligious and anti-Christian, because he expressed himself less provocatively.[47] The book's treatment of religious themes indeed tends to be drowned out by its expansive and often tedious discussions of more prosaic matters.[48]

Digression on Socrates

Smith's silence concerning Jesus is paralleled by his silence in *The Wealth of Nations* concerning Socrates, which is striking because the book refers to such a large group of Greek philosophers and rhetoricians: Thales, Pythagoras, Democritus; Timaeus, Isocrates, Hippias of Elis, Gorgias, Protagoras, Plato, Aristotle; Carneades, Dionysius of Halicarnassus, Polybius, Zeno of Elea, Zeno of Citium, Epicurus, Epictetus, Diogenes, and Plutarch. Socrates clashes with the spirit of the book for at least five reasons. First, Socrates was a beggar who boasted of his poverty, whereas Smith proudly emphasizes the wealth of ancient teachers (I.x.c.39).[49] Second, Socrates expressed deep reservations about "the many," whereas *The Wealth of Nations* deprecates the distinctiveness of the philosopher (I.ii.4) and consistently speaks up for "the great body of the people." Smith indeed chastises Socrates, along with Aristippus, Swift, and Voltaire, for having shown "the most improper and even insolent contempt of all the ordinary decorums of life and conversation" (*TMS* VI.i.10). Third, Socratic philosophy is essentially contemplative, whereas Smith's philosopher is imbued with "powers" (*WN* I.i.9).[50]

Fourth, Socrates was, like Jesus, a charismatic or "dazzling" figure, a martyr whose heroic death left a lasting hold on human consciousness: "Had the enemies of Socrates suffered him to die quietly in his bed, the glory even of that great philosopher might possibly never have acquired that dazzling splendour in which it has been beheld in all succeeding ages" (*TMS* VI.iii.5).[51] Smith invokes the Socratic daimon to illustrate the great pretensions that even the wise may concoct. If Smith faults Socrates for pretending to converse with the god-daimon, and Alexander for fancying himself a god (*TMS* VI.iii.28), what did he think about Jesus' claim to be the Son of the living God? The ease with which people are dazzled by excessive presumption helps explain "the frequent and often wonderful success of the most ignorant quacks and impostors, both civil and religious" (*TMS* VI.iii.27).

Finally, the Socratic dialectic clashes with Smith's efforts to construct "systems" or "machines," partly because it suggests that the whole is fundamentally mysterious.[52] As Pamphilus says at the beginning of Hume's *Dialogues*: "To deliver a System in conversation scarcely appears natural." Insofar as the myriad manifestations of the "Adam Smith Problem" point to puzzles that cannot easily be digested by Smith's systems, however, Socrates is vindicated. Relentless reflection on Smith may produce more awareness of fundamental problems than confidence in the ultimately tentative solutions he proposes: "bettering our condition," the "invisible hand," and "natural liberty" raise more questions than they answer.

History, God, and Prophecy

> Christianity, like other monotheisms which depict God acting on the
> world by means of covenant, incarnation or prophecy, at a point in
> time, leaving the promise of his acts to be fulfilled at another point in
> the future, utterly transforms the nature of world and time. There now
> comes to be a cosmic past, present and future, constituted by divine
> acts which, because they are unique and unrepeatable, are particular
> and so constitute a time-scheme. —Pocock, "Civic Humanism"

Joseph Cropsey has provocatively stated that the replacement of nature by history constitutes the "fissure, narrow but bottomless, that divides capitalism from communism" (*Political Philosophy*, p. 74). Cropsey and other scholars have discussed the four-stages theory, recognizing Smith's anticipations of Marx's historical materialism, but perhaps none has adequately conveyed the centrality of historical analysis to the entirety of Smith's corpus, especially with respect to the religious question. The various sorts of histories provided by Smith and Marx are intransigently secular. Neither author leaves room for a history infused by Providence or for the disparagement of history in light of the eschaton and God's glory.[53] As Löwith remarks in discussing Voltaire, "The inauguration of the philosophy of history was an emancipation from the theological interpretation and anti-religious in principle" (p. 104).

As was noted above, *The Wealth of Nations* provides a huge parade of historical figures; the silence about Jesus is remarkable even from a secular point of view. Given the profusion of historical detail, it is surely no accident that Smith never even alludes to biblical events such as the fall, the flood, God's covenant with Abraham, the revelation to Moses, and the birth, death, and resurrection of Jesus. According to Smith, "The two greatest and most important events recorded in the history of mankind" were the discovery of America and the discovery of a sea passage to the East (*WN* IV.vii.c.80).[54] Smith suggests that the greatness of these events lies in their "commercial benefits," although he concedes that "no human wisdom can foresee" their long-term impact (IV.vii.c.80). As is the case with all of the book's intimations of the limitations to "human wisdom," divine revelation is implicitly excluded as a possible remedy.

Secular factors, albeit infused with military as well as economic elements, likewise prevail in Smith's selection and portrayal of the first three "great revolution[s] in the affairs of mankind of which history has preserved any distinct or circumstantial account": Philip's conquest of the Greek republics, Rome's ascendancy over Carthage, and the fall of the Western empire (V.i.a.29,30,36). Smith's account is erroneous, however, insofar as history has preserved a "distinct or circumstantial account" of another "great revolution in the affairs of mankind" between the two latter: so great and so distinct, even from a secular perspective, that it still provides the bifurcation of Western history into before and after. Smith is so determined to deny the divine Jesus that he denies even the human Jesus.[55]

In explaining the causes of the three revolutions, Smith emphasizes the existence of secular "causes" that are determinative of "fate" and "fortune" (V.i.a.30,34,36), eschewing any recourse to an inscrutable God. Departing strikingly from Augustine, Machiavelli, Hobbes, Montesquieu, and Gibbon, Smith is silent about the possible connection between both the rise and fall of ancient Rome and the rise of Christianity.

Rome's fall is explained in secular terms; Constantine is mentioned, but only for the decision to disperse the great legions "in small bodies through the different provincial towns" (V.i.a.36).[56] Smith refers later to the moment "when christianity was first established by law" (V.i.f.20), but says nothing about why this occurred.[57]

Smith's silence about the origin of Christianity is accentuated by his intense attention to its later development. This attention is unflattering, but allows Christianity a grand historical role. For example, Smith states that the Crusades were "the most destructive frenzy that ever befell the European nations." It goes without saying that Smith is silent about the possible benefit of converting infidels. With the calm voice of economics, he condemns the Crusades on account of "the great waste of stock and destruction of inhabitants which they occasioned" (III.iii.14). But the most exalted denunciation in his entire corpus is applied to the medieval Church, which, during its peak, was "the most formidable combination that ever was formed against . . . the liberty, reason, and happiness of mankind" (V.i.g.24).

The Four Stages, Divine Debt, and the Grip of the Past

In addition to sundry reflections about the actual course of world history, Smith provides the abstract and theoretical four-stages theory. Its vision of human destiny is wholly secular, nay, economic: "improvement" is defined by wealth. There is not a single indication in the book that there might exist a divine plan that infuses, transcends, or eclipses "the natural progress."[58] The "original destination of man" was "to cultivate the ground" (*WN* III.i.3), not the Garden of Eden. The final destination is not Divine Judgment or the Kingdom of God but the endless march of commercial and technological progress. The "conveniency and luxury" of the town (III.i.2) thus eclipse not only the pastoral simplicity celebrated in the Old Testament but the "beauty," "pleasures," and "tranquillity of mind" of the agricultural life.[59]

Near the conclusion of Book III, Smith provides one of the work's only explicit digressions:

> It does not, perhaps, relate to the present subject, but I cannot help remarking it, that very old families, such as have possessed some considerable estate from father to son for many successive generations, are very rare in commercial countries. In countries which have little commerce, on the contrary, . . . they are very common. The Arabian histories seem to be all full of genealogies. (*WN* III.iv.16; cf. *TMS* VI.ii.1.13)

Especially in light of the mention of Esau in the preceding paragraph, one is reminded of Jewish "histories" laden with genealogies (cf. *LJA* iv.44–

45). The "great shepherd or herdsman," we have seen, is "revered" for "the immemorial antiquity of his illustrious family" (*WN* V.i.b.11). The backward-lookingness so essential to biblical religion, if not to politics and religion generally (consider the opening question of Plato's *Laws*), is, according to the four-stages theory, "barbarous" rather than civilized. In discussing feudal entails, Smith brands the presumption "that the property of the present generation should be restrained and regulated according to the fancy of those who died perhaps five hundred years ago" as "the most absurd of all suppositions" (III.ii.6). What does this imply for Jews whose whole lives are "restrained and regulated" by far older writings? The abstract and impersonal character of Smith's "natural progress," furthermore, clashes with the Bible's focus on individuals and specific events: prophets receive revelation; God makes covenants with particular individuals and peoples; there is no general course to human affairs independent of God's will; the crucial divisions are between Jew and Gentile, Christian and pagan, and righteous and unrighteous, not between civilized and barbarous; particular genealogies take the place of Smith's succession of nameless generations.

Feudal/shepherd authority, like the authority of the biblical God, is monopolistic: a visible and deep dependence on one "lord," like the God to Whom we owe all thanks and Whom we love with all our hearts. In the absence of commerce and manufacturing, the shepherd chief or feudal lord/priest is solely responsible for the maintenance of his subordinates, who are dependent on his "bounty" (III.iv.5–7). Because of the division of labor, the individual in a commercial or civilized society is even less self-sufficient—standing "at all times in need of the cooperation and assistance of great multitudes" (I.ii.2)—but is subject to many rather than one. Dependence is increased, but it is depersonalized and decentralized. The tradesman or artificer, likewise, though "in some measure obliged" to all of his customers, "is not absolutely dependent upon any one of them" (III.iv.12); even great wealth does not enable a man to command a dozen people because he only gives to them "in exchange for an equivalent" (V.i.b.7). Such exchange, however, is impossible with the biblical God. What we receive cannot possibly be repaid; we owe in return uncompromising obedience, devotion, and prayer, if not sacrifices; we are permanently in debt. Smith's aversion to the latter is perhaps suggested by his query: "What can be added to the happiness of the man who is in health, who is out of debt, and has a clear conscience?" This condition, Smith optimistically observes, "may very well be called the natural and ordinary state of mankind" (*TMS* I.iii.1.7). Here again we see the potential tension between nature and the Bible: both Abraham and Job surely suffered because of their debt to God.

Locke's famous "appeal to heaven," which he first employs with reference to the biblical Jephthah, raises similar questions. As Locke elaborates it, the appeal is the resort to force for which one will answer in the next world.[60] Locke tacitly denies the implication that one "appeals" to heaven for a response in this world: a heavenly answer to the question of who is right. Such an answer could be a communication obviating the need for violence, or divine intervention determining the outcome of combat. Locke fails to mention that Jephthah, expecting the latter, offered to sacrifice the first "creature" that left his house to greet him on his successful return; he succeeded on the battlefield, but the sacrifice fell on his only child.[61] Smith might say that paying on delivery is still paying.

As we have seen, "the natural course of things"—"the gradual improvements of arts, manufactures, and commerce"—terminated a Church empire that "must have endured forever" if attacked solely by human wisdom and virtue (V.i.g.24–25). Smith's explanation of the disruption of the "natural progress" by feudalism further illustrates the antagonism that may arise between nature and religion. The first chapter of Book III examines "the natural progress of opulence" whereby agricultural development precedes that of the town, but the remainder of Book III addresses Europe's deviation from the natural path because of primogeniture and entails, "human institutions" that perpetuated the concentrated ownership of land (III.i.4,9, III.ii.2,3,5). These institutions, although "reasonable" in the chaotic circumstances that hatched them, were subsequently an obstacle to progress: "Laws frequently continue in force long after the circumstances, which first gave occasion to them, and which could alone render them reasonable" (III.ii.3–4,6). Because of the link between religion and reverence, however, the tenacity or stickiness of "human institutions" reaches its peak with religion. In explaining the place of Latin in the university curriculum, Smith observes that "the reverence of the people naturally preserves the established forms and ceremonies of religion, long after the circumstances which first introduced and rendered them reasonable are no more" (V.i.f.20). The irreligiosity of this formulation is accentuated by its context, the book's sole discussion of "the Bible" and "divine inspiration."

Even if Smith's materialistic analysis of authority is flawed because of the way it discounts the contributions of opinion,[62] it subverts many of the opinions that supported traditional authority. Although Smith's scattering of his discussions of feudalism (Book III), the four-stages theory (V.i.a–b), and religion (V.i.g) obscures their connection and softens the demystification of authority characteristic of all three, *The Wealth of Nations* might tend to weaken lingering "reverence" for the Bible along with reverence for Church, clergy, lords, and kings.[63] By delicately link-ing such authority with a "barbarous" stage of social development, Smith simultaneously explains its origins and intimates its obsolescence; one wonders whether Smith's historical materialism is partly rhetorical.[64] Burke, not Smith, is the conservative: "We [English] fear God; we look up with awe to kings . . . with duty to magistrates; with reverence to priests; with respect to nobility."[65]

The Subordination of Will, Word, Prophecy, and Plan

The history conveyed by *The Wealth of Nations*, as we have seen, completely excludes divine plans, intentions, or foresight; with this exclusion necessarily comes the exclusion of any exaltation individuals would obtain from their participation in such phenomena. This pro-cedure is paralleled by Smith's de-emphasis of human plans, intentions, and foresight. History for Smith may reveal the "cunning of reason" (Medick, p. 229), but without Hegel's world-historical individuals or ruling *Geist*. Contemporary scholarship in history and social science likewise excludes the divine dimension, and generally minimizes the role played by the comprehensive designs of individuals.[66] An analogy in intellectual history would be the tendency to treat thought as derivative from a historical context. Winch, for example, places Smith in a "quint-essentially" eighteenth-century context; Heilbroner and Thurow assert that "Smith wrote about a world that has long since vanished" (p. 23). Insofar as one perceives the world in narrow terms, one will be more struck by the extent of change. Ironically, because of the absence of God, the world portrayed in *The Wealth of Nations* is more like the world as viewed by Smith's readers today than the world as seen by Smith's contemporaries.[67]

Contemporary academic historicism certainly assumes that the con-text within which to locate human thought is not a Christian context of "Creation, Covenant, Christ, Church, [and] Consummation."[68] The bib-lical religions, moreover, have themselves been infused with histor-icism. It is tempting to say that Smith has contributed as an architect to the emergence of the various historicist strands; it is safe to say that we have moved further along the lines that distinguish his approach to history from classical and biblical approaches. There is of course no doubt that eighteenth-century Europe was more orthodox in its Chris-tianity than were many of its leading philosophers.

The surface of Smith's own writings seems radically anti-prophetic, and theoretical rather than practical: an "inquiry" into wealth, the "the-ory" of moral sentiments, the "principles" that direct "philosophical enquiries." These titles suggest detached investigation rather than a call to arms, and the texts yield a similar impression. In conveying each of his major works as a "system," Smith provides a representation or model of what is, not a prophetic call to action.[69] For all his deference to the "natural" and "ordinary," however, Smith admits that some of his proposals are utopian (*WN* IV.ii.43, V.iii.68) if not the offspring of "the most visionary enthusiast" (IV.vii.c.66).

If the system of natural liberty "establishes itself of its own accord" (*WN* IV.ix.51), enlightenment would be necessary only to remove the systems of "preference or restraint." Although both of Smith's books generally mute the contribution of "opinion" as a causal force in human affairs, *The Theory of Moral Sentiments* acknowledges that religion may breed opinions that disrupt our "natural" moral sentiments. Did Smith de-emphasize opinion in general for the sake of taming specifically religious opinions? Smith in *The Wealth of Nations* clearly goes out of his way to avoid introducing religious opinions and sentiments to explain phenomena—for example, the pay of curates, the success of the Reformation—with which they seem to be associated. In explaining the unique power of Catholicism, Smith ignores the power of God's words, whether real or imagined, and invokes the "ties of private interest" that bound the people to the clergy (V.i.g.24) and the institutional structure that linked the clergy's "self-interest" with its "industry and zeal" (g.2). Smith looks to the "natural course" rather than to divine or even human words. As he says earlier in the book, "We must in all cases attend to the nature of the thing, without paying any regard to the word" (IV.v.a.40). Smith's words strive to deconstruct *the* word and perhaps words generally.[70] Despite his praise of Voltaire,[71] Smith exhibits little or no interest in the Enlightenment call to "*écrasez l'infâme*" by means of philosophy. History as Smith presents it is explicable without reference to the words of either philosophers or prophets.

Despite Smith's indifference to such words, *The Wealth of Nations*, as we have seen, subtly calls attention to certain kinds of philosophic powers.[72] In conjunction with the early chastening of the philosopher's "vanity" (*WN* I.ii.4), these passages suggest that philosophy in the form of technological science will be an indispensable cog in a society's productive apparatus. With the "progress of society," philosophy, like every other "employment" or "trade," becomes increasingly specialized and "more work is done upon the whole" (I.i.9). One can easily agree with Smith that a greater *quantity* of work will be done; but how can more attention be paid to "the whole"? Can the philosopher continue "to observe every thing" (I.i.9) and to attain "comprehensive" knowledge (V.i.f.51)? The burgeoning division of labor might make it impossible for an individual to grasp the whole even of the human sciences, not to say all sciences.[73] But perhaps *The Wealth of Nations* does not so much deny or eliminate philosophy as transform and hide it; perhaps modern social science is part of this philosophical legacy. Within *The Wealth of Nations*, philosophy's empire, in the form of technology and the science of political economy, is quite visible; perhaps it possesses a deeper empire masked by the book's ubiquitous naturalism and historicism. Smith's danglers and paradoxes—not to mention the sheer breadth of his inquiries—point to a whole more complex than the wholes that contemporary social science considers.

Within the historical horizon of *The Wealth of Nations*, as we have seen, the decisive battle against Christianity has already been won, though by commerce rather than philosophy. There seems to be no place for prophets or philosophers to legislate comprehensively for humanity. Whatever uncertainty there might be about Smith's final views on these matters, Marx intransigently asserts and argues the epiphenomenal nature of philosophy and religion. Even Marx, however, finds it necessary to combat the ideological illusions perpetrated by bourgeois political economy that mask the fundamentally oppressive nature of capitalism; communist consciousness, though an offshoot of proletarian consciousness, must struggle to enlighten the proletariat.

Smith's exhortations to defer to "nature" and "circumstances" can be interpreted as Machiavellian exhortations to permit human necessities or needs ("necessaries, conveniencies, and amusements") to be met without distortions arising from thoughts about the superhuman. Both of Smith's books insist that the whole—the cosmos as well as society—is adequately cared for; Smith tries to discourage people from thinking about it. One might suppose that he is trying to restore an encompassing "natural" horizon for human life free of philosophical and theological intrusions, especially intrusions that encourage people to rebel against the cycles of growth and decay integral to the "progress of opulence." Or is Smith trying to create a horizon that misrepresents the frenzied motion of capitalist society as natural?

The "education" required under the system of natural liberty is limited to reading, writing, and arithmetic (with some elementary mechanics and geometry), and will be left largely to private teachers. Nature again comes to the rescue: Smith praises ancient teachers who attained "that natural authority, which superior virtue and abilities never fail to procure from young people, towards those who are entrusted with any part of their education" (V.i.f.43,45). When Smith defers or refers to the "wisdom" of legislators and statesmen, it is always to a manifestly worldly wisdom.[74] His references to "human wisdom" all stress what is beyond its purview.[75] The breach is filled by nature's wisdom, whose means, though discrete, are as ingenious as its ends are modest.

CHAPTER EIGHT

The Theological-Political Problem

SMITH'S THEMATIC TREATMENT of religion (*WN* V.i.g), whose motif may be said to be the fusion of politics and religion, is perhaps the most craftily composed section of his entire corpus. As a result, although the rejection of Christianity is unambiguous, it is presented with a mix of blatant and subtle devices, and the analysis of some related matters is hard to pin down. The line of argument is exceedingly complex and has produced distortions in the interpretations of careful scholars. Rhetoric or "eloquence" indeed receives more attention in this section than anywhere else in *The Wealth of Nations*. The reader likewise encounters more analysis of authority and the institutional arrangements that sustain it.

The True Religion

The third Part of Book V, chapter 1, is "Of the Expence of publick Works and publick Institutions"; its first two Articles concern commerce and "the Education of Youth"; the third is entitled "Institutions for the Instruction of People of all Ages." This Article begins with the observation that such institutions "are chiefly those for religious instruction," whose "object is not so much to render the people good citizens in this world, as to prepare them for another and a better world in a life to come" (*WN* V.i.g.1). Having explored the work's mixture of indifference and hostility toward doctrines of the afterlife,[1] we might wonder why the sovereign's duties under the system of natural liberty would include preparation for the next world. Not surprisingly, the one subsequent reference to the afterlife in the Article indicates merely that clerical doctrine is adhered to (and clerical authority thereby sustained) out of fear of "eternal misery" (g.17). The Article conveys an extensive analysis of clerical authority and the problems it poses, but, like the work as a whole, gives no advice for entering the kingdom of heaven. The instruction of people of all ages may be necessary under the system of natural liberty, but for wholly worldly purposes.

The Article does allude to "the true" religion. In the middle of a lengthy quotation from Hume's *History of England*, we read that the

> interested diligence of the clergy is what every wise legislator will study to prevent; because, in every religion except the true, it is highly pernicious, and it has even a natural tendency to pervert the true, by infusing into it a strong mixture of superstition, folly, and delusion. (*WN* V.i.g.6)

By mentioning but not identifying "the true" religion, Hume implies that determining which religion is true is impossible, imprudent, unimportant, or irrelevant;[2] by avoiding the phrase "the true religion," Hume intimates the disjunction between truth and religion. Smith does not remedy Hume's silence. In Smith's index to *The Wealth of Nations*, the entry for "religion" includes the "Origin of persecution for heretical opinions," and the entry for "persecution" is "*Persecution* for religious opinions, the true cause of": we will learn about "the true cause" of persecution rather than the true religion.[3]

Smith in his own name never even refers to the true religion. He refers instead to the "pure and rational religion" (V.i.g.8), but, imitating Hume, he neither identifies any actual religion as this rational religion nor specifies its content. What he does say, however, strongly implies that it is not one of the biblical religions.[4] The rational religion is free of any "absurdity, imposture, or fanaticism" (g.8), ills that characterize Catholicism, Calvinism, and perhaps Protestantism as a whole.[5] It is something "wise men have in all ages of the world wished to see established" (g.8); that is, this religion can be specified without reference to biblical revelation.[6] The rational religion is something that "positive law has perhaps never yet established" (g.8); the "perhaps" softens the implied exclusion of the Christian churches—Anglican, Lutheran, and Calvinist in addition to Roman Catholic and Greek Orthodox—that the Article elsewhere identifies as established.[7] The gulf between the "pure and rational religion" and extant religions is further accentuated by Smith's claim that the former "might in time probably" emerge after a series of hypothetical (and unlikely) developments. One of these hypothetical conditions is government's leaving each man free "to chuse his own priest and his own religion," which would "no doubt" result in the existence of "a great multitude of religious sects" (g.8).[8] So much for the inherent attractiveness of the true and catholic religion.[9]

Politics and Religion

Although the Article on religion peaks with Smith's famous denunciation of the Catholic church (*WN* V.i.g.24), it begins with a general discussion of why established religions tend to "call upon the civil magistrate to persecute . . . their adversaries" (g.1). Smith proceeds to explain the general origins of religious establishments. "Times of violent religious controversy have generally been times of equally violent political faction"; the political "party" therefore allies with a contending "sect"; the sect allied with the conquering party finds its "influence and authority with the great body of the people" enhanced, and thus insists that the civil magistrate silence opposing sects and furnish it an "independent provision" (g.7), i.e., state funding. In sum, "politicks . . . called in the aid of religion" (g.8).

The calm and abstract tone of this presentation would suggest that Smith is not emphatically concerned with a particular set of established churches—the Christian churches that are the only established churches mentioned in *The Wealth of Nations*. Smith thus does nothing to elaborate his reference in the education Article to the time "when christianity was first established by law" (V.i.f.20). Whatever answers he provides about *why* Christianity was established must be subsumed under the general account of how politics "called in" religion. The quoted passages of Hume invoke "religious" views to explain establishment (g.6); Smith implicitly denies that Christianity had a unique, divine beginning, or even a special secular beginning befitting its distinctive content. Christianity is reduced to a mere instance.

The specification of the aim of "religious instruction" as preparing people for "a life to come" implies that religion as such subordinates this world to the next world. Or does the whole investigation presuppose the existence of a specific religion that has conveyed such instruction on an impressive scale? Smith's four-stages theory, curiously, does not stipulate any association of the individual stages with particular religions or kinds of religion.[10] The theory, moreover, is missing from the religion Article. In examining the other duties of government (especially defense, justice, and education), Smith explains how the duties and expenses vary from one stage to the next. The silence in the religion Article suggests that the sovereign's duty regarding the instruction of people of all ages has been conditioned if not created by historical developments that cannot be deduced from the "natural progress of opulence"; one is again led to suspect that Smith, in erasing prophecy, has deliberately exaggerated.

The religion Article is likewise distinguished from the rest of the first chapter of Book V by the paucity of its attention to the ancients, to Greece and Rome. Does this suggest that something happened in the aftermath of antiquity that changed the rules of the game?[11] In place of the four-stages theory and antiquity, the Article provides a detailed history and analysis of the politics of Christian churches and a *general* analysis of religious "establishment," that is, of the relationship between religion and politics.

The religion Article does not explain why "violent religious controversy" and "violent political faction" usually coincide. That Smith may perceive some essential kinship if not identity here is suggested in the first place by the development of his terminology: from explaining the alliances of party and sect (V.i.g.7), the Article proceeds to identify party and sect (g.29,33). If sects are parties, what is it that motivates the clergy? The Article begins by identifying the object of religious instruction as preparing people more for the next world than for being "good citizens in this world," but perhaps its true result (if not its object) is making people good citizens under priestly rule. Fear of hell intimidates the people (g.17), but the motivations of the clergy come to light as worldly, characterized by the pursuit of such things as wealth, ease, and power—the ends that political economy investigates and promotes.[12] By citing Machiavelli to explain the contribution of the Dominicans and the Franciscans to reviving "the languishing faith and devotion of the catholick Church" (g.2), Smith calls to mind the spirit of Machiavelli's elaboration: the new orders ensured that

> the dishonesty of the prelates and heads of the religion did not ruin it, for living still in poverty and having such credit with peoples in confessions and sermons, they gave them [i.e., the people] to understand that it is evil to speak evil of evil and that it is well to live in submission to them [i.e., the prelates], and if they [i.e., the prelates] make errors to leave them to be punished by God; and so they do the worst they can, because they do not fear that punishment they do not see and do not believe in. This renovation, therefore, has maintained and maintains this religion.[13]

The initially confusing parade of third-person plural pronouns delays but ultimately only enhances the impact of Machiavelli's accusation; likewise, the accusation emerges from what starts out as an apparently sympathetic appraisal of the Catholic renewal. Smith puts his own twist on the reasons why the two orders strengthened the Church, but the true thrust of his comment that the orders revived "languishing faith and devotion" is revealed when one examines his source.

When Smith refers to "countries where there is an established or governing religion" (*WN* V.i.g.16), one wonders just how "governing" a religion can be. An answer soon appears: "The authority of religion is superior to every other authority" (g.17). Hume referred to the clergy's "address in governing the minds of the people" (g.5). Throughout the Article, Smith associates clergy with phenomena suggesting their special authority: "authority and influence with the inferior ranks of people" (g.1.), "influence and authority with the great body of the people" (g.7), "influence over the common people" (g.22), "the minds of the people" (g.23), "absolute command . . . over the great body of the people" (g.25), "influence over the minds of the common people" (g.38). Indeed, the Article concludes with a reference to the clergy's "weight and authority" (g.42). Smith could hardly be more emphatic about religion's grip on the masses: "Almost all religious sects have begun among the common people, from whom they have generally drawn their earliest, as well as their most numerous proselytes" (g.11). As expounded in *The Wealth of Nations*, the relationship between politics and religion is equally overlap, interplay, and fusion.

These passages are likewise a belated concession to the dependence (not acknowledged in the rest of *The Wealth of Nations*) of authority upon opinion.[14] With opinion comes the word: prophecy, rhetoric, and propaganda. Fear of "eternal misery" promotes belief in "every part" of Church doctrine (V.i.g.17), although the afterlife must itself be a "part" of that doctrine, nay, from Smith's point of view, a mere figment of the imagination.

If the authority of the Catholic church was "established" on a "system of opinions" (V.i.g.29), one must consider the contribution of opinion to authority generally. One might even entertain the following hypothesis about the relationship between Christianity and modernity. If Christianity succeeded in governing human minds on an unprecedented scale, it was partly by means of a doctrine that every human soul is potentially worthy of immortal happiness.[15] In the lectures, Smith explains the special appeal of monotheism to slaves, who were excluded from the protection of local gods (*LJA* iii.97–98). Judaism therefore made progress among the Roman slaves, but "when the Christian religion was spread abroad, which put all men on an equality without any of these foolish restrictions with regard to meats, the progress it made amongst these folks was most astonishing" (99–100).[16]

If Christianity thus succeeded in co-opting or enfranchising the people, perhaps philosophers saw an opportunity (if not a duty) to "recapture" the people for the city of man, for this world. Because the equality of souls coexisted in medieval times with such a pronounced social hierarchy,[17] one could say that modern political philosophy helped transform equality in word to equality in deed. If this story is plausible, there are certainly many indications of it in *The Wealth of Nations*. The system of natural liberty is "obvious and simple"; the three duties of the sovereign under it are "plain and intelligible to common understandings";[18] it provides security and economic liberty to "every man."[19] To the extent that Smith speaks on behalf of a particular class among "the three great, original, and constituent orders of every civilized society" (I.xi.p.7), he (like Jesus and Marx) speaks on behalf of "those who live by wages" (p.9), the "lower ranks," who constitute the "far greater part of every great political society"; the connection between the welfare of this "part" and the welfare of "the whole . . . seems at first sight abundantly plain" (I.viii.36).[20] In the spirit of Locke's flirtation with viewing mankind as "one fellowship and society," a "great and natural community," Smith inclines to a universalistic focus on "the great society of mankind" (*WN* V.i.f.31; *TMS* VI.ii.2.4). A society is "great" by virtue of its large population (*WN* I.viii.57).

Sophistry, rhetoric, and "eloquence" are discussed elsewhere in *The Wealth of Nations*,[21] but they are especially prominent in the Article on religion: whence the clergy's extraordinary "influence" over the popular mind, if not from their words? Eloquence indeed seems to be the chief component of their "arts of popularity," their "arts of gaining proselytes" (V.i.g.1,29). Priests are obviously not the only practitioners of rhetoric, and *The Wealth of Nations* generally links rhetoric with philosophy. Whereas ancient teachers instructed the youth, however, priests instruct people "of all ages." Smith nevertheless praises "the antient philosophers" for being much superior to any modern teachers in their "empire . . . over the opinions and principles of their auditors" (V.i.f.45). Several factors distinguish ancient teachers from modern priests. Apart from their association with the young, the ancients operated privately, without public subsidy, and more or less as individuals; as a result, they were subject to "competition" and the forces of demand, unlike the multinational monopoly of the Catholic priests. Smith does not, however, explain the clergy's authority primarily in terms of their message. Rather, he provides a detailed and complex analysis of the structure of churches and societies, to which we now turn.

Priestly Austerity and Gentlemanly Authority

The Article on religion begins with a general account of what might be called the dialectic of religious establishment. After his brief acknowledgment that religious instruction is preparation for the next world, Smith focuses on the teachers' mode of "subsistence." Teachers who derive their subsistence from "the voluntary contribution of their hearers" will likely demonstrate "exertion . . . zeal and industry" far beyond those of teachers with an independent provision (*WN* V.i.g.1). The clergy of an "established and well endowed religion," as a result, "frequently become men of learning and elegance, who possess all the virtues of gentlemen"; for this reason, however, they lose their "authority . . . with the inferior ranks" and will be easily challenged by "enthusiasts," though not before they have called in government to persecute the challengers (g.1). Smith later explains the origins of establishment. Clergy allied with the victorious political party ask it to eliminate their adversaries and to "bestow an independent provision on themselves"; they thus compromise the future "authority of their order" for the sake of their "own ease and comfort" (g.7).[22] Smith's framework here has a distinctively economic flavor, which serves first and foremost to remove God from the picture—hence the claim that clerical zeal and industry are "perhaps" the "original causes" of a religion's "success and establishment" (g.1). But the framework eclipses the contribution even of religious sentiment as stirred by charisma, piety, ceremony, and doctrine.[23] Smith's explanations of how authority (including clerical authority) derives from a "monopoly" over subsistence (III.iv.7, V.i.b.7, V.i.g.22) are here supplemented with an account of how authority may be acquired by means of exertion, zeal, and industry. In rising to wealth and greatness, however, the clergy may undermine their authority. Smith goes so far as to liken the established church attacked by new enthusiasts to the "indolent, effeminate, and full fed nations" of southern Asia "invaded by the active, hardy, and hungry Tartars of the North" (V.i.g.1). By the end of the first paragraph, Smith has already raised a crucial problem of aristocracy: whether "gentlemen" naturally possess the qualities that would enable them to rule. Smith proceeds to explain clerical authority by means of a comprehensive analysis of social class.

Within a hypothetical investigation of what might have happened "if politicks had never called in the aid of religion" (V.i.g.8), Smith switches to a manifestly non-hypothetical voice:

> In every civilized society, in every society where the distinction of ranks has once been completely established, there have been always two different schemes or systems of morality current at the same time; of which the one may be called the strict or austere; the other the liberal, or, if you will, the loose system. (*WN* V.i.g.10)[24]

Generally speaking, the "common people" adopt the austere system, and the "people of fashion" adopt the liberal system. The two systems are principally distinguished by their respective condemnation and indul-

gence of the "vices of levity," vices that ordinarily "arise from great prosperity, and from the excess of gaiety and good humour." The liberal system therefore tolerates a certain amount of luxury, "disorderly mirth,"
intemperate pursuit of pleasure, and breaches of chastity (g.10). In suggesting the reasons for the difference, Smith resorts to his typical reductionism and functionalism: "The vices of levity are always ruinous to
the common people" (g.10). Smith proceeds to explain the relevance of
the two moralities to religion. Because "almost all religious sects" both
begin and multiply "among the common people," the sects almost constantly adopt the austere system, and even exaggerate or enhance its
rigor in order to obtain the people's "respect and veneration" (g.11).[25]
Clerical authority thus derives from exertion, zeal, and industry fused
with austerity.

The account of the two moralities serves to explain what was simply
asserted in the Article on education: that "modern" moral philosophy
was "ascetic," identifying virtue with the "penance and mortification . . .
of a monk" (V.i.f.30). Smith there lauds the Greek emphasis on "the
liberal, generous, and spirited conduct of a man" and brands the modern
philosophy as "corrupted" and "debased" (V.i.f.30–31). In *The Theory of
Moral Sentiments*, Smith illustrates in great detail the "esteem," "admiration," and "worship" naturally bestowed on wealth and greatness.
Although Smith labels this worship "corruption," he vindicates it because of its contribution to creating and maintaining social subordination, order, and rank (*TMS* I.iii.3.1–2, VI.ii.1.20). Combining the two
works, we might identify two paths to authority: that of the gentleman,
based on wealth and greatness, and that of the priest, based on poverty
and humility. In *The Wealth of Nations*, the puzzling praise of the
"liberal" and "generous," in conjunction with the contrast between liberal and austere moralities, highlights the connection between modern
liberalism and the ancient virtue of liberality or generosity: their common opposition to Christian asceticism.[26] Bourgeois virtue is ascetic but
worldly, thus combining the Christian and the Greek views; the result
(optimistically) is austerity without fanaticism.

In the religion Article, Smith seems to side with the "austere" rather
than the liberal morality. Most obviously, the liberal system is described
as frivolous, not as noble; it is the morality of the "people of fashion." *The
Wealth of Nations* as a whole, moreover, has more the spirit of austerity
than of liberality. But because the instruction of the "people of all ages"
under the system of natural liberty inculcates no hope for "a better world
in a life to come," one may infer that Smith did not expect to convey
unmanageable despair about the quality of life in this world.[27] As we have
seen, the accumulation of capital helps create a "progressive" state of

society in which the masses are "cheerful" and "hearty" rather than "miserable" and "melancholy" (*WN* I.viii.43).[28] Insofar as virtue decays without the press of necessity, however, permanent prosperity would create a problem analogous to the one faced by established churches.[29] But the problem might disappear if scarcity is permanent, that is, if people have an infinite capacity for "conveniences and ornaments," the "desires which cannot be satisfied" (I.xi.c.7), and if even necessity derives as much from convention as from nature (V.ii.k.3). In any case, the growing wealth and comfort of "the great body of the people" would presumably loosen the hold of fanaticism along with self-restraint. Perhaps Smith hoped that the austerity of bourgeois virtue, bolstered by the dismal science of political economy, could consolidate the defeat of the Church by commerce and supplant clerical "authority and influence" over the "minds of the people."

The system of natural liberty, however, does *not* require the extirpation of religion. Like Rousseau in the *Social Contract* (IV:viii), Smith stops short of endorsing Bayle's public atheism.[30] Rousseau's civil religion, however, still retains the substance of religion: doctrine, worship, and ceremony. What might be dubbed Smith's social or sociological religion is the purely worldly contribution to social "order" brought by the austere morals of small sects (V.i.g.12). But we need to review the conditional nature of Smith's discussion. If politics had never called in religion, "it would *probably* have dealt equally and impartially with all the different sects."[31] This policy "no doubt" would have produced a "great multitude" of sects, and possibly the "pure and rational religion" (g.8). The sheer multiplicity of sects, in any case, would produce several good effects, which Smith proceeds to elaborate with his observation about the two systems of morality (g.10–11).[32] Precisely the rigor and the austerity of the small sects enables them to combat the anomie of the masses in a commercial society. A "man of rank and fortune is by his station the distinguished member of a great society, who attend to every part of his conduct, and who thereby oblige him to attend to every part of it himself"; he is "obliged to a very strict observation" of the morals prescribed to him by "the general consent of this society" (g.12). The "man of low condition" lacks such membership, so only while he remains in a country village is it possible for him to have "a character to lose." Once in a great city, "he is sunk in obscurity and darkness," and because "his conduct is observed and attended to by nobody," he is likely to sink into "every sort of low profligacy and vice." The best remedy is to join a small religious sect, in which "the morals of the common people have been almost always remarkably regular and orderly," though likewise "rather disagreeably rigorous and unsocial" (g.12).

In several respects, this analysis replaces theology with sociology.[33] From a Christian point of view, everyone is potentially "the distinguished member of a great society," the kingdom of heaven or city of God; everyone likewise has a soul rather than "a character to lose"; because of God's ever-present attention and love, no one who loves and trusts in God would be "sunk in obscurity and darkness" with his conduct "observed and attended to by nobody";[34] it is rather the godless who live in "darkness." Biblical morals, furthermore, are prescribed by God rather than by the "general consent" of society. Human approval and disapproval, as in *The Theory of Moral Sentiments*, serve to replace divine approval and disapproval.

Small sects function thus as a remedy, but because they "have frequently been rather disagreeably rigorous and unsocial" (*WN* V.i.g.12), further "remedies" are needed. First is the "study of science and philosophy," for "science is the great antidote to the poison of enthusiasm and superstition" (g.14).[35] Second is "the frequency and gaiety of publick diversions"—painting, poetry, music, dancing, and drama—to "inspire" "gaiety and good humour," thus dispelling "that melancholy and gloomy humour which is almost always the nurse of popular superstition and enthusiasm" (g.15).[36] Scholars tend to mistake the first of these for the usual Enlightenment call for a full-scale philosophic assault on superstition. Even the judicious Cropsey says that Smith "proposed that the universities be employed as instruments for the broadest dissemination of science and philosophy, the antidotes to superstition and enthusiasm and the props of free government" (*Polity*, p. 100). Smith does indeed propose that the state render "the study of science and philosophy . . . almost universal" among "the superior ranks," on the assumption that where these people are immunized to the poison of enthusiasm and superstition, the "inferior ranks could not be much exposed" (*WN* V.i.g.14). We may infer, however, that science and philosophy will *not* be imparted to the masses by the state; the job of dispelling the melancholy and gloomy humor that underlies superstition falls rather to the "publick diversions" (g.15) that, perhaps, more directly attack the troublesome "humours." Consistent with the spirit of the education Article, of course, the state will merely implement examinations and leave teaching in private hands. Nowhere in the Article explicitly devoted to the universities does Smith argue that the state should require them to dispense science and philosophy. He does call for the removal of scholarships, privileges of graduation, and the like; he also laments that the education of "gentlemen and men of fortune" was long monopolized by an institution whose original purpose was preparing churchmen (V.i.f.35); he laments the focus on spirits rather than bodies (f.26). But his solution to these and other difficulties is what today would be called privatization, not public indoctrination with science.[37]

There remains a small public commitment to "facilitate" and "encourage" elementary education for the common people, and to "impose" it on them (V.i.f.54–55), including the substitution of geometry and mechanics for Latin (f.55). Without public institutions for education, "no system, no science would be taught for which there was not some demand; or which the circumstances of the times did not render it, either necessary, or convenient, or at least fashionable to learn" (*WN* V.i.f.46). With the above exceptions, this is Smith's solution. Smith recommends deference to whatever is made "necessary," or even "fashionable," by "circumstances," i.e., the circumstances of this world (f.32,35). Smith puts his faith in them rather than in God or His revelation, although one suspects that these circumstances are not immune to manipulation by Machiavellian politicians and philosophers.

Smith quietly points out that the "improvements which, in modern times, have been made in several different branches of philosophy, have not, the greater part of them, been made in universities"; the richer the university, the less responsive to "the current opinions of the world" (V.i.f.34). One may infer that privatization and competition would cause philosophy or "science" to replace Scholasticism in the universities. In the religion Article, Smith invokes the advantages of universities as the home for a "teacher of science" only in opposing the Church as such a home (g.40). In both Articles, Smith stresses how well philosophy fared in Greece and Rome, without either universities or churches (g.40), indeed without any "public" support (f.41–43); "demand" and "competition" produce "talent" and "perfection" (f.45).

At the end of the education Article, Smith does issue a call for public enlightenment. Apart from the intrinsic detestability of the "gross ignorance and stupidity" that afflict the masses because of the division of labor, government itself would derive "advantage" from their instruction: "The more they are instructed, the less liable they are to the delusions of enthusiasm and superstition, which, among ignorant nations, frequently occasion the most dreadful disorders" (*WN* V.i.f.61). The instruction Smith has in mind is presumably not the "instruction" he immediately proceeds to discuss in the next Article—preparing people for the next world—because that is a cause of rather than a remedy for superstition and enthusiasm. Smith's call for instruction would then refer back to elementary education (f.54–55), not ahead even to "science and philosophy" (V.i.g.14), the learning of which is to be required of the upper ranks. Or does the remark also look ahead to the instruction Smith soon provides about the true nature of clerical authority (especially the "interests" that sustain it), instruction that would help its recipients unmask "the interested complaints of faction and sedition" (V.i.f.61)? Although "the natural course of things" broke the back of the Catholic church, it seems that nature could not remedy the ills of religion without rhetorical and technological assistance from philosophy. Might Smith's exaggerated claims on behalf of nature constitute such assistance? Unlike Marx, Smith does not predict an end to religion, even biblical religion.

All things considered, there would seem to be no need (on Smith's view) for public dispensing of philosophy in a non-Christian world. Smith's proposal for using philosophy as an "antidote" to superstition, moreover, is contingent on the hypothetical existence of a multiplicity of sects. We may conclude that, short of the "pure and rational religion" completely purged of fanaticism, Smith's ideal would be a large number—perhaps two or three thousand (V.i.g.8)—of small sects of strict morality whose fanaticism is tempered by science and public diversions. Compared to the other proposals in *The Wealth of Nations* admitted to be utopian—full freedom of trade, union between Britain and its colonies, and so on—Smith's hypothetical discussion of religious toleration is more detailed and far more complex (if not confusing) in its blurring of what is actual, what might have been possible, and what might now be possible. One wonders if the multiplicity of sects was approximated in pagan Rome, whose policy of incorporating new gods was lauded by some of Smith's predecessors. In any case, the sociological side of religion for Smith replaces its theological side, as if toleration would produce indifference to God. The potential connection between such indifference and toleration has been often discussed, though with disagreement about which comes first.[38]

Church Organization and History

In addition to its abstract account of politics and religion, the religion Article analyzes the institutional structures of Catholicism, Lutheranism, Anglicanism, and Calvinism. That the Catholic church could have dominated Europe the way that it did must seem almost miraculous in light of the tendency for established religions to lose their authority. Smith mentions several factors that might explain the peculiar staying power of the Church.

In general, established clergy lose the "arts of popularity" because they evolve into gentlemen (V.i.g.1); establishment thus entails a sacrifice of future authority for present "ease and comfort" (g.7). Smith proceeds quickly to explain the distinctiveness of the Roman church. The "powerful motive of self-interest" perpetuates the "industry and zeal of the inferior clergy"; the subsistence of parochial clergy depends partially on the "voluntary oblations of the people," enhanced by confession; the mendicant orders are wholly dependent and therefore find themselves in the situation characteristic of "the hussars and light infantry of some armies"—"no plunder, no pay." The "great dignitaries" of the Church become "gentlemen and men of the world" (like established clergies in general), but the lower clergy stay hungry (g.2). This economic model of Catholic success calls our attention to the organizational structure that keeps the inferior clergy obedient to the great dignitaries and thereby strengthens the bonds that tie the people to the highest officials of the Church.

Smith thus highlights the subsistence mode of the inferior clergy as an institutional structure distinguishing the Catholic church. There is a second institutional factor that applies less distinctively to Catholicism—unity. The "interested and active zeal" of clergy is dangerous only when there are very large sects whose clergy act "by concert, and under a regular discipline and subordination" (V.i.g.8). The clergy of every established church constitute a "great incorporation"; they "can act in concert, and pursue their interest upon one plan and with one spirit" (g.17). But Smith presents only the Catholic church as achieving unity on an international scale, and his description of this is fraught with the military metaphor he introduced in likening the inferior clergy to "hussars and light infantry." As the pope acquired the power of distributing Church benefices, the European clergy became "a sort of spiritual army." Although that army was dispersed in various countries, its "movements and operations could now be directed by one head, and conducted upon one uniform plan"; each "detachment" was thus "dependent upon a foreign sovereign" (g.21). Smith's first remark about the organization of the reformed churches, on the other hand, emphasizes that there was "no general tribunal, which, like that of the court of Rome . . . could settle all disputes among them, and with irresistible authority prescribe to all of them the precise limits of orthodoxy" (g.33). One could say that the Catholic church pioneered the multinational corporation.

We may infer, however, that the two institutional factors (unity and the clergy's mode of subsistence) would not alone have sufficed to make the Church the "single greatest combination ever formed": it was the combination of "spiritual" and "temporal" authority that so elevated the Church. Here we confront a particular rather than a general circumstance. In the aftermath of the chaos brought to Europe by the barbarian invasions, land—the great source of authority and order—was up for grabs (*WN* III.iii.1, III.ii.3, III.iv.7). Under these circumstances, the

Church was granted large tracts of land (out of "mistaken piety") and its wealth was augmented by tithes. This wealth constituted the "formidable" arms of the clergy; as with the barons, these arms enabled them to keep the peace in their dominions. Their "hospitality and charity" thus brought them great "temporal force," but also "increased very much the weight of their spiritual weapons," enhancing the "respect and veneration" felt for them by the common people (V.i.g.22). This exceptional power was a fusion of bread and spirit: in Smith's words, of "private interests" and "delusions of superstition" (g.24).[39] We may presume that the Catholic superstitions were no more captivating than those of other religions except insofar as they were enhanced by the zeal and industry of the inferior clergy.[40] Uniquely Catholic, however, were the "ties of private interest" that came from feeding the people. Because of these ties, the Church would have endured forever if attacked only by "the feeble efforts of human reason" (indeed, by "all the wisdom and virtue of man"), but the "natural course of things" (the "gradual improvements of arts, manufactures, and commerce") came to the rescue and destroyed "the whole temporal power of the clergy" (g.24–25). What interest has joined, let no philosopher rend asunder. Laments about the weakness of human reason, wisdom, and virtue might of course be biblical, contrasting human frailty with divine greatness and thus illustrating the need for divine revelation and dispensation. In Smith's account, however, human reason and virtue are impotent with respect to nature as expressed through commerce and interest.

Smith's inquiry into the Church's rise and fall is the peak of the religion Article, if not of *The Wealth of Nations* as a whole. The long and fascinating discussion of rational religion, religious toleration, the multiplying of sects, the two schemes of morality, and public diversions emerges to answer a hypothetical question: What might have happened if politics had *not* called in religion? Smith concludes his answer with the observation that where the law is neutral between religions, there would be no need for the clergy to have "immediate dependency" on the sovereign, who would be required only to keep the peace—"but it is quite otherwise in countries where there is an established or governing religion" (V.i.g.16). This introduces an emphatically non-hypothetical discussion of church-state relations and launches Smith on a comprehensive history of Christian politics.

For the sovereign to be secure in the face of "an established or governing religion," he must have influence over its "teachers" (V.i.g.16), i.e., the clergy. Their interest, which is "to maintain their authority with the people," clashes with the sovereign's, and the authority of religion "is superior to every other authority" (g.17). Smith briefly explains why the sovereign cannot simply "instruct" the people in return, and concludes that the sovereign must attempt to influence the clergy by means of "fears and expectations" (g.18). Smith proceeds to his well-known contrast between "management and persuasion" ("always the easiest and safest instruments of government") and "force and violence" (the "worst and the most dangerous" instruments), which, because of our "natural insolence," are generally preferred (g.19). Smith heartily recommends that the sovereign attempt to manage rather than to intimidate an established clergy.[41] Regarding Christian clergy, it seems, the available means of management is just the "preferment" the sovereign may bestow (g.19), i.e., the sovereign's ability to influence the assigning of benefices (g.20): interest is again the key. Even in the "antient constitution of the Christian church," the sovereign's means were lacking, and the growing power of the pope sealed the sovereign's weakness (g.20–21). Hence the unprecedented sway of the Church (g.22–24) and also its termination by commerce, which augmented the management tools of European sovereigns "even before the time of the reformation" (g.26–28).

Although the authority of religion is supported by "the fears it suggests" (V.i.g.17), Smith alleges that the sovereign cannot remove these fears by his own program of instruction. Smith himself eschews (except minimally in *Essays on Philosophical Subjects*) engaging in a direct campaign to neutralize religious fears or even to refute theological doctrines; his indirectness thus parallels the course he recommends for the sovereign—managing the clergy rather than either intimidating them or going directly to the people.[42] Smith's campaign against the biblical religions proceeds indirectly: casually, quietly, and intermittently. Machiavelli and Hobbes directly attempted to replace fear of God with fear of the prince, to supplant fear of powers invisible with that of powers visible. The philosopher Adam Smith can of course neither manage nor coerce his readers; his only weapon is "persuasion." Ironically, he tries indirectly but persistently to persuade his readers that philosophers (along with gods and prophets) do not shake the world with words.

Smith traces the unique power of the Catholic church to its hold over the "interest" of the people. As a result, commerce, the agent of nature, accomplished what philosophy could never have accomplished. The defeat of medieval Christendom is attributed to nature, not human initiative; to commerce, not the sermons of reformers, the schemings of princes, the discoveries of scientists, and the writings of philosophers. In Smith's account, the decisive battle has already been fought.[43] But to the extent that he exaggerates the kingdom of nature and the impact of commerce, his own philosophy emerges as a weapon in the war against the imagined kingdom of God. If fear of damnation still gripped the "great body of the people," would Smith's preferred techniques of management suffice? Would Smith's own writings help to tame this fear or to efface the longing for another world? Do they teach others how to do those things? Does Smith exaggerate the contribution of crude "interests" to clerical motivation and influence in order to combat clerical power, if not the religious impulse itself? Does Smith generally exaggerate the sway of interest (and the possibility that management can replace rule), in order to consolidate the liberation of the "minds of the common people" from Christianity? To what degree do the common people—as distinguished from economic, political, and intellectual elites—need to be "enlightened"? In the spirit of the chronology provided by *The Wealth of Nations*, we might suppose that Smith's "persuasions" are a mopping-up operation, to secure the battlefield as the smoke clears. Whatever the causes of the Church's rise and fall, it is doubtless the case that Smith's science of political economy tries to remove the ideological breeding-ground for any further religious outbursts.

The Reformation

In *The Wealth of Nations*, the saga of politics and religion ends not with commerce but with the Reformation. Smith's analysis of the Reformation's success is both secular and unflattering:

> The reason of the new doctrines recommended them to some, their novelty to many; the hatred and contempt of the established clergy to a still greater number; but the zealous, passionate and fanatical, though frequently coarse and rustick eloquence with which they were almost every where inculcated, recommended them to by far the greatest number. (*WN* V.i.g.29)

Consistent with the Article's emphasis on the contribution of opinion to the "arts of gaining proselytes" (g.1), Smith here accentuates the vulgar character of the reformers' "eloquence."[44] The least important factor was the "reason" of the new doctrines; Smith is silent about their truth. Needless to say, the Reformation further strengthened the hand of the sovereigns against the Church (g.30)—the situation of the buyers improved with the break-up of the Catholic monopoly.

The fusion of politics and religion is suggested not only by Smith's identifying Lutheranism and Calvinism as the two main "parties or sects" spawned by the Reformation, but by his explanation of their emergence. Disputes among the reformers concerning "the government of the church, and the right of conferring ecclesiastical benefices" were perhaps the disputes "most interesting to the peace and welfare of civil society" and "gave birth *accordingly* to the two principal parties or sects" (V.i.g.33). It is the disputes about matters central to "the peace and welfare of civil society," not disputes about worship, piety, and salvation, that spawn sects that are thus indistinguishable from parties; Smith's subsequent explanation of why certain presbyterian clergy are so effective at converting people likewise ignores religious content (g.38). Although Smith does not erase Luther and Calvin the way he erases Moses and Jesus, he erases the theological concerns that dominated their lives.

Smith's elaboration of the ways the disputes about Church government were resolved focuses on the problem of how "gentlemen" can maintain authority with the people. We may infer from his discussion that neither the Lutherans nor the Calvinists eliminate the problem. Smith categorizes Lutheranism and the Church of England as "episcopal" and argues that the sovereign's status as the "real head" of the church is "favorable to peace and good order."[45] Because of the power of the state, the clergy cultivate the favor of the sovereign, the court, the nobility, and the gentry. Although the clergy occasionally employ the "vilest flattery," they frequently employ the arts esteemed by "people of rank and fortune": "knowledge in all the different branches of useful and ornamental learning," "decent liberality of . . . manners," "social good humour of . . . conversation," and open contempt for the austerities inculcated by fanatics. By courting the higher ranks, however, they are likely to lose their authority with the lower and to become vulnerable to the attack of "the most ignorant enthusiast" (V.i.g.34). Because they look up to worldly elites, such clergy will have trouble ruling the people.

Smith proceeds to evaluate two institutions characteristic of Calvinist or "presbyterian" churches: popular election of pastors and "perfect equality among the clergy" (V.i.g.35). Smith frowns on the former but smiles on the latter. Because elections cause the clergy to meddle in a "factious and fanatical" way, magistrates were occasionally led to assume appointment rights in order to preserve the peace (g.36). The equality of "jurisdiction" and "benefice," by contrast, seems to calm the agitated furies of clerical ambition. The clergy cultivate their superiors by "nobler and better arts": learning, regularity, and duty. As a result,

> there is scarce perhaps to be found any where in Europe a more learned, decent, independent, and respectable set of men, than the greater part of the presbyterian clergy of Holland, Geneva, Switzerland, and Scotland. (*WN* V.i.g.37)[46]

By the standards of *The Wealth of Nations*, this is lavish praise, and the passage accentuates Smith's seriousness about the common people's

need for "instruction." Although these clergy, like the Lutherans, cultivate their superiors, they do so by means of more austere arts: regularity
and duty as opposed to "liberality," "good humour," and contempt of
austerity. One might describe such clerics as middle-class gentlemen.

This impression is confirmed by Smith's subsequent remarks. The
equality of the benefices means that none can be large; because only "the
most exemplary morals can give dignity to a man of small fortune," a
minister of modest means naturally avoids the "vices of levity and
vanity" (V.i.g.38).[47] As a result, the common people "look upon him with
that kindness with which we naturally regard one who approaches somewhat to our own condition, but who, we think, ought to be in a higher."
Kindness provokes kindness and diligent instruction. These clergy, consequently, "have more influence over the minds of the common people
than perhaps the clergy of any other established church"; only in presbyterian countries do "we ever find the common people *converted, without
persecution,* compleatly, and almost to a man, to the established church"
(g.38). Such a clergy is, as it were, poised between the people and the
upper ranks. They maintain their hold over the people because they
resist the temptation to indulge in material perquisites that lie beyond
the reach of the people: recall Smith's claim that an established clergy
trades its "future . . . influence and authority" for present "ease and
comfort" (g.7). These presbyterian clergy, however, maintain some elevation over the people, and they cultivate the "nobler and better arts,"
including "learning." This very elevation is enhanced by the modesty of
their incomes: the common people almost feel sorry for them

One may infer that Smith would favor a synthesis of episcopal and
presbyterian institutions: the sovereign on top (as opposed to the popular
election of pastors); equality and mediocre benefices to keep the clergy
close to the people and to reduce the prizes for clerical ambition. Smith
presumably is happy that reformed clergy (compared with the "inferior"
Catholic clergy) are less dependent on their flock for subsistence. Indeed,
the religion Article ends with a return to the question of the mode of
clerical subsistence, for "the proper performance of every service seems
to require that its pay . . . should be, as exactly as possible, proportioned
to the nature of the service" (g.42). As before (I.x.c.34), Smith's elaboration portrays the "nature of the service" in wholly secular terms. The
point here is that the recipients of high incomes are prone to "festivity,"
"vanity," and "dissipation." Such actions and attitudes in a cleric destroy
the "sanctity of character" that, as perceived by the common people, can
alone enable him to perform his "duties with proper weight and authority" (V.i.g.42).

Religion, Regime, and Faction

> For forms of government let fools contest;
> Whate'er is best administer'd is best;
> For modes of faith let graceless zealots fight;
> His can't be wrong whose life is in the right.
> —Pope, *Essay on Man*

According to Harvey C. Mansfield, Jr., Hobbes abandoned the Aristotelian notion of "regime"—that rulers "promote themselves in a partisan view of the whole that is typically theirs"—because it was appropriated by religious parties acting with tyrannical zeal.[48] As we have seen, Smith departs from the classical approach to regimes even more than Machiavelli, Hobbes, Locke, Montesquieu, and Hume did, and he struggles to combat religious interpretations of the cosmos and humanity's place within it. As we will now explore, Smith's account of faction reveals linkages between politics and religion, and suggests remedies with an economic flavor. Religious faction is especially acute because partisanship in the service of God cannot always be tempered by human concerns. The pursuit of salvation or piety, perhaps even more than the pursuit of glory, empire, or political hegemony, is poorly suited to the marginalism essential to the economic realm of marketplace bargaining and cost-benefit analysis.

Apart from the discussion of Calvinism and the factiousness it breeds when clerics are elected by the people (V.i.g.35–36), Smith says little about the desirability of elections; he combats the Calvinist vision of rule by a godly or saintly elect by completely ignoring it. He nevertheless addresses some general problems posed by faction and fanaticism: "The good temper and moderation of contending factions seems to be the most essential circumstance in the publick morals of a free people" (V.i.f.40). Religion, however, seems to be the greatest source of faction and fanaticism. Smith invokes "good temper and moderation" several times in the religion Article: the clergy's interested "zeal" is dangerous where there are a small number of sects, but where there are many, the teachers must learn "candour and moderation"; the multiplicity of sects might even produce "that pure and rational religion, free from every mixture of . . . fanaticism" (V.i.g.8). But the situation is acceptable even if the many sects do not develop "good temper and moderation," provided the magistrate keeps the peace among them (g.9).

In *The Theory of Moral Sentiments*, faction looms even more prominently as an evil, and is again linked with religion and fanaticism. The impartial spectator is never "at a greater distance than amidst the violence and rage of contending parties" who may impute their prejudices to God Himself: "Of all the corrupters of our moral sentiments, therefore, faction and fanaticism have always been by far the greatest" (III.3.43), and these corrupters are easily fused with "false notions of religion" (III.6.12). In a section of the book added in 1790, however, Smith presents a different assessment, identifying the disposition to admire (and even to "worship") wealth/riches and greatness/power as "the great and most universal cause of the corruption of our moral sentiments" (I.iii.3.1–2). This contradiction, which emerges from Smith's warning us of the morally corrupting effects of the ends to which his own science of political economy is devoted, suggests that such corruption is an antidote to the more dangerous corruption caused by faction, fanaticism, and religion. Smith proceeds to specify that it is "the great mob of mankind"—as opposed to the "select" few who exalt "wisdom and virtue"—who exalt wealth and greatness (I.iii.3.2). Worship of the biblical God by the "great mob" is apparently more dangerous than worship of political and economic status.[49] Smith's remarks also suggest that religion is not "necessary both to establish and to maintain the distinction of ranks and the order of society" (*TMS* I.iii.3.1).[50] For Marx, of course, religious and political faction is superstructure built upon a "base" of economic faction—in modern society, the class struggle between capital and labor—and will therefore disappear under communism.

Insofar as Smith emphasizes wealth over political goods like greatness and power, he leads us to replace God with mammon. But because his political economy's eclipse of religion is so much broader and deeper than its eclipse of politics, one might say that his chief concern is reorienting politics from religion to economics.[51] In any case, Smith's discussions of faction suggest numerous linkages between politics and religion. Given his tendency to identify sects and parties (*WN* V.i.g.29,33; *TMS* VI.iii.28), it is not surprising that he implicitly defines a "heretic" as a person who belongs to the "weaker party" once violence has commenced (*TMS* III.3.43). In defending his utopian proposal to unite England with its Irish and American colonies, he dwells on the ills of fanaticism and faction and hints at their sources in politics and religion. Just as union with England delivered Scotland from an oppressive aristocracy based on "the natural and respectable distinctions of birth and fortune," it would liberate Ireland from the "much more oppressive aristocracy" based on "the most odious of all distinctions, those of religious and political prejudices" (*WN* V.iii.89). Here again, Smith extols wealth over religion and politics, though his earlier account of the "respectable" distinctions of birth and fortune was not particularly respectful (V.i.b.7,8,11). Smith goes on to state that religious and political prejudices, more than any other distinctions, "animate both the insolence of the oppressors and the hatred and indignation of the oppressed" (V.iii.89). We may infer that political and religious domination is more thymotic than the political authority derived from wealth and the "command" embodied in exchange value.

Union will deliver the American colonies not from an "oppressive aristocracy" but from "those rancorous and virulent factions which are inseparable from small democracies"; separation from Britain would inflame the problem by removing the coercive power by which faction was previously restrained. Smith continues with the only mention of "impartial spectator" in *The Wealth of Nations*: the "spirit of party" is generally weaker in an empire's *provinces* because their distance from the capital, "from the principal seat of the great scramble of faction and ambition, makes them enter less into the views of any of the contending parties, and renders them more indifferent and impartial spectators of the conduct of all" (*WN* V.iii.90). Small democracies are apparently afflicted by "rancorous and virulent factions" because people's humors are continually agitated by their proximity to the "great scramble of faction and ambition." From Smith's reservations about democracy, coupled with his apparent indulgence of the natural aristocracy—those "ambitious and high-spirited men" who will "draw the sword in defence of their own importance" (IV.vii.c.74)—one may infer that Smith wishes "the great body of the people" to be absorbed in bettering their condition by lengthy, laborious industry and to be insulated from the intoxicating elixirs of politics: "splendour and glory," the "dazzling objects of ambition," the "dazzling object" amid "the confused scramble of politics and war," "a thousand visionary hopes of conquest and national glory," "the splendid and showy equipage of empire," and so on.[52] The parade of such terms is even longer in *The Theory of Moral Sentiments*: "dazzling splendour," the "dazzling tumult of war," "the splendour of great actions," "splendid and dazzling actions," the "most glittering and exalted situation," "extravagant projects," "noble and magnificent objects," "the giddy admiration of shining accomplishments," "foolish wonder and admiration," "dazzling colours," "enthusiastic and rapturous veneration," "splendid characters," and "foolish admiration."[53]

The project of counteracting the human propensity to fanaticism pervades Smith's corpus. Smith tends to elevate the gradual, the ordinary, the pedestrian, the predictable; in his words, "the solid and the profitable" as opposed to "the grand and the marvellous" (*WN* II.ii.77).[54] Smith's campaign against fanaticism seems to be directed primarily against the biblical religions and secondarily against politics, war, philosophy, and eros; even within the sphere of economics, Smith's bourgeois virtue entails the demotion of "extensive projects," "golden dreams" (*WN* II.ii.69), monopoly, pageantry, the precious metals, "glittering baubles," and wild speculation. Religion is the most potent adversary because the most "dazzling objects" of all are God and Heaven. What Smith says of society may be applied to the universe: the center or "capital" is "the principal seat of the great scramble of faction and ambition." Smith tries to divert attention from the center because the stakes there are so high; the deist God is of course more remote than the biblical God.

God and Heaven, of course, could be construed so as to temper human pursuit of other dazzling objects. As we will see, Smith in *The Theory of Moral Sentiments* explains but does not really indulge our hope for an afterlife in which "modest, silent, and unknown merit" will equal or transcend the "splendid and dazzling actions" of this world (III.2.33); he likewise ignores the possibility that an appeal to a divine judge or "spectator" could be used to temper human discord. Smith instead provides an atheistic system of natural liberty that uses the market not only to enforce impartiality but to equalize the fates of "modest" bourgeois virtue and "dazzling" actions.

In the end, Smith's perspective on faction (not to say religion) is Machiavellian. Smith adapts Machiavelli's doctrine of the two humors: the few who want "to command and oppress" and the many who want to be left alone.[55] The few are motivated by ambition and avarice for great things; the many are motivated by avarice for small things and cherish security. For both Smith and Machiavelli, the clergy is an elite that speaks persuasively in the name of the many. There is no necessity that either order receive moral edification; their clash can instead be "managed" for the common good, by institutions and princely prudence for Machiavelli, almost by nature for Smith. But Smith condemns and/or ridicules avarice and ambition much more often than Machiavelli does.

Departing from Machiavelli's gleeful exhortation to conquer fortune, Smith soberly accommodates his readers to enslavement in the "chains" of nature, though that enslavement is fused with the technological mastery of nature. By abandoning the contract theorists' premise of natural freedom and equality—that no one may be subject to another without his own consent—Smith aligns his politics with his metaphysics. In *The Wealth of Nations*, Smith combats the human tendency to interfere with the "natural course" of labor and capital,[56] "natural liberty" (including free international trade), and "the natural progress of opulence." Can Smith squelch the human impulse to escape nature's chains in pursuit of wholeness and transcendence? The replacement of nature by history was launched by Rousseau along with a more radical doctrine of popular sovereignty, a more radical insistence on the continued participation of citizens in *ruling*, and the promise of being subject only to laws legislated by oneself. In light of Rousseau, and with a glance ahead to Marx's historical materialism, Smith's books almost seem to invite the search for what Arendt and Strauss call an "Archimedean point" outside of nature.[57] In Cropsey's words, the alternatives would be a divine will above nature, as Scripture teaches, or a "human will alongside it," as Kant teaches (Cropsey, *Political Philosophy*, pp. 84, 88). Smith tries to eliminate the former without bringing on the latter. "Natural liberty" is a theological, political, and philosophical puzzle.

CHAPTER NINE

Religion and Moral Sentiments I

Religion and the "Adam Smith Problem"

In light of the sustained attention devoted to alleged contradictions between Smith's two books, it is remarkable that the discrepancy between them regarding religion has been so little explored. Are modern scholars moved more by the contrast between selfishness and benevolence than by the contrast between an atheistic universe and a theistic one? Given the orientation of modern economics, of course, it is no surprise that the absence of God in *The Wealth of Nations* causes little concern. *The Theory of Moral Sentiments*, on the other hand, is full of God, and features little of the blatant irreligiosity of *The Wealth of Nations*.

On close inspection, however, it is clear that even in *The Theory of Moral Sentiments* the biblical religions are rejected. The differences from *The Wealth of Nations* are twofold. First, there is much more apparent borrowing from Christianity; certain forms of religion appear as socially useful or necessary despite their falsity; perhaps Smith tempers his suggestions of their falsity in order to preserve their utility. Second, there is a powerful residue of deism that has survived the purgation of biblical elements.

It might be alleged that discrepancies exist because Smith changed his mind during the seventeen years between the publication of his two books.[1] Regarding religion, Smith made some serious alterations in the text of *The Theory of Moral Sentiments*, especially in the edition appearing in the year of his death, 1790; in general, these alterations constitute a subtle departure from orthodoxy.[2] When carefully examined, however, they reflect not a change in Smith's views of the truthfulness of the doctrines in question, but a change in circumstances. One obvious factor is Smith's old age in 1790. Like Hume, it seems, Smith did not find God as he went to meet his maker. My suspicion is that he wrote more frankly as death approached;[3] there is no way to confirm this, but his conspicuous concern with avoiding notoriety for religious unorthodoxy suggests that my view is at least plausible.[4] The most telling consideration, however, is that even with the modifications, *The Theory of Moral Sentiments* is much more pious than *The Wealth of Nations*.[5] If Smith had become an atheist between 1759 and 1776, the alterations in the 1790 edition of *The Theory of Moral Sentiments* should have been more radical. One likewise would have expected the change of view to be reflected in Smith's revisions of *The Theory of Moral Sentiments* between 1759 and 1776. Smith's 1790 additions, finally, include theological observations—about the "benevolent wisdom of nature" (VI.ii.1.20) and the melancholy that may emerge from "the very suspicion of a fatherless world" (VI.ii.3.2)—that are implicitly denied by *The Wealth of Nations*.[6]

One is left with the supposition that the theological clash between the two books results primarily from the rhetorical and thematic differences between the two disciplines, political economy and moral philosophy.[7] Because Smith suggests that moral philosophy encompasses political economy (*TMS* VII.iv.34,37), there should not be any simple contradictions among the premises and the conclusions of the two disciplines. One may therefore hypothesize that the broader scope of the parent discipline requires a loftier rhetoric to sustain it, whereas the system of natural liberty can be adequately defended in worldly terms. Since the concerns of *The Wealth of Nations* are so much more modest than those of *The Theory of Moral Sentiments*, they can be promoted without recourse to God. Even nature, however, is portrayed more resplendently in *The Theory of Moral Sentiments*. This leaves two possibilities: the agenda of *The Wealth of Nations* can be sustained without supposing a nature with high purposes, so that its rhetoric is not required to make a case for such purposes; or the agenda of *The Wealth of Nations* can substitute for that of *The Theory of Moral Sentiments*, and be spared the need to lie about nature and God. *The Wealth of Nations* formulates a science of society that, without God or an afterlife, attempts to promote order and progress by harmonizing the interests of individual and society.

The greater religiosity of *The Theory of Moral Sentiments* corresponds to its greater kinship with ancient thought, which is treated sympathetically. In almost all respects, the sights of *The Theory of Moral Sentiments* are set higher than those of *The Wealth of Nations*: toward nobility, virtue, happiness, love, benevolence, God, and Heaven.[8] The withering of both religion and politics is only anticipated. We will begin by examining Smith's sights at their highest.

God: Existence and Attributes

Although absent from *The Wealth of Nations*, God is nearly ubiquitous in *The Theory of Moral Sentiments*. But what kind of God? On close inspection, one finds not the biblical God—the God of Abraham, Isaac, and Jacob—but the deist God.[9] In *The Wealth of Nations*, the closest approximation is "the Deity" included by the Greeks among the parts of the great system of the universe. Unlike this Deity, the God of *The Theory of Moral Sentiments* may be the creator of the universe; but neither disrupts what Smith calls the "great machine of the universe," with its "secret wheels and springs" (*TMS* I.i.4.2). Smith flirts with the possibility that God is active in the afterlife, but removes God from involvement in this life: Smith leaves little or no room for the biblical phenomena of revelation, covenant, miracles, prayer, and particular Providence.

Creation

Smith refers frequently to "God" or "the Deity." Of the myriad other terms Smith employs, most have a strong deist (and Stoic) flavor: God as nature's "Director," "Conductor," "administrator," "Author," and "Architect."[10] Only the last two suggest God's creative role (completely ruled out in *The Wealth of Nations*), but both stop short of the biblical notion of creation *ex nihilo*: architect and author employ preexisting materials such as language, paper, and pen.[11]

In *The Theory of Moral Sentiments*, Smith alludes to God as creator on three different occasions. The least committal comes in a hypothetical examination of the question of why we ought to obey "the will of the Deity." Smith's concern here is with the typology of theories of virtue, and he reduces the "system" identifying virtue as "obedience to the will of the Deity" to the system either of prudence (obey because of reward and punishment) or of propriety—obey because "there is a congruity and fitness that a creature should obey its creator" (*TMS* VII.ii.3.20). This analysis would apply to various accounts of deities and their commands, not just to the biblical God; Smith does not here assert or even imply that such a creator exists.

Smith adopts a more pious tone in the other references (earlier in the book) to God as creator. In one instance, Smith passionately exclaims: "How unnatural, how impiously ungrateful not to reverence the precepts that were prescribed to him by the infinite goodness of his Creator, even though no punishment was to follow their violation" (III.5.12). The context of this observation is again hypothetical, however. The paragraph begins as follows:

> When the general rules which determine the merit and demerit of actions, come thus to be regarded as the laws of an All-powerful Being, who watches over our conduct . . . they necessarily acquire a new sacredness from this consideration. That our regard to the will of the Deity ought to be the supreme rule of our conduct, can be doubted of by nobody who believes his existence. (*TMS* III.5.12)

Smith's point is the utility to morality, not the correspondence to reality, of faith in "an All-powerful Being" (not specifically the biblical God) who enforces morality. Smith argues that the imperative to obey is indubitable for the believer. Such an imperative would apply only if the creator's will has been adequately communicated, but Smith neither argues belief in the creator nor claims knowledge of its precepts.

The third example (presented first by Smith) is the most suggestive of the Bible:

> The all-wise Author of Nature has . . . taught man to respect the sentiments and judgments of his brethren. . . . He has made man, if I may say so, the immediate judge of mankind; and has in this respect, as in many others, created him after his own image, and appointed him his vicegerent upon earth, to superintend the behaviour of his brethren. They are taught by nature to acknowledge that power and jurisdiction. (*TMS* III.2.31)

Smith says nothing about the "many" other respects in which man has been created in God's image. Smith certainly allows human beings to judge and superintend each other. Smith equates the human judging faculty, however, with the impartial spectator, who, as we shall soon explore, is more of a substitute than an agent for God.

This whole paragraph was added in the 1790 edition. It replaces some paragraphs from the same chapter that were added in the second edition. The replaced passages include the claim that the impartial spectator is the "substitute of the Deity" (*TMS*, p. 130). The wording allows two interpretations: the impartial spectator is the agent of the Deity, or the impartial spectator is substituted by Smith *for* the Deity. The latter seems closer to the mark, given Smith's strenuous efforts in *The Theory of Moral Sentiments* to provide a psychology that explains religion as a natural outgrowth of morality.[12] The clause about creation (III.2.31) is preserved almost intact from the earlier editions. The excised passages, however, prepared the attribution of human "vicegerency" with one of Smith's most provocative remarks about revelation:

> If those infinite rewards and punishments which the Almighty has prepared for those who obey or transgress his will, were perceived as distinctly as we foresee the frivolous and temporary retaliations which we may expect from one another, the weakness of human nature, astonished at the immensity of objects so little fitted to its comprehension, could no longer attend to the little affairs of this world; and it is absolutely impossible that the business of society could have been carried on, if, in this respect, there had been a fuller revelation of the intentions of providence. (*TMS*, p. 128)

This theme is not addressed anywhere else by Smith. The passage seems friendly to Christianity, for it could be used to defend revelation against the charge of vagueness or uncertainty;[13] it also might suggest that the Bible is compatible with the worldly power of inter-human fear and the high status accorded human judgments by Smith's theory. The removal of the passage is thus consistent with the generally less orthodox tone of the 1790 edition. It could not be clearer in *The Wealth of Nations* that Smith's priorities lay with "the little affairs of this world" and "the business of society." In both works, furthermore, human "retaliations" are hardly portrayed as "frivolous and temporary." For these and other reasons, it seems that Smith thought that human beings created God in the image of a human judge. According to *Essays on Philosophical Subjects*, the earliest belief in gods arose from the attribution of the human capacities of willing and designing to the "irregular" events of nature (Astronomy III.2).

Christian Precepts and the Necessity of Grace

Further indications of Smith's insincerity in voicing the claim that man was created in God's image are suggested by Locke's identification of the biblical injunction, "Whoso sheddeth man's blood, by man shall his blood be shed," as "the 'great law of nature'" that entitles everyone to "execute" the law of nature by killing murderers.[14] As Richard Cox has argued, examining the biblical quotation (Genesis 9:5–6) and its context reveals Locke's departure from the Bible: beyond the absence from the Bible of the general concept of the "law of nature," the Bible explicitly attributes the human right to execute to the Noahic covenant, implying that the right is not coeval with humankind.[15] Smith follows Locke in stating that "as every man doth, so it shall be done to him, and retaliation seems to be the great law which is dictated to us by Nature" (*TMS* II.ii.1.10). In the Bible, unlike the *Second Treatise*, God's grant of capital punishment is explained in terms of man's creation in God's image

(Genesis 9:6). This rationale is missing from Locke's granting of this right. Smith defers to nature, which dictates retaliation, without regard to the Bible, and our creation in God's image is invoked not to condemn murder but to permit human judgments of condemnation.

Locke, having given almost total predominance to the Old Testament over the New Testament in the *Second Treatise*, defers to nature's "great law" of retaliation without so much as a nod toward the Christian injunction to turn the other cheek. Smith's exploration of this tension provides a compelling indication of his muted yet decisive rejection of Christianity. The closest Smith comes to mentioning Jesus is a reference to "our Saviour" that serves to ridicule Jesus' most famous imperative:

> A very devout Quaker, who upon being struck upon one cheek, instead of turning up the other, should so far forget his literal interpretation of our Saviour's precept, as to bestow some good discipline upon the brute that insulted him, would not be disagreeable to us. (*TMS* III.6.13)[16]

The silence in Smith's corpus as a whole accentuates the ridicule contained here. To maintain that silence, Smith elsewhere in *The Theory of Moral Sentiments* mistranslates two references to "Jésus-Christ" in a long quotation from Jean Baptiste Massillon, a French bishop.[17] The ridicule is more complex and more radical than it first seems. The obvious point is that Smith sides with the retaliation approved by our "natural sentiments" (III.6.13) rather than with the characteristically Christian response. Smith, however, proceeds to deny that the retaliating Quaker acted virtuously: because his actions were contrary to his own (albeit "wrong") sense of duty, the Quaker lacked "the sentiment of self-approbation" essential to virtuous action (III.6.12).[18] The chapter housing these passages is the only chapter or section of Smith's corpus that begins with the word "religion"; it ends with "self-approbation." This is one of many indications that Smith substitutes human judgment for God's. Humankind can "approve" of itself; it need not feel sinful and abject in light of God's perfection.

The passages immediately preceding Smith's mention of "our Saviour" reinforce the anti-Christian drift. Smith's first hypothetical example of how nature may prevail over "a wrong sense of duty" is the "bigoted Roman Catholic" whose compassion led him to save some Protestants from the St. Bartholomew's Day massacre (III.6.13).[19] So much for the way of love and peace. In the chapter beginning with "religion," "Christianity" is identified as a sect (III.6.1) and thereafter represented by bigotry and bloody persecution coupled with ridicule of Jesus. In the paragraph preceding his mention of "our Saviour," Smith blames "False notions of religion" for causing the "gross perversion[s] of our natural sentiments" that may arise from a misguided sense of duty. Smith then discusses Voltaire's *Mahomet,* a play in which two people are "instigated by the strongest motives of a false religion, to commit a horrid murder, that shocks all the principles of human nature" (III.6.12). Can there be any doubt that Christianity, mentioned along with its Savior in the next paragraph and linked with a horrible massacre, is for Smith likewise a false religion?[20]

The most orthodox presentation of the Creator comes in a passage present in the first five editions but excised in 1790.[21] Smith says that when thinking of themselves in light of God's holiness, people will probably fear that "vice should appear to be more worthy of punishment than the weakness and imperfection of human virtue can ever seem to be of reward." When preparing to confront "his infinite Creator," a man is likely to perceive no "reason why the divine indignation should not be let loose without any restraint, upon so vile an insect." Happiness, consequently, is dependent upon God's mercy rather than God's justice. Even the individual's "repentance, sorrow, humiliation" and contrition seem inadequate "for appeasing that wrath which . . . he has justly provoked." As a result,

> some other intercession, some other sacrifice, some other atonement, he imagines, must be made for him, beyond what he himself is capable of making, before the purity of the divine justice can be reconciled to his manifold offences. The doctrines of revelation coincide, in every respect, with those original anticipations of nature; and, as they teach us how little we can depend upon the imperfections of our own virtue, so they show us, at the same time, that the most powerful intercession has been made, and that the most dreadful atonement has been paid for our manifold transgressions and iniquities. (*TMS*, p. 92)

This passage, subsequently excised, certainly expresses the Christian view that Jesus' sacrifice was an act of divine mercy and grace bringing redemption and atonement (for human sin). On closer inspection, the passage serves equally as a psychological explanation of characteristic Christian tenets. In stating that the doctrines of revelation coincide "in every respect" with the "original anticipations of nature," Smith implies that revelation is not inherently mysterious, that it can be deduced from wholly secular phenomena.[22] Whether the revelation is genuine or imagined, the psychological explanation stands. Without the passage, there is little to give *The Theory of Moral Sentiments* a specifically Christian blush; Smith refers to God rarely as Creator or Judge, but never as Redeemer. Without the passage, the naturalistic explanation of the specifically Christian doctrine is moderated, but the widespread naturalistic explanation of religion in general remains intact; the impression of biblical religion as a mere "instance" grows.

The excised passage capped an argument that people, regardless of considerations about punishment's social utility, wish to see injustice punished. As evidence, Smith invokes the human longing to see that happen in the afterlife.[23] Thus, "nature teaches us to hope, and religion, we suppose, authorizes us to expect, that it will be punished even in a life to come." (Characteristically, the qualifying phrase "we suppose" was added in the third edition.) The hope comes unqualifiedly from nature; the expectation is *thought* to be justified by religion. The excised passage about atonement that concluded this analysis was replaced in the final edition by a single sentence: "In every religion, and in every superstition that the world has ever beheld, accordingly, there has been a Tartarus as well as an Elysium; a place provided for the punishment of the wicked, as well as one for the reward of the just" (II.ii.3.12). The specifically Christian doctrines are replaced with a generalization applicable to all religions, nay, to all superstitions. For Smith, Tartarus and Elysium have the same status as Heaven and Hell.[24]

The excised discussion of atonement is in a sense supplanted by some remarks added in 1790 to the next section:

> As, in the ancient heathen religion, that holy ground which had been consecrated to some god, was not to be trod upon but upon solemn and necessary occasions, and the man who had even ignorantly violated it, became piacular from that moment, and until proper atonement should be made, incurred the vengeance of that powerful and invisible being to whom it has been set apart; so, by the wisdom of Nature, the happiness of every innocent man is, in the same manner, rendered holy. (*TMS* II.iii.3.4)

As is marginally the case even in *The Wealth of Nations*, Smith retains the vocabulary of the holy and the sacred on behalf of justice (cf. *TMS* III.5.2, VI.ii.Intro.2). The holiness, of course, is here attributed to nature's wisdom rather than God's, and *The Theory of Moral Sentiments* shows at length that it will be respected even in this world: awe of human beings will replace awe of God. Smith has substituted praise of paganism for the excised Christian passages, and their removal further tips the balance in the book from Christian humility to pagan pride. These passages are kindred to the spirit of prayer, devotion, sacrifice, and worship. Earlier, Smith identifies as the "natural and ordinary state of mankind" the "happiness of the man who is in health, who is out of debt, and has a clear conscience"; despite "the present misery and depravity of the world, so justly lamented," such happiness is enjoyed by "the greater part of men" (I.iii.1.7). The Jewish, Christian, and Islamic view that we are never free of our debt to God is thus rejected for what is "natural and ordinary." As for the "present . . . depravity" of the world, Smith nowhere even mentions original sin or the Fall.[25] Smith sides with the natural sentiments that exalt worldly accomplishments—including even the arts of "subsistence," "conveniency," and "ornament"—rather than with "worship" and "the duties of devotion" (III.2.34–35).[26] Religion, as presented in *The Theory of Moral Sentiments*, is a valuable prop to morality, provided, among other things, that it identifies "the obligations of morality" as "the first duty" and does not teach people "to regard frivolous observances, as more immediate duties of religion, than acts of justice and benevolence" (III.5.13). The horizon is purely human.

The Deist God and Its Cosmos

The treatment of God in even the 1790 edition of *The Theory of Moral Sentiments* would be unthinkable in *The Wealth of Nations*. Consider the following passage added along with the rest of Part VI in 1790:

> The idea of that divine Being, whose benevolence and wisdom have, from all eternity, contrived and conducted the immense machine of the universe, so as at all times to produce the greatest possible quantity of happiness, is certainly of all the objects of human contemplation by far the most sublime. (*TMS* VI.ii.3.5)

Although Smith here praises contemplation of the "idea" of a being, he does not assert or argue the reality of such a being.[27] The being in question, moreover, is not the biblical God but the Stoic God with a utilitarian and technological gloss.[28] The universe has been so contrived and conducted "from all eternity"; it was not created as Genesis says. There is little that is mysterious about this being, or about the "machine" that is the universe, and such notions leave little or no room for miracles.[29] The Fall and the Flood, moreover, suggest clearly enough that God's intention is not to "produce the greatest possible quantity of happiness" at "all times." Biblical religion is eschatological: a drama of Fall and Redemption, an expectation that this world will ultimately be supplanted by the Kingdom of God. Smith flirts instead with the Stoic vision of "that great chain of causes and effects which had no beginning, and which will have no end" (VII.ii.1.37).[30]

The deist God, unlike the biblical God, does not become jealous or angry. In Smith's only reference to "inspired writers," he notes their emphasis on "the wrath and anger of God" (II.i.5.9). In the next paragraph, he refers to the principles upon which "a perfect being would approve of the punishment of bad actions." Smith implies that this perfect being would punish simply out of concern for "the welfare and preservation of society" (10); that is, it would not punish to secure human salvation or perfection, to tame human pride, to express offense, or to procure devotion, worship, and piety. When Smith in *The Theory of Moral Sentiments* once describes the immoral as "enemies of God," he qualifies the phrase with an "if I may say so" (III.5.7).

Given the similarities between the biblical God and Jupiter, Smith's analysis in *Essays on Philosophical Subjects* suggests that the biblical God was perceived as wrathful because of the fearful and precarious character of primitive life. This prospect is preserved in *The Theory of Moral Sentiments*:

> Men are naturally led to ascribe to those mysterious beings, whatever they are, which happen, in any country, to be the objects of religious fear, all their own sentiments and passions. . . . During the ignorance and darkness of pagan superstition, mankind seem to have formed the ideas of their divinities with so little delicacy, that they ascribed to them, indiscriminately, all the passions of human nature, those not excepted which do the least honour to our species, such as lust, hunger, avarice, envy, revenge. (*TMS* III.5.4)

Is the biblical God, from Smith's point of view, just one among a collection of "mysterious beings . . . which happen, in any country, to be the objects of religious fear"?

Like the *Essays*, *The Theory of Moral Sentiments* suggests the preferability of theism, i.e., a deistic theism, to polytheism/superstition. As we have seen, the essays are strangely silent about the biblical God, Who seems to combine the unitary and creating character of the theist God with the human involvement characteristic of polytheism. Not long after the above passage from *The Theory of Moral Sentiments*, Smith proceeds to address this theme. There is a clash between our "natural sentiments," which make us want to see all forms of virtue rewarded with worldly success, and "the natural course of things," which tends to reward only certain classes of virtue (III.5.9). As a result, human beings, "like the gods of the poets," are "perpetually interposing" on behalf of all virtue; because of the inevitable failure of this endeavor, "we naturally appeal to heaven, and hope, that the great Author of our nature will himself execute hereafter" what he has caused us to wish to promote; "thus we are led to the belief of a future state" (10). The interposing gods are creatures of the poets, created to fulfill a natural human longing. From Smith's point of view, what distinguishes them from the interposing God of the Bible? Smith's explanation of why we "naturally appeal to heaven" is equally an explanation of why we would naturally *create* heaven in our imaginations.

In the essays, Smith indicates that the theistic God is concerned essentially with the welfare of the universe, not with individual beings (Physics 9). There seems to be no place in *The Theory of Moral Sentiments* for either particular Providence—the God who has counted "even the hairs of your head" (Matthew 10:30)—or a personal relationship between the individual and God.[31] The one example of prayer in *The Theory of Moral Sentiments* is the unfortunate Johanna of Castile: her husband died, and a monk told her about a king revived fourteen years after his death by the prayers of his queen (III.3.33).

One passage suggests that Smith thought that the idea of particular Providence was already in decay. Smith describes how a humane European might react to an earthquake destroying China:

> He would, I imagine, first of all express very strongly his sorrow for the misfortune of that unhappy people, he would make many melancholy reflections upon the precariousness of human life, and the vanity of all the labours of man, which could thus be annihilated in a moment. He would, too, perhaps, if he was a man of speculation, enter into many reasonings concerning the effects which this disaster might produce upon the commerce of Europe, and the trade and business of the world in general. (*TMS* III.3.4)

As Macfie and Raphael point out, it is striking that the "man of speculation" would comment on the commercial rather than the theological implications of the catastrophe.[32] Smith thus hints that the outlook of his contemporaries already bears the marks of secularization. From Smith's point of view, of course, there might be nothing theological about which to speculate.

Smith indicates that the European described above, after his brief excursus on "all this fine philosophy," would "pursue his business or his pleasure . . . with the same ease and tranquillity" (III.3.4). In the chapter on the invisible hand, Smith articulates the "splenetic philosophy" that dwells on the vanity of human labor and the precariousness of human life (IV.1.8–9), but he proceeds to the invisible hand, Providence, the defense of civilization, and the "love of system" conducive to "the public welfare" (IV.1.10–11).

Cosmic Wisdom and the Argument from Design

In light of the above discussion, it might seem that the religious language in *The Theory of Moral Sentiments* is a combination of rhetoric on behalf of morality and raw material to illustrate a psychology of religion. This interpretation, however, must be reconciled with the passages that directly assert and argue the reality of the Deity and its care for mankind. In the first, Smith attempts to explain the "final cause" of the "irregularity" in our moral sentiments whereby actions are judged with reference to their consequences. The chapter begins with the anti-biblical assertion that "Fortune . . . governs the world" (II.iii.3.1). But Smith proceeds quickly to a very optimistic assessment of the cosmos:

> Nature, however, when she implanted the seeds of this irregularity in the human breast, seems, *as upon all other occasions*, to have intended the happiness and perfection of the species. . . . *Every part of nature*, when attentively surveyed, equally demonstrates the providential care of its Author, and we may admire the wisdom and goodness of God even in the weakness and folly of man. (*TMS* II.iii.3.2)

The second passage unfolds on behalf of the all-important proposition that the rules the human "moral faculties" prescribe must be "regarded as the commands and laws of the Deity" (III.5.5–6), even though these faculties are grounded in sentiment or passion. In arguing for the authority of the rules, Smith extols the goodness of the cosmos as strongly as he does anywhere in his corpus.

> The happiness of mankind, as well as of all other rational creatures, seems to have been the original purpose intended by the Author of nature, when he brought them into existence. No other end seems worthy of that supreme wisdom and divine benignity which we necessarily ascribe to him; and this opinion, which we are led to by the abstract consideration of his infinite perfections, is still more confirmed by the examination of the works of nature, which seem *all* intended to promote happiness. (*TMS* III.5.7)

A few lines later Smith refers to "the scheme which the Author of nature has established for the happiness and perfection of the world." In these passages, Smith provides an argument to support his assertions about God's purposes: the argument from design, from "examination of the works of nature." Smith nowhere argues the existence of God on the basis of miracles or specific instances of revelation, so the argument from design is crucial. We have good reason, however, to suspect that the confident expressions of the world's "happiness and perfection" are exaggerated and partly rhetorical.[33] Most obviously, there is not a single such sunny statement in *The Wealth of Nations*. Smith's opposition to even the posthumous publication of Hume's *Dialogues Concerning Natural Religion*, with its critique of the argument from design, might suggest that Smith held the argument useful to morality but defective. *The Theory of Moral Sentiments* is in fact pervaded by statements about the purposes and "wisdom" of both nature and God, but, as several scholars have noted, these statements are divided between more and less optimistic assessments.[34] The most optimistic portrayals are issued on morality's behalf.

The optimistic statements include the above-discussed claims about "happiness" and "perfection" (II.iii.3.2, III.5.7); Smith elsewhere identifies nature's "end" as "the order of the world, and the perfection and happiness of human nature" (III.5.9) and invokes "that benevolent wisdom which directs all the events of human life" and which allows only those misfortunes "indispensably necessary for the good of the whole" (VII.ii.1.45). The bleaker statements include Smith's specifying nature's "favorite" and "great ends" as "self-preservation and the propagation of the species" (II.i.5.10); when Smith identifies nature's "two great purposes" with the "wisdom of God," they are the "support of the individual, and the propagation of the species" (II.ii.3.5). By acting always "with the strictest economy" (VII.iii.3.3), nature indeed serves as a model for bourgeois virtue.[35]

One passage added for the 1790 edition is particularly revealing when compared to *The Wealth of Nations*. Smith is explaining why, among the people with whose welfare we become concerned because of "their extraordinary situation," we show more respect and sympathy for the greatly fortunate than for the greatly unfortunate. The reason is that our respect for the fortunate contributes to an end—society's "peace and order"—that is even more important than "the relief of the miserable," despite the moralists who "exhort us to charity and compassion":

> Nature has wisely judged that the distinction of ranks, the peace and order of society, would rest more securely upon the plain and palpable difference of birth and fortune, than upon the invisible and often uncertain difference of wisdom and virtue. The undistinguishing eyes of the great mob of mankind can well enough perceive the former: it is with difficulty that the nice discernment of the wise and virtuous can sometimes distinguish the latter. In the order of all those recommendations, the benevolent wisdom of nature is equally evident. (*TMS* VI.ii.1.20)

The Wealth of Nations likewise identifies birth and fortune as "the principal causes which naturally establish authority and subordination" (*WN* V.i.b.11), more operative than wisdom and virtue because more "plain and palpable" (b.5), but does not invoke nature's "benevolent wisdom." The discussion in *The Wealth of Nations*, furthermore, is bounded by remarks drastically more cynical than anything that appears in *The Theory of Moral Sentiments*: "The affluence of the few supposes the indigence of the many" (*WN* V.i.b.2); "civil government . . . is in reality instituted for the defence of the rich against the poor" (b.12). The reference to nature's "benevolent wisdom" added in 1790 rules out the possibility that Smith simply adopted a bleaker, godless view of things as he aged. The change in tone would then reflect the different subject matter of the two books and/or their different rhetorical tasks. In addition to Smith's total silence about God in *The Wealth of Nations*, there is only one reference to the "wisdom of nature." This wisdom, as we have seen, supports bodily preservation, and the parallel on the social level is "the natural progress of a nation towards wealth and prosperity" (*WN* IV.ix.28). The argument for laissez-faire exalts nature's wisdom to temper the pretensions of human wisdom, but the wisdom of this godless nature is less exalted and benevolent than nature in *The Theory of Moral Sentiments*.[36]

In the 1790 edition, Smith argues that "universal benevolence"—one's good will embracing "the immensity of the universe"—brings no "solid happiness" to someone who doubts that all the inhabitants of the universe are under God's "immediate care and protection." To such benevolence, the "very suspicion of a fatherless world, must be the most melancholy of all reflections," and that gloom cannot be lifted even by "the splendour of the highest prosperity" (*TMS* VI.ii.3.1–2). Given that the world of *The Wealth of Nations* is unambiguously fatherless, and that melancholy and gloom are the roots of "superstition and enthusiasm" (*WN* V.i.g.15), Smith would be compelled to discourage "universal benevolence." He encourages the individual to tend to his own "little department" (*TMS* VII.ii.1.44, VI.ii.2.4). He explicitly discourages us from attempting to "superintend" society, and he implicitly discourages us from embracing the cosmos with love rather than with resignation. The challenge for Smith's political economy is to dissuade people from tinkering with a "system" or "machine" that lacks a divine maker; if the economy is a machine, why not redesign it to our own specifications? In *The Theory of Moral Sentiments*, Smith appeals to the benevolent wisdom of nature and God to tame the dissatisfaction naturally aroused in our moral faculties by the "natural course of things"—that justice but not benevolence may be publicly enforced; that wealth and greatness, despite being "mere trinkets of frivolous utility," are admired and even worshiped; that vice often triumphs and virtue often fails; that results, not intentions, are judged. Smith indicates that the frustrations deriving from the latter two circumstances are sources of religion. As Cropsey observes but does not elaborate, "Nature is divided, but not equally divided against itself. The cause of unmitigated virtue can be heard only upon a change of venue to a jurisdiction in a world beyond nature."[37]

In contrast to Enlightenment philosophy generally and *The Wealth of Nations* in particular, the perspective on religion in *The Theory of Moral Sentiments* is almost tragic: "We are led to the belief of a future state, not only by the weaknesses, by the hopes and fears of human nature, but by the noblest and best principles which belong to it, by the love of virtue, and by the abhorrence of vice and injustice" (*TMS* III.5.10). Like contemporary sociobiologists, Smith must provide a functionalist or Darwinian explanation, first, of why people yearn for and believe in a more exalted universe and, second, of the human mind, which can discover and demonstrate the universe's Darwinian character.[38] Unlike the sociobiologists, however, Smith in *The Theory of Moral Sentiments* tries to shield the misguided sensibility from the harsher reality that explains it; he is less confident that publicizing his insights would be "adaptive." He argues strenuously, though not so strenuously as the Stoics (VII.ii.1.45), on behalf of resignation, tranquillity, happiness, and peace of mind,[39] and thus tempers his Machiavellianism with classical and Christian elements. The identification of happiness with tranquillity and resignation suggests that happiness would be available even in the bleaker version of the cosmos if people believed this version to be their "permanent situation." The more dismal vision in *The Wealth of Nations* is conveyed primarily by indirect means—for example, irony, the "scientific" tone, and the judicious allocation of attention (including repetition and silence)—and therefore may be more effective in reorienting human horizons than a frontal assault that cannot but highlight the alternatives.

This World Versus the Next World

The positive outlook on the afterlife conveyed in *The Theory of Moral Sentiments* clashes resoundingly with its treatment in *The Wealth of Nations*, where "modern" moral philosophy is condemned as "debased" because of its monastic, otherworldly orientation. The two books alike attribute to ancient moral philosophy the notion that virtue is productive of happiness in this life (*TMS* VII.ii.1.28). But *The Theory of Moral Sentiments* includes passages on the afterlife that seem irreconcilable with *The Wealth of Nations*. The most spectacular is the following:

> Our happiness in this life is thus, upon many occasions, dependent upon the humble hope and expectation of a life to come: a hope and expectation deeply rooted in human nature; which can alone support its lofty ideas of its own dignity; can alone illumine the dreary prospect of its continually approaching mortality, and maintain its cheerfulness under all the heaviest calamities to which, from the disorders of this life, it may sometimes be exposed. (*TMS* III.2.33)

This passage concludes Smith's discussion of the plight of an innocent man so vehemently condemned by his fellows that his conscience—the "supposed impartial and well-informed spectator . . . the man within the breast"—joins in the condemnation (III.2.32). The passage explains the longing for the afterlife without asserting its existence. Indeed, Smith refers to the "everlasting infamy" to which the innocent man can be reconciled only by religion (III.2.12), not to heaven and hell. The book does leave room for the soul, unlike *The Wealth of Nations*—where the single discussion of the soul is implicitly disparaging—but never suggests its immortality. The closest Smith comes is his explanation of our ability to "sympathize" with the dead. The melancholy that the living attribute to the dead arises from "our lodging, if I may be allowed to say so, our own living souls in their inanimated bodies, and thence conceiving what would be our emotions in this case"; this "illusion of the imagination" is what makes death appear so terrible (*TMS* I.i.1.13). Smith thus qualifies ("if I may be allowed to say so") his only allusion to transmigration; would not the Christian vision of eternal reward or punishment likewise count for Smith as "an illusion of the imagination"?[40]

The question remains, however, whether *The Wealth of Nations* can be reconciled with the claim that belief in the afterlife "can alone support" human dignity and maintain our happiness despite inevitable mortality and unpredictable calamities.[41] The passage continues in Smith's tragic voice. In a complex sentence, Smith first describes the different features of the longed-for "world to come": "exact justice" will be done to all; each will be ranked with his true moral and intellectual equals; the unlucky individual of "modest, silent, and unknown merit" will equal or transcend those "who, from the advantage of their situation, had been enabled to perform the most splendid and dazzling actions." The sentence culminates with the assertion that this doctrine is

> in every respect so venerable, so comfortable to the weakness, so flattering to the grandeur of human nature, that the virtuous man who has the misfortune to doubt of it, cannot possibly avoid wishing most earnestly and anxiously to believe it. (*TMS* III.2.33)

Given the complete absence of the doctrine from *The Wealth of Nations*, and the diatribe therein against the "modern" version of it, one might suppose that Smith simply gave up on comforting the weakness or flattering the grandeur of human nature. The virtuous man necessarily wishes "earnestly and anxiously" to believe the doctrine, but Smith refrains from arguing or even asserting its truth. The general tone of *The Theory of Moral Sentiments*, however, is sympathetic; without a careful study of the book, a virtuous reader's belief would not be shaken. In both books, Smith tries to tame human intoxication with "splendid and dazzling actions," as if to fill the breach left by his expulsion of traditional religions.[42] The virtue defended in both books is likewise lauded for its power in achieving worldly success, though the success appears primarily as wealth in one and esteem or love in the other.

Smith does not here claim that any and every doctrine of the afterlife is a friend of morality, and this provides a way of reconciling the two books. When Smith finishes his sympathetic sentence, he proceeds immediately to explain why such a venerable doctrine has provoked derision: because some of its "most zealous assertors" had alleged a scheme of rewards and punishments that clashes with "our moral sentiments" (*TMS* III.2.33). As an example of the erroneous version, Smith (in 1790) provides the notorious quotation from Massillon, who was chiding a regiment of soldiers for what they had done "in vain, for the world":

> You suffer always in vain for the life to come, and frequently even for this life. Alas! the solitary monk in his cell, obliged to mortify the flesh and to subject it to the spirit, is supported by the hope of an assured recompence, and the secret unction of that grace which softens the yoke of the Lord. . . . The best days of your life, however, have been sacrificed to your profession, and ten years service has more worn out your body, than would, perhaps, have done a whole life of repentance and mortification. Alas! my brother, one single day of those sufferings, consecrated to the Lord, would, perhaps, have obtained you an eternal happiness. (*TMS* III.2.34)

There are thus two versions of the afterlife with which Smith is especially concerned: the venerable version that emerges from and harmonizes with our "natural" moral sentiments and the monastic version. In *The Wealth of Nations*, Smith extols the worldly focus of the ancients on human "happiness and perfection," on "the liberal, generous, and spirited conduct of a man," and condemns the otherworldly focus of the moderns on "penance and mortification," i.e., "the austerities and abasement of a monk" (*WN* V.i.f.30). The latter corresponds precisely to Massillon.[43] Just as Smith criticizes economic arrangements in the name of natural paths and plans, he criticizes the monastic orientation that has obscured our natural moral and religious sentiments. One again suspects that he was aware of the difficulties of his attempt to keep (or to render?) mankind comfortably ensconced within the chains of nature.[44]

In responding to Massillon in the name of "our natural sense of praiseworthiness," Smith fuses pagan worldliness with modern commercialism as noble antagonists of monasticism:

> To compare, in this manner, the futile mortifications of a monastery, to the ennobling hardships and hazards of war . . . is surely contrary to all our moral sentiments; to all the principles by which nature has taught us to regulate our contempt or admiration. It is this spirit, however, which,

while it has reserved the celestial regions for monks and friars, . . . has condemned to the infernal all the heroes, all the statesmen and lawgivers, all the poets and philosophers of former ages; all those who have invented, improved, or excelled in the arts which contribute to the subsistence, to the conveniency, or to the ornament of human life. (*TMS* III.2.35)

Smith concludes with the book's sole quotation from Voltaire (from *La Pucelle d'Orléans*), to illustrate the antipathy aroused by the monastic outlook that condemns the worldly to "the infernal": "Vous y grillez sage et docte Platon, Divin Homere, eloquent Ciceron, etc." (*TMS* III.2.35).[45] The quoted passage, of course, does not quite establish that the place Voltaire refers to (the French "*y*") is the Christian Hell. Smith presumably endorses Voltaire's implied ridicule, and he tries to carve out an otherworldly doctrine exempt from it. In choosing between the two doctrines of the afterlife, Smith invokes nature, sentiment, and the needs of this world, not God or the Bible.

The economic alternative is usually in the background of Smith's defense of "this world." Smith identifies the following attributes of France and England as "*the* real improvements of the world we live in" that have "benefited" mankind and "ennobled" human nature: "internal happiness and prosperity"; land cultivation; the advance of manufacturing and commerce; numerous and secure ports and harbors; and "proficiency in all the liberal arts and sciences" (VI.ii.2.3). Smith traces Mandeville's "licentious system" to the "popular ascetic doctrines . . . which placed virtue in the entire extirpation and annihilation of all our passions" and claims that Mandeville easily proved that such annihilation would halt "all industry and commerce, and in a manner . . . the whole business of human life" (*TMS* VII.ii.4.12). It is Smith, however, who here identifies industry and commerce as the "whole" business of human life.[46]

Given Smith's favorable regard for "the natural principles of religion" (*TMS* III.5.13), one might infer that the praised doctrine of the afterlife belongs to natural religion. The claim that the virtuous man "cannot possibly avoid wishing most earnestly and anxiously to believe it" is akin to the vision in *The Wealth of Nations* of a "pure and rational religion, free from every mixture of absurdity, imposture, or fanaticism, such as wise men have in all ages of the world wished to see established" (*WN* V.i.g.8). One suspects that this pure and rational religion whose establishment the wise have always desired includes the "doctrine" of the afterlife that the virtuous always wish to believe. The wise wish the virtuous to believe things that will support virtue. Because *The Wealth of Nations* says nothing of the content of this "rational religion," however, and given the almost irresistible tendency for religions to become established, perhaps the wise will be satisfied if the established religion is free of "absurdity, imposture, or fanaticism." The natural system of political economy, unlike the natural system of moral sentiments, neither spawns nor requires natural religion.

Apart from the utility of the afterlife to remedy the failings of the impartial spectator, *The Theory of Moral Sentiments* is replete with more usual assertions of the boost given to morality by belief in the afterlife. Thus, "the same great principle which can alone strike terror into triumphant vice, affords the only effectual consolation to disgraced and insulted innocence" (III.2.12). In addition, Smith argues that reverence for the "rules of morality" is enhanced by the opinion that they are "the commands and laws of the Deity, who will finally reward the obedient, and punish the transgressors."[47] This opinion is initially "impressed by nature" and only later "confirmed by reasoning and philosophy" (III.5.3):

> That the terrors of religion should thus enforce the natural sense of duty, was of too much importance to the happiness of mankind, for nature to leave it dependent on the slowness and uncertainty of philosophical researches. (*TMS* III.5.4)[48]

Appearances to the contrary notwithstanding, Smith is not here humbling philosophy to exalt biblical revelation. Smith explained the rules in question as generalizations derived from particular verdicts of the "natural sense of duty" (III.5.4), that is, from sentiment, not the Bible; Adam disobeyed a rule that had nothing to do with the "natural sense of duty." The fear of punishment and the hope for reward likewise arise naturally. Smith goes on to say that the "natural hopes, and fears, and suspicions, were propagated by sympathy, and confirmed by education" (III.5.4), that is, not by revelation and the power of the Word.[49] Regarded as the laws of an enforcing deity, the rules of morality "necessarily acquire a new sacredness"; thus religion (where its natural principles are not corrupted) "enforces the natural sense of duty" (III.5.12–13).

In *The Wealth of Nations*, where there is no God and no function for religion beyond the purely sociological, there is little or no appeal to duty; the breach is filled by "interest." *The Theory of Moral Sentiments* provides ample social-psychological explanation for belief in the afterlife and ample justification for the social utility of the belief. Instead of endorsing the reality of the afterlife, however, the book displays the human "arms," both physical and emotional, that support morality.

From a Christian point of view, of course, there is one instance of death and ascension to heaven of special relevance to the promise of eternal life: the crucifixion and resurrection of Jesus. As we have seen, *The Wealth of Nations* totally ignores Jesus' life and death in its explanations of the rise of Christianity. *The Theory of Moral Sentiments* is likewise silent, but explores several other deaths that made their mark on history.[50] Perhaps the most revealing discussion occurs in the section added in 1790 where Smith observes that the "excessive presumption" and "excessive self-admiration" of certain men may "dazzle the multitude"—hence the frequent success "of the most ignorant quacks and impostors, both civil and religious." When joined with great merit, this excessive presumption has often procured "the most noisy fame, the most extensive reputation—a fame and reputation, too, which have often descended to the remotest posterity" (*TMS* VI.iii.27). When "crowned with success," the presumption could produce "a vanity that approached almost to insanity": Alexander the Great thinking himself a god, Socrates "fancying that he had secret and frequent intimations from some invisible and divine Being," Caesar thinking himself descended from Venus. Smith continues with the only reference in his writings to prophets or prophecy: "The religion and manners of modern times," however, "give our great men little encouragement to fancy themselves either Gods or even Prophets" (VI.iii.28). The "modern" religion, however, was founded on a grander claim than that of Alexander, Socrates, or Caesar.

Smith here provides a remarkable generalization: "Great success in the world, great authority over the sentiments and opinions of mankind have very seldom been acquired without some degree of this excessive self-admiration." Among those "who have brought about the greatest revolutions, both in the situations and opinions of mankind," Smith includes (along with warriors, statesmen, and legislators) the "founders and leaders of the most numerous and successful sects and parties"; their presumption helped them "to command the submission and obedience of their followers" (VI.iii.28). Thus we finally encounter the forbidden fruits of the Smithian world: prophecy, the Word, Jesus, great individuals who bring "new modes and orders."[51] Smith's chapter on self-command, one of the great bourgeois virtues, is indeed his most revealing statement about those who command others. All this was added for the 1790 edition, calling into question the impersonality and gradualism characteristic of human history as portrayed in *The Wealth of Nations*. To what extent did Smith intend to initiate and/or join a great revolution in "the situations and opinions of mankind"?

CHAPTER TEN

Religion and Moral Sentiments II

Morality, Authority, and Fanaticism

Smith's whole approach to morality prepares the abandonment of reliance on revelation or authority.[1] *The Theory of Moral Sentiments* is primarily an analysis of the nature and causes of moral sentiments. While identifying the "natural" forms of the moral mechanism, however, Smith does introduce a normative standard, for the moral mechanism is grounded in a more or less beneficent nature, more or less connected with a deity. This deity, however, is not the biblical God, and the moral mechanism substitutes for authoritative revelation about right and wrong. Although Mandeville's writings exude vastly more impiety than Smith's, Mandeville explicitly exempts the content of biblical revelation from his account of the sources of moral judgment: in explaining how human beings come to "distinguish between Virtue and Vice," he indicates that the men he will discuss are "neither Jews nor Christians" but "meer" men "in the State of Nature and Ignorance of the true Diety."[2]

Smith identifies moral sentiments as the "principles by which nature has taught us to regulate our contempt or admiration" (*TMS* III.2.35). In ruling out reason as the ultimate source of moral judgment, Smith also rules out revelation: the "first perceptions of right and wrong" (from which reason induces general rules) are the object of "immediate sense and feeling"; only sentiment can "render any particular object agreeable or disagreeable to the mind for its own sake" (VII.iii.2.7). As we have seen, the severing of morality from authority if not sanctity is carried to the extreme in the account of moral philosophy presented in *The Wealth of Nations* (V.i.f.25). Within these constraints (and sometimes beyond them), Smith in *The Theory of Moral Sentiments* generally preserves an air of righteousness, conveying that "warmth in the cause of virtue" whose absence in Hume was criticized by Hutcheson.[3] It seems that for the sake of the "ought" Smith exaggerates the "is" with some of the inflated rhetoric about nature and God; this rhetoric counteracts the demoralizing potential of Smith's reductionistic explanations of our moral sentiments; perhaps Smith is more concerned than nature is with human "happiness and perfection." In Cropsey's words, Smith is attempting to carve out a sphere for the noble while conceding the "ultimate indifference of nature to nobility."[4] For Smith, this project is in some ways facilitated by the removal of the biblical religions, which are unambiguous casualties of his reductionism. But Smith's project is also threatened by their removal, because it is religion that "gives the greatest authority to the rules of duty" (III.6.12).

Precisely the naturalness of moral sentiments reduces the need for them to be presented with all the trappings of authority. The impartial spectator emerges naturally as what today would be called an internalized social conscience (III.1.2–3, III.3.3,21–26,38). Smith proffers this "great discipline which Nature has established for the acquisition" of every virtue as a substitute for "abstruse syllogisms of a quibbling dialectic" (III.3.21). Nature takes the place of philosophy and religion, not to say formal education, though nature's lessons are best absorbed when the particular sentiments become encapsulated in general rules to which people may be habituated (III.4.7,12). In the end, however, the "exciting" of the proper "emotions" is paramount; Smith is especially critical of the casuists' proclivity for "abstruse and metaphysical distinctions" (VII.iv.32). Nature's morality, unlike Christian morality, does not need sacred or authoritative texts for support. There is only one reference to the Bible in the entirety of Smith's book: "In the Decalogue we are commanded to honour our fathers and mothers." Because nature (looking out for "the continuance and propagation of the species") has generally rendered "parental tenderness a much stronger affection than filial piety," "moralists . . . exhort" us with reverse emphasis (III.3.13). Smith's point seems to be that the author of the Decalogue, like any proper moralist, acknowledges the pressures of nature even while trying to moderate them.

The theory of the impartial spectator allows an appeal beyond actual sentiments of approbation and disapprobation to "natural" sentiments, an appeal beyond praise and blame to the praiseworthy and the blameworthy. Smith concedes that different societies and eras spawn divergent moral sensibilities, but argues that a nation's general "situation" generally spawns "suitable" mores (V.2.13). "Of all the corrupters of moral sentiments," however, "faction and fanaticism have always been by far the greatest" (III.3.43). A related threat to our moral sentiments is the "wrong sense of duty" or "erroneous conscience" attributable to religion:

> False notions of religion are almost the only causes which can occasion any very gross perversion of our natural sentiments in this way; and that principle which gives the greatest authority to the rules of duty, is alone capable of distorting our ideas of them in any considerable degree. In all other cases common sense is sufficient to direct us. (*TMS* III.6.12)

Here again we see the potentially tragic dimension to Smith's outlook: a most needful thing can also be a most harmful thing.[5]

The impartial spectator, though a remedy for the conflicts of daily life, is "never at a greater distance than amidst the violence and rage of contending parties"; the impartial spectator does not prevent contending parties from imputing their prejudices to God and viewing Him "as animated by all their own vindictive and implacable passions" (*TMS* III.3.43). But insofar as people naturally "ascribe to those mysterious beings . . . which happen, in any country, to be the objects of religious fear, all their own sentiments and passions" (III.5.3–4), the spread of tranquillity will temper religious fanaticism.[6] Recall that science/philosophy aims "to sooth the imagination" (*Astronomy* II.12) and constitutes "the great antidote to the poison of enthusiasm and superstition" (*WN* V.i.g.14). Smith concedes, however, that the "systems" provided even by worldly philosophy can be a breeding ground for fanaticism (*TMS* VI.ii.2.15).[7]

One suspects that the chief obstacle to Smithian tranquilizing was the Christian vision of the afterlife. Smith says that "the great source of both the misery and disorders of human life, seems to arise from over-rating the difference between one permanent situation and another" (*TMS* III.3.31). Heaven and hell, however, are the permanent situations whose difference cannot be overrated. After digressing to criticize Aristotle's account of virtue as a mean (*Proleg.*, 43–44), Grotius states that one cannot "too much seek after the blessings that shall abide forever, nor fear too much the everlasting evils, nor have too great hatred for sin" (45). As Löwith observes in interpreting Augustine, "What is at stake in this short interval of human existence is the alternative between being eternally blessed or being condemned."[8] For Smith, these stakes are too high; hence his flirtation with Stoicism, which views life as a "mere twopenny stake; a matter by far too insignificant to merit any anxious concern" (*TMS* VII.ii.1.24). With lower stakes, one can avoid the extremes of both melancholy/superstition and enthusiasm.[9] Smith prefers that our significance be underestimated rather than overestimated, to counter what Carl Becker describes as the Christian announcement that "the life of man has significance, a universal significance transcending and including the temporal experience of the individual" (p. 128). Smith sacrifices eternity to combat fanaticism.

The Mechanism Within

In Part VII of *The Theory of Moral Sentiments*, "Of Systems of Moral Philosophy," Smith provides a historical overview that is pregnant with hints about the religious implications of the psychological approach. Smith begins by specifying the two "questions which ought to be examined in a theory of moral sentiments"—In what does virtue "consist," i.e., What qualities count as virtues? and "By what power or faculty in the mind" is that content determined?[10] The second question is addressed in the third section of Part VII. Smith states that whereas the first question has "influence upon our notions of right and wrong in many particular cases," the second—the determination of the "contrivance or mechanism within" from which the different notions arise—is a "mere matter of philosophical curiosity." Though the second question is "of the greatest importance in speculation," it is of "none in practice" because it cannot influence our notion of particular rights and wrongs (VII.iii.Intro.3).[11] Several difficulties with this disparagement are quickly evident. First, as Campbell points out, this question provides the thematic focus of Smith's book (p. 50). Smith's outline of his own account of the principle of approbation specifies the "sources" of approbation—propriety, merit, general rules, and utility (VII.iii.3.16)—that are examined successively in the first four Parts of the book.[12] Second, Smith's elaboration of the "mechanism" generating moral approval and disapproval is laden with glowing accounts of virtue and the noble, exhortations to moral action, and demonstrations that morality generally leads to success and happiness. In addition to its "theoretical" character, therefore, *The Theory of Moral Sentiments* seems to imitate the "practical" function of the "books of morality" discussed in the ultimate section of the work: using "embellishments of eloquence" to "inflame our natural love of virtue, and increase our abhorrence of vice" (VII.iv.33,6). Third, the chapter on reason as the principle of approbation ends with an explanation of why controversy may persist despite Hutcheson's compelling delineation of the respective provinces of reason and sentiment: either because of inattention to his writings or because of "a superstitious attachment to certain forms of expression, a weakness not very uncommon among the learned, especially in subjects so deeply interesting as the present, in which a man of virtue is often loath to abandon, even the propriety of a single phrase which he has been accustomed to" (*TMS* VII.iii.2.9). Lo and behold, the theoretical issue (regarding the "mechanism within") involves "superstitious attachment" in "deeply interesting" matters. The chapter indeed touches on some weighty controversies. The paragraph immediately preceding the above passage begins with the bald claim that "pleasure and pain are the great objects of desire and aversion" (VII.iii.2.8), a claim that indicates Smith's ultimate agreement with writers from whom he rhetorically disengages, explicitly Epicurus but also Hobbes and Mandeville.[13]

Smith's psychological perspective on morality is both a consequence and a precondition of his rejection of God's word. "Forms of expression" may thus have an urgent practical bearing. In our day, most of the concerns of philosophers are indeed mere matters of "philosophical curiosity," but how true was this in Smith's day? Smith surely looked forward to a time when philosophy/science could proceed without theological encumbrances (*WN* I.i.9, V.i.f.26,28,34). Smith labors mightily to detach moral philosophy from metaphysics:

> The beauty of a plain, the greatness of a mountain, the ornaments of a building, the expression of a picture, the composition of a discourse, the conduct of a third person, the proportions of different quantities and numbers, the various appearances which the great machine of the universe is perpetually exhibiting, with the secret wheels and springs which produce them; all the general subjects of science and taste, are what we and our companion regard as having no peculiar relation to either of us. We both look at them from the same point of view, and we have no occasion for sympathy, or for that imaginary change of situations from which it arises, in order to produce, with regard to these, the most perfect harmony of sentiments and affections. (*TMS* I.i.4.2)

It is both difficult and urgent, according to Smith, to achieve this harmony of outlook on a personal "injury" or "misfortune" (hence the need for the impartial spectator); if these are not greeted with indignation and fellow feeling, respectively, "we become intolerable to one another." On the other hand, he asserts:

> Though you despise that picture, or that poem, or even that system of philosophy, which I admire, there is little danger of our quarreling upon that account. Neither of us can reasonably be much interested about them. They ought all of them to be matters of great indifference to us both. (*TMS* I.i.4.5)

We may infer that two people will not quarrel over "the conduct of a third person," for example, his religious or sexual practices.[14] Once the universe is recognized as a "great machine," why feud over the precise nature of its "secret wheels and springs"? On Smith's definition of interest, different preferences for "systems of philosophy" are not occasion for conflict; it is Smith's hope that people will similarly lose "interest" in each other's religion and therefore perhaps in their own. The great challenge for Smith is to preserve justice, benevolence, love, happiness, and nobility in a mechanistic universe about which people will not quarrel.

As we have seen, Smith scatters hints that "the propensity to truck, barter, and exchange" is ultimately a form of ambition, the desire to "lead and direct" other people. In laying bare this connection in the lectures, Smith says the following:

> Men always endeavour to persuade others to be of their opinion even when the matter is of no consequence to them. If one advances any thing concerning China or the more distant moon which contradicts what you imagine to be true, you immediately try to persuade him to alter his opinion. And in this manner, every one is practising oratory on others through the whole of his life. (*LJA* vi.56)

Smith's writings never so forthrightly acknowledge the power of this disinterested desire to persuade.[15] Smith tries to deflect the impulse to persuade toward economic activities centered on the trucking disposition. He tries to deflect it away from religion, where it may be expressed as prophecy, proselytizing, or persecution, and away from politics, where it may spur people to become princes, conquerors, legislators, or founders. This attempted deflection helps to explain the emphasis on unintended consequences that links Smith's interpretations of economics, politics, history, law, and morality: people more easily "accommodate" themselves to *impersonal* constraints.[16] By means of both the impartial spectator and the system of natural liberty, Smithian man naturally, gradually, and continuously learns to assimilate the perspectives of other individuals where it is really necessary: regarding concrete "interests."

Hobbes and his critique of religion figure prominently in the discussion leading up to Smith's concession that the elevation of sentiment over reason may breed controversy. Immediately after the assertion about "mere . . . philosophical curiosity," Smith mentions Hobbes and his followers (Pufendorf and Mandeville) as those who deduce "the principle of approbation from self-love" (*TMS* VII.iii.1.1). The second chapter, on reason as "the principle of approbation," likewise begins with Hobbes's doctrine of absolute sovereignty (VII.iii.2.1). Smith continues with a striking assertion about Hobbes's intention:

> It was the avowed intention of Mr. Hobbes, by propagating these notions, to subject the consciences of men immediately to the civil, and not to the ecclesiastical powers, whose turbulence and ambition, he had been taught, by the example of his own times, to regard as the principal source of the disorders of society. His doctrine, upon this account, was peculiarly offensive to theologians. (VII.iii.2.2)[17]

However accurate, this account of the historical context of Hobbes's teaching suggests a context for Smith's teaching: Smith wants to complete the liberation of the conscience from "ecclesiastical powers" by subjecting it to nature (via the impartial spectator) rather than to the sovereign.[18] Consider how the discussion proceeds. Hobbes's doctrine offended not only theologians but "all sound moralists" because it supposed that "there was no natural distinction between right and wrong," which depended "upon the mere arbitrary will of the civil magistrate" (VII.iii.2.2).[19] To combat Hobbes, the search was launched for a faculty by which the mind, "naturally" and "antecedent to all law or positive institution," distinguished right and wrong, virtuous and vicious (VII.iii.2.3). The first nominee was reason. The account based on reason was "true in some respects" but "rather hasty in others." It was nevertheless "more easily received at a time when the abstract science of human nature was but in its infancy, and before the distinct offices and powers of the different faculties of the human mind had been carefully examined and distinguished from one another" (VII.iii.2.5). Smith concludes by explaining the true relationship between sentiment and reason in moral judgment, according to which reason has a role but sentiment is primary (VII.iii.2.6–8). The final chapter of the section expounds the systems, including Smith's own, that make sentiment "the principle of approbation." In a somewhat technical discussion, Smith refers explicitly to Hutcheson (VII.iii.3.4–8) and Locke (6); he refers to Hume's system without naming him (17).[20]

Smith thus regards the great philosophical tradition of British empiricism—"the abstract science of human nature"—as having been spawned by Hobbes's attempt (precipitated by the social turmoil that ecclesiastical "turbulence and ambition" occasioned) to liberate the conscience from religion. Was the abstract science of human nature an attempt, while minimizing the collateral damage inflicted upon morality, to destroy the breeding ground of Christian delusions?[21] In concluding his discussion of Mandeville, Smith explains that "moral philosophy" cannot depart as "far from all resemblance to the truth" as natural philosophy. Giving an account of "the origin of our moral sentiments" is like describing "what passes in our neighborhood," where we may "examine things with our own eyes"; giving an account of "the causes of the great phenomena of the universe" is like a traveler describing "some distant country." Resembling "indolent masters who put their trust in a steward who deceives them," however, we are "liable to be imposed upon" even in moral matters—but not by the inculcation of radical falsehood (VII.ii.4.14). Smith's analysis applies to moral philosophy constituted by investigation into the "nature and origin of our moral sentiments," but not to teleological or theological theories, which can speak more authoritatively about good and evil. Smith intimates the novelty of his definition of moral philosophy. Part VII is entitled "Of Systems of Moral Philosophy," but in the body of the chapter, Smith immediately replaces "moral philosophy" with "theory of moral sentiments." Smith also has to strain to represent all previous moral philosophers as purveyors of a "system"; he himself praises Cicero and Aristotle for proceeding unsystematically (VII.iv.5–6).

Several objections may be leveled at Smith's procedure in Part VII. First, some of the writers he explicates (Plato, Aristotle, and Epicurus) engage in a kind of moral philosophy that transcends theorizing about the "nature and origin" of moral sentiments. Second, Smith's analysis is radically ahistorical. Smith indicates that Part VII takes up "the most celebrated and remarkable" moral theories (VII.i.1). By placing them side by side, Smith implies that moral philosophy from Plato to Smith is essentially the same enterprise; he appears to ignore the ancient/modern split so prominent in *The Wealth of Nations*;[22] he includes no distinctly Christian, Jewish, or Islamic version among "the most celebrated and remarkable" theories. Smith goes so far as to claim that "every system of morality that ever had any reputation in the world has, perhaps, ultimately been derived" from the principles he has presented. Thus, all the systems are "founded upon natural principles"; they differ and err insofar as they derive "from a partial and imperfect view of nature" (*TMS* VII.i.1); even though Smith initially condemns the "licentious" system of Mandeville as "wholly pernicious," he later concedes that it "in some respects bordered on the truth."[23] One may infer that revelation-based "systems" are excluded from consideration because they fail to bow before nature. Although everyone agrees that obeying the Deity's will is the "first rule of duty," people differ widely in specifying the "particular commandments" the Deity has imposed (III.6.12). Smith ignores the revealed will of God, and in its place tries to constitute nature as a united moral front: hence the eclecticism of Part VII. Surely morality as conveyed in the Bible—or in the works of Augustine, Aquinas, Luther, and Calvin—bears little resemblance to a "theory of moral sentiments." That Smith's whole attempt to reconstitute moral philosophy as moral psychology has an anti-Christian animus is further suggested by the fact that whereas consideration of ancient thinkers dominates Smith's account of the first question (What qualities count as virtues?), the ancients are absent from his account of the second question: What internal "contrivance or mechanism" generates moral judgments? On Smith's presentation, the abstract science of human nature is a post-Christian and perhaps even an anti-Christian phenomenon.

Smith casts the ancient/modern issue in yet a new light in the conclusion of the book, when he returns from the principles of approbation to the content of morality as embodied in "practical Rules." Smith distinguishes two approaches. The ancients wrote like critics, employing a "loose method" and therefore not providing a "complete system."[24] The "exact" or precise approach, analogous to that of the grammarian, is in turn represented by two schools, Christian casuistry and natural jurisprudence. Only casuistry is rejected. The casuist goal was "to prescribe rules for the conduct of a good man" (VII.iv.8); Smith's criticism is that the casuists tried futilely "to direct by precise rules what it belongs to feeling and sentiment only to judge of" (33); the impartial spectator is thus a direct substitute for the casuists' rules (VII.ii.1.22). Smith extols the ancients' ability to inspire virtue; they "inflame our natural love of virtue" and "may often help us both to correct and to ascertain our natural sentiments"; this approach does "whatever precept and exhortation can do to animate us to the practice of virtue" (VII.iv.6), presumably eclipsing the effects of prophetic exhortation. The endorsement is perhaps softened, however, in light of the general limits to what "precept and exhortation" can accomplish, as Smith hints a few pages earlier.[25] Be this as it may, we are left with praise of a pagan approach and criticism of a Christian approach; praise of passion, criticism of "rules."

Religion and Natural Jurisprudence

Although the ancients as presented by Smith in the final chapter are not in any way supplanted by Christian casuistry, their approach does ultimately come to light as incomplete when contrasted with the second school of precise or systematic morality, natural jurisprudence. "Ethics," the ancient approach, and jurisprudence remain the "two useful parts of moral philosophy," as opposed to casuistry, which "ought to be rejected altogether" (*TMS* VII.iv.34). Because it is third in the series, one wonders about the degree to which jurisprudence, like the "abstract science of human nature," is an essentially post-Christian phenomenon. Natural jurisprudence is an inquiry into "the natural rules of justice independent of all positive institutions"; it attempts to provide "a theory of the general principles which ought to run through and be the foundation of the laws of all nations." Smith laments that "it was very late in the world before any such general system was thought of, or before the philosophy of law was treated of by itself, and without regard to the particular institutions of any one nation" (VII.iv.37). Most biblical law, of course, is emphatically the law of a "particular . . . nation." One suspects, moreover, that treating "the philosophy of law . . . by itself" entails treating it free of God and revelation, free of divine law. Smith's whole corpus is indebted to Montesquieu's quest for the spirit/mind of the law as a replacement for divine and even natural law. Unlike the legislator of Plato and even Rousseau, the legislator of Smith and Montesquieu need not present himself as an agent of God: Smith completely severs the link between God and law. In removing God and prophecy, Smith also removes comprehensive human legislating and the quest for the best regime. Smith turns Montesquieu into a science or system, with help from political economy, the "abstract science of human nature" (as perfected by Hume), and Grotius.

Although Smith praises Grotius as the pioneer of jurisprudence, Grotius displays vastly more deference than does Smith to Christianity and the Bible (the contrast between Smith and Pufendorf is equally dramatic). Grotius provides detailed discussions of biblical law, and acknowledges biblical events and concepts that Smith minimizes or erases: Adam and Eve, the Flood, Babel, the Decalogue, prophecy, miracles, oaths, Providence, repentance, sin, Jesus, the Sermon on the Mount, charity, the Resurrection, and eternal life. Despite his frequent invocations of the Bible, however, it is not clear that Grotius regards the Bible as authoritative, as the revealed will of God. In the spirit of Smith's call for examining law "by itself," Grotius labors hard to remedy the treatment of the law of war by "doctors of law" and theologians, who "intermingle and utterly confuse what belongs to the law of nature, to divine law, to the law of nations, to civil law, and to the body of law which is found in the canons."[26] These writers, being insufficiently touched by the "illumination of history" (*Proleg.*, 38), perhaps failed to realize that the eras of ancient Greece and Rome were "better times" and their citizens "better peoples" (46). Cicero is the first and last authority cited in the work.

Grotius is well known for alleging that his approach to law—perhaps especially his emphasis on life, property, and contracts (what Smith calls "mere justice")—would possess validity even if there were no God or if God lacked concern for human affairs. Although Grotius states that these suppositions "cannot be conceded without the utmost wickedness" (*summo scelere*), he does not insist that they are false or suggest that they could only be believed by the wicked (*Proleg.*, 11). Perhaps the essence of Grotius's claim is that wickedness would run rampant in the absence of faith. Grotius argues vigorously for religion's civic utility, and sketches four self-evident principles that ground "true religion, which is the same at all periods and times."[27] Perhaps he hoped that his pioneering emphasis on property at the expense of virtue and the regime would help temper the religious persecution and warfare so prominent during his times.[28]

As we have seen, Smithian laws are intended to secure life, property, and contracts, not virtue or piety. In building his science of natural jurisprudence and his account of governmental duties upon the quasi-materialistic four-stages theory, Smith supplants divine revelation and Thomistic natural law along with ancient philosophical dialectics and modern theories of the social contract.[29] Smith faults ancient ethics, such as Cicero's *Offices* and Aristotle's *Ethics*, because it failed to investigate justice with the heightened precision that distinguishes justice from the other virtues (*TMS* VII.iv.37, III.6.10–11). In Smith's account, precision was introduced to moral philosophy by Christian casuistry, but found its proper home in jurisprudence. Smith's sciences adopt and augment the precision of casuistry, but they promulgate "rules" of systems rather than rules of commanders (divine or human). Smith introduces the conspicuously technical material of *The Wealth of Nations* to explain "the rules which men naturally observe" in exchanging commodities (*WN* I.iv.12): nature's rules, i.e., the natural order, replace laws that are willed.[30]

Perhaps Christianity also contributed to the universal, trans-political orientation that would enable Smithian jurisprudence to supplant ancient approaches and to overcome Montesquieu's insistence on the irreducible diversity of regimes, climates, and *moeurs*. In *The Theory of Moral Sentiments*, Smith explicitly makes benevolence the supreme virtue and reveals the Christian roots of this doctrine. We proceed now to examine how the book incorporates and modifies Christian doctrine and borrows from Christian psychology.

God, Conscience, and the Impartial Spectator

The Impartial Spectator as Substitute

Smith identifies the impartial spectator with the conscience (*TMS* III.2.32, III.3.4) and substitutes it for casuist (VI.ii.1.22), God, and priest. As we have seen, in the second through the fifth edition, Smith identifies the impartial spectator as "the substitute of the Deity." Although this passage was removed from the final edition, it adequately conveys the tone of the whole book. The impartial spectator is the voice of the "ideal man within the breast" (III.3.26), not the voice of God. A human being's greatest desire is to act in such a manner that "the impartial spectator may enter into the principles of his conduct" (II.ii.2.1), not to act in a manner pleasing to God. To live well, it seems, we need not God but the impartial spectator: no one "ever trod steadily and uniformly in the paths" of virtue "whose conduct was not principally directed by a regard to the sentiments of the supposed impartial spectator, . . . the great judge and arbiter of conduct" (VI.Conc.1).[31] Indeed, "if we place ourselves completely in his situation" and "listen with diligence and reverential attention . . . his voice will never deceive us" (VI.ii.1.22). The impartial spectator is apparently untainted by original sin.

A person who grew up lacking contact with other people would only experience the sentiment of approbation that derives from "utility," from the likely effects of his actions on his "happiness or disadvantage." He would possess these weak sentiments of taste rather than the strong sentiments of propriety and merit because the latter "suppose the idea of some other being, who is the natural judge of the person that feels them" (*TMS* IV.2.12). Human moral psychology is thus the breeding ground for religion in more ways than one: God can be interpreted as an exaggerated version of a quasi-natural phenomenon, the impartial spectator. Smith of course prefers a spectating God to an intrusive God. But his theory of our "natural sentiments," by so thoroughly explaining the human moral experience in social terms, allows man rather than God to reign supreme as the "natural judge"; the different claims to human virtue are adjudicated before a human judge.[32]

Smith, however, does not sever the connection between religion and morality: he refers to the impartial spectator as the "demigod within the breast" (III.2.32, VI.iii.18,25). This element of transcendence surely provides morality with a rhetorical boost, compensating for the implied inadequacy of enlightened self-interest.[33] Morality for Smith retains its character as a struggle or ascent. Thus, the individual who looks beyond the judgments of other people to those of the impartial spectator, the magnanimous individual "who desires virtue for its own sake," acts from "the most sublime and godlike motive which human nature is even capable of conceiving" (VII.ii.4.10).[34] Smith allows, moreover, the appeal not only from actual human judgment to the impartial spectator, from praise to the praiseworthy, but from the impartial spectator to God. Because the "demigod within the breast" is "partly . . . of mortal extraction," the impartial spectator, though constitutive of "our natural sense of praise-worthiness and blame-worthiness," may be overcome by "the vehemence and clamour of the man without" (III.2.32). The virtuous will thus appeal beyond the sphere of praise and blame, but they cannot simply transcend it because the impartial spectator, unlike God, derives from it; this dependence presumably constitutes the "mortal" side of the impartial spectator's genealogy. It is precisely the condemned innocent who can only be consoled by an appeal beyond the impartial spectator to God. Smith's discussion of these matters culminates with his stunning depiction of the virtuous person's need to believe in an afterlife where people will be judged according to their real worthiness (III.2.33). The "great judge" (III.3.4, VI.Conc.1) thus falls short of the "great Judge" (II.iii.3.2, III.3.43) or the "all-seeing Judge" (III.2.12, III.2.33).

In the other set of references to the impartial spectator as a "demigod" (added for the final edition), Smith likewise flirts with transcendence: "the great demigod within the breast" is responsible for the construction of "the idea of exact propriety and perfection" (VI.iii.25). That this demigod operates without revelation is indicated first by Smith's claim that such an idea "exists in the mind of every man," formed gradually from his observations of others (25). In estimating their own merit, people "naturally" (i.e., without revelation) appeal both to "the idea of exact propriety and perfection" and to the standard of what is "commonly attained in the world" (23).[35] Smith's subsequent remarks, however, highlight the resemblances between moral and religious striving. The "wisest and best of us," insofar as we look to the higher standard, "see nothing but weakness and imperfection; can discover no ground for arrogance and presumption, but a great deal for humility, regret and repentance" (24). The wise and virtuous individual strives continuously to imitate the "divine artist" by delineating and achieving "this archetype of perfection" (25). Smith of course says nothing to suggest that divine grace could help the wise, the virtuous, or the "impartial" to overcome their limitations.

The impartial spectator replaces the priest along with God, conscience, and casuistry. As we have seen, Smith traces the "abstract science of human nature" to Hobbes's attempt to liberate human consciences from "ecclesiastical powers" (VII.iii.2.2,5). But Smith does not explain how these powers exerted their hold over the conscience until the concluding section of the book, in his discussion of casuistry:

> What seems principally to have given occasion to the cultivation of this species of science was the custom of auricular confession, introduced by the Roman Catholic superstition, in times of barbarism and ignorance. (*TMS* VII.iv.16)[36]

In explaining the impact of casuistry and confession, Smith reveals the psycho-social groundwork for his own theory of moral sentiments. In confession, people reveal to the priest secret actions and thoughts that might deviate from "the rules of Christian purity." In determining the penance necessary to "absolve them in the name of the offended Deity" (VII.iv.16), the priest discharges an invaluable psychic function:

> The consciousness, or even the suspicion of having done wrong, is a load upon every mind, and is accompanied with anxiety and terror in all those who are not hardened by long habits of iniquity. Men, in this, as in all other distresses, are naturally eager to disburthen themselves of the oppression which they feel upon their thoughts, by unbosoming the agony of their mind to some person whose secrecy and discretion they can confide in. (*TMS* VII.iv.17)

The natural and worldly phenomenon of guilt is thus the foundation of confession. Smith specifies that what balances the shame from the confession is the pleasure brought by the priest's sympathy; such sympathy makes people feel "that they are not altogether unworthy of regard." A "numerous and artful clergy" thus "insinuated themselves into the confidence of almost every private family." Being learned and well-mannered by the standards of "those times of superstition," the clergy came to be regarded as "the great directors" of moral duties (VII.iv.17). In referring to the penance necessary to absolve parishioners "in the name of the offended Deity," Smith characteristically suggests his distance from Christian doctrine. A believer would presumably say that priests absolved "in the name of God" or perhaps "in the name of the Deity, who had been offended." As it stands, the Christian God is just a particular "offended Deity."[37]

A few paragraphs later, Smith (in the final edition) added a digression on what could be dubbed the human propensity to believe. This digression elaborates the fusion of politics and religion so prominent in the religion Article of *The Wealth of Nations* and completes Smith's secular explanation of Christianity's triumphs. Although "the wisest and most experienced" people are generally the least credulous, there is scarcely a man "who is not more credulous than he ought to be" and who therefore often believes "tales, which not only turn out to be perfectly false, but which a very moderate degree of reflection and attention might have taught him could not well be true" (*TMS* VII.iv.23).[38] The political dimension is indicated by Smith's argument that the man whom we believe becomes, with respect to the matters in question, "our leader and director." In *The Wealth of Nations*, Smith elaborates the political (and economic) roots of clerical motivation. In *The Theory of Moral Sentiments*, he suggests that the clergy's success in propagating "tales" can be understood in terms of the "natural disposition . . . to believe" (VII.iv.23).

But perhaps the ultimate foundation of their power is the "anxiety and terror" human beings experience when they do wrong. Throughout *The Theory of Moral Sentiments*, Smith explains this anxiety and terror in secular terms, as reflecting a fear of human beings rather than of God. In fact, Smith's theory of moral sentiments appropriates the psychological lessons regarding both love and fear that can be gleaned from a secular explanation of Christianity's success.

Love

The twin passions of love and fear were central to Machiavelli's analysis of politics, but Smith departs from Machiavelli in elevating love over fear. One might say that Smith revives Christian love against its disparagement in the political philosophy of Machiavelli and many of his successors, notably Hobbes, Spinoza, and Mandeville. The most striking contrast on this score between Smith's two books is occasioned not by the thematic prominence in *The Theory of Moral Sentiments* of sympathy and fellow feeling, but by the insistence that the experience of these sentiments is constitutive of human fulfillment. In light of *The Wealth of Nations*, the rhetoric on behalf of love in *The Theory of Moral Sentiments* is shocking: "Nothing pleases us more" than observing in others "a fellow-feeling with all the emotions of our own breast" (*TMS* I.i.2.1); a human creature's "most agreeable hope, and . . . most ardent desire" is "to be observed, to be attended to, to be taken notice of with sympathy, complacency, and approbation" (I.iii.2.1); the "chief part of human happiness" comes from the "consciousness of being beloved" (I.ii.5.1); the generous and just man can look forward to "cheerfulness, serenity, and composure" because of his "friendship and harmony with all mankind" (II.ii.2.4); Epicurus failed to understand that the sentiments incited in other people by our virtues are the objects of a "much more passionate desire or aversion" than are the other consequences of being virtuous (VII.ii.2.12).

It is passages such as these, coupled with the book's related praise of benevolence, that provoked investigation of an "Adam Smith Problem." Even if careful analysis reveals no simple contradiction between the two books, there remains a change of emphasis that has been inadequately explained by contemporary scholars who deny the existence of the "Problem." These scholars have likewise neglected the religious angle. From a Christian point of view, our greatest "hope" and "desire" are for being approved of, noticed, observed, "attended" to, and loved by God, not by human beings. In *The Theory of Moral Sentiments*, the need for human love replaces the need for God's love, just as in *The Wealth of*

Nations the social utility of religion is reduced to the moral benefits available to the common people who belong to small sects, in which conduct and character are "observed and attended to" (*WN* V.i.g.12). According to *The Theory of Moral Sentiments*, esteem and love are perhaps the prime support—both motive and reward—for virtue. Recall that Epicurus, in emphasizing the contributions virtue makes to the individual's ease, safety, and advantage, incorporated the esteem virtue generates. By making esteem not only intrinsically desirable but also the overriding end, Smith can complement the Epicurean virtues ("caution, vigilance, sobriety and judicious moderation") integral to *The Wealth of Nations* with the "great," "awful," and "respectable" virtues emphasized by the ancient propriety-based systems, and with the "soft," "amiable," and "gentle" virtues (benevolence, humanity, charity, love) emphasized by the modern merit-based systems.[39] Smith's transcendence of Epicurus, moreover, is ultimately effected within the confines (suitably masked) of materialism, hedonism, and atheism. Smith departs from the ancients in a Christian direction by according such high status to *caritas* and by rejecting the superiority of the detached life of the philosopher.

It might seem that the exalted status of human love in *The Theory of Moral Sentiments* results from the abandonment of a divine love allegedly available to every human being,[40] as if a substitute were needed for the hunger whetted by the Christian promise. Smith proffers human love as a counterweight to several things: Christian promises of divine love and eternal life, the immorality of Epicurus and Machiavelli, and worldly ambition generally.[41] For human love to discharge this far-reaching responsibility, Smith must appeal beyond actual esteem first to the hypothetical esteem of the impartial spectator and ultimately, on behalf of the innocent person subjected to widespread condemnation, to the afterlife. Smith emphasizes horizontal transcendence—appeal to the impartial spectator, who is but "the representative of mankind"—rather than the vertical transcendence to God, to the superhuman. Smith's "wise man," like Plato's philosopher, transcends the praise and blame of "the many," but only by appealing to a moderately enlightened version of their praise and blame. In *The Wealth of Nations*, love and the non-Epicurean virtues (along with happiness, tranquillity, and the noble) recede in importance, permitting Smith to abandon God and the afterlife.

Fear

Fear of God plays a minimal role in *The Theory of Moral Sentiments*. In the *Essays*, Smith attributes polytheism to the fear and insecurity that pervade primitive life. Theism emerged along with greater security as the natural order became more apparent. Smith in *The Theory of Moral Sentiments* reiterates the connection of fear, superstition, and primitive society (III.5.4), and the book as a whole gives not the slightest indication that we have anything to fear (or to hope for) from God in this life. Smith explains both the origin and the utility of the fear of punishment after death, but he scarcely indulges it (III.5.10). The utility is not hard to see:

> The idea that, however we may escape the observation of man or be placed above the reach of human punishment, yet we are always acting under the eye, and exposed to the punishment of God, the great avenger of injustice, is a motive capable of restraining the most headstrong passions. (*TMS* III.5.12)

The afterlife is for Smith an "idea," not a reality. The passage that most indulges the human sense of deserving and expecting divine punishment was removed for the final edition.[42] Anticipating the Kantian moral law, Smith departs from the likes of Machiavelli, Hobbes, Spinoza, Mandeville, and Hume in struggling to bolster the individual's reverent regard for the welfare of others.

Fear of human beings partially fills the breach left by the removal of the fear of God. Unlike Machiavelli, however, Smith presents this fear as natural rather than the product of political manipulation, and as a wholehearted ally of morality. Smith could hardly give more sway to the fear experienced as a result of acting immorally. The person who violates "the more sacred laws of justice," when he considers what other people would feel in response, will experience "all the agonies of shame, and horror, and consternation"; even "his own thoughts can present him with nothing but what is black, unfortunate, and disastrous, the melancholy forebodings of incomprehensible misery and ruin." Such "remorse" is "the most dreadful sentiment" that a human being can experience. Smith's analysis of remorse is subtle and complex:

> It is made up of shame from the sense of the impropriety of past conduct; of grief for the effects of it; of pity for those who suffer by it; and of the dread and terror of punishment from the consciousness of the justly-provoked resentment of all rational creatures. (*TMS* II.ii.2.3; cf. II.iii.2.5)

The shame, grief, and pity, one suspects, would not create unbearable agony without the fear of punishment that, as it were, gives them teeth. But without fear of the God who cannot be deceived and who threatens eternal torment, can we expect that such a level of horror will consistently accompany injustice? Smith tries to convince us that the impartial spectator will suffice. Doing something despicable will lead a person to misery even if "he should have the most perfect assurance that what he had done was for ever to be concealed from every human eye." Looking back upon his action, such a person adopts the perspective of the impartial spectator and thus feels "abashed," "confounded," and ashamed. If his crime were really enormous,

> he could never think of it, as long as he had any sensibility left, without feeling all the agony of horror and remorse; and though he could be assured that no man was ever to know it, and could even bring himself to believe that there was no God to revenge it, he would still feel enough of both these sentiments to embitter the whole of his life. . . . These natural pangs of an affrighted conscience are the daemons, the avenging furies, which, in this life, haunt the guilty. (*TMS* III.2.9)

Smith admits, however, that the person whose heart had "grown callous by the habit of crimes," who showed "a complete insensibility to honour and infamy, to vice and virtue," might be immune from the avenging furies (III.2.9,11).

Perhaps the biggest problem for Smith's position is the Machiavellian one, nicely restated by Locke:

> Great robbers punish little ones to keep them in their obedience, but the great ones are rewarded with laurels and triumphs, because they are too big for the weak hands of justice in this world. (*Second Treatise*, sec. 176)

A few sentences after the sole mention of Machiavelli in *The Theory of Moral Sentiments*, Smith observes that "the violence and injustice of great conquerors are often regarded with foolish wonder and admiration; those of petty thieves, robbers, and murderers, with contempt, hatred, and even horror upon all occasions" (VI.i.16).[43] Because Smith, like Machiavelli, appears to deny the existence of an omniscient, omnipotent, and punishing God, he must beware providing encouragement to Machiavellian "princes."

Smith's fullest analysis of the problem comes earlier:

> In many governments the candidates for the highest stations are above the law; and, if they can attain the object of their ambition, they have no fear of being called to account for the means by which they acquired it. They often endeavour, therefore, not only by fraud and falsehood, the ordinary and vulgar arts of intrigue and cabal; but sometimes by the perpetration of the most enormous crimes . . . to supplant and destroy those who oppose or stand in the way of their greatness. (*TMS* I.iii.3.8)

Smith here acknowledges the tendency but tries to combat it, first by pointing out that such attempts usually fail, and second by arguing that even if they succeed, honor is "polluted and defiled by the baseness of the means." The man in question may attempt, "by the hurry of public business, or by the prouder and more dazzling tumult of war" to "efface . . . the remembrance of what he has done," but the attempt will fail:

> Amidst all the pride of conquest and the triumph of successful war, he is still secretly pursued by the avenging furies of shame and remorse; and, while glory seems to surround him on all sides, he himself, in his own imagination, sees black and foul infamy fast pursuing him, and every moment ready to overtake him from behind. (*TMS* I.iii.3.8)

Smith's moral theory combats the Machiavellian temptation by upgrading the human need for love and esteem, by identifying happiness with tranquillity, and by arguing that happiness is easy to achieve; he mixes in vestiges of biblical perspectives and much strenuous rhetoric of his own on behalf of morality. These weapons are largely absent from *The Wealth of Nations*; their place is taken by *homo economicus*, bettering one's condition, and the sobering rhetoric of political economy.

Ancients and Moderns Revisited

Smith explicitly contrasts ancient and modern in categorizing the virtues. Of the three specifications of the content of virtue addressed in Part VII—propriety, benevolence, and prudence—Smith clearly treats the Epicurean system based on prudence as rhetorically useful but morally inferior to the other two (*TMS* VII.ii.4.4–5). Although the chapter expounding propriety systems concludes by mentioning the "modern" versions articulated by Clarke, Wollaston, and Shaftesbury (VII.ii.1.48–49), the chapter is dominated by Plato, Aristotle, and the Stoics; Smith later simply identifies the propriety systems as "ancient" (VII.ii.4.2). The non-Epicurean ancients thus emphasize the "great," "awful," and "respectable" virtues: self-command, fortitude, magnanimity, "the contempt of all outward accidents, of pain, poverty, exile, and death" (VII.ii.4.2). The benevolent systems are evidently post-Christian, beginning with Neoplatonists "about and after the age of Augustus" and continuing with "many ancient fathers of the Christian church" and several post-Reformation "divines of the most eminent piety and learning."[44] Smith characterizes the virtues emphasized by these systems as the "soft," "amiable," and "gentle" virtues: benevolence, humanity, charity, "kindness and general love towards those we live with" (VII.ii.4.2,5).[45]

This bifurcation of the virtues has its roots in the two chief sources of approbation and disapprobation, the sense of propriety and the sense of merit (I.i.3.5–7). The sense of propriety is the foundation for the virtues derived from the agent's toning down his own sentiments in order to facilitate sympathy. These virtues comprise "the great, the awful and respectable, the virtues of self-denial, of self government, of that command of the passions which subjects all the movements of our nature to what our own dignity and honour, and the propriety of our own conduct require." The sense of merit is the foundation of the virtues derived from the spectator's efforts to enter the actor's sentiments (i.e., to "sympathize" with the actor): "the soft, the gentle, the amiable virtues, the virtues of candid condescension and indulgent humanity" (I.i.5.1). Smith continues with his well-known claim that "to feel much for others and little for ourselves, . . . to restrain our selfish, and to indulge our benevolent affections, constitutes the perfection of human nature (I.i.5.5). The two categories of virtue seem to be on a par. But the picture becomes more complex when Smith introduces Christianity: "As to love our neighbour as we love ourselves is the great law of Christianity, so it is the great precept of nature to love ourselves only as we love our neighbour" (I.i.5.5). That is, Christian benevolence requires us to elevate our love for our neighbor; the ancient systems of propriety require us to lower our concern for ourselves. Happily, both revelation and nature combat human selfishness, but not with equal efficacy. Smith tentatively identifies "the great law . . . dictated to us by Nature" as "retaliation" (II.ii.1.10); because of his later ridicule of "our Saviour's precept"—turning the other cheek (III.6.13)—it is clear that regarding retaliation he sides with nature rather than Christianity. Smith of course acknowledges neither the grace that perfects nature nor the distinction between original and fallen nature.

With respect to loving one's neighbor, which he identifies as Christianity's "great law," Smith's departure is less pronounced. There are, however, many indications of a departure. For example, Smith states:

> Every man is, no doubt, by nature, first and principally recommended to his own care; and as he is fitter to take care of himself than of any other person, it is fit and right that it should be so. (*TMS* II.ii.2.1)

We must wonder first whether nature's "great precept" (to love oneself only as one loves one's neighbor) meshes with nature's allowing each to tend "first and principally" to himself; nature's imperative may be farther from Christianity's than it earlier appeared to be. But Smith here goes beyond describing nature's imperative to judging it as "fit and right." Given Smith's rejection of the Christian God, of course, one would not expect him to maintain Christian benevolence in an unadulterated form. Smith acknowledges the connection between the "first precept" of Christianity—"to love the Lord our God with all our heart, with all our soul, and with all our might"—and the second, "to love our neighbour as we love ourselves" (III.6.1).[46] Both precepts are clearly abandoned in *The*

Wealth of Nations; in *The Theory of Moral Sentiments*, the love of God is muted and the second precept is diluted with admixtures of Stoicism and Epicureanism, if not Hobbes and Mandeville.

Smith occasionally intimates reservations about even nature's precept that we "love ourselves only as we love our neighbour." Smith appropriates nature for his own theory of the impartial spectator, producing a synthesis of Christian benevolence and Stoic "apathy"; at times he seems to favor one, at times the other, though his harshest language is reserved for Christianity. From his point of view, however, both go too far in attempting to equalize concern for self and other. The impartial spectator is the solution: "It is only by consulting this judge within . . . that we can ever make any proper comparison between our own interests and those of other people" (III.3.1). The impartial spectator does what the "feeble spark of benevolence" cannot; it teaches the individual that he is "but one of the multitude, in no respect better than any other"; only the impartial spectator can show us "the real littleness of ourselves" (III.3.4). This lesson taught by the impartial spectator replaces Christian equality before God as well as the natural equality derived by Hobbes, Locke, and Rousseau from the "state of nature." Smith's theory requires neither divine revelation nor the social contract. The "man within" who enables us to look at ourselves as others see us—and who thereby makes it possible for "the natural misrepresentations of self-love" to be "corrected" (III.3.4)—emerges automatically if not inevitably from the interaction between us and the man without.[47] As depicted by Smith, people generally (and consequently the impartial spectator) allow an individual that degree of self-preference associated with liberalism: in "the race for wealth, and honours, and preferments," an individual may run "as hard as he can" within the limits of "fair play" (II.ii.2.1).

Smith proceeds to elaborate a thesis implicit in this passage: that nature programs human beings as liberals rather than as Stoics or Christians. Smith's theory ingeniously incorporates the discrepancy between "our passive feelings" and "our active principles." The former embody a gross selfishness: whereas a humane European's anticipation of losing his little finger would produce a sleepless night, "he would snore with the most profound security" despite the death of a hundred million Chinese in an earthquake. But would this man sacrifice the Chinese to save his finger? "Human nature startles with horror at the thought, and the world, in its greatest depravity and corruption, never produced such a villain as could be capable of entertaining it" (III.3.4).[48] Given the lack of emotional concern for the unknown Chinese, it is not benevolence that prevents their sacrifice. It is, rather, the impartial spectator—"reason, principle, conscience, the inhabitant of the breast, the man within, the great judge and arbiter of our conduct"—who intrudes "whenever we are about to act so as to affect the happiness of others" to remind us that "we are but one of the multitude" (III.3.4). The key here is that selfishness is combated in the sphere of action rather than feeling.[49] Without "the great Judge of hearts" (II.iii.3.2–3) to inspire and enforce it, benevolence cannot bear the weight assigned to it by Christianity. Smith concludes his discussion of the earthquake by characterizing the operative remedy for self-love as "the love of what is honourable and noble, of the grandeur, and dignity, and superiority of our own characters" (III.3.4). He resorts to pagan magnanimity rather than to the Bible.

He proceeds, however, to imply the superiority of his own theory of the impartial spectator to both Christian and ancient doctrines. He refers to "two different sets of philosophers" who have tried "to teach us this hardest of all the lessons of morality," namely, to "correct the inequalities of our passive feelings."

> One set have laboured to increase our sensibility to the interests of others; another, to diminish that to our own. The first would have us feel for others as we naturally feel for ourselves. The second would have us feel for ourselves as we naturally feel for others. Both, perhaps, have carried their doctrines a good deal beyond the just standard of nature and propriety. (*TMS* III.3.7–8)

As is evident from our discussion above (of *TMS* I.i.5.5), the first is Christian and the second ancient. Smith identifies the second as "all the ancient sects of philosophers," especially the Stoics (III.3.11), but he leaves the first anonymous. His silence about Christianity is perhaps occasioned by the nasty evaluation that unfolds. He mentions Pascal in a footnote as an example of "those whining and melancholy moralists, who are perpetually reproaching us with our happiness, while so many of our brethren are in misery." Smith offers several arguments against this view. The first is that, taking "the whole earth at an average, for one man who suffers pain or misery, you will find twenty in prosperity and joy, or at least in tolerable circumstances" (III.3.9).

The spirit of these "whining and melancholy moralists" is surely akin to the monastic "penance and mortification" Smith denounces in *The Wealth of Nations* and the "melancholy and gloomy humour" identified there as the "nurse of popular superstition and enthusiasm." Especially in *The Theory of Moral Sentiments*, Smith presents a world far brighter than the vale of tears. In his thematic treatment of the non-Epicurean ancients, Smith says that "the spirit and manhood of their doctrines make a wonderful contrast with the desponding, plaintive, and whining tone of some modern systems." This praise refers specifically to ancient attempts to belittle such evils as poverty, banishment, blindness, deafness, old age, death, pain, torture, and sickness,[50] and calls to mind the "ancient" ideal—"the liberal, generous, and spirited conduct of a man"— that Smith briefly extols at the expense of monasticism (*WN* V.i.f.30).

Smith thus prefers ancient manliness to Christian whining: he prefers nature's law (decrease concern for oneself) to Christianity's (increase love for one's neighbor). But as we have seen, the ancient approach too is flawed: "Both, perhaps, have carried their doctrines a good deal beyond the just standard of nature and propriety" (*TMS* III.3.8). Although Stoic severity is a useful counterpoise to monasticism, its annihilation of individuality is ultimately too severe. According to the Stoics, the individual "ought to regard himself, not as something separated and detached, but as a citizen of the world, a member of the vast commonwealth of nature" (III.3.11).[51] The Stoics err especially in not recognizing the propriety of giving special consideration to family and friends, although it is often appropriate for the individual to exhibit "stoical apathy and indifference" toward his own concerns (III.3.13,16). As Smith spells out in his comprehensive discussion of Stoicism in Part VII, the Stoics too quickly ascend from our individual concerns to contemplate "that benevolent wisdom which directs all the events of human life"; they try "to eradicate all our private, partial, and selfish affections," not simply to moderate them by means of the impartial spectator.[52] That is, the Stoics combat selfishness by a vertical transcendence to God and the cosmos; Smith combats it primarily by a horizontal transcendence to the human spectator.

Smith's broadest evaluation of the Stoics is quite critical: "The plan and system which Nature has sketched out for our conduct, seems to be *altogether* different from that of the Stoical philosophy" (*TMS* VII.ii.1.43). This degree of rejection is surprising for a number of reasons: Smith identifies propriety and the impartial spectator as central Stoic concepts (VII.ii.1.20–21); the private vice–public benefit thesis derives from the Stoic view of Providence (I.ii.3.4); *The Theory of Moral Sentiments* is pervaded by quasi-Stoic statements about the "benevolent wisdom" of the whole;[53] and Smith pays more attention to the Stoics than to any other philosophers. Does Smith flirt with Stoicism to temper his rejection of Christianity?[54] In the fight against Christianity, Smith is able to employ potent Stoic rhetoric against selfishness (VII.ii.1.20) while allowing self-preference: "Every man, as the Stoics used to say, is first and principally recommended to his own care" (VI.ii.1.1).[55] Smith draws on the Stoics, not Christianity, to encourage resignation to the unavoidable ills of this world (III.3.30–31). The Christian version is too otherworldly and therefore monastic; the Stoics dispense with the afterlife and are therefore manly, but they are too oriented toward cosmic Providence.[56] The Christian stakes are too high, which produces fanaticism; the Stoic stakes are too low, which produces "apathy." Severed from Providence, Smith's Stoicism ultimately takes the form of bourgeois virtue (III.3.16,31).

We have seen that Smith links manliness and worldliness in the fight against monasticism. His praise of manliness is accompanied by praise of *thymos* and pride that is anti-Christian in spirit. In choosing between pagan pride and biblical humility, Smith comes down on the side of the ancients: "In almost all cases, it is better to be a little too proud, than, in any respect, too humble" (VII.iii.52).[57] In defending *thymos* and regard for one's "rank and dignity,"[58] Smith departs from Hobbes as well as Christianity. Smith comments on the kinship between pride and the "magnanimity" of Aristotle, a philosopher who "certainly knew the world" (*TMS* VI.iii.44), i.e., this world. Smith quotes from *Hamlet* to illustrate that the proud man dies "with all his sins upon his head" (45), evoking Smith's praise of Hume's notoriously unrepentant death.[59] In *The Theory of Moral Sentiments*, Smith never in his own name refers to sin. Apart from the *Hamlet* quotation, Smith refers only to "what in their [the casuists'] language are called the sins of concupiscence" (VII.iv.32), and Smith is no fan of the casuists. When Smith says that "the great secret of education is to direct vanity to proper objects" (VI.iii.46), he splashes Christian humility with the cold water of Mandeville.[60]

Smith, of course, does not simply dismiss Christian humility: the impartial spectator shows us the "real littleness of ourselves." But this means the littleness of the individual, not of "the multitude" (III.3.4). The individual must bow before his fellows, but the species need not abase itself before God. Smith here resembles Hobbes. The biblical Leviathan was "the king of the proud," portrayed by God in order to humble Job; Hobbes's Leviathan-sovereign is necessary to tame the pride of glory-seeking individuals. Although the book as a whole proffers the human Leviathan in place of God, with man as maker displacing God as Creator, Hobbesian individuals must ultimately abandon another form of pride: being made in the image of God and possessing a higher dignity than inanimate nature, plants, and animals. For Hobbes, life is "but a motion of limbs" and human behavior is explicable by the physics of "appetites and aversions." By rejecting ancient teleological views that structure a hierarchy of man and beast (*TMS* I.ii.1.3), Smith too discourages us from gloating about our superiority to non-human life.[61] Both Smith and Hobbes nevertheless encourage us to *exercise* our superior rationality in procuring "commodious living" by means of "necessaries, conveniencies, and amusements."

Smith makes further concessions to Christian humility. The equality taught by the impartial spectator requires a softening of Aristotle's crowning virtue of magnanimity, built on the sense of deserved superiority.[62] Shame and remorse are therefore much elevated in comparison to Aristotle's *Ethics*, in which shame is explicitly excluded from the list of moral virtues.[63] The greater egalitarianism of *The Theory of Moral Sentiments* perhaps also contributes to the de-emphasis (though clearly not the abandonment) of the distinction between noble and base, and to Smith's confidence that nature can teach virtue without significant assistance from law, training, and formal education. In the name of equality, moreover, Smith seems to reject the ancients' exaltation of the philosopher. Smith translates Plato's *sophia* as "prudence" (VII.ii.3.6), not wisdom, and asserts that "the most sublime speculation of the contemplative philosopher can scarce compensate the neglect of the smallest active duty" (VI.ii.1.6). Smith nevertheless preserves elements of the ancient view: "A philosopher is company to a philosopher only" (I.ii.2.6). More strikingly, he states:

> To a real wise man the judicious and well-weighed approbation of a single wise man, gives more heartfelt satisfaction than all the noisy applauses of ten thousand ignorant though enthusiastic admirers. He may say with Parmenides, who, upon reading a philosophical discourse before a public assembly at Athens, and observing, that, except Plato, the whole company had left him, continued, notwithstanding, to read on, and said that Plato alone was audience sufficient for him. (*TMS* VI.iii.31)

Smith insists that the "wise man" is above the praise and blame of the many, but not above what the many should approve and disapprove.[64]

Smith retains a place even for "mortification," though in a moral rather than a theological sense.[65] The most suggestive usage comes early in the book when Smith describes the "dread of death" as "the great poison to the happiness, but the great restraint upon the injustice of mankind"; "while it afflicts and mortifies the individual, [it] guards and protects the society" (I.i.1.13). We again confront the prospect that the unhappiness of individuals is the price exacted by nature for the survival and progress of the species; the fulfillment of nature's purpose—the preservation and propagation of species—creates obstacles to human "happiness and perfection." *The Theory of Moral Sentiments* in fact wavers between accentuating and disparaging the fear of death.[66] By not following Hobbes in making this fear the overarching motivation, Smith converts self-preservation into species preservation, and leaves room—without invoking Heaven—for a non-mercenary morality of justice, nobility, and courage.

All this suggests the ultimate vindication of Christian benevolence. Smith once identifies benevolence as "the supreme virtue" (VII.ii.3.15); he concedes that "proper benevolence is the most graceful and agreeable of all the affections"; the benevolence system tends "to nourish and support in the human heart the noblest and the most agreeable of all affections" (VII.ii.3.4,14). Smith surely respects the benevolence system's vision of perfect virtue: "directing all our actions to promote the greatest possible good" and "regarding one's self but as one of the many" (VII.ii.3.11). Smith himself asserts that "man was made for action, and to promote by the exertion of his faculties such changes in the external circumstances both of himself and others, as may seem most favourable to the happiness of all" (II.iii.3.3). The Christian implications of this sympathy for benevolence are accentuated by Smith's harsh criticism of the Greeks for practicing infanticide and of Plato and Aristotle for condoning it (V.2.15).[67]

Even if Smith too posits the happiness of mankind as the ultimate goal, he recommends that the goal be pursued indirectly. Nature provides for the whole of the species, but by directing each individual first and primarily to his own "department." The excesses of selfishness are curbed by outward punishment for injustice, the worldly success that generally accrues to a just individual, and the powerful inner voice of the impartial spectator. This relationship between the individual good and the collective good is summarized by the metaphor of the invisible hand. Its one mention in *The Theory of Moral Sentiments* fittingly comes in the thematic treatment of utility:[68] despite great inequality and the greed of the rich, the lowly enjoy an equal share of "real happiness." Or do they simply subsist and propagate (IV.1.10)? Our natural moral sentiments, of course, are for Smith only marginally utilitarian; at times they are counter-utilitarian. But these anti-utilitarian sentiments ultimately serve nature's utilitarian end, species preservation and propagation.[69] Unlike Nietzsche, Smith treats individuals as nature's vehicle to enhance the species. Christian equality before God is in a sense reborn as the natural imperative of species growth. Although it remains the job of philosophy to comprehend nature's wisdom, Smith strives to counteract extant philosophies that have had unsalutary effects and to discourage the incompetent—i.e., almost everyone—from dwelling on "the whole." The discourses of Parmenides are perhaps better addressed to "Plato alone" than to the "ignorant" multitudes in the "public assembly."[70]

Smith's apparently neutral stance between the two great moral systems, benevolence and propriety, is further complicated by the historicist dimension of his analysis. In general, social morality constructively emerges in response to the "circumstances" and "situation." The basic contrast Smith delineates between civilized and primitive moralities corresponds almost exactly to the contrast between the great, awful, and respectable virtues of ancient propriety and the soft, amiable, and gentle virtues of modern benevolence. In civilized nations, the virtues grounded in humanity predominate; in "rude and barbarous nations," the virtues grounded in self-command and self-denial (V.2.8). The differentiation arises for the simple reason that life is easy for the civilized and difficult for the primitive. Even within a civilized society, it is unlikely that the same person will perfect both types of virtue. Although the same natural disposition facilitates their acquisition, they are actualized by different circumstances. The "gentle virtue of humanity" is most readily actualized in ease, tranquillity, and leisure; the "austere virtue of self-command" is most readily actualized under the hardships of war, faction, insolence, envy, injustice, dangers, and injuries (III.3.34–38).

Smith indeed provides historical background for his discussion of the ancients. The age "in which flourished the founders of all the principal sects of ancient philosophy" was rent by war and faction, such that "the most perfect innocence . . . could give no security to any man." Like the American savage, the ancient philosophers prepared a "death song." Because they portrayed virtue as "the certain and infallible road to happiness even in this life," they had to show that happiness was largely (the Academics and the Peripatetics) if not totally (the Stoics) independent of "fortune" (VII.ii.1.28).[71] On the one hand, all this would lead Smith to accord higher status to the gentle virtues: the excesses of Stoic self-denial and apathy would not seem suitable to the circumstances of Smith's time; Smith prefers soft tranquillity and peace to harsh deprivation and war. On the other hand, Smith promises no end to war, and bourgeois virtue itself incorporates not only self-denial and self-command but the amoral selfishness endorsed by Epicurus, Machiavelli, Hobbes, and Mandeville. The Christian precepts to love thy neighbor and to turn the other cheek would seem to be inadequate in any foreseeable circumstances, from Smith's perspective, though they point in the right direction. Civilization and the conquest of nature may usher in a gentler, more humane era. In this sense, to paraphrase Nietzsche, the capitalist movement is heir to the Christian movement.

CHAPTER ELEVEN

Karl Marx on the Withering of Religion and Politics

SMITH (in *The Wealth of Nations*) and Marx reject religion without the manifest ambiguities that characterize their posture toward politics and political philosophy.* The linkages between religion and politics, however, are more manifest in Marx's presentation. The "materialistic connection of men with one another," which is "determined by their needs and their mode of production . . . presents a 'history' independently of the existence of any political or religious nonsense which would especially hold men together."[1] Political and religious "nonsense" is part of the superstructure, not the base (the mode of production). The conceptual linkage between religion and politics reflects Marx's view, derived in part from Feuerbach, that the state, God, and Jesus embody an alienated essence that human beings must reappropriate.[2]

---

* Unless otherwise indicated, references to Marx's *Capital* are to Volume I, translated by Ben Fowkes (New York: Random House, 1976). For example, 10:7 means chapter 10, section 7. Chapter and/or section citations are occasionally provided for other works as well, to facilitate the use of different editions. The references to Engels are to *Socialism: Utopian and Scientific* (1880), reprinted in *The Marx-Engels Reader*, 2d ed., edited by Robert C. Tucker (New York: W. W. Norton, 1978). This reader is also the source for the cited speeches and letters of Marx, and for other works of Marx (or Marx and Engels) that will be identified by the following short titles:

1844	"Economic and Philosophic Manuscripts of 1844."
CM	*The Communist Manifesto* (1848).
CW	*The Civil War in France* (1871).
GI	*The German Ideology* (1845–46).
Gotha	"Critique of the Gotha Program" (1875).
JQ	"On the Jewish Question" (1843).

Religion

Marx's rejection of religion is still more intransigent than Smith's. The disappearance of all fundamental antagonisms that allows the state to wither would likewise erase any lingering religious sentiments—any longing for a world more perfect than this one, for a God that will punish those who prosper in this world by unrighteous means, for a superhuman entity that transcends the perishability and the flux of all things human. Consequently, Marx never flirts with theism and doctrines of the afterlife as Smith does in *The Theory of Moral Sentiments*, where he implies that religious longings are coeval with humanity. Like Smith, Marx rejects the Bible and medieval Christendom in the name of progress, but only Marx condemns the way that the past dominates the present in a capitalist society.[3]

With Smith, as we saw, the invisible hand is a signpost for profound theological, philosophical, and political questions that cannot be tidily disposed of. Marx, by contrast, promises that "the religious reflections of the real world" will vanish once "the practical relations of everyday life between man and man, and man and nature, generally present themselves to him in a transparent and rational form."[4] Marx's early remark that atheism is "meaningless" implies that the religious longing itself, the very question of God, is a sign of alienation (1844, p. 92). Communism solves the antinomies of both philosophy and society.[5]

Even in *The Wealth of Nations*, Smith praises religious toleration and the "pure and rational religion" (V.i.g.8). Marx, on the other hand, calls for liberation "from" religion and therefore criticizes the religious freedom guaranteed by liberal society. Religion is simply a "defect," the opiate of the people.[6] Smith is comparably insistent only on liberating humanity from superstition and fanaticism. Smith also retains vestiges of the classical and Christian exaltation of contemplation, in contrast to Marx's exaltation of production, revolution, and the transcendence (*Aufhebung*) of the whole philosophic tradition.

In contrast to the tradition of political economy, however, Volume I of *Capital* is replete with references to Christian terminology and concepts—the Lamb of God, prayer, the soul, God's eternal will, transubstantiation, various saints, the Bible, "the water of everlasting life," the afterlife, the last judgment, God the Father and God the Son, transmigration, salvation, divine law, Jehovah and the chosen people, Moses and the prophets, Adam and original sin,[7] charity, celibacy, and monasticism—not to mention the occasional quotations from both Testaments of the Bible and from Luther.[8] Because the tone is so contemptuous, the book's rejection of the religious tradition is more blatant than Smith's. Like Smith, Marx is engaged in a minor campaign to purge the remnants of Christian superstition, the major campaign having been provided (from Marx's perspective) by developments in the mode of production.[9] The deepest purpose of this campaign, however, is to neutralize not the religious opiate but the capitalist opiate. Robert Paul Wolff puts it as follows: "Writing for an audience that had been reared on the mysteries and incantations of Christianity, he [Marx] invoked its most powerful metaphors to force upon his readers a self-awareness of their complicity in the inversions and fetishism of capitalist market relations" (*Money-bags*, p. 81). In the Preface to *Capital*, Marx wryly remarks that "nowadays atheism itself is a *culpa levis*, as compared with the criticism of existing property relations" (p. 92).

It is nevertheless easy to catalog ways in which Marxism resembles religion. Although, like Smith, Marx denies that prophets have helped to shape human history, he seems to have synthesized the vocations of scientist, revolutionary, and prophet. Twentieth-century communism suggests a similar paradox. The forms of authority and political organization introduced by communism, despite their novelty, resemble the Catholic church as described by Smith.[10] Communism was an international movement, if not a "spiritual army, dispersed in different quarters" able to operate "upon one plan and with one spirit" (*WN* V.i.g.21,17). Its adherents and agents challenged political establishments around the globe in the name of the toiling masses, thus competing for "authority and influence" with "the inferior ranks" (*WN* V.i.g.1,7); they likewise displayed an "austerity" of the sort cultivated by reform-minded churches and movements in Christendom, and developed corresponding forms of popular "eloquence" (V.i.g.11,29). The ruling communist elites, finally, resisted for many years the temptation to indulge their "own ease and comfort" at the expense of the long-run "authority of their order" (V.i.g.7).

With the spread of liberation theology, we witness the remarkable coincidence of Catholic priest and Marxist revolutionary (not to mention Reverends Ernesto Cardenal and Miguel D'Escoto, who served as Sandinista ministers). Like Jesus, Marx and his successors address their call primarily to the lowly, the poor, the toiling masses. Marx's secularized eschatology promises them ultimate deliverance from evil, a transformation of worldly life vastly more pronounced than anything envisioned by classical political philosophy, liberalism, or classical political economy; Marx himself refers to communism as "heaven on earth."[11] Marx's revolutionary praxis provides the proletarians not only with an almost supernatural demon to be exorcised—capital, a "vampire" and "animated monster" (*Capital*, pp. 302, 342, 367, 416)—but also with human scapegoats (recalcitrant capitalists) to be "expropriated" along the way. The proletarians are asked to lodge a kind of faith in the materialist dialectic of history and perhaps even in the Party members who, unlike "the great mass of the proletariat," have the advantage of "clearly understanding the line of march, the conditions, and the ultimate general results of the proletarian movement" (*CM*, p. 484). Whether or not Marx was "the deity of a new world religion" (Blanshard, p. 69), the cult of personality—the worship of such figures as Lenin, Stalin, Mao, Ho Chi Minh, and Castro—has been a conspicuous feature of communist governments. And *Capital*, as the "Bible of the working class,"[12] surely requires interpreters who have plumbed the depths of classical political economy, Hegel, and other complex matters.

Insofar as Smith stands to capitalism in roughly the same way as Marx stands to communism, comparing the two authors may benefit practice as well as theory. One must nevertheless acknowledge that the analogy is flawed, primarily because Smith, although an advocate of "the system of natural liberty," postdates many of the economic developments we associate with capitalism, whereas Marx writes in a decidedly precommunist age.[13] In addition, assessing two theorists who focus so much on historical development and its laws requires attention to the changes— especially those related to the French Revolution and the Industrial Revolution—that occurred in the roughly seventy-five years that separated Smith and Marx.[14] Assessing them is further complicated by the growing discrepancies between capitalism and Smith's "system of natural liberty."

The most fundamental distinction between the two authors is in fact their different weighting of nature and history; they differently draw the line between what is permanent and what can be changed; Smith seems to accommodate nature as much as he battles it. First of all, Smith is less confident that the course of history can be foreseen. More important, he seems to rule out any radical amelioration of the human condition. Nature's empire, as depicted in both of Smith's books, is in many ways ubiquitous, and although Smithian nature itself incorporates historical change—society's "natural progress" through the four stages—the arena for change initiated by mankind is much more constrained than is the arena envisioned by Marx. The sphere of change Smith acknowledges would include several developments: the technological and economic mastery of nature, which had grown enormously and might continue indefinitely; human liberation from the tyranny of feudal aristocracy and the Church, and perhaps from religious persecution; the gradual securing of life and property against the depredations of both rulers and subjects; and a pacifying of international relations due to the dismantling of mercantilism and a greater equality of power among states. But as we have seen, Smith offers little or no room for the higher freedom envisioned by Rousseau's political philosophy, Kant's moral philosophy, and Marx's "realm of freedom."[15] Humanity will continue to bow before nature, especially nature's economic laws.

Smith's conservatism is most visible in his Stoic calls for resignation, tranquillity, and contentment; he argues that "the great source of both the misery and disorders of human life seems to arise from over-rating the difference between one permanent situation and another" (*TMS* III.3.31). With an eye to history, one may accuse Smith of "over-rating" the goods previously brought by commerce and those that might follow from its ongoing development, fueled by laissez-faire reforms. But whatever the evils of nineteenth-century capitalism, one may more plausibly accuse Marx of exaggerating the likelihood of capitalism's quick demise and, more important, the blessings that would follow from its forcible overthrow.

Whereas capitalism "drowned the most heavenly ecstasies of religious fervor, of chivalrous enthusiasm, of philistine sentimentalism in the icy water of egotistical calculation" (*CM*, p. 475), Marx infused the icy prose of political economy with the fire of world revolution. Marx's tale of the burgeoning conflict between the two great classes, on which the whole of human destiny hinges, reinfuses human life with the urgency of the Christian drama of Heaven and Hell; Marx raises the stakes that Smith strove quietly to lower.[16]

If Marx infused the "dismal science" with what Smith calls the "poison of enthusiasm" and fanaticism, Smith may have helped to prepare the way, and not only by pioneering the science. First, Smith, like many other modern thinkers, encourages the indefinite augmentation of the power of the human species vis-à-vis nature. Smith can invoke nature but not God to limit human freedom and to tame mankind's hubristic drive for cosmic sovereignty. The political economy of both Smith and Marx effaces divine command as well as the more general possibility that mankind is beholden to something superhuman. Second, the tranquillity and the resignation extolled in *The Theory of Moral Sentiments* clash with the restless and interminable effort to "better one's condition" described and encouraged in *The Wealth of Nations*.[17] Finally, Smith encourages political theorists to exploit the human intoxication with power over things, despite the ultimately futile character of such power, to bolster patriotism and to effect social reform (*TMS* IV.1.11). The "systems" provided by modern social science can thus be a breeding ground for a new kind of "fanaticism" (VI.ii.2.15). Smith suggests ways of preventing priests—but not political economists—from exploiting the likely debilitation of the workers under the system of natural liberty.[18]

Of the historical phenomena that seem to have obstructed Smith's project, perhaps three are worthy of special mention: the nationalism and egalitarian republicanism unleashed by the French Revolution, the scientific prophesying of Karl Marx, and the social disruptions triggered by the capitalist dynamic of competition, accumulation, and technological progress. Smith may have tried to preempt the first two phenomena, but he strove to encourage the last.

Politics and Economics

Mystifications and Inversions

Marx uses historical materialism to replace political philosophy as well as religion. Politics itself, as part of the superstructure, is erased as an independent historical variable. Marx predicts that the state, an instrument of coercion used by one class to exploit other classes, will disappear in the aftermath of the revolution along with class distinctions, scarcity, religion, and tension between the public and the private.

According to Trotsky, communism will demonstrate that the human race has "ceased to crawl on all fours before God, kings, and capital."[19] Although historical materialism enabled Marx to dismiss the traditional concerns of philosophy and religion, the obfuscations of political economy were a more serious obstacle. As Wolff points out, Marx's theoretical analysis and critique of capitalism is more than five thousand pages long (*Understanding Marx*, p. 3). Wolff argues elsewhere that *Capital* is fundamentally a work of demystification. Philosophy and religion had already been "dramatically demystified" by Kant, David Strauss, and especially Feuerbach; the effect was "to blow away the clouds of incense, revealing the church in its true nature as a secular institution, created by man as an instrument of domination." Politics was demystified by the French Revolution, although "popular sovereignty stepped forward as the new sophistry by which power misrepresented itself as authority" (Wolff, *Moneybags*, pp. 39–40). Marx's great project was thus to demystify political economy, a task rendered especially challenging because the capitalist economic order and the men who wrote about it appeared to be so down-to-earth and transparent.[20]

Marx's famous discussion in *Capital* of "fetishism" begins with the claim that the commodity, though it "appears at first sight an extremely obvious, trivial thing," is actually "a very strange thing, abounding in metaphysical subtleties and theological niceties" (p. 163). That is, "just as man is governed, in religion, by the products of his own brain, so, in capitalist production, he is governed by the products of his own hand" (p. 772). The liberty and the equality promised by modern democratic politics, what Wolff calls the "sophistry" of popular sovereignty, are fraudulent because of the continued dominion of capital. In a famous passage, Marx explains that the sphere of "circulation or commodity exchange," where "everything takes place on the surface and in full view of everyone," is "a very Eden of the innate rights of man," of "Freedom, Equality, Property, and Bentham." But Marx invites his readers to accompany the worker "into the hidden abode of production" to reveal "the secret of profitmaking" and therewith the exploitation and oppression essential to capitalism.[21]

Marx proceeds to dispel the "mystery" of wages and profits by showing that although there *appears* to be "an exchange of equivalents," the capitalist is actually appropriating unpaid labor.[22] Proletarians, when contrasted with the oppressed classes of old—serfs and slaves—appear to enjoy freedom and equality, and this illusion is part of the genius of capitalism.[23] Wage-labor remains a system by which surplus labor is "extorted" from the "immediate producer." Capitalism, moreover, surpasses the earlier systems, which were "based on directly compulsory labor," in its "energy and its quality of unbounded and ruthless activity"; in precapitalist systems, use value took precedence over exchange value and the imposition of labor was "restricted by a more or less confined set of needs."[24] Capital's insatiable appetite for profit and accumulation compels unrelenting appropriation of the laborers' time and energy.

In the course of capitalism's development, according to Marx, it further distinguishes itself from earlier systems of exploitation. Technology makes the individual laborer an "appendage of the machine"; by displacing workers, it also causes pauperism to increase more quickly than population and the total wealth. In a word, the bourgeoisie is "unfit to rule because it is incompetent to assure an existence to its slave within his slavery, because it cannot help letting him sink into such a state that it has to feed him, instead of being fed by him." The proletarians, an "immense [*ungeheuern*] majority" in 1848, grow ever larger because of the inevitable shrinkage of the capitalist class.[25]

The economic realm built on private property, competition, the free market, and freedom of contract is thus not something to be insulated from political control in the name of freedom. Indeed, communism will end the "anarchy" that characterizes the operation of the capitalist economy as a whole and its recurring crises. This anarchy, however, has paradoxically coexisted with tyranny in the factory and the workshop, where the worker is forced to labor ever longer and harder under the most stultifying and unhealthy conditions.[26] Having fulfilled its historic mission of socializing mankind and radically developing the forces of production, capitalism is now a "fetter" that must be, and will be, "burst asunder." Once efficiency has done its work, freedom can come into its own.[27]

The inexorable, impersonal dynamics of the capitalist system constituted the economic machine whose laws were analyzed by the political economist. Marx's "critique" of these laws shows that they generate "contradictions" that now necessitate the transformation of the system, just as feudalism had generated the first phase of capitalism (manufacturing), which in turn generated the era of machinery and giant industry.[28] The pending transformation, though dictated by economic laws of "iron necessity" (*Capital*, Preface, p. 91), will be consummated politically as Marx explains these laws to the proletariat (and to defectors from the ruling class) and thus incites them to seize their destiny (*CM*, pp. 481, 484).

Perhaps the most impressive (if not visionary) feature of the posited reinversion of living labor and capital—which Marx describes as accumulated, congealed, or "dead" labor-power—is that labor will no longer be undertaken out of necessity and unfreedom, as a means to subsist, but freely as an end in itself.[29] This contributes crucially to overcoming the alienation denounced in Marx's early writings: by engaging in free, conscious production, we will actualize our "species-being" (1844, pp. 75–76). Aggression, coercion, and clashes of interest will have disappeared. In the famous formula for the final stage, "from each according to his ability, to each according to his needs" (Gotha, p. 531), Marx promises that these needs will be met without "exchange"; production and consumption will thus be mediated without either coercion or appeals to self-interest. Marx of course faults Smith for his identification of labor with toil and trouble (*Capital*, pp. 137–38n16), and Marxists take special glee in ridiculing the alleged existence of a trans-historical "propensity to truck, barter, and exchange."[30] For Smith, labor is largely instrumental, a means to an end; such a view meshes easily with the old-fashioned notion of a hierarchy of activities and perhaps of classes or human types (e.g., citizens and workers), hierarchies that Marx condemns. Smith, although he laments and calls for remedies to the debilitation of the workers caused by the division of labor, hints that such debilitation might be the price for the full development of a "few" (*WN* V.i.f.51).[31] Marx promises that communism will entail "the casting off of all natural limitations" (*GI*, p. 192), the full and free development of everyone, supposing that free development will always be full development and that the development of one person will never clash with that of another. The "realm of freedom" would ensure the flowering of "human energy which is an end in itself."[32]

If Marx had to choose between full development for some and partial development for all, however, he might hesitate.[33] After recounting Aristotle's speculation that intelligent tools might enable craftsmen to dispense with slaves, Marx exclaims: "Oh those heathens! They understood nothing of political economy and Christianity." They were ignorant of political economy, one may infer, because they did not realize that machinery "is the surest means of lengthening the working day" (*Capital*, pp. 532–33). They were ignorant of Christianity because although they "may perhaps have excused the slavery of one person as a means to the full human development of another," they "lacked the specifically Christian qualities which would have enabled them to preach the slavery of the masses in order that a few crude and half-educated parvenus might become 'eminent spinners', 'extensive sausage-makers' and 'influential shoe-black dealers' " (p. 533).[34] Marx projects the means/end rationalization of social hierarchy onto history, where the slavery and misery of the past are in a sense vindicated by the resplendent future they prepared. "What use is it to lament an historical necessity?"[35]

Smith's major project, of course, is to protect the economy from unnecessary political intrusion. Along with this comes substantial demystifying, especially in *The Wealth of Nations*. The targets—religious, political, and economic elites—are similar to Marx's, though only with respect to religion is the attack taken as far.[36] We have explored Smith's subtle demystification of priests, "whining and melancholy" Christians, Jupiter, heaven and hell, metaphysics, landlords, hereditary aristocrats, primogeniture, entails, ancient education in "music," the philosopher's "vanity," royalty, Parliament, statesmen enticed by the "wheel of the great . . . lottery" of politics, European colonialism and imperialism, Alexander the Great, Caesar, Jesus, Socrates, Rousseau, and even the great demystifier, Mandeville. Within the economic sphere, the dominant targets are mercantilism—its doctrines about money and the balance of trade, and its chief beneficiaries, the "merchants and master manufacturers"—and other institutions that restrain trade or promote monopoly. Although Smith's political economy erases God and tolerates kings, it certainly bows before private property in the means of production and its ceaseless "accumulation." But perhaps "capital," as the great provider of commodities, is more the servant of the people than their master.

Regarding the crucial political phenomena of authority, rank, and subordination, Smith in a sense demystifies their alternatives along with them. Smith eschews the philosophical and religious considerations that were (and are) used either to exalt or to denounce authority and subordination, although the historical social science he substitutes shows their prevalence, power, and perhaps permanence.[37] Apart from his strong reservations about the division of labor, Smith seems indifferent to the Marxian vision of transforming labor from the realm of necessity to the realm of freedom. He nevertheless emphasizes the differences between wage-laborers and serfs or slaves. Smith treats the struggle between workers and owners over wages and working conditions as a competitive one that the side with the greater bargaining power will win; he concedes that the master has the edge, and thinks that in the long run the workers can only look forward to a subsistence wage.[38] On all these questions, however, Smith leaves an opening for the Marxian critique. Smith concedes that civilized countries differ from their colonies because "rent and profit eat up wages, and the two superior orders of people oppress the inferior one" (WN IV.vii.b.3). He also insists that

> what improves the circumstances of the greater part can never be regarded as an inconveniency to the whole. No society can surely be flourishing and happy, of which the far greater part of the members are poor and miserable. It is but equity, besides, that they who feed, cloath and lodge the whole body of the people, should have such *a share of the produce of their own labour* as to be themselves tolerably well fed, cloathed and lodged. (WN I.viii.36)

Smith attacks not only the mercantilist policies that benefit the few at the expense of the many, but the underlying principle that production rather than consumption is "the ultimate end and object of all industry and commerce" (IV.viii.49).

The "Public Power" Under Communism

In calling for "social" ownership and control of the means of production, Marx stands Smith on his head and paradoxically reasserts the hegemony of politics over economics. In the short term, the economy will be run politically, in Marx's sense of the term. The proletariat, organized as ruling class—the infamous dictatorship of the proletariat—will expropriate the capitalists, redistribute wealth, and improve conditions in the workplace. Only down the road, when classes and their attendant antagonisms have disappeared, will the state wither away. Throughout this whole development, however, the processes of production will be directed by a collective will, intelligence, and plan.

The gigantic question that Marx does not answer is precisely how, by what institutional mechanism, production (and societal activities generally) will be coordinated.[39] Marx here defers to history. He is first and foremost someone who uncovers society's "economic law of motion," not a founder, a legislator, or even a prophet.[40] His analysis, of course, also promises to help liberate mankind from the allegedly "natural" economic laws—for example, supply and demand—that have hitherto stood in the way of human freedom and fulfillment. Marx supposes that communism, as it develops historically, will shape the "public power" into its appropriate forms. More persuasive, however, is Marx's related attempt to describe and explain the myriad ways in which the development of capitalism has both revealed the shape of the communist future and created its preconditions: the gigantic increase in social productive forces, the overcoming of "national divisions and antagonisms," the evisceration of religion and the family, the socialization of labor, and even the formation and empowerment of a "universal" proletarian class.[41] Capitalism "is like the sorcerer, who is no longer able to control the power of the nether world whom he has called up by his spells"; the bourgeoisie "produces . . . its own gravediggers" (*CM*, p. 483); the revolution will "set free the elements of the new society with which old collapsing bourgeois society itself is pregnant" (*CW*, p. 636). In the Preface to *Capital*, Marx observes that although a society must pass through all "the natural phases of its development," it may—presumably by means of Marx's analytical contributions—"shorten and lessen the birth pangs" (p. 92).

Whether or not one is a dialectical materialist, one can discern anticipations of Marx not only in Smith and Hegel, but in the whole tradition of modern political thought. According to Arendt, Marx, in hoping for and/or predicting the withering of "the whole public realm," merely "summed up, conceptualized, and transformed into a program the underlying assumptions of two hundred years of modernity."[42] Even by Marx's day, capitalism had legislated reforms that anticipated communism: mandatory public education for children, provision for worker safety, and, most important, limits on the working day.[43] But we must examine Marx's comments about decision making under communism in order to assess the plausibility, nay, the sanity, of the most radical, universal, and confident call for revolution ever to gain a worldwide following.

The dilemma is encapsulated in a famous passage from *The German Ideology*:

> In communist society, where nobody has one exclusive sphere of activity but each can become accomplished in any branch he wishes, society regulates the general production and thus makes it possible for me to do one thing today and another tomorrow, to hunt in the morning, fish in the

afternoon, rear cattle in the evening, criticize after dinner, just as I have a mind, without ever becoming hunter, fisherman, shepherd or critic. (*GI*, p. 160)

We need not dwell here upon the main theme of the passage—the overcoming of the specialization imposed by the division of labor—despite the seeming absurdity of the prediction that "each can become accomplished in any branch." Distracted by the prospect of hunting, fishing, etc., people often lose sight of the gigantic paradox, nay, riddle, that I can do "as I have a mind" (*"wie ich gerade Lust habe"*) despite or, rather, because "society regulates the general production" (*"die Gesellschaft die allgemeine Produktion regelt"*). How can radical individual liberty— "the *free* development of each," the "full and *free* development of every individual"[44]—coexist with the attempt to "regulate national production upon a common plan" (*CW*, p. 635); with "the associated producers, rationally regulating their interchange with Nature, bringing it under their common control" (*Capital*, vol. III, p. 820); with "production by freely associated men . . . under their conscious and planned control"; with the "conscious attempt to control and regulate the process of production socially" (*Capital*, pp. 173, 477); with centralizing and concentrating production "in the hands of the State" or "a vast association of the whole nation" (*CM*, p. 490); with "social regulation of production" according to a "definite" and "predetermined" plan?[45] In other words, how are labor and production to be not only planned and "associated" but also free?[46]

The *German Ideology* vision might be plausible if social act· vity were confined to hunting, fishing, herding, and criticizing, but communism presupposes the technological developments already achieved by capitalism and promises further increases in social productivity.[47] Technological progress and economic growth would be essential for the evolution of a classless world society in which everyone achieves "full development": there would be need for wheelchairs (if not artificial limbs), eyeglasses, insulin, incubators, kidney dialysis machines, and who knows what else. In his "Critique of the Gotha Program," Marx identifies the first phase of communism as the dictatorship of the proletariat. The distributive principle of this phase, to each according to his work (with deductions for community expenses such as relief, insurance, and reinvestment), still bears the mark of the "bourgeois" right to equality: although it "recognizes no class differences," it recognizes the unequal productive capacities and unequal needs of individuals. Only in a higher phase "can the narrow horizon of bourgeois right be crossed in its entirety" by establishing the famous principle: "From each according to his ability, to each according to his needs" (pp. 528–31). We may infer that achieving the realm of freedom, where human energy is developed as "an end in itself," would require interminable progress in the campaign to master nature and to extinguish the thrall of necessity. The other dramatic change must come in "human nature" as competitive, aggressive, and egoistic impulses disappear in response to changes in the mode of production.[48]

The question about the nature of the "public power" is thus vexing not only regarding the dictatorship of the proletariat—under which old-fashioned oppression must be used to eliminate the former oppressors—but even regarding the classless, stateless society in which "the government of persons is replaced by the administration of things, and by the conduct of processes of production" (Engels, p. 713). This formulation might render Marx's promise in *The German Ideology* intelligible, if machines took care of all basic needs, leaving the people who were not "administering" the machines freedom to hunt and fish as they desired.[49] Down the road, Marx states, the "public power will lose its political character," that is, its class-based oppressive character.[50] But how will this "public power" be exercised? Let us first examine the *Manifesto*, where Marx issues his most vigorous and public summons to the revolution.

The immediate aim of the Communists is the "conquest of political power by the proletariat"; the revolution's first step is "to raise the proletariat to the position of ruling class, to win the battle of democracy" (*"die Erkämpfung der Demokratie"*). The proletariat will then use its political supremacy to expropriate the capitalists and "to centralize all instruments of production in the hands of the State."[51] Marx proceeds to spell out ten subsidiary measures, including the centralization of credit, communication, and transportation "in the hands of the State." One obvious effect of all this is a dramatic explosion of political authority, but Marx has said almost nothing about the institutional mechanisms or forms by which that authority will be exercised.[52] With the expropriation of land and capital, and the rejection of "bourgeois" political institutions, can there be any private powers to counterbalance the newly engorged "public power"?[53]

For Marx, the "liberal movement," as the struggle by the bourgeoisie against feudal aristocracy and absolute monarchy (*CM*, p. 494), was a step on the journey to communism, and Marx cherishes its political fruits insofar as they can facilitate proletarian revolution. In the third part of the *Manifesto*, Marx identifies liberalism with representative government, "bourgeois competition, bourgeois freedom of the press, bourgeois liberty and equality," and ridicules the German philosophers who borrowed (from French socialism) the "traditional anathemas" against liberalism without recognizing that "the pending struggle in Germany" was precisely to establish the bourgeois arrangements.[54] Years later (in 1875), Marx complains that the political demands of the "Gotha Program" merely recite "the old democratic litany"—the "pretty little gewgaws" of "suffrage, direct legislation, popular rights, a people's militia"—already realized in Switzerland and the United States, "democratic republic[s]" built on "the so-called sovereignty of the people." Such demands are inappropriate in a "police-guarded military despotism" such as Germany. Marx also complains that they do not point to "the revolutionary dictatorship of the proletariat" (Gotha, p. 538).

The most complete description in Marx's published writings of communist "public power" occurs in *The Civil War in France*, composed in 1870–71 during the Franco-Prussian War and a French workers' revolt that temporarily established the "Paris Commune." According to Marx, the organization of the workers in the Commune was "the political form at last discovered under which to work out the economic emancipation of labor" (*CW*, p. 635); according to Engels, the Commune was an example of the "dictatorship of the proletariat."[55] A full twenty-two years after the call for world revolution in the *Manifesto*, four years after the publication of Volume I of *Capital*, Marx thus enlightens the public about communism's "political form"; such are the advantages of being a historical materialist and political economist rather than a political philosopher.[56] Marx at least describes the institutional structure of the Commune in some detail. The Commune (i.e., the government of the French territory in the hands of the Paris-based revolutionaries) consisted of "municipal councilors, chosen by universal suffrage in the various wards, responsible and revocable at short terms"; magistrates and judges were "elective, responsible, and revocable." The Commune functioned as a supreme authority, combining legislative and executive functions: all the tasks of state and municipal "administration," including the police, were subordinate to it (*CW*, p. 632).[57] On the question of centralization, Marx also provides a sketch. The commune form—"self-government of the producers"—was to be mimicked in the provinces; district delegates assembled in a central town of the province to manage local affairs and to send deputies to the "national delegation" in Paris, each of whom was "at any time revocable and bound by the . . . formal instructions" of the constituents (p. 633).[58] On the structures for determining economic activities, Marx says little beyond the claim that with land and capital as "mere instruments of free and associated labor," "united cooperative societies" will "regulate national production upon a common plan" (p. 635). One wonders especially how the liberty of the individual or even of a local cooperative will harmonize with economic planning on a global level. Recent events have confirmed that Leninist "centralism" is not a solution to such difficulties.

Marx does not worry that a government like the Commune, shorn of most of the safeguards that characterize liberal or "bourgeois" democracy, will abuse its prerogatives. Marx asserts that universal suffrage in electing the communes will serve the people "as individual suffrage serves every other employer in the search for the workmen and managers in his business"; companies generally know whom to install where, and how to correct mistakes promptly (*CW*, p. 633). The conflict over "place, pelf, and patronage" that corrupts the bourgeois state (p. 630) will be eliminated because all governmental positions will be remunerated at workers' wages (p. 632). The Commune even operated somewhat in the spirit of the First Amendment: it disestablished and disendowed the churches, and because it did not "pretend to infallibility," it "published its doings and sayings" (p. 640). All this belies frequently voiced charges that Marx either altogether denied the relevance of political institutions, viewing man simply as an economic animal, or that he favored authoritarian politics.

Three things chiefly distinguish the Paris Commune from liberal democracy, especially as articulated in *The Federalist*. First is the absence of any "trustee" features of the representation: the Commune lacked institutions designed to increase the chances that people of special moral or intellectual excellence would hold office, or to provide a stability that would insulate government from the fluctuations of the popular temper. Might not training, specialization, and a certain level of native intelligence be necessary for someone to comprehend and to help supervise the complex operations of a modern economy?[59] Second is the diminished presence of restraints on political authority to counteract the vices, especially ambition, of officeholders. The primary restraint is the increasing of the people's immediate power over them (for example, the recall), which only aggravates the third and most important difference between the Paris Commune and liberal democracy: the absence of checks against majority tyranny, whether economic, cultural, or spiritual. The dangers posed by majority tyranny and predatory officeholders are mitigated in America by federalism, bicameralism, the separation of powers, checks and balances, constitutionalism, the rule of law, judicial review, a Bill of Rights, political parties, property rights, and occasional dilutions of the representative principle (for example, in judicial selection and tenure). Although Marx mentions that the Commune "published its doings and sayings," *The Civil War in France* is silent about freedom of speech and press; the right of the people to assemble, to petition, and to organize political parties; and matters of criminal justice, among them, trial by jury, habeas corpus, and seaches and seizures. Needless to say, Marx is unimpressed by the "pompous catalog of 'the inalienable rights of man.'"[60]

The fundamental reason for Marx's lack of attention to the question of communist political institutions and his willingness to abandon liberalism's limitations on governmental power is his belief that there are no permanent antagonisms based on class, scarcity, or human psychology (for example, innate "propensities" toward greed, competition, or domination). Communist citizens will certainly not fight about philosophy and theology.[61] Madison's critique of "pure democracy" (as opposed to republican or representative democracy) emphasizes the permanence of class antagonisms, and not only the ones based on property.[62] Thus, the "latent causes of faction are . . . sown into the nature of man" (*Federalist* 10). On the assumption that neither the rulers nor the ruled will be angels or even philosophers (nos. 49, 51), *The Federalist* recommends, among other things, political structures that manipulate but therefore incorporate ambition and self-interest, whereas Marx promises the eclipse of such mediating motivations even in economic relations. In addition to more detail about the nature of the public power under communism, Marx should have provided something that covers the same ground as *The Theory of Moral Sentiments*: an investigation of the depths of human psychology and sociality to show us why reasonable people can expect the sort of regeneration necessary to produce "communist man"; to show us why communism can dispense with nationality, religion, moral philosophy, traditional family arrangements, bourgeois safeguards against government (in the short run), and, ultimately, coercion as such. The numerous twentieth-century marriages of Marxism and psychoanalysis reflect this need, although they lead down the path of "revisionism."[63]

History has put an ironic gloss on these objections to Marx. An obvious aggravating circumstance is that Marxist revolutions have erupted and prevailed not in mature capitalist societies but in semi-capitalist and Third World nations. The forbidden fruit of brutal centralized authority has been tempting both economically, as a means for rapid "accumulation" and technical progress, and politically, to contend with a sizable peasantry that obstructs the development of the "universal class."[64] Social regulation of production, on the whole, has thus far been conducted hierarchically, with a premium on specialization and technical skill as well as political status.[65] Marx cannot escape blame for such evils. He described the transition between capitalism and socialism as a "dictatorship," insisted that communism is not a philosophy but a "historical

movement going on under our very eyes,"[66] and called for the "expropriation" of an entire class. Marx implicitly applied the Machiavellian judgment that "the end justifies the means" to the logic of the whole historical process, and many of his revolutionary successors have explicitly
employed it to justify their "inhuman cruelties."

The position of Lenin constitutes a final irony. Though typically
exalted by communist governments to the level of Marx himself
("Marxism-Leninism"), he is reviled by many Western Marxists, especially those of an intellectual bent. The key bone of contention, not
surprisingly, is the theory and practice of the "vanguard." But there
should be little dispute about the intelligence and care with which *State
and Revolution* fleshed out Marx's theory of the "public power" under
communism: how the masses can participate in the planning and control of "socialized production"; how and why the state will ultimately
wither away. Perhaps the crucial consideration is that capitalism itself,
by virtue of factories, railroads, telephones, and the post office, has made
state power mostly reducible to "such simple operations of registration,
filing, and checking that they will be quite within the reach of every
literate person."[67]

Lenin's remarks on the vanguard have clear roots in Marx's treatment
of the relationship between the Party and the proletariat, and might seem
to have been required by the immature development of Russia in 1918.
The skimpiness of Marx's account of the public power under communism gave the Party great leeway; people will continue to disagree about
whether this reveals Marx's foolishness, prudence, or "historical sense."
In any case, the knowledge necessary to plan and regulate a modern
economy would presumably owe something to the thousands of pages of
Capital. Perhaps one's faith in Marx's genius would incline one to defer
not only to the "ideologists" who have "raised themselves to the level of
comprehending theoretically the historical movement as a whole," but
to the Party, which enlightens the proletariat about "the line of march,
the conditions, and the ultimate general results of the proletarian movement."[68] It would be difficult to deny that Marxist ideology has been
widely employed to legitimize "ruling classes."

Many have recoiled from the Leninist vanguard to the more friendly
terrain of market socialism (for example, Yugoslavia), democratic socialism, or the Scandinavian welfare-state. Transforming ownership to
workers' cooperatives—or less comprehensive measures that increase
workers' control and expand the social "safety net"—obviate the need for
a centralized, planned economy and can coexist with the political institutions of liberal democracy. But such arrangements entail a substantial departure from Marx because they would perpetuate so many of the

"alienating" features of capitalism: competition, conflicts of interest, the profit motive, inequalities due to nature and luck, consumerism, and the continued subordination of labor to necessity.[69] Although the first two volumes of *Capital* barely mention "socialism," "communism," "revolution," or *The Communist Manifesto*, Marx continues to insist that reform is not enough and that a successful "revolt" against and "overthrow" of capitalism by the workers is inevitable.[70]

Smith and Marx: A Concluding Assessment

People awed by the wisdom of either Smith or Marx are often contemptuous of the wisdom of the other. Marx's disciples, however, better appreciate the full range and depth of their master's insights. With an eye to his manifest political and intellectual impact, one may dub Marx the patron philosopher of the twentieth century: there is perhaps no Western author or philosopher whose words have been more studied and invoked. A thorough and open-minded comparison of Smith and Marx would enlighten their disciples not only about the wisdom of their preferred antagonist but also about philosophical possibilities that transcend both.

However wise Smith may appear regarding the human condition, one cannot simply pronounce him the victor. For regarding the subject matter that dominates his published output—determination of "the nature and causes of the wealth of nations"—Marx challenges him on his own ground, assessing a broader range of economic theories and analyzing a more developed economy. To the extent that there are economic "laws" in our world, Marx may have better described them. In the major capitalist economies of today, the degree of governmental intervention and the scale of corporate organization are much greater than Smith recommended. Irrespective of this, a full evaluation of their competing theories would be an enormous undertaking requiring a high level of economic expertise. In the view of most contemporary economists, both *The Wealth of Nations* and *Capital* suffer from serious empirical and theoretical shortcomings.

On behalf of Smith's disciples, however, we must acknowledge that the recent movements in the communist world toward both political freedom (*glasnost, demokratizatsiia*) and the free market (*perestroika*) give fresh life to the old argument that democracy and capitalism are mutually supporting. In addition, for those in capitalist countries who lament the excessive power and perquisites of the corporate class, one can imagine remedies beyond plant-closing laws, redistributive taxation, and the welfare-state. Workers' cooperatives and schemes for employee ownership can be set up voluntarily within a capitalist framework;[71] possible reductions in remuneration would presumably be compensated by reductions in "alienation." Neoconservatives tend to paint liberal and radical critics of capitalism as an elite that objects to the tone of a society dictated by mass tastes. Whether or not this is a fair criticism, one must acknowledge the virtues as well as the vices of consumer sovereignty, of voting with one's wallet. The constraints deriving from the majority's decisions in the marketplace are not necessarily worse than the constraints deriving from its dominance of the political process. Capitalism may help to minimize the subjection of the individual to the coercive dictates of government, democratic or otherwise.

It is obviously tempting to evaluate Marx in light of subsequent historical developments, for Marx's core concern is to illuminate history's "line of march." At first glance, Marx seems oddly refuted: the proletariat did not rise to overthrow the mature capitalism of Western Europe and the United States, and communist regimes were established in less-developed countries. One possible explanation of this is especially ironic: that Marx's rhetoric and ideas have been powerful enough to escape the fetters allegedly dictated by the mode of production. Marxism-Leninism evolved from revolutionary ideology to ruling ideology in Russia, China, Cuba, Vietnam, and Nicaragua; it was imposed by conquest in Eastern Europe, and it has thrived as a revolutionary force in the Third World. The survival of mature capitalism might have a similarly paradoxical explanation, insofar as clever capitalists and their political "lackeys" used the knowledge provided by Marx to address the grievances of workers. Consider Cropsey's elaboration of the impact of legislation:

> Marx made concessions, but absolutely insufficient ones, to such simple and undialectical influences as laws—laws to limit the length of the working day, laws to encourage or compel collective bargaining, to enact workmen's compensation, progressive income taxation, unemployment insurance, old-age benefits, laws to regulate securities exchanges, to promote full employment, to protect competition, to control the money supply, to support agriculture, to relieve the sick, to suppress the adulteration of food, to compel the young to submit to be educated, to insure savings, and a thousand other laws, not the least of which is the law that puts lawmaking under the influence of the reigning multitudes that he mistook for a pauperized proletariat.[72]

Some of the measures spelled out in the *Manifesto* have been adopted throughout the capitalist world. Are we ruled exclusively by "capital"?

Marx's analysis of the dynamics of capitalism incorporates a theory of wages built upon the doctrine that the "value" of labor-power, like the value of any other commodity, is its cost of production, that is, whatever is necessary to sustain and reproduce the working class. But Marx admits that unlike the value of other commodities, the value of labor-power "contains a historical and moral element."[73] Workers must be paid as much as is necessary to induce them to provide the required effort, but habits and expectations may dictate an amount well above physical subsistence. Is this the great wedge through which such old-fashioned things as opinion and will can overcome the economic laws of "iron necessity"? Smith presented workers and capitalists as simply dickering over the division of the pie, a perspective Marx adopts in analyzing the struggle concerning the length of the working day.[74]

On a more philosophical level, credit must be given to the central Marxian contention that capitalism and its "laws" came into being and will pass away. Although this is a possibility generally neglected by people intoxicated with capitalism, the doctrine may be regarded as applied Platonism; Smith himself quietly toys with the prospect of civilization's perishability.[75] It is Marx, not Smith, who exudes confidence that the capitalist episode will have the happiest possible ending. This is a foolish assumption, even if we must acknowledge the nobility of Marx's vision of saturating the economy with "consciousness and planfulness" (Trotsky's phrase) on our infinite journey toward the realm of freedom.

The unshakable devotion in the capitalist world to economic growth, technological progress, creature comforts, and individual gratification should, despite their legitimate allure, be questioned, although not only from a Marxian viewpoint. One must never lose sight, moreover, of the evils that may emerge from the pressure to "accumulate" capital and to maximize profits. The study of Smith's texts is unlikely to vanquish the disorienting and demoralizing effects of modern capitalism: the uncertainties of the business cycle; the disruptions entailed by unemployment; the impersonal power of immense, bureaucratic corporations; the rapid mobility of things and people, which undermines community; extreme urbanization; the constant change of products and culture; and the gradual erosion of civic virtue by greed and cynicism.[76]

Much of what is fueled in capitalism by consumerism and the profit motive, however, is likewise required by Marx's call for the realm of freedom, the "full and free development" of the entire species, and "the casting off of all natural limitations" (*GI*, p. 192). Exploding population, production, and consumption will eventually threaten irreversible damage to global ecology. Capitalism has done much to propel the world down this path, but Marx seems to call for its ceaseless continuation. The environmental record of the Soviet bloc, needless to say, has been appalling.

Although there are traces of an ecological vision in Marx, centered around redressing the imbalance between town and country,[77] the conquest of nature and of necessity will take its toll on the environment. Population growth, furthermore, will at some point make it impossible for all human beings to enjoy "full and free development," but how can it be restricted without compromising the "productive" freedom that defines our "species-being"?[78] Perhaps Marx's trenchant critique of capitalism can open up broader questions about modernity as a whole and, therewith, a broader spectrum of possible remedies—beyond "proletarian revolution" and seizing the means of production—to the ills of capitalism. Neither Smith nor Marx suffices as a comprehensive guide to present action, and environmentalism may be a necessary complement to both.[79]

To say that neither Smith nor Marx can plausibly serve as a comprehensive guide implies that there is a sphere within which individuals and peoples can deliberate about their destinies, a sphere constricted by Smith and in a sense eliminated by Marx. Both thinkers pioneered the development of modern social science by substituting empirically based modeling or system building for the theological, metaphysical, and moral frameworks that housed most previous social thought.[80] As we have seen, Smith mutes questions that Marx simply dismisses. And although Marx unmasks some of the intellectual blinders promoted (if not always initiated) by Smith and augmented by subsequent economists, he augments other blinders in fully absorbing philosophy into a historical dialectic based on the mode of production. Marx recommends but does not really argue that nature should be conquered; that virtue should be eclipsed by freedom and prosperity as social goals; that spirituality, the Bible, and concern for the superhuman should be abandoned; that humanity should proceed relentlessly toward a globalized economy and the development of its species-identity at the expense of more local attachments. On the whole, he assumes rather than argues that human history has not been decisively shaped by the plans and projects of "great men," and that the pursuit of knowledge can and will perfectly harmonize with the needs of society. Smith, however, leads his readers—at least when they are sufficiently attuned to the various contradictions, "vestiges," and "danglers"—to investigate alternatives to the above propositions.

To the extent that there is no inexorable path of social development, we must do our best to contemplate the fundamental choices or alternatives that lie before us, including those that are not immediately visible. There would therefore be a need for political philosophy—including comprehensive reflection about the good life, the good society, and the forms of government—beyond inquiry, however sophisticated, concerning society's "economic law of motion" and the "nature and causes of the wealth of nations." Moving beyond Smith and Marx will require reconsideration of the relationship between a variety of disciplines, including political science, sociology, economics, philosophy, theology, and history.[81] The comparison of the two thinkers would be an excellent starting point and would focus attention on the urgent question of how to manage mankind's growing technological capabilities.

Serious deliberation about fundamental alternatives clashes with Marx's utopianism as well as his determinism. As we have seen, Smith's moral philosophy and political economy both incorporate conflict along with cooperation, vice along with virtue, and reform along with conservation. The system of natural liberty supposes, like *The Federalist*, that people are neither angels nor devils. Marx, on the other hand, presents capitalism as thoroughly exploitative or oppressive, and promises total harmony under communism.

Mainstream economics as such embodies a very traditional piece of wisdom: benefits often come with costs, and "trade-offs" are the rule not the exception. In considering economics as the science of choosing among scarce resources toward competing ends, we may conceive "science" and "resources" in a more old-fashioned way and thus minimize the tendency in the discipline toward materialism and positivism.[82] Who can deny that there are competing ends worthy of pursuit and that the relevant resources (including time) are often scarce?[83] Modern economics, for all its bourgeois character, is here in league with some basic tenets of pre-Marxian philosophy and religion: this world is essentially imperfect, and there is consequently a place for the virtue of moderation.[84] The seeds of pessimism or resignation planted by *The Wealth of Nations* grew into the "dismal science" with Malthus and Ricardo, and were then "burst asunder" by Marx.[85] Perhaps there is a happy medium between the Marxian effort to reduce philosophy to the agenda of a party preaching world revolution and the Smithian emphasis on its tranquilizing effects.

Near the end of his life, Michael Harrington declared that he had only "two cheers" for socialism. Such lowering of the stakes helps reduce the choices about capitalism to sane proportions. One must likewise commend the efforts of Michael Walzer and many others who are indebted to Marx—no thinker receives equal accolades in *Spheres of Justice*—but who accept the permanence of the political "sphere" and therefore strive to specify the nature of the public power under socialism.[86] On the Right, economic conservatism centered on opposition to "big government" coexists uneasily with social conservatism, and the spirit of Adam Smith needs to be better integrated with that of Aristotle and Aquinas. Leo Strauss identified "economism" with "Machiavellianism come of age," and attempted to strip the intellectual blinders imposed by modernity, but how would he assess the economism of Smith against that of Marx? How can one employ ancient thought to address the complex economic issues that agitate contemporary politics: for example, inflation, unemployment, trade deficits, budget deficits, tax reform, industrial safety, minimum-wage legislation, strikes, union busting, health insurance, deposit insurance, leveraged buyouts, junk bonds, rent control, anti-trust policy, and a huge array of environmental issues?[87] Many people hold confident positions on such matters, despite the inadequacy of their knowlege and tools of analysis, to say nothing of their historical and philosophical sensibilities. We confront again the dilemma posed by the disproportion between the complexity of modern life and the limitations of an individual mind that must deliberate as citizen if not ruler. We may have no alternative but to muddle through.

Marx in *Capital* strove with unbelievable perseverance and penetration to lay bare the dynamic of capitalism in all its complexity; the work is truly a "great book." But given the confident tone of the *Manifesto*, one would assume that all the knowledge necessary to consummate the revolution was on hand in 1848. Unlike Smith's writings, which leave clues as to their own shortcomings, Marx's writings do not point to other books as means to perfect one's knowledge of "the whole." Marx seems to promise a world that has overcome its paralyzing and mystifying complexity, a world in which each human being can and will possess the ultimate wisdom.[88] Marx's disparagement of philosophy conceals the possibility that we remain ignorant of what Socrates calls "the greatest things." Such ignorance spurs the continued pursuit of wisdom and may serve as a check on the tyrannical inclinations of subjects and rulers who presume that they possess adequate answers to the most basic questions.[89] Marxist scholars limit their opportunity to appraise non-Marxian answers to such questions and to learn from the past insofar as they assume that philosophy and religion are just the ideological manifestations of alienation and class struggle.

Marx's complaint that philosophers have interpreted the world rather than changed it has been the subject of countless intoxicated recitations, matched by pretentious musings about "praxis." The Marxian experiment in expropriation, from which many countries are now struggling gamely to extricate themselves, has dramatically failed to refute the core proposition of *The Wealth of Nations*: there is no "human wisdom or knowledge" that would render a government capable of properly "superintending the industry of private people" (IV.ix.51, IV.ii.10). Smith's lament about the imperfection of human knowledge points to the need for philosophy or revelation, a need that Marx simply dismisses. However much we can learn from Marx, we must condemn him for inciting world revolution on the basis of counterfeit wisdom.

Reference
Matter

Notes

CHAPTER ONE *Introduction*

1. On Smith's debt to Hume—perhaps the philosopher who most directly prepared Smith's emphasis on history and social science—see Forbes; Haakonssen; Teichgraeber, *Free Trade*; and Winch, *Smith's Politics*, pp. 8–9, 34, 38–45, 52–53, 70–76, 81–83, 99–100, 124–30, 135–36, 156–59, 162–63, 171, 176–77.

2. According to William Letwin, "All the efforts of seventeenth and eighteenth century economic writers culminated in *The Wealth of Nations*. Everything useful that they did, Adam Smith incorporated; everything worth doing that they left undone, he accomplished" (p. 221). In Phyllis Deane's words, the book served as "the undisputed, internationally accepted, bible of the new science of political economy" (p. 6).

3. On the contributions of Jeremy Bentham and J. B. Say to the purification of economics, see Halévy, pp. 15, 94–95, 158–59, 268–72, 371–72, 433, 492–506; and Flubacher, pp. 112–15, 159–64. On post-Smithian developments in Scottish political economy, see Burrow et al., pp. 25–26, 37, 44–57, 61, 67, 87; and Chitnis, pp. 117–27.

4. An examination of Mill's *Principles of Political Economy* would nicely complement my discussions of the interplay of economics with philosophy, politics, and religion in Locke, Smith, Malthus, Ricardo, and Marx. Although Mill's treatise is generally neglected by contemporary economists, social scientists, and politicians, it was very prominent in the nineteenth century. For a partial assessment, see Bonar, pp. 248–64; Burrow et al., pp. 65–159; Duncan, pp. 1–54, 209–315; Flubacher, pp. 139–52; Ryan, *Property and Political Theory*, pp. 142–93; and Winch, "Introduction."

5. According to Hans Medick, Smith is not only "der Stammvater der anglo-schottischen politischen Ökonomie" but also "eine Schlüsselfigur in der Entstehungsgeschichte der übrigen Sozialwissenschaften, der Politischen Wissenschaft ebenso wie der Politischen Soziologie" (p. 178); Smith conceived himself as the Newton of the social sciences (p. 247). According to James Farr, Smith "plays a very visible hand in the emergence of modern political science" (p. 51).

6. Although economists Robert Heilbroner and Lester Thurow warn us about the limited relevance of the GNP (pp. 68–70), they proceed to identify "well-being" with the GNP and other purely economic factors (pp. 126, 212, 216). They even refer to a table depicting "real per capita disposable personal income" over time as "the curve that represents our real well-being" (p. 125).

7. Kristol, *Reflections*, p. 188. But cf. p. 116; and Kristol, *Two Cheers*, pp. 56, 253. Also cf. Friedman, *Capitalism*, pp. 15, 33–34, 178, 187, 192; Friedman, *Free to Choose*, pp. 88–89, 109, 119, 120, 216; and Hayek, pp. 41, 87, 96, 111, 145, 161, 232, 283, 385, 400–402.

8. Medick, p. 178; Myers, pp. 110–11; Raphael, p. 90; Winch, *Smith's Politics*, p. 10. Although he ignores the religious contradictions, McNally provides some ingenious arguments to reconcile the two books (pp. 178, 189, 209–20, 225–28, 244). Richard Teichgraeber has dissented from the consensus among modern scholars, complaining about the "perfunctory treatment" of the *Problem*, and providing a helpful summary of its original formulations by Oncken, Paszkowski, and Zeyss (Teichgraeber, "Rethinking," pp. 106–8, 123). For a more comprehensive overview of scholarly positions on the *Problem*, see Dickey, pp. 579–87.

9. As Smith wrote in 1788 to his publisher Thomas Cadell, "I am a slow, a very slow workman, who do and undo everything I write at least half a dozen of times" (*Correspondence*, #276, 15 March 1788). Cf. Medick, p. 182.

10. Letwin invokes Smith's uncanny success at systematizing to explain his status as the founder of scientific economics (pp. 221, 226–28). Cf. Hollander, pp. 21, 305, 313–14; and Skinner, p. 182.

11. Montesquieu, *Pensées*, quoted in Pangle, p. 13.

12. The well-known trio of essays in *EPS* that illustrate "the principles which lead and direct philosophical enquiries" stress the connection between philosophy and coherence. See Astronomy II.7,9,12, III.1,3, IV.13,15,24,32,35,43,50,65,75; and Physics 2,8,9,11.

13. Although Winch denies the original version of "*das Adam Smith Problem*" (*Smith's Politics*, p. 10), he stresses the difficulty of "understanding the connections between the overlapping sub-systems that compose Smith's highly ambitious and systematic enterprise—the most ambitious enterprise to be carried through to near-completion in an age and place that was notable for the compendious quality of its intellectual projects" ("Smith's 'enduring particular result,'" p. 253).

14. Viner, *Long View*, p. 214, emphasis in original. In Teichgraeber's words, "A great many doors lead into Smith's mind" (*Free Trade*, p. 125).

15. Winch, *Smith's Politics*, pp. 155, 171. Smith defines these two forms of

discursive argument in his rhetoric lectures. "Didactick . . . proposes to put before us the arguments on both sides of the question in their true light, giving each its proper degree of influence," whereas the "Rhetoricall . . . endeavours by all means to perswade us; and for this purpose it magnifies all the arguments on the one side and diminishes or conceals those that might be brought on the side conterary to that which it is designed that we should favour"; the primary purpose of didactic is instruction, not persuasion (*LRBL* i.149–50).

16. See, for example, Marx, *Capital*, vol. II, pp. 276, 290, 297, 448, 454, 465.

17. Marx, *Werke*, 26.2.162, quoted by Dumont, who agrees that Smith "juxtaposed esoteric and exoteric views" (pp. 91, 97). Vernard Foley, in part inspired by Eric Havelock's studies of Greek anthropology, argues that Smith's teaching was "consciously, systematically, and secretly modeled" on pre-Socratic vortex physics (p. xi). Although Foley appreciates the subtlety of Smith's religious unorthodoxy, and proceeds with ingenuity and extensive research, the argument as a whole is unconvincing.

18. Wolff, *Moneybags*, pp. 43, 28; indeed, the paradigm is Socratic irony (pp. 25–31). McCloskey's *The Rhetoric of Economics*, despite its powerful critique of "positivism" and "modernism" in contemporary economics, is blind to the rhetoric that launched both mainstream and radical economics.

19. As Hume asks, "Why rake into those corners of nature which spread a nuisance all around? Why dig up the pestilence from the pit in which it is buried?" He concludes, "Truths which are *pernicious* to society, if any such there be, will yield to errors which are salutary" (*ICPM*, IX:ii, p. 99, emphasis in original).

20. Smith's *Correspondence*, #165, 15 August 1776, #172, 5 September 1776. Smith also opposed the posthumous publication of Hume's letters: "Many things would be published not fit to see the light" (#181, 2 December 1776). Cf. Bryson, pp. 230–31.

21. Smith's *Correspondence*, #178, 9 November 1776.

22. Viner conveys the basic theological contrast between the two books (*Long View*, pp. 216–17, 221–24, 229–30) but, as will be demonstrated, not without distortion. Though Medick strives relentlessly to explain the inter-relation of the parts of Smith's corpus, he depreciates *das Problem* (p. 178) because he pays minimal attention to Smith's treatment of religion.

23. "The close conjunction of economics and political philosophy, even or perhaps especially if tending towards the eclipse of the latter, is a powerful fact of political philosophy" (Cropsey, *Political Philosophy*, pp. 53–54).

24. Winch, *Smith's Politics*, pp. ix–x, 86–87, 164–65, 183. Winch rightly criticizes Cropsey for treating the proposition that "capitalism is the embodiment of Smithian principles" as an "axiomatic premise" (p. 16; cf. p. 142; and McNally, pp. 152–54). Other scholars with more or less "historical" orientations—including Laurence Dickey, Knud Haakonssen, Istvan Hont, Michael Ignatieff, David McNally, Nicholas Phillipson, Richard Teichgraeber, and Pocock himself—have subsequently focused their attention on

Smith. Cropsey, by contrast, pays homage to that great critic of historicism, Leo Strauss. On Strauss's relevance for political economy, see Minowitz, "Machiavellianism."

25. Winch, *Smith's Politics*, pp. 6, 180. Winch's argument is complemented neatly by McNally, who stresses the difference between the "agrarian capitalism" lauded by Smith (and many of his predecessors) and the "industrial capitalism" extolled—and perhaps more rigorously analyzed—by Ricardo, Bentham, and Say (McNally, pp. 12, 230–33, 248, 262, 265–66; cf. pp. 252–54 on the political features of Smith's political economy). For a recent formulation, not discussed by Winch, of the deflection thesis, see Dumont (pp. 7, 24, 26, 33), who dubs *WN* "the birth registration" of a new category of analysis, "the economy." Although Winch approvingly cites Albert Hirschman, he does not address Hirschman's charge that Smith was responsible for a narrowing of thought whereby the discipline of economics gained its independence (Hirschman, p. 112). Pocock argues that "the dialogue between polity and economy remained a dialogue" throughout the eighteenth century (*Virtue, Commerce*, p. 70). The dialogue continues in *WN*, but one voice tends to drown out the other.

26. *WN* V.i.a.5,28, V.i.g.19, I.viii.41, III.ii.9, IV.vii.b.55, IV.iii.c.9, V.i.f.25; unfortunately, these examples concern violence, war, injustice, and slavery. Smith describes post-feudal commercial society and its mercantilist political economy as "our own times" (*WN* IV.Intro), and freely invokes "present" phenomena along with the distinction between "ancient" and "modern"; he also makes frequent reference to "the present century" when discussing economic data such as grain prices and interest rates (*WN* I.viii.34, I.ix.9,11, I.xi.g.6,14,16,17,20, I.xi.h.11, I.xi.m.11, I.xi.n.4–5, IV.v.a.5, IV.v.b.5). But he rarely refers to centuries by number, and never binds a philosophical doctrine with a specific century (the closest he comes is *TMS* VII.iv.7; regarding the influence of historical circumstances on intellectual developments, see *TMS* VII.ii.1.28, VII.ii.4.12, VII.iii.2.2, VII.iv.16; *WN* Intro.7–8, IV.i.5–6,10, IV.ix.3–4; and Astronomy III.1–5).

27. Smith also published two reviews in the *Edinburgh Review*, an essay in *The Philological Miscellany* on the origin of languages, the letter about Hume in *Scots Magazine*, and a brief dedication to William Hamilton. All but the language essay and the Hume letter are included in the Oxford edition of *EPS*. For a fuller description, see pp. xiii–xiv above.

28. Rae, p. 434; Raphael, pp. 27–28; Winch, *Smith's Politics*, p. 3.

29. My references to Smith's "corpus" or "writings" exclude the lectures.

30. See, for example, Haakonssen, pp. 83–189; Teichgraeber, *Free Trade*, pp. 121–69; and Winch, *Smith's Politics*, pp. 46–146.

31. John Gunnell has made powerful arguments against assuming the existence of a "tradition" subsuming the authors commonly examined in textbooks on the history of political philosophy. He says little, however, to establish that such a tradition does not exist ("Myth," pp. 122–34; "Political Theory," pp. 339–61; *Between Philosophy and Politics*, pp. 21–22, 95–98, 108, 113, 115). Smith refers to all of the above-mentioned authors in addition

to some of their classical counterparts: Plato, Aristotle, Polybius, and Cicero. (In *WN*, Smith refers to "the very respectable authority" of the first three and Cicero is cited approvingly; cf. *TMS* VII.1, VII.ii.1, VII.iv.3.) In making comparisons between Smith and earlier writers, I do not mean to imply that Smith always had the particular writer in mind; cf. Winch, *Smith's Politics*, pp. 17–18. Even if the comparison of particular positions does not always demonstrate the process by which later positions emerged from earlier ones, such comparison will help us in assessing the adequacy of the different views.

32. As we shall explore in Chapters 6–10, the economic ends also clash with the spiritual goals of the *respublica Christiana* as envisioned in the Middle Ages.

33. My chapters and sections will usually take up *WN*, the work that constitutes Smith's prime legacy, before *TMS*.

CHAPTER TWO *The Ends and Forms of Government*

1. *WN* IV.Intro.1. Smith says little to elaborate the latter phrases. On the original meanings of "political economy," see Bonar, pp. 59, 152; Letwin, p. 217; and McNally, pp. 69–72.

2. *WN* I.xi.c.7, II.ii.7. Cf. *LJA* vi.16,18–20; *LJB* 209–11; and Plato's *Republic*, 369d, 372e. Albion Small is pleased that Smith thus bursts from the narrow confines of "economics," which treats the accumulation of capital as an end in itself, to sociology, which looks at material things as objects of consumption by the people (p. 3). For Smith, indeed, it is "perfectly self-evident" that "the interest of the producer ought to be attended to, only so far as it may be necessary for promoting that of the consumer," and he therefore excoriates mercantilism for treating production "as the ultimate end and object of all industry and commerce" (*WN* IV.viii.49).

3. Cf. *WN* V.i.f.7 on interest "vulgarly understood." Whereas Ricardo, in *The Principles of Political Economy and Taxation*, casually but repeatedly identifies wealth with human well-being (pp. 53, 61, 80, 109, 181, 194–95, 210, 231, 263, 277), Malthus, as befits an Anglican minister, is more careful (*An Essay on the Principle of Population*, XVI, p. 103). Cf. Burrow et al., pp. 72–74. Nowadays, talk of "the quality of life" is beginning to complement that of "the standard of living," but economists are prone to overlook the distinction. When Thurow looks beyond "output" as a criterion of "welfare," he looks primarily to distribution (p. 225); he elsewhere claims that the following "important question" is outside the scope of economics: "Is the good society a laissez-faire society or one in which government intervenes to produce a 'good' distribution of income?" (p. 27). Even when articulating "non-economic" questions, Thurow thus defines "the good society" and "welfare" in terms of income-distribution patterns. Some leading political economists convey a similar sensibility: "When questions of distribution arise, and the problem is to choose between Pareto-efficient points, economists frequently throw up their hands and state that the problem is 'political'" (Alt and Chrystal, p. 240).

4. WN II.ii.86, II.iii.20, III.iv.15, IV.vii.b.64, V.ii.c.6. Smith does occasionally lament the bloodier forms of injustice (WN IV.i.32, IV.vii.a.15, IV.vii.c.80).

5. Feudalism and its attendant disorders were indeed ended by "the gradual improvements of arts, manufactures, and commerce"—i.e., by "the *natural* course of things" (WN III.ii.1, III.iii.12, III.iv.4,9–10, V.i.g.24–25).

6. Cf. Haakonssen, p. 122; and Pangle, p. 116. In explaining Smith's ranking of intelligence above courage, Phillipson brilliantly suggests that in "commercial civilization, wisdom rather than the classic martial and political virtues was the true touchstone of virtue" ("Adam Smith," p. 181; cf. "Enlightenment," p. 38). As we will see, Smith puts his own stamp on the Enlightenment project of reconciling philosophy and society. Heilbroner's penetrating analysis of the "economic" rationale behind Smith's delineation of public and private spheres overlooks this remarkable governmental duty to "superintend" character (*Behind the Veil*, pp. 140–41).

7. Marx grasps the spirit of Smith's educational program better than Michael Ignatieff does (p. 120). Marx comments: "For preventing the complete deterioration of the great mass of the people which arises from the division of labor, Adam Smith recommends education of the people by the state, but in prudent homeopathic doses" (*Capital*, vol. I, ch. 14, p. 484). According to Himmelfarb, however, Smith's program required a higher degree of government involvement in education "than anything that had ever existed before" (p. 59).

8. As Pangle points out, however, Montesquieu's account is itself a departure from the ancients. By praising music only as a corrective to the excesses of civic or military virtue, Montesquieu contradicts the cited Platonic passages where music is portrayed as the peak of civic education and a stepping-stone to virtue (Pangle, pp. 65–66; cf. Lowenthal, pp. 276–80, 269–71). Both Montesquieu and Smith rely on commerce rather than music to mitigate militarism. According to Montesquieu, military/gymnastic training emerged as a substitute for the despised arts of commerce (*Spirit of Laws*, IV:8, p. 39). Cf. Pocock, *Machiavellian Moment*, pp. 491–93.

9. WN Intro.4, I.xi.d.3, II.iii.31, III.i, IV.i.33, IV.ix.28, V.i.a.1–3,6,8,11, 36,42–44, V.i.f.51. The four-stage categorization has roots in Montesquieu and echoes in many of Smith's contemporaries—Turgot, Ferguson, Millar, and James Steuart. In arguing that Smith extolled agrarian rather than industrial capitalism and that Smith was "profoundly critical of commercial society" (p. 227), McNally overlooks the privileged position of commercial society in Smith's four-stage schema. Dickey errs in the opposite direction by contending (on the basis of the 1790 edition of TMS) that Smith's alarm about moral decay within commercial societies peaked in the 1780s (p. 608; cf. pp. 598–99).

10. Heilbroner confuses the commercial stage with the system of natural liberty ("Paradox of Progress," p. 535). In good Marxist fashion, he faults Smith for eschewing "a logic . . . in the historical scheme capable of transcending or transforming" the bleak world portrayed in WN (p. 533), i.e.,

for overlooking any "social dynamics" that could produce "a fundamental change in socio-economic structure" (p. 537).

11. Cf. Ferguson, *Essay*, IV:ii, p. 186. For a more complete discussion of Smith on ancient civilization, see Haakonssen, pp. 180–81.

12. "Regime means simultaneously the form of life of a society, its style of life, its moral taste, form of society, form of state, form of government, spirit of laws" (Strauss, *Political Philosophy*, pp. 33–34). Cf. pp. 84–86; and *Natural Right*, pp. 135–38. For Smith's use of the term *"politeia,"* see *LJB* 203, which will be discussed at the end of this chapter.

13. Machiavelli, *Discourses*, I:2. Cf. Hobbes, *Leviathan* (pp. 238, 240, 380); Pufendorf, *De Jure Naturae et Gentium, VII:* v; the brief Chapter X of Locke's *Second Treatise* ("Of the Forms of a Commonwealth"); Montesquieu, *Spirit of Laws*, XI:9; and Hegel, *Philosophy of Right*, secs. 273–74, and "Introduction" to *Philosophy of History*, pp. 44–47.

14. Engels, *Socialism: Utopian and Scientific*, pp. 689, 713.

15. In Arendt's judgment, Montesquieu was "the last political thinker to concern himself seriously with the problem of forms of government" (p. 202). Compared with *WN*, *The Spirit of the Laws* draws more on classical sources, defers more to religion, and devotes more attention to regimes, political institutions, Aristotelian virtues, legislators, and the corrupting effects of wealth.

16. See Hume, "Of Civil Liberty" and "Idea of a Perfect Commonwealth," in *Essays*; on Hutcheson, see Winch, *Smith's Politics*, pp. 48, 55–56; on Ferguson, see the discussion of his *Institutes of Moral Philosophy* in Sher, pp. 192–94.

17. In analyzing the other governmental duties—defense, justice, and public works (including education and religion)—Smith acknowledges variation based on the different "periods" or "states" of society, but never refers to the "form of government." Some contemporary political economists are more neglectful than Smith. Consider the following theoretical generalizations, which imply that all governments are democratic: "Economic policy is . . . political because it reflects decisions made by elected politicians in an institutional context"; "decisions about economic policy are made in the political arena by incumbent elected politicians"; "if electorates had completely stable preferences, governments (or at least their policies) would never change" (Alt and Chrystal, pp. 33, 101, 192).

18. The danglers may be construed as threads that clash with the larger fabric of Smith's design. Kristol refers to *WN*'s "crosscurrents" and "countercurrents" (*Reflections*, p. 164).

19. In a more typical formulation, Smith explains that because the government of England has never been "very parsimonious," parsimony "has at no time been the characteristical virtue of its inhabitants" (*WN* II.ii.36). On Montesquieu's account of government's formative role, see Pangle, pp. 185–87, 280; and Shklar, pp. 51–52, 103–5.

20. Economics continues to presuppose this independence and, like contemporary social science generally, treasures its freedom from any naturalis-

tic, theological, or metaphysical baggage. Cf. Dumont, pp. 24, 33, 41; and Foley, p. 193. On the contribution of the Physiocrats to portraying the economy as a self-regulating whole, see Bonar, p. 195; Caton, *Politics of Progress*, p. 413n2; Deane, pp. 4–6; Halévy, pp. 267–72; Hirschman, p. 94; Hollander, pp. 44–52, 78–92, 166, 316–17; Letwin, p. 217; and McNally, pp. 85–86, 110–14, 142. According to Winch, "Smith did not invent what is now called economic analysis, though he did extend and give it academic respectability by absorbing it into a larger class of metaphysical and human speculation" ("Smith's 'enduring particular result,'" p. 268). Or did Smith's attention to the "metaphysical and human" department contribute to liberating economic analysis from its fetters?

21. According to Robert E. Lane, "The market leads people to think about processes of allocation and deserts, whereas politics leads people to think about outcomes of allocation" (p. 390). Also consider Hayek's remarks about why economists emphasize the "need for an impersonal mechanism" to coordinate human activities (pp. 4, 26, 29, 87, 137, 385).

22. Cf. *WN* II.ii.23,29,86. Also cf. I.viii.40 on the "proper rate" of human procreation; I.viii.57 on the "proper division and distribution of employment"; and IV.i.9 on how free trade supplies all commodities "in the proper quantity."

23. Cf. *TMS* III.5.6 on the subtle difference between laws enacted by governments and the laws of physics. Also cf. pp. 132–34 below; and Bonar, pp. 194–96, 212–13.

24. Cf. Cropsey, *Polity*, pp. 72–79, on how Smith's theory of natural wages, profits, and rents substitutes convention and competition for virtue and the idea of "congruence" with human nature. McNally too discerns that convention enters into the determination of these natural rates, but argues that distributive justice is likewise a factor (pp. 210, 214–20, 225–28). Cf. Hollander, pp. 117–21.

25. Consider Smith's use of the phrase "naturally, or rather necessarily" (*WN* I.i.7, IV.ii.4) and of related phrases about nature and necessity (IV.i.30, V.i.h.2, V.i.g.23).

26. The classic statement on Smith's departures from pure laissez-faire is Viner, *Long View*, pp. 231–45. Also see Hollander, pp. 217, 257–58; and Rosenberg, "Smith and Laissez-Faire."

27. Cf. *WN* III.iii.12, V.iii.7, IV.vii.b.2.

28. *WN* V.i.a.2,4,41, V.i.g.16,17,41; *TMS* II.iii.2.4, III.3.42, VI.ii.2.2, VI.ii.3.3. Hume, like Smith, rejects social-contract theory, but he admits that the question—"to whom is allegiance due" or "who is our lawful sovereign"—is "often the most difficult of any, and liable to infinite discussions" ("Of the Original Contract," *Essays*, p. 481). But cf. *Treatise*, III.ii.10, p. 557.

29. When Smith asserts that the "republican form of government seems to be the principal support of the present grandeur of Holland" (*WN* V.ii.k.80), the context is again economic: Smith is exonerating Holland for taxing

necessities. Republican government is here indicated by the prominent governmental role of the great mercantile families, as opposed to nobles and soldiers. Cf. Forbes, p. 197.

30. Campbell, p. 206; Cropsey, *Polity*, pp. 65–66; Raphael and Macfie, p. 19. Cropsey, invoking Smith's praise of Holland, suggests that Smith may have tempered his praise of republicanism for prudential reasons.

31. Rousseau, *Second Discourse*, pp. 149, 179.

32. Smith follows the *Second Discourse* on some crucial matters: isolating morality from philosophy and linking it instead with sentiment (pity/ sympathy) and the common man; emphasizing history rather than abstract philosophy; viewing government as a project of the rich against the poor. See pp. 39–46 below. Smith replaces the general will with the invisible hand and the impartial spectator as devices for harmonizing the individual and society.

33. Smith's authorship of the letter, according to John Bryce, was widely known prior to Dugald Stewart's attribution (*EPS*, p. 230).

34. For Cropsey's dazzling hints about this, see *Political Philosophy*, pp. 70, 74, 82, 84. West errs in alleging that Smith, despite his criticisms of the *Second Discourse*, would have been sympathetic to the *Social Contract* (West, p. 69).

35. Ricardo's *Principles* employs the terms "free" and "despotic" without any attempt to define them.

36. The despotic forms have a spectrum of their own, ranging from "the gentle and mild government of Paris, to that of the violent and furious government of Constantinople" (*WN* V.i.g.19), with Spain and Portugal presumably closer to the latter end (IV.vii.b.52).

37. The political involvement of the people in "free countries" (cf. *WN* V.i.f.61) may explain Smith's assertion that the "good temper and moderation of contending factions seems to be the most essential circumstance in the public morals of a free people" (V.i.f.40).

38. Smith nevertheless insists that "the ordinary laws of justice" may be ignored in the name of "public utility . . . only in cases of the most urgent necessity" (*WN* IV.v.b.39).

39. Montesquieu, *Spirit of Laws*, I:12; cf. Pangle, pp. 41, 46, 54, 89, 102, 109–112, 142.

40. *WN* III.iv.12, IV.vii.b.2, IV.vii.c.54, V.iii.7.

41. Winch, *Smith's Politics*, pp. 40, 95; cf. Burrow et al., p. 31; Forbes, p. 198; and Skinner, p. 101. Hutcheson, in defining a "free people" as one whose "important interests are well secured against any rapacious or capricious wills of those in power," departs explicitly from the Greek and Roman identification of the term with the people's exercise of political power (*A System of Moral Philosophy*, II, p. 282, quoted in Teichgraeber, *Free Trade*, p. 29). Adam Ferguson, by contrast, claims that "liberty is never in greater danger than it is when we measure national felicity by the blessings which a prince may bestow, or by the mere tranquillity which may attend on

equitable administration" (*Essay*, VI:v, pp. 269–70). As Sher documents (pp. 193, 197–98, 265–66), Ferguson elsewhere joins Smith and Hume in adopting Montesquieu's identification of liberty and security.

42. The silence in Smith's writings is partially remedied in the lectures, where he states that "no government is quite perfect, but it is better to submitt to some inconveniences than make attempts against it" (*LJB* 95). Smith concludes, however, that "whatever be the principle of alledgiance, a right of resistance must undoubtedly be lawfull, because no authority is altogether unlimited" (*LJB* 98). Cf. Pocock, *Virtue, Commerce*, p. 48.

43. *WN* I.x.c.12,59, IV.ii.42, IV.v.b.16, IV.vii.b.44, IV.ix.3,51.

44. Robert Nozick here parts company with Smith: "Taxation of earnings from labor is on a par with forced labor" (p. 169).

45. Cf. *WN* III.iv.24, IV.vii.c.103, V.i.e.26. McNally uses such passages to support his ingenious thesis that Smith's "natural aristocracy" was a political elite constituted by "country gentlemen and farmers" whose public spirit would help them counteract the corrupting influence of merchants and manufacturers (pp. 190–92, 220–25, 265). McNally stresses, however, that Smith favored not the hereditary nobility prone to indolence but the "progressive" or "improving" gentry who had developed mercantile habits of "order, economy, and attention" and who undertook capital investments in the land they leased to wealthy farmers (pp. 154, 203–4, 230, 232–33). Cf. Winch, *Smith's Politics*, pp. 140–41.

46. *WN* I.viii.13, I.x.b.40, I.xi.m.9, II.v.31–32, IV.iii.c.2. Smith's famous defense of standing armies, however, indicates that political force and liberty are not simply opposed to one another (V.i.a.41).

47. See, for example, Hume, "Of Civil Liberty," in *Essays*.

48. Cf. Cropsey, *Polity*, pp. 69–70. The above passage, added in the final edition of *TMS*, characteristically serves to demystify passages in prior editions that were less unambiguous in rejecting the pretensions of traditional aristocracies (I.iii.2.4).

49. As usual, this political observation occupies a small portion of a larger argument with an economic focus: pecuniary considerations dictate that Great Britain either unite with its colonies or liberate them. On the prospects for representative institutions in larger societies, see *WN* IV.vii.c.75,77.

50. Cf. the argument in Plato's *Laws* that citizens should not be craftsmen: citizenship alone is a demanding art (*technē*), and almost no one can labor "with precision" at two pursuits or arts (864d).

51. Stewart, IV.6, p. 311. Some of Stewart's own writings were accused of "unhinging established institutions" (Burrow et al., pp. 32–39; Chitnis, pp. 23–24).

52. Stewart, IV.2,4, pp. 309–10. Phillipson argues that the 1707 Union with England made it natural for Scottish thinkers to focus on social, economic, and cultural conditions rather than constitutional forms, and to abandon the "civic humanist" exaltation of autonomy and political participation ("Enlightenment," pp. 21–25, 33). In Pocock's words, the Scottish

Enlightenment, in emphasizing communication, sentiments, sympathy, and *doux commerce*, replaced the polis with politeness and *oikos* with economy ("Cambridge paradigms," p. 242).

53. Cropsey exaggerates in saying that Smith intended his writings to "cause a new polity to come into being" (*Polity*, p. 56).

54. *WN* IV.ii.43, IV.iii.68, IV.vii.c.66. On the gulf between the best and the actual, also see IV.v.b.40, 53, IV.ix.4, V.i.f.43,59, V.i.g.8. Smith does once suggest, perhaps ironically, that the system had been a reality: "In what manner the natural system of perfect liberty and justice ought gradually to be *restored*, we must leave to the wisdom of future statesmen and legislators to determine" (IV.vii.c.44); cf. IV.ii.43 on the prospects for free trade being "restored."

55. "The ideas of the profligate Mandeville seem" in Rousseau "to have all the purity and sublimity of the morals of Plato" (Letter 12). Foley comments about this strange observation: it "would seem . . . as if Smith is attempting to use the fame and reputation of Rousseau and Plato to reduce the risks which he will later run by adopting the principles of Mandeville" (p. 119).

56. West goes too far, however, in suggesting that Smith's chief concern was with Rousseau's "literary style" (p. 69).

57. Ferguson, *Essay*, III:ii, p. 123. Edmund Burke, of course, emphasizes the "principle of growth" rather than transformative foundings or fixed forms of government, and endorses "prescription" as the title to both government and property.

58. The warnings were added for the 1790 edition of *TMS*, apparently with an eye toward events in France. In the earlier editions, Smith's praise of the "spirit of system" as a spur to good citizenship was more wholehearted (IV.i.11).

59. Haakonssen, p. 91. Winch agrees that the raffle passage is cynical and perhaps ironic (*Smith's Politics*, p. 156).

60. Smith explains that despite his "very advanced age," he retained the concluding promise published more than thirty years before when he "entertained no doubt of being able to execute every thing which it announced" (*TMS* Advert.2). For a philosopher, perhaps time is the scarcest commodity.

61. The qualifying phrase, "at least," suggests that *WN* provides a partial account of justice—presumably the article on the "expence of justice" (V.i.b).

62. *LJA* iv.3–179; *LJB* 18–64. Also see Winch, *Smith's Politics*, pp. 57–63.

63. *TMS* VII.iv.37, VI.ii.Intro.2. Cf. Smith's claim that the deliberations of the legislator "ought to be governed by general principles which are always the same" (*WN* IV.ii.39).

64. "How great soever the variety of municipal laws . . . their chief outlines pretty regularly concur, because the purposes to which they tend are everywhere exactly similar" (Hume, *ICPM*, III:ii, p. 33). Montesquieu, by contrast, emphasizes the variety of regimes, climates, and manners.

65. Grotius, *The Law of War and Peace*, I.3.6–10, II.9.6, III.15.8,10, III.20.3–4.

66. Grotius, *Proleg.*, 1, 17–18, 21–25, 28, 53; *The Law of War and Peace*, II.2.19–22, II:22, III.3.2, III.11.19, III.15.10–11, III.25.1.

67. On the relationship between police and justice in the lectures, also see Haakonssen, pp. 95–96.

CHAPTER THREE *Justice*

1. *WN* I.x.c.12,27,59, IV.v.b.16, IV.vii.c.44, IV.ix.3.

2. Locke removes the rosy veil in his chapter on conquest (secs. 175–76, 180). Charles Lindbloom errs in implying that Locke and Smith assumed that the original distribution of property and land was always peaceful (pp. 45–46); cf. Alt and Chrystal, p. 17. Hont and Ignatieff present a subtler view: "The world whose economic problems Smith set out to solve was a world where land was already private property" (p. 43). Even Burke, who greatly surpassed Smith in sympathy for the traditional aristocracy, conceded that Europe's landlords were indebted to the "barbarous conquerors" who ushered in the feudal era (*Reflections*, p. 346).

3. *WN* I.vi.4,5,8, I.viii.2. At one point Smith even states that in civilized countries "rent and profit eat up wages, and the two superior orders oppress the inferior one" (IV.vii.b.3). Cf. the claim in the lectures that "a porter or day-labourer must continue poor forever" (*LJB* 286).

4. *WN* I.vi.5, I.vi.8. Cf. Hollander, pp. 148–54, 185; McNally, pp. 255–61; and Meek, *Smith, Marx*, p. 7.

5. Locke, *Second Treatise*, secs. 36–37, 40, 42–43.

6. The impartial administration of justice is thus the foundation of "the liberty of every individual, the sense which he has of his own security" (*WN* V.i.b.25; cf. IV.v.b.39). As we have seen, however, "the natural liberty of a few individuals" must yield to "the security of the whole society" (II.ii.94).

7. *LJA* iv.19, v.114–19,127–29; *LJB* 15–18. Hume, "Of the Original Contract," *Essays*, pp. 468–71. According to James Steuart, "The rights of kings . . . are to be sought for in history; and not founded upon the supposition of tacit contracts between them and their people" (*Inquiry*, II:xiii, p. 209). For a detailed discussion of Smith's position in the lectures, see Haakonssen, pp. 127–33.

8. Cf. Hume, *Treatise*, III.ii.2, pp. 491–92.

9. Cf. *TMS* II.i.5.9; and Hume, *Treatise*, III.ii.2, p. 493.

10. Smith faults Rousseau for exaggerating the positive features of primitive life (Letter 11).

11. Government arose not "from any consent or agreement . . . but from the natural progress which men make in society" (*LJA* iv.19). Cropsey overstates Smith's insistence on consent (*Political Philosophy*, p. 70). He nevertheless conveys a profound explanation for Smith's abandonment of consent: that Smith, unlike Rousseau and Kant, did not seek to liberate "the inner drives of every man in the interest of the moral will" (pp. 70, 74; cf. Forbes, p. 195). Rosenberg likewise exaggerates: "Smith strongly rejects all views that allow one group of people, on whatever pretext, the right to make

important decisions affecting the lives of others" ("Smith and Laissez-Faire," p. 28).

12. *WN* V.i.b.25, IV.ix.51, II.ii.94, IV.ii.42, IV.v.b.16; cf. pp. 25–26 above. Smith's "natural liberty" calls to mind Hobbes's specification of the "Liberty of Subjects" as their "liberty to buy, and sell, and otherwise contract . . . ; to choose their own aboad, their own diet, their own trade of life" (*Leviathan*, ch. XXI, p. 264). On Smith's departure from Rousseau's "moral freedom," see pp. 24–25 above; and *Social Contract*, I:i, I:viii (pp. 47, 56).

13. Smith's lectures, as usual, are more blunt: "Laws and government may be considered . . . as a combination of the rich to oppress the poor, and preserve to themselves the inequality of the goods which would otherwise be soon destroyed by the attacks of the poor, who if not hindered by the government would soon reduce the others to an equality with themselves by open violence" (*LJA* iv.22–23). Smith, however, continues by suggesting that the rich acquired their wealth in a peaceful manner (iv.23). In explaining why there would be little accumulation in the "infancey of society," furthermore, the lectures state that "the indolent, which would be the greatest number, would live upon the industrious" (*LJB* 287–88).

14. Smith confronts Machiavellianism even more directly when he explains and evaluates the admiration of "the great mob" for mighty conquerors (*TMS* VI.iii.30); cf. *TMS* III.5.1 on the "coarse clay of which the bulk of mankind are formed." Tacitly elaborating his thesis that "economism" is "Machiavellianism come of age" (*Political Philosophy*, p. 49), Leo Strauss says of Machiavelli: "Accepting the ends of the demos as beyond appeal, he seeks for the best means conducive to those ends" (*Thoughts*, p. 296). Smith's discussion of authority in *WN* V ultimately acknowledges that the authority bred by wealth is the subject of "constant complaint" (V.i.b.7); cf. the other complaints of "philosophers" and "moralists" (*WN* I.xi.b.26; *TMS* I.iii.3.1,4, II.iii.3.1).

15. Despite the fact that the transition from a hunting society to a shepherding society brings with it the introduction of government and inequality, Smith does not indicate why and how this evolution occurs. Haakonssen argues that even the lectures are vague on this point (p. 156).

16. Characteristically, the account of these matters in *TMS* is more indulgent. Whereas in *WN*, Smith flatly attributes the authority of birth to ancient wealth, in *TMS* the rank and "superiority" of "the young nobleman" are attributed to "the virtue of his ancestors." The subsequent discussion is not free from irony, however (*TMS* I.iii.2.4).

17. Burke insists that "there is no qualification for government, but virtue and wisdom, actual and presumptive," but differs from Smith in deferring to the presumptive virtue and wisdom of conventional aristocrats; nobility is "a graceful ornament to the civil order" (*Reflections*, pp. 139, 245). Cropsey simply asserts that "the hereditary nobility has the role, in Smithian society, of guaranteeing the general liberty by standing between the monarch and absolute power" (*Polity*, p. 68; cf. Forbes, p. 196). Smith wrote nothing to suggest this, though the lectures (in the course of criticizing

polygamy) argue that nobles can secure "the people's liberty" by leading their resistance to an oppressive king or foreign invaders (*LJA* iii.41–45; *LJB* 115–16). *WN*'s harsh portrayal of primogeniture and entails (III.ii.3,6) suggests that Smith had second thoughts about the view stated in the lectures. But he remained sympathetic to the hereditary principle in monarchies, whereby succession is based on a "plain and evident difference which can admit of no dispute" as opposed to "doubtful distinctions of personal merit" (*WN* III.ii.3).

18. Cf. *WN* IV.vii.c.69 and V.i.g.19 on how intermediate leaders are rewarded by those on top for extracting revenue from those on the bottom.

19. Dumont, p. 208nn. On the emergence of authority, subordination, and rank from economic inequality, also see Hume, *ICPM*, III:ii (p. 25) and VI:ii (pp. 71–72). Compared to Smith and Hume, Locke takes a much less detached tone: "A Man can no more justly make use of another's necessity to force him to become his Vassal, by with-holding that Relief, God requires him to afford to the wants of his Brother, than he that has more strength can seize upon a weaker, master him to his Obedience, and with a Dagger at his Throat offer him Death or Slavery" (*First Treatise*, sec. 42).

20. Burke, *Reflections*, p. 171. On Burke's praise of Smith, see Himmelfarb, p. 66.

21. "Smith makes full use of the ambivalence of the word 'Nature' to cover both what can be explained and what can be morally justified" (Winch, *Smith's Politics*, p. 65). It is Cropsey, however, who has best explained this ambivalence (*Polity*, pp. 38–40; *Political Philosophy*, pp. 62, 72–73, 87–88). Also see Campbell, pp. 56–57.

22. Hume, "Of the First Principles of Government," *Essays*, p. 32.

23. Haakonssen, p. 131. Winch more thoroughly argues the position taken by Haakonssen (*Smith's Politics*, pp. 168–70). Whereas Winch includes the various human emotions under the rubric "opinion," I use the term in a more Platonic sense (*doxa*): what today might be called doctrine, ideology, or *Weltanschauung*. In *WN*, the connection between opinion and authority is prominent only in the discussion of religious authority. See pp. 169–70 below; and *TMS* I.iii.2.2–4, VI.iii.28–30.

24. *WN* IV.vii.b.2; *TMS* I.iii.3.1–2, VI.iii.30.

25. Aristotle himself laments that nature's failure to match slavish bodies with slavish souls makes it difficult to identify the natural slave (*Politics*, 1254b26–1255a1).

26. *WN* V.i.b.7. Cf. IV.vii.c.74, V.i.a.41; and pp. 27–28 above on the "natural aristocracy." As we will see, Smith looks favorably upon the bourgeois virtues (frugality, industry, skill, etc.) cultivated during the final social stage and insists that possession of them generally produces success. In a sense, they are the modern-day version of the "first cause" of subordination, superiority of wisdom and virtue. As distinguished from the virtues of traditional aristocracies, bourgeois virtue produces rather than consumes wealth.

27. As Himmelfarb observes, Smith presents the differences among these social orders as "functional rather than hierarchic" (p. 54). Meek shows how Smith's classificatory scheme exalted the workers—whose status as a "great,

original, and constituent" order was previously denied—and even prepared Marx's doctrine of surplus value, by emphasizing the productivity of labor (compared with land and nature) and by linking profit with the employment of wage-labor (*Smith, Marx*, pp. 6–7). Also see Caton, "Preindustrial Economics," pp. 850–51, and *Politics of Progress*, pp. 527–29.

28. *WN* IV.viii.30. Cf. IV.vii.c.87, IV.viii.49.

29. Smith's explicit evaluation of aristocratic privilege is likewise both negative and indirect. In *WN*'s sole mention of natural law, Smith quickly establishes its clash with primogeniture (III.ii.3). In criticizing the related institution of entails, Smith describes the "exclusive privilege of the nobility to the great offices and honors of their country" as an "unjust advantage" that has been "usurped" (III.ii.6).

30. *WN* I.viii.36, I.x.c.12, III.ii.6, III.iii.12, IV.viii.30, IV.vii.c.87, IV.ix.3.

31. Cf. Haakonssen, pp. 4–49; and Teichgraeber, *Free Trade*, pp. 29–48, on the influence of Hume and Hutcheson on *TMS*.

32. Cf. *TMS* I.i.3.1, III.4.8, VII.ii.1.3.

33. Compare *TMS* VII.iii.3.16 with the titles of I.i and II.i.

34. The sympathy process obviously involves the mind, requiring an imaginary change of situation (*TMS* I.i.2.2, I.i.4.5): animals would not be capable of sympathy in the sense relevant for moral sentiments. Rousseau, by contrast, stresses that pity, the natural sentiment that tempers natural selfishness, is possessed by animals (*Second Discourse*, p. 95).

35. *TMS* III.2.25. Cf. III.5.5 on the moral faculties' "right" to restrain our other faculties and appetites.

36. *TMS* III.1.2–3, III.3.3, III.3.21–26, III.3.38. In Hume's words, the "constant habit of surveying ourselves, as it were in reflection, keeps alive all the sentiments of right and wrong"; social interaction teaches us to transcend that "position and point of view which is peculiar to ourselves" (*ICPM*, IX:i, p. 96, IV:ii, p. 55). Cf. *ICPM*, pp. 48, 54, 93; and *Treatise*, III.i.2.

37. *TMS* II.i.2.3, II.i.4.1, IV.2.8,10.

38. *TMS* III.2.9,11, VII.iii.3.8,14.

39. Locke's posture differs strikingly: "He that will impartially survey the Nations of the World . . . will have but little Reverence for the Practices which are in use and credit amongst Men" (*First Treatise*, sec. 58).

40. Viner strangely claims that he was unable to find "even a casual reference in *TMS* to the moral sentiments being influenced by changes in the physical or political environment or of their being different in different countries or at different stages of history" (*Role of Providence*, p. 84).

41. On the lengthy account of such matters in Smith's lectures, and its roots in Grotius, Hutcheson, and Hume, see Haakonssen, pp. 99–132; and Teichgraeber, *Free Trade*, pp. 20–32, 49–72, 102, 156–57.

42. Cf. *TMS* II.iii.2.4; Campbell, pp. 189–91; and Haakonssen, p. 100.

43. Aristotle, *Politics*, 1280a7–1284b34. Cf. *LJA* v.102,125–26; Haakonssen, p. 128; and Hont and Ignatieff, p. 25. In Plato's *Laws*, "political justice" entails giving "greater honors/offices [*timē*] to those who are greater as regards virtue" (757c). Smith faults Plato's *Laws* for addressing "police"

rather than justice (*TMS* VII.iv.37), but it is Smith who excludes "political justice."

44. Macpherson, *Possessive Individualism*, p. 64. Cf. McNally, pp. 210, 214–20, 225–28; and Hayek, pp. 36, 232, 385.

45. *TMS* II.ii.1.3,5, VI.ii.Intro.2, III.6.10–11, VII.iv.7.

46. *TMS* II.ii.2.1, III.1.3, III.2.32, III.3.3,21–22,25, 38, III.4.6,7,12.

47. Cf. Haakonssen's discussion of utility and natural justice (pp. 121–25).

48. Smith would seem to prefer "rule" utilitarianism to other forms of utilitarianism. See Campbell and Ross, p. 73.

49. *TMS* II.ii.3.4, VII.ii.3.12–13,16–18, VII.ii.4.8.

50. Michael Novak actually misquotes the sentence in attempting to document Smith's liberal individualism (p. 147). Cropsey (*Polity*, p. 10) and Anspach (p. 194) nicely interpret the message of the actual passage.

51. Cf. Phillipson, "Enlightenment," pp. 35–39, on the problems posed by reducing virtue to propriety; and Pocock, *Virtue, Commerce*, pp. 56, 103–4, on the connections between propriety and property.

52. But see *TMS* III.3.31; on liberty and licentiousness, see *WN* V.i.a.41.

53. See Cropsey, *Polity*, p. 38; *Political Philosophy*, pp. 62, 65; and pp. 199, 201, and 203 below.

54. Haakonssen, pp. 83–86, 91. Anspach beautifully brings home the economic flavor of Smith's analysis here (pp. 191–92).

55. Smith is of course famous for recommending that you rely on "interest" and "self-love" rather than "friendship" and "benevolence" in procuring your dinner (*WN* I.ii.2). Cf. pp. 71–72 below; cf. *LJB* 301 on why bartering is "mean" and disinterested giving is "always generous and noble." Burke, in his notorious "Thoughts and Details on Scarcity" (1795), outdoes even Smith in severing beneficence from justice and government. Burke accentuates the sanctity of the wage levels determined by the free market ("the laws of commerce" are "the laws of God") and radicalizes Smith's critique of the Poor Laws by insisting that government *never* provide relief for the poor: the magistrate enforces not mercy but justice, and his interference would be "a violation of the property which it is his office to protect." Charity is "a direct and obligatory duty" for the individual but not the state (pp. 145–47, 156–57; cf. pp. 133–36, 140–42, 150–51, 166–69; and Himmelfarb, pp. 61, 67–71). Burke thus departs from his famous and more characteristic principle that the state is a partnership in "every virtue, and in all perfection" (*Reflections*, p. 194).

56. In distinguishing commutative and distributive justice, Smith mentions Grotius and describes commutative justice with a phrase—"abstaining from what is another's" (*TMS* VII.ii.1.10)—that Grotius uses to identify the general aim of law (*Proleg.*, 8, 10, 44). Also see *The Law of War and Peace*, I.2.1, II.1.4, II.2.6,18, II.22.10; and Hont and Ignatieff, pp. 29–36. Grotius occasionally adopts a more classical posture toward virtue (*Proleg.*, 9, 32, 54; *The Law of War and Peace*, II.1.9).

57. Pocock, "Cambridge paradigms," p. 249; cf. p. 246; and *Virtue, Commerce*, pp. 43, 104.

58. Compare *TMS* II.ii.3.4–9 on the public enforcement of justice with *TMS* I.iii.2.1–2, I.iii.3.1–2, II.i.5.10, II.iii.3.2, III.3.4,27,31, IV.1.8–11, V.2.12–14, VI.ii.1.20, VI.iii.30.

CHAPTER FOUR *'Homo Economicus'*

1. According to Socrates, appetite is "most of the soul . . . and by nature most insatiable for money" (*Republic*, 442a).

2. *WN* I.viii.44, II.iii.31,36, III.iii.12, IV.v.b.43, IV.ix.28. In general, *WN* identifies "interest" with ease and riches (III.ii.9, V.i.f.7).

3. *WN* I.xi.c.7, I.x.b.2,24,30–31, III.iv.10, IV.vii.c.66, IV.ix.47, V.i.g.25, V.ii.k.3,29.

4. "In bourgeois society, psychology replaced biology as the basis of 'need' satisfaction" (Bell, p. 224).

5. One may say "sublimated" because of the near invisibility of the quest for esteem in *WN* despite its centrality in *TMS*'s explanation of the pursuit of wealth. Cf. Ernest Becker: "The amassing of a surplus . . . goes to the very heart of human motivation, the urge to stand out as hero, to transcend the limitation of the human condition and achieve victory over impotence and finitude" (p. 31). Heilbroner employs Freudianism more crudely than Becker because he combines it with Marxism: "The pleasures of adult domination," the drives for prestige and power, are a "delayed enactment of repressed infantile fantasies" (Heilbroner, *Behind the Veil*, pp. 19, 38; cf. p. 46).

6. The distinction between the appetitive and spirited faculties is perhaps further weakened by the following consideration. To the extent that the spirited faculty's function is "to defend us against injuries" (*TMS* VII.ii.1.4), it can be explained as subordinate to the Darwinian imperatives of preservation and propagation. Cf. Smith's claim that resentment "seems to have been given us by nature for defense" (II.ii.1.4). For Montesquieu, Pangle suggests, "the desire to display superiority originates in an extreme and perverted development of the pleasure men take in contemplating the personal power which insures their security" (p. 180).

7. *WN* I.x.b.24,30–32. For further vestiges of conspicuously "non-economic" motivations, see *WN* I.x.b.2, III.i.5, V.ii.k.80. As Danford suggests, however, perhaps no amount of money could deter men like Alcibiades, Caesar, and Napoleon from pursuing honor, glory, and empire; the economistic assumption that all goods are commensurable undercuts certain types of social hierarchy and cleavage (Danford, pp. 681–82, 686–88, 691–92, 694). But cf. Aristotle, *Politics*, 1267a32–36.

8. *WN* IV.vii.c.74–75, V.i.a.14, V.i.f.60. See pp. 18–19 and 95–97 below.

9. Cf. Locke, *Second Treatise*, secs. 42–43.

10. Cf. Hayek's argument that if we appealed to benevolence rather than self-interest, we might not receive assistance from those who disapprove of our purposes (p. 141); also cf. E. Becker, p. 81.

11. Cf. Aristotle's thesis that "immediately from birth certain things diverge, some toward being ruled, others toward ruling" (*Politics*, 1254a23).

12. See pp. 41–46 above. "The idea that division of labour in society is analogous to the division of functions among the organs of a living individual body did not occur to Adam Smith, and he does not even trace out the division of labour, like Aristotle, in the family" (Bonar, p. 156). Bonar's only mistake here is assuming that Smith's writings broadcast all of his thoughts. Consider *WN* IV.ix.28 on "the political body" and Himmelfarb, p. 54; and cf. Danford, pp. 677–82.

13. Cf. Locke's famous argument that the private appropriation of land via labor increases "the common stock of mankind"; the person who encloses ten acres "may truly be said to give ninety acres to mankind" (*Second Treatise*, sec. 37). Marx's notion of "species-being" helped inspire his vision of a communist society in which "different geniuses and talents" are brought into a "common stock" without either coercion or exchange. Cf. "Critique of the Gotha Program," pp. 530–31 (in Tucker).

14. See *WN* V.i.f.43 and pp. 156–57 below.

15. The concluding chapter of Ricardo's *Principles*, a prosaic discussion entitled "Mr. Malthus's Opinions of Rent," ends abruptly and on a strangely philosophical note: "Value in use cannot be measured by any known standard; it is differently estimated by different persons." Marx contrasts the "writers of classical antiquity, who are exclusively concerned with quality and use value" and the political economists, who, because of their orientation toward quantity (the unceasing accumulation of wealth) and exchange value, view the division of labor as a means to cheapen commodities and accumulate capital (*Capital*, vol. I, ch. 14, sec. 5, pp. 486–87). In non-capitalist societies where use value predominates, "surplus labour" will be "restricted by a more or less confined set of needs" (ch. 10, sec. 2, p. 345). By observing that the *Republic*'s division of labor made the laborer "adapt himself to the work, not the work to the laborer," however, Marx indicates a kinship between Platonism and capitalism (*Capital*, ch. 14, sec. 5, p. 487n57). On the Physiocrats' orientation toward use value, see Dumont, p. 85. On Ricardo and J. B. Say, see Halévy, pp. 320–22, 495.

16. Bell, p. 223. Cf. Friedman, *Capitalism*, pp. 15, 178; *Free to Choose*, p. 119.

17. Cf. *WN* I.v.4 on "the higgling and bargaining of the market." Also cf. McNally, pp. 210–13; and Phillipson, "Enlightenment," p. 36.

18. Strauss, *Political Philosophy*, p. 49. Caton contrasts Hobbes's posture toward progress with the more heroic posture adopted by Bacon and Descartes (Caton, *Politics of Progress*, pp. 48–49, 64–66).

19. Smith does acknowledge the possible limits of "political arithmetic" (*WN* IV.v.b.30); cf. Deane, p. 13; Letwin, pp. 99–146; Medick, p. 243; and pp. 132–34 below. *TMS*, moreover, abandons the quantitative orientation of Hutcheson, whose utilitarianism included a series of equations constituting "a universal Canon to compute the morality of any action" (*Inquiry*, III:xi–xii). Bentham's "calculus of pleasures and pains" is still more notorious.

20. *Leviathan*, ch. X, p. 150, ch. XIII, p. 184. Hobbes stresses the economic ills of the state of nature as well as the threat posed to bare preservation:

people will not "plant, sow or build" (p. 184); because the fruit of "Industry" is so insecure, there will be "no Culture of the Earth; no Navigation, nor use of the commodities that may be imported by Sea; no commodious Building; no Instruments of moving, and removing such things as require much force" (p. 186). Hobbes defines taxes as "wages, due to them that hold the public sword, to defend Private men in the exercise of several Trades, and Callings" (ch. XXX, p. 386). Cf. *Leviathan*, pp. 227, 376, 387; *De Cive*, XIII:4–6,14; and Macpherson, *Possessive Individualism*, pp. 23–24, 95–96.

21. Both Hobbes and Smith, needless to say, abandon Aristotle's teleological understanding of *dynamis* and *energeia*. Cf. Aristotle, *Nicomachean Ethics*, 1098a16–17, 1168a6–8; and Macpherson, *Democratic Theory*, pp. 8–9.

22. According to Schumpeter, indeed, it is the everyday economic tasks that have provided the human race with its "elementary training in rational thought and behavior" (pp. 122–24).

23. Machiavelli, *Discourses*, III:1; cf. Montesquieu, *Spirit of Laws*, VI:5, XXI:20, XXII:13. Rousseau removes war from the state of nature partly by removing foresight (along with vanity and dependence) (*Second Discourse*, p. 117), all of which Smith tries to restore in a peaceful, capitalist form.

24. *WN* II.iii.42, V.i.f.30,50–51, V.i.g.10, V.iii.1.

25. Under feudalism, "personal dependence characterizes the social relationships of material production" (*Capital*, vol. I, ch. 1, sec. 4, p. 170).

26. Cf. Aristotle's famous doctrine that man, by virtue of his *logos*, is "much more a political animal than any kind of bee or herd-animal" (*Politics*, 1253a7–10).

27. *New York Review of Books*, 24 April 1986, p. 46. Cf. Foley, p. 118; and Haakonssen, pp. 49–50.

28. Hirschman, pp. 100, 15. Hirschman's larger concern is to explain how commerce and avarice became honorable in "the modern age after having stood condemned or despised . . . for centuries past" (p. 9).

29. Hirschman, pp. 32, 35, 41, 43, 60–61, 71–96.

30. Hirschman does not comment on the differences between the forms of "social thought" that Smith presents and the forms presented by Hobbes, Locke, and Montesquieu. As we have seen, Smith's political economy is concerned with the means to wealth and does not deliberate about ends; rather than argue the virtues of wealth, Smith seduces or lulls his readers with the magnificent complexity of the mechanism whereby it is produced.

31. Hirschman, pp. 107–8. Milton Myers is still more guilty of overlooking the differing possible constituents of self-interest (p. 29).

32. In the words of Stephen Holmes, "Smith recognizes the essential untidiness of human psychology" (p. 40). Holmes provides a succinct and penetrating account of Smith's posture toward the various dimensions of "interest."

33. Weber, *Protestant Ethic*, pp. 17, 163. Cf. Montesquieu: "The spirit of commerce brings with it the spirit of frugality, economy, moderation, work, wisdom, tranquillity, order, and rule" (*Spirit of Laws*, V:6, p. 48).

34. *WN* II.iii.12,14–16,19–20,35–38. Also consider Smith's tendency to

define "good conduct" as frugality and "misconduct" as prodigality (II.iii.26–32,36). Mandeville, by contrast, praises prodigality and disparages frugality (*Fable*, vol. I, pp. 104–6).

35. Montesquieu argues that "gaining little" is compensated "only by gaining continuously." As a result of believing that one's wealth is secure, furthermore, "one dares to expose it in order to acquire more" (*Spirit of Laws*, XX:4, p. 340).

36. Cf. pp. 27–28 and 31–32 above on the natural aristocracy's pursuit of "importance."

37. The contrast here is with the aristocratic airs of "the young nobleman" (*TMS* I.iii.2.4) and with the "frivolous accomplishments" admired in "the superior stations of life" (I.iii.3.6). The implications for the natural aristocracy of *WN* are unclear. Cf. Skinner, p. 172.

38. Cf. Dickey, pp. 589–99. From the premise that the "good sense and happiness of individuals largely consists in their having middling talents and fortunes," Montesquieu arrives at the un-Smithian recommendation that laws in a democracy attempt some equalization of rich and poor (*Spirit of Laws*, V:3, p. 44, V:6); Montesquieu also worries that frugality will be undermined by envy of luxuries (V:4). Rousseau recommends preventing extreme inequality, without any provisos about the form of government ("Political Economy," p. 221). Both theorists here follow Plato (*Laws*, 744d). Unlike Smith, Aristotle praises the middle class for the sake of the regime (*Politics*, 1295a25–1297a13), not the economy.

39. Machiavelli, *Prince*, chs. 15–16. Smith's lectures provide telling evidence that his wording in *TMS* was neither careless nor ignorant. In discussing ancient republics, Smith employs the Greek word (*eleutheriotes*), equates it with liberality, and explains that it was used to distinguish the gentleman from the slave (*LJA* iv.70).

40. Marx, needless to say, criticizes Smith for not recognizing labor as "man's normal life activity" (*Capital*, vol. I, ch. 1, sec. 2, pp. 137–38n16). Arendt characterizes the "modern" ideal of abundance without labor as "the age-old dream of the poor and destitute," which would be a "fool's paradise" if realized (pp. 126, 129, 133). The above passage from *TMS*, however, embodies this ideal more fully than anything written by Marx, the main suspect in Arendt's critique of the *animal laborans* (see Arendt, p. 104).

41. Cf. Caton, "Preindustrial Economics," pp. 840, 851; *Politics of Progress*, p. 355; Gilder, pp. 37, 312; and Hollander, pp. 212–17, 220–23, 229, 233–41.

42. See pp. 89–93, 102–9, 121–29, 183–87, and 210–11 below. Such undertakings are fueled by people's "absurd presumption" in their own good fortune (*WN* I.x.b.26).

43. In arguing that "population regulates itself by the funds which are to employ it," Ricardo follows Smith, but he makes the erotic dimension more explicit: "So great are the delights of domestic society" that "an increase of population follows the amended condition of the labourer" (*Principles*, II, p. 41, XXXII, p. 278).

44. We have it on the authority of Allan Bloom that these three philosophers are "all highly erotic authors" (Washington *Post*, 13 July 1987, sec. C).

45. Cf. *TMS* III.2.7,20,32 on the wise man's greater attachment to praiseworthiness than to praise, and his consequent kinship with the impartial spectator.

46. As if to call attention to these issues, Smith makes provocative claims about philosophy in the first two chapters (*WN* I.i.9, I.ii.4–5), after which it is almost invisible until it dramatically resurfaces in Book V—in a confrontation between "antient" and "modern" (V.i.f.23–35).

47. The thesis of restless dissatisfaction is a kind of touchstone for modern political philosophy: Machiavelli, *Discourses*, I:37, II:Proem; Hobbes, *Leviathan*, ch. XI (pp. 160–61); Locke, *Essay Concerning Human Understanding*, II:21, secs. 29–31; Mandeville, *Fable*, vol. I, p. 242, vol. II, p. 181. Hume's version frames the problem that political economy must solve: the "avidity . . . of acquiring goods and possessions" is "insatiable, perpetual, universal, and directly destructive of society" (*Treatise*, III.ii.2, pp. 491–92).

48. By contrast, Mandeville disparages the contribution of "those that enquire into the Reason of Things" to inventions and "improvements" (*Fable*, vol. II, p. 144); see pp. 112–13 below on the debate over Smith's awareness of the Industrial Revolution.

49. Even in *WN*, Smith likens commerce to war: foreign trade can be "a species of warfare of which the operations are continually changing, and which can scarce ever be conducted successfully, without an unremitting exertion of vigilance and attention" (V.i.e.30). Cf. III.iv.3, V.i.e.26.

50. The remaining religious competitors to bourgeois virtue are superstition, fanaticism, "zeal," and "enthusiasm," which will be discussed in Chapters 6–10.

51. Smith passes over the Epicurean critique of religion, although in *WN* and *EPS* he comes close to adopting it. He also ignores the Epicurean exaltation of the philosophic life. Cf. Blumenberg, pp. 151, 157, 165–66.

52. This formulation, though it perhaps disparages the contemplative ideal, suggests a teleological dimension missing from Epicurus's "atomical philosophy" (*TMS* VII.ii.2.14).

53. Cf. Lucretius, *The Nature of Things* (V:1423–33): "Then, it was hides; now, gold and purple trouble and fret men's lives. . . . What harm to lack our gold, our purples stiff with rich brocade, while we have plain, coarse cloth to keep us warm? Yes, all for nothing we wretched men toil on forever, and waste our lives on foolishness; clearly, because we never learned the limits of having, and where true pleasure's growth must end." On the differences between ancient and modern materialism, see Blumenberg, pp. 154–55, 165, 168–69, 181–82; Strauss, *Natural Right*, pp. 112–15, 167–76, 188–89; and Strauss, *Spinoza's Critique*, p. 29.

54. Cf. *TMS* VII.ii.2.11, VII.ii.4.5.

55. As Buchan put it, "In many respects, Adam Smith was a chaste disciple of Epicurus, as that philosopher is properly understood" (Rae, p. 433).

56. Astronomy III.7. Tocqueville invokes Plato's historical triumph over

the ancient materialists to show the greater appeal, if not the greater validity, of anti-materialism (*Democracy in America*, II.ii.15, p. 545).

57. Cf. Himmelfarb's chapter entitled "An Odd Lot of Disciples," especially her discussion of Burke and Paine (p. 86).

58. See pp. 52–56 above and 226–34 below.

59. John Dunn errs seriously by overlooking that this is a formulation of Stoic views rather than Smith's own (Dunn, p. 128).

60. *TMS* VI.ii.3.2–3; cf. II.i.5.10, II.ii.3.4,5, II.iii.3.2, III.5.7,9, VI.ii.Intro.3, VI.ii.1.20.

61. Marcus, of course, being "absolute sovereign of the whole civilized part of the world," had "no peculiar reason to complain of his own allotment" (*TMS* VII.ii.1.35,37).

62. To receive sympathy, indeed, one must lower one's passion to a "pitch" that others can share (*TMS* I.i.4.7).

63. Thus, "the greater part" of the misfortunes experienced by "the greatly unfortunate" arose because they did not know "when it was proper for them to sit still and to be contented" (*TMS* III.3.31). Cf. I.iii.1.7, III.3.9,29.

64. Mandeville explicitly opposed serenity and tranquillity to people's concern with "mending their condition"; contentment is thus "the bane of industry" (*Fable*, vol. I, p. 242).

CHAPTER FIVE *International Relations*

1. See, for example, Aristotle's *Politics*, 1323a14–1325b31, 1333a31–1334b28.

2. On the nineteenth-century interpretations emphasizing Smith's pacifism and hostility to government, see Earle, pp. 222, 225–26, 244n64.

3. Smith occasionally links and even conflates war and politics (*WN* III.iv.24, IV.iii.c.11, IV.vii.c.107).

4. *WN* IV.ii.24,30, IV.v.a.36. Smith acknowledges other "political" considerations that would warrant departures from free trade: when tariffs can be prudently used to induce other countries to remove their tariffs (IV.ii.37–39); when free trade needs to be restored with "reserve and circumspection" (IV.ii.37,40,43).

5. Cf. Ferguson, *Essay*, pp. 61, 225, 232, 237. On martial spirit, civic humanism, and the militia debate in Scotland, see Phillipson, "Enlightenment," pp. 36–37; Pocock, *Machiavellian Moment*, pp. 426–32; Sher, pp. 39, 215–20, 326–27; and Winch, *Smith's Politics*, pp. 103–20, 175.

6. *WN* V.i.a.1,41, V.i.b.2, V.i.f.40, V.iii.89–90. One wonders whether rulers who perpetrate and perpetuate violence and injustice can be counted on to protect their subjects from the same.

7. "Moveable effects, such as silver, notes, letters of exchange, shares in companies, ships, and all commodities, belong to the whole world, which, in this regard, comprises but a single state of which all societies are members" (Montesquieu, *Spirit of Laws*, XX:23, p. 352). Smith refers to bullion as the money of "the great mercantile republick" (*WN* IV.i.24).

8. Hollander helpfully observes that when Smith recognizes a conflict between defense and opulence, "the foregone opportunities (i.e. the alternative costs) in following the former objective are made quite explicit" (p. 267).

9. The depoliticization and internationalization conveyed by *WN* anticipate not only current scholarly literature on "interdependence," but modern political science generally. This is strikingly illustrated in the study of international relations, where scholars investigate questions about the causes of war, or the factors producing stability in the international "system," as though they were not essentially citizens of a particular state or regime. Even in the field of "international security," with its intensely military focus, Western scholars waver, speaking sometimes as world citizens, as Westerners, or as citizens of a particular country.

10. Locke, *Second Treatise*, secs. 128, 172. Aristotle and Rousseau characteristically differ from Smith on other related themes: they reject commerce as vulgar and slavish, they have reservations about technological progress, they extol self-sufficiency as a public goal, and they insist that citizens participate in ruling and in the military.

11. When Rome's extension of citizenship to its allies reached a certain point, "any rabble" could "drive out the real citizens" (*WN* IV.vii.c.77). Smith nowhere elaborates the distinction between a rabble and a citizenry; he argues, at the conclusion of *WN*, for the extension of Britain's systems of taxation and representation to its colonies inhabited by people of British or European stock (V.iii.68).

12. In the absence of the hypothetically best policy, states (especially small ones) might have no choice but to restrict grain exportation (*WN* IV.v.b.39).

13. The discoveries under consideration figure equally prominently in Marx's world history (*The Communist Manifesto*, pp. 474–75 [in Tucker]). The ever-increasing globalization of the economy is an essential prerequisite of communism—a stateless world community. Marx would have to reject, however, Smith's contention that "no human wisdom can foresee" the long-term benefits or misfortunes that "may . . . result from those great events" (*WN* IV.vii.c.80). Cf. Winch's discussion of "accident and local circumstances" (*Smith's Politics*, p. 182).

14. Cf. *Federalist* 10 on the "extended sphere"; and Phillipson, "Adam Smith," p. 197.

15. Cf. Locke's famous claim that God gave the earth "to the use of the industrious and rational . . . not to the fancy and covetousness of the quarrelsome and contentious" (*Second Treatise*, sec. 34).

16. Might not an army procure slaves? Cf. Aristotle, *Politics*, 1256b23–25. Smith's lectures specify that the original form of slavery was the enslavement of people captured in war (*LJA* iii.145).

17. Smith does concede that a wealthy nation is "the most likely to be attacked" (*WN* V.i.a.15). See *LJB* 288 on the impulse, under primitive conditions, to pillage and plunder; cf. pp. 109–13 below. In commenting on Smith's labor theory of value, Dumont remarks—as it were, in *vox eco*-

nomica—that "acquiring" and "producing" differ "only through a nuance" (p. 190).

18. Viner argues that the linkage of these terms ("power and plenty," "wealth and strength," etc.) was common during the mercantilist era (*Long View*, p. 289). On eighteenth-century perceptions of the contributions of wealth to national power, see Hollander, p. 264; and McNally, pp. 118–21. I am indebted to Judith Shklar for the observation that a wealthy nation's greatness and power, even if held quietly in reserve, would still deter aggression.

19. Strauss, *Thoughts*, p. 293. According to Strauss, Machiavelli rejects classical political philosophy "because it does not accept as authoritative the end which all or the most respectable states pursue. That end is the common good conceived of as consisting of freedom from foreign domination and from despotic rule, rule of law, security of the lives, the property and the honor of every citizen, ever increasing wealth and power, and last but not least glory or empire" (*Thoughts*, p. 256). Smith accepts these ends as authoritative, but with honor, glory, and empire supplanted not only by wealth and power but by "esteem"—the reorientation whereby Machiavellianism "came of age"? See pp. 63–86 above and 104–9 below.

20. "In one sense, economic growth, by holding out a promise of plenty for the citizenry, has been the 'moral equivalent' of war that William James once sought. Previous wealth had been gained by plunder, annexation, expropriation; now societies were being mobilized for a concerted internal effort, rather than for war against a neighboring state" (Bell, pp. 237–38). For Marx, of course, capitalist wealth remains "expropriation."

21. Steuart, *Inquiry*, II:xiv, p. 218; cf. *WN* IV.i.13. Rousseau too differs from Smith by praising Sparta (*Social Contract*, III:xv).

22. Dumont states flatly that the mercantilists "considered economic phenomena from the point of view of the polity" (p. 34); cf. Earle, p. 219; and Pocock, *Machiavellian Moment*, p. 425. Viner, however, critiques the common view that mercantilism valued "power" more than "plenty" (*Long View*).

23. Smith proceeds to argue that gold and silver are not necessary for this purpose (*WN* IV.i.20–30).

24. Foley strangely downplays Smith's appreciation of "the laissez-faire side of physiocracy" (p. 135).

25. *WN* Intro.8, I.x.c.26, II.v.37, III.i.1–4,8–9, III.iii.17–20, III.iv.18–24, IV.vii.c.81, IV.ix.3–4,39. Cf. Caton, *Politics of Progress*, p. 418; and McNally, pp. 228–31, 234–50. For Smith's critique of actual nations who favored agriculture, see *WN* IV.ix.40–49.

26. *WN* IV.iii.a.1,3, IV.iii.c.10,12.

27. *WN* IV.iii.c.11, IV.vii.c.16,18,56,60,84.

28. Smith elsewhere concedes that the country in which the merchant resides usually derives the greatest benefit from foreign trade (*WN* IV.i.31). Smith invokes the invisible hand specifically to allay suspicion that the individuals who sink their capital into foreign trade promote their own interests at the expense of the nation's (IV.ii.4.9).

29. This passage seems to refute Haakonssen's suggestion that (for Smith) "the more we trade with our enemies, the better we shall be able to defend ourselves against them" (pp. 179–80).

30. Smith would perhaps approve of contemporary Japan, which, despite (or because of?) its mercantilist policies, advances its economy but not its military with all the fervor of empire.

31. "Smith was looking forward to an international division of labor in which developed economies like England would use their manufacturing capacity to draw themselves forever beyond the closed limits of nature" (Hont and Ignatieff, p. 22).

32. For a fuller treatment of some of these themes, see Minowitz, "Invisible Death."

33. "The great body of the people becomes altogether unwarlike" (*WN* V.i.a.4,6,15).

34. Smith acknowledges but depreciates the threat posed by Caesarism (*WN* V.i.a.36,41, V.i.f.59), even suggesting that a standing army can promote "liberty" by rendering the sovereign secure enough to tolerate some "popular discontent" and "tumult" (V.i.a.41). Cf. Ferguson, *Essay*, pp. 61, 225, 232, 237; Phillipson, "Enlightenment," pp. 36–37; Pocock, *Machiavellian Moment*, pp. 426–32; Sher, pp. 39, 215–21, 326–27; and Winch, *Smith's Politics*, pp. 103–20, 175.

35. *WN* V.i.f.51, V.i.a.2,4,6–7,9–10,43. Smith thus anticipates contemporary laments about the tension between prosperity and military spending, not to mention the related crises in public finance (*WN* V.ii.k.79–80, V.iii.4,10–13,26,37,40–41,50,52,56–57,68,92). Cf. Pocock, *Virtue, Commerce*, pp. 48–49, 68–69, 100, 109–16, 123; Pocock, *Machiavellian Moment*, pp. 437–46, 450–61, 470–73, 496–500; Tawney, pp. 85–88; and Winch, *Smith's Politics*, pp. 121–45. It is Marx who consummates the eclipse of politics by economics in international matters: the problems of war, defense spending, and Caesarism will disappear consequent to the disappearance of oppression, class conflict, and the state. Smith and Marx differ less in cynicism regarding the past and present than they do in optimism regarding the future.

36. The "essential difference" between militias and armies, however, can be overcome: a militia that engages in "several successive campaigns . . . becomes in every respect a standing army" because the troops are both "exercised" in their arms and "habituated to . . . prompt obedience" (*WN* V.i.a.27).

37. It is not necessary to belabor the tension in Hobbes and Locke between the principles of liberalism (individual "preservation" and "consent") and the pressures of national defense. Even Rawls has trouble: despite his strong defense of pacifism (pp. 381–82), he argues that conscription is permissible if "demanded for the defense of liberty" anywhere in the world (p. 380). Rousseau's social contract escapes these dilemmas because Rousseau elevates the general will above the individual and exalts small societies, patriotism, and courage. According to Hegel, international relations involves the "moment"

wherein the state's "absolute power against everything individual and particular, against life, property, and their rights, even against societies and associations—makes the nullity of these finite things an accomplished fact and brings it home to consciousness"; war "deals in earnest with the vanity of temporal goods and concerns" and thus shows the absurdity of regarding "the security of individual life and property" as the state's ultimate purpose (*Philosophy of Right*, secs. 323–24). Cf. Marx, "On the Jewish Question," p. 44 (in Tucker).

38. See pp. 18–20 above.

39. *WN* IV.vii.c.75,77, V.i.a.29,35–36,41; *LJA* iv.88–95,169; *LJB* 39–43,334–36,338. On the connection between war, commerce, and the ancient-modern contrast, see Adam Ferguson's *Essay* (IV:ii, pp. 185–86); Rousseau's *Social Contract* (III:xv); and Haakonssen (pp. 159–64, 179–81).

40. *WN* I.viii.26, IV.i.32, IV.v.b.6, IV.vii.c.80,100–101; *TMS* V.2.9.

41. *WN* IV.vii.a.1–3,15,17, IV.vii.b.58–64, IV.ix.47. *WN* does not indicate how the ancients acquired their slaves.

42. These circumstances further augment the importance of inculcating armies with "regularity, order, and prompt obedience to command," to the further detriment of individuality.

43. In the lectures, Smith portrays ancient battle in a harsher light: "Modern armies . . . are less irritated at one another because fire arms keep them at a greater distance. When they always fought sword in hand their rage and fury were raised to the highest pitch, and as they were mixed with one another the slaughter was vastly greater" (*LJB* 350). Hume too emphasized the fury of ancient battles; in addition, he attributed the near-constant warring of the ancient republics to, among other things, their "martial spirit" and "love of liberty" ("Of the Populousness of Ancient Nations," *Essays*, pp. 404–6). Neither Smith nor Hume approaches Hegel's praise of gunpowder as "one of the chief instruments in freeing the world from the domination of physical force" (*Philosophy of History*, p. 402). Hegel argues that "the principle of the modern world—thought and the universal—has given courage a higher form, because its display now seems to be more mechanical, the act not of this particular person, but of a member of a whole. . . . It is for this reason that thought has invented the gun . . . which has changed the purely personal form of bravery into a more abstract one" (*Philosophy of Right*, sec. 328).

44. See, for example, Plato's *Laws*, 676b–677a, and *Statesman*, 271d–272b. Smith flirts with the ancient view in the lectures, where he acknowledges a "fated dissolution that awaits every state and constitution whatever" (*LJB* 46). *WN* casually notes that two hundred years is "as long as the course of human prosperity usually endures" (III.iv.20) and concludes by exhorting Britain to recognize the "real mediocrity of her circumstances." We are a long way from "The Wonderful World of Adam Smith" described by Heilbroner in *The Worldly Philosophers*.

45. Marx, *Capital*, vol. I, ch. 14, p. 468n19. Smith's prescience is also challenged by Blaug (p. 39), Caton ("Preindustrial Economics," pp. 838–39,

848, 852–53, and *Politics of Progress*, pp. 355–57, 371, 519), and Kindleberger (pp. 1–25); it is defended by Hartwell (pp. 33–41) and Meek (*Smith, Marx*, pp. 16–17). For a balanced overview, see Hollander, pp. 105, 110–13, 215–17, 220–26, 236–41.

46. On Smith and Watt, see Bonar, p. 183; Graham, p. 141; and Hollander, pp. 214n18, 217n28, 239–40.

47. Also see *WN* I.viii.57, I.xi.o.4, II.Intro.4, II.ii.7, IV.viii.1, IV.ix.41, V.ii.c.15. Smith's letter to the *Edinburgh Review* praises the *Encyclopedia* for conveying a Baconian account of the "genealogy and filiation" of the different arts and sciences, especially the "mechanical arts" (Letter 6).

CHAPTER SIX *The Invisible Hand*

1. Both Novak (p. 113) and Cropsey (*Political Philosophy*, p. 82) overlook the appearance of the phrase in *EPS*.

2. Macfie's article, "The Invisible Hand of Jupiter," is brief and superficial (*Journal of the History of Ideas* 32 [1971]: 595–99). Cropsey's article, "The Invisible Hand: Some Moral and Political Considerations," is brief and deep, but it pays scant attention to Smith's specific discussions of the invisible hand (*Political Philosophy*, pp. 76–89). Viner's *Role of Providence*, even in the long chapter entitled "The Invisible Hand and Economic Man," says little about the theological implications of Smith's invisible hand; basing his conclusions on *TMS*, Viner treats Smith as a Providentialist thinker, failing to appreciate the atheism of *WN*. In an earlier work, however, Viner does delineate the basic cosmological contrast between the two books (*Long View*, pp. 215–31).

3. Gus Tyler, in a recent polemic entitled "The Myth of Free Trade," offers a particularly egregious misinterpretation. Tyler claims that Smith "saw economics as a subhead of theology—as a modern way to prove the existence of God 'by design'," writing *WN* to demonstrate the benevolent will of "the Great Designer"; to interfere with the invisible hand is thus a sin (Tyler, p. 213). Tyler errs by projecting the deism of *TMS* onto the policy analysis of *WN*; Bryson (pp. 23, 55) and Deane (pp. 7–8, 13) likewise conflate the cosmologies of the books. Even in *TMS*, however, Smith only minimally invokes the vocabulary of "sin," and never on behalf of free trade.

4. Contemporary calls for "situating" the liberal "self" often dwell upon the self's place in society rather than in the cosmos, but Smith illuminates both dimensions.

5. On the "futility of individual life," and its implications for economics as well as theology, political philosophy, and art, see Arendt, pp. 18–19, 56, 97, 106–7, 135, 173, 176–77, 313–15. Arendt argues that accumulation, even though it is constantly challenged by human mortality, can—unlike property—"be as infinite as the life process of the species"; "only if the life of society as a whole . . . is considered to be the gigantic subject of the accumulation process can this process go on in full freedom and at full speed, unhampered by limitations imposed by the individual life-span and individ-

ually held property" (p. 116). On the rootedness of property (in contrast to the abstraction of wealth), see Arendt, pp. 61, 68–69, 110, 125–26; and Ryan, *Property*, p. 48.

6. Astronomy Intro.1,7, II.12. Paradoxically, Smith's investigation in *EPS* of "the nature and causes" of wonder, surprise, and admiration shows that philosophy, the science that seeks the natures and the causes of things, is ultimately but a means to soothe the imagination prone to disturbance by the three passions. The implication is that we have easier access to human psychology than we do to the "connecting principles of nature." (Cf. Lindgren, p. 14; Raphael, pp. 108–10; *TMS* VII.ii.4.14, VII.iii.2.5; and the Introduction to Hume's *Treatise*, pp. xvi–xvii.) Smith does not indicate whether the investigation of the three passions is prompted by some second-order psychic distress equivalent to the distress occasioned by natural events whose "hidden chains" we do not immediately comprehend. Further inquiry is needed regarding the enormous implications, for Smith's project, of Hume's critique of causation. See Wightman's general introduction to *EPS*, pp. 15–21; and Bonar, pp. 111–12.

7. This proposition seems to mean, for example, that a phenomenon producing an immediate sensation of fear will subsequently produce a stable opinion about the phenomenon that renders that phenomenon genuinely fearful. The alleged connection between passions and opinions is also visible in Smith's explanation of why people, especially primitives, lash out at inanimate objects that have caused harm. Among the civilized, the reaction is "checked by reflection," but the savage "waits for no other proof that a thing is the proper object of any sentiment, than that it excites it" (Astronomy III.2). Cf. *TMS* II.iii.1.1 and the related allusion to Exodus at II.iii.1.3 (p. 95n2). See also Hume, *ICHU*, X, p. 125, and "Of Superstition and Enthusiasm," *Essays*, pp. 73–74.

8. Hobbes, Mandeville, Voltaire, and Hume all employ the concept of invisible power/causes to explain religion (Hobbes, *Leviathan*, ch. XII, pp. 169–70, 176; Mandeville, *Fable*, vol. II, p. 214; Hume, *The Natural History of Religion*, pp. 26, 30–32, 38, 47; *ICHU*, VII, p. 81). Voltaire traces the origin of polytheism to feelings of "weakness and dependence," accompanied by the sense of "an invisible power everywhere"; worship is rooted in fear (*Philosophical Dictionary*, pp. 245, 351).

9. As Hume put it, the "generality of mankind never find any difficulty in accounting for the more common and familiar operations of nature, such as the descent of heavy bodies, the growth of plants, the generation of animals. . . . It is only on the discovery of extraordinary phenomena, such as earthquakes . . . that they find themselves at a loss" and "have recourse to some invisible intelligent principle" (*ICHU*, VII, pp. 80–81; cf. *WN* V.i.f.24 on plants and animals). Cf. Ferguson, *Essay*, II:ii, p. 90.

10. Novak gives a misleading impression in attributing to Smith the liberating insight that "human beings can gain some measure of control over the economic system" (p. 77).

11. As Cropsey asserts, Smith is "articulating man entirely within nature, yet declining to see a question of man's freedom vis-à-vis nature"; Cropsey points out that "a purely mechanical principle such as that of evolution through natural selection is compatible with a teleology of nature but does not presuppose a will in nature" (*Political Philosophy*, p. 88). Hayek credits the thinkers of the Scottish Enlightenment with discovering that "an evident order which was not the product of a designing human intelligence need not therefore be ascribed to the design of a higher supernatural intelligence" (p. 59). Cf. Carl Becker, pp. 161–62; and Bonar, p. 174.

12. "Political" liberty would include the "natural liberty" of Hobbes, Locke, and Rousseau that underlies the liberal doctrine of government by consent, as well as the ancient conception that a class may determine the essential features of a society by ruling it in broad daylight. "Spiritual" liberty (e.g., Kantian "autonomy" or Augustinian "free will") would entail exercise of those human faculties that transcend the mechanistic necessity of inanimate nature and the instinct-dominated existence of plant and animal life. See pp. 22–31, 40 above, and 131, 186–87 below.

13. Philosophers are even prone to "give up the evidence of their senses to preserve the coherence of the ideas of their imagination" (Astronomy IV.35). Cf. Strauss's interpretation of Epicurus: in order for science/philosophy to eliminate the noxious fear of gods, "the world itself must be of such a nature that we would not fear finding ourselves confronted with surprising, dangerous occurrences. A soothing regularity and necessity must prevail" (*Spinoza's Critique*, p. 41); also see Blumenberg, pp. 157–59; and pp. 86–89 above. On the Epicurean nature of the psychology presented in *EPS*, see Foley, p. 47.

14. The contrast with Rousseau's picture of primitive life is obvious. Cf. Smith's letter to the *Edinburgh Review*, par. 12. Rousseau's savage lives within himself, lacks foresight, and has no thought of the divine (*Second Discourse*, pp. 116–17, 179, 202).

15. If Wightman is correct in arguing that the essays were composed prior to the publication of *TMS* in 1759 (*EPS*, pp. 5–11), we have one more piece of evidence that Smith did not simply become less orthodox with age. Spinoza makes the key point without introducing a distinction between polytheism and monotheism: when the Jews could not "understand any phenomenon, or were ignorant of its cause, they referred it to God" (*Theologico-Political Treatise*, I [p. 21]; cf. Preface, VI [pp. 3, 81]).

16. Physics 9. In Hume's *Dialogues Concerning Natural Religion*, Cleanthes explains that the "whole of natural theology" resolves into the proposition that "the cause or causes of order in the universe probably bear some remote analogy to human intelligence" (XII, p. 88). Cf. *ICHU*, XI, p. 154; and Blumenberg, p. 159.

17. The biblical God also differs from the pagan god of Plato and Timaeus by creating *ex nihilo*. Smith notes that this pagan god relied on external matter (Physics 9) and eternal "essences" (Logics 2).

18. "The biblical world is not a world in the sense of a 'universe,' i.e., everything combined into one whole, but a creation with beginning and end" (Löwith, p. 158). Cf. Blumenberg, p. 316.

19. Smith chides the ancient Athenians for offering sacrifices to the rainbow (*Astronomy* III.2).

20. Cf. *TMS* III.5.4; and pp. 196–98 below. Unlike Smith, Spinoza implies that the New Testament is more refined than the Old: "Religion was imparted to the early Hebrews as a law written down, because they were at that time in the condition of children, but afterwards Moses . . . predicted a time coming when the Lord should write His law in their hearts" (Spinoza, *TPT*, XII, p. 165; cf. pp. 18–19, 38–39, 64, 88, 93, 95, 158–59; but see Strauss, *Spinoza's Critique*, p. 20). Despite the great length of the astronomy essay, Smith is silent about the pagan deifications of heavenly bodies. Spinoza, by contrast, emphasizes the differences between the visible gods of the Gentiles and the invisible God of the Jews (*TPT*, VI, p. 82).

21. According to Alexander Pope, who in Smith's judgment is "the most elegant and harmonious of all the English poets" (*TMS* III.2.19), "All are but parts of one stupendous Whole, Whose body Nature is, and God the soul" (*Essay on Man*, I:267–68; cf. I:50–51, I:288–94, IV:113–14).

22. The beauty bestowed by utility is the last of the four sources of approbation systematically expounded in the first four Parts of the book. The previous three are propriety, merit, and the general rules derived from them (*TMS* VII.iii.3.16).

23. Cf. *TMS* III.3.31 on "the vanity of all the labors of man." Ernest Becker articulates a Freudian version of these Smithian themes: "Man is a robustly active creature; activity alone keeps him from going crazy. If he bogs down and begins to dwell on his situation, he risks releasing the neurotic fear repressed into his unconscious—that he is really impotent and will have no effect on the world" (p. 136). According to Becker, "All power is in essence power to deny mortality. . . . Power means power to increase oneself, to change one's natural situation from one of smallness, helplessness, finitude, to one of bigness, control, durability, importance" (p. 81; cf. pp. 96, 124).

24. Cf. pp. 68–69 above; and Harpham, pp. 772–73.

25. Smith here flirts with the famous Socratic vision—alluded to in *EPS* (Logics 4)—of philosophy as learning to die (Plato, *Phaedo*, 64a; *Laws*, 803b, 903b; *Republic*, 485a–486b, 604b–c). Cf. the discussion above (pp. 66, 69) of Smith's striking lament—"For to what purpose is all the toil and bustle of this world?" (*TMS* I.iii.2.1)—and his moving description of the harsh conditions that prompt the savage to compose a "song of death" as preparation for possible capture by an enemy (V.2.9). But also consider his argument that we are horrified by death only because we succumb to an "illusion of the imagination" (I.i.1.13).

26. "The rich man consumes no more food than his poor neighbour," however superior its quality and preparation (*WN* I.xi.c.7). Cf. Ecclesiastes 5:11: "When riches multiply, so do those who live off them; and what advantage has the owner, except to look at them?" Marx would emphasize

that ownership of land, the fundamental "means of subsistence," brings great wealth only because the landlord induces large numbers of people both to work the land and to turn over its produce.

27. *WN* III.iv.10,15. Cf. *TMS* IV.1.6 on the people who "ruin themselves" by squandering their money on "trinkets of frivolous utility" (toys and baubles). Also see *WN* III.iii.12, III.iv.4; and McNally, pp. 187–93.

28. *WN* III.ii.7,19, III.iv.3, IV.vii.b.1,3,16, V.ii.a.19. Cf. I.vi.8.

29. It is difficult to dispute Raphael's judgment that "the *TMS* passage on the invisible hand is extravagant in its picture of natural equality" (p. 79). Cf. Danford, p. 691; Viner, *Role of Providence*, pp. 87–88; and Hume, *ICPM*, III:ii, pp. 24–25. In criticizing ambition with reference to "ease of body and peace of mind," Smith plays the Epicurean. See pp. 86–89 above.

30. As was discussed above (pp. 65–70), *TMS* optimistically assesses the economic circumstances of "the meanest labourer," but associates "bettering one's condition" with the substitution of "toil" and "anxiety" for "leisure," ease," and "careless security " (I.iii.2.1). Also see III.3.31 and III.3.9 on the easy availability of happiness.

31. In the theodicy that concludes the *Essay on the Principle of Population*, Malthus strives to counteract the bleakness of the main theme—that population inevitably grows beyond what the food supply can sustain—by arguing that the discrepancy between food and population spurs the "unremitted excitements" without which mankind would likely have remained in "the savage state" (XVIII, pp. 120–21). Marx would agree with Smith on the quasi-inevitability of economic and technological progress, though Marx stresses the dialectical (rather than linear) character of the developmental path. Marx would deny, however, that progress is a "deception" perpetrated by nature: Marx has no doubts about the ultimate goodness of progress, and seeks rather to combat the deception perpetrated by bourgeois ideologists, like Smith, who condone the continued ownership (by a small class) of land and the other means of production.

32. Cf. Smith's assumption that people strive ceaselessly to better their condition because they are never satisfied with their situation (*WN* II.iii.28).

33. Cf. Kant: "Man wishes concord; but Nature knows better what is good for the race; she wills discord. He wishes to live comfortably and pleasantly; Nature wills that he should be plunged from sloth and passive contentment into labor and trouble" ("Idea for a Universal History," 4th Thesis, p. 16).

34. Cf. pp. 19–20, 67–68, and 109–13 above; also see Bell, p. 222; and Rosenberg and Birdzell, pp. 144, 261.

35. Smith wavers between what would today be called an "absolute" definition of national wealth (as implied by his various endorsements of population growth) and a "per capita" definition focusing on average income. In arguing that Smith generally favors the latter, Hollander beautifully links Smith's posture toward population growth with his posture toward unemployment, his endorsement of economic growth, and his tempered assessment of luxuries (pp. 246–56, 277–80, 307–8). Cf. Viner, *Role of Providence*, p. 102. Population growth is of course a boon to social science insofar as

increasing sample size can negate the distorting impact of human individuality. In a formulation especially relevant to economics, Smith observes that "though the principles of common prudence do not always govern the conduct of every individual, they always influence that of a majority of every class or order" (*WN* II.ii.36).

36. *WN* I.viii.23–27, 38–39. Cf. Heilbroner, "Paradox of Progress"; and Winch, *Smith's Politics*, p. 176: " 'Spontaneous harmony' and 'sunny optimism' are . . . a travesty" of Smith's position. To the extent that people are satisfied by a vision of preservation and propagation, of course, they need not despair about the stationary state.

37. Recall Smith's claim that what counts as a necessity is determined by national "custom," the "established rules of decency," in addition to "nature"—the "commodities indispensably necessary for the support of life" (*WN* V.ii.k.3). Cf. *WN* I.viii.35; *TMS* VII.ii.4.11; and Marx, *Capital*, vol. I, ch. 6, p. 275. Ricardo follows Malthus in insisting that "the comforts and well-being of the poor cannot be permanently secured" without an "effort . . . to regulate the increase of their numbers" (*Principles*, V, p. 61).

38. Hume, "Of Superstition and Enthusiasm," *Essays*, p. 73.

39. Ibid., p. 74. *WN* generally pairs "enthusiasm" with superstition and its "melancholy" humors (*WN* V.i.g.8,14–15). On the connotations of "enthusiasm" in the eighteenth century, see Bryson, p. 247n2.

40. Contrast *TMS* I.i.1.13, II.ii.2.21, III.3.33 with I.iii.2.12, III.2.11, III.3.6, VI.iii.7, VII.iv.13.

41. In the prosaic language of Ricardo: "Man from youth grows to manhood, then decays, and dies; but this is not the progress of nations" (*Principles*, XIX, p. 177).

42. Cf. Cropsey, *Political Philosophy*, pp. 62, 64, 67. As the ultimate equalizer of rich and poor, might death serve the *TMS* invisible hand? Or are people usually distressed by the thought that nature summons even kings "from their exalted stations to that humble, but hospitable, home, which she has provided for all her children" (*TMS* I.iii.2.2)?

43. Locke, *First Treatise*, sec. 59; *Second Treatise*, sec. 7.

44. According to Montesquieu, the law of nature "fait que tout tend à la conservation des espèces" (*L'Esprit des Lois*, X:3). In philosophizing about Genesis, Kant observes that "the individual must consider as his own fault, all the evils which he suffers; and yet at the same time, insofar as he is a member of a whole (a species), he must admire and praise the wisdom and purposiveness of the whole arrangement" ("Conjectural Beginnings of Human History," Remark, p. 60).

45. For a more aesthetically oriented version of the love of system, see Smith's Imitative Arts, II:30.

46. Marx denounces the "utopian socialists" for their "fanatical and superstitious belief in the miraculous effects of their social science"—for naively pushing their "system" as "the best possible plan of the best possible state of society" (*The Communist Manifesto*, III:3), but is not Marx intoxicated with the investigation of societies' "economic law of motion"? We may today

observe the "spirit of system" in the newfangled obsession of empirically oriented social scientists (and economists generally) with models and methodology rather than facts. Regarding the economics profession, see Kuttner, pp. 76–77; cf. Weber on the "romanticism of numbers" (p. 71). One also wonders about the implications of "number crunching."

47. Cf. Haakonssen, p. 90. In the words of Michael Novak, Smith tried to understand the world "not from the top down, but from the bottom up. . . . The best way to make the economic system rational is not to impose upon it the rationality glimpsed in the minds of one person or a few, but to empower the individual rationality of every individual" (p. 79). Novak overlooks, however, that *WN* removes the central direction of an overarching mind from the universe as well as from the economy.

48. See pp. 39–44 above. In his essay on the origin of languages, Smith explains how grammatical regularities emerged "without any intention or foresight in those who first set the example" (Languages 16).

49. Libertarianism is usually fueled by two things: the passionate belief in individual autonomy, independence, and self-sufficiency; and the passionate belief in the efficiency of the free market and voluntary arrangements generally. We could dub those inspired by the latter considerations as economist-libertarians. As a rule, they are intoxicated with Smith's "spirit of system"— the ingenuity of the various schemes that can replace the imposition of collective arrangements.

50. Cf. *TMS* VII.ii.1.46 on the Stoics. It was Edmund Burke, surprisingly, who (in "Thoughts and Details on Scarcity") linked God, economics, and the invisible hand. Workers should be grateful "to the benign and wise Disposer of all things, who obliges men, whether they will or not, in pursuing their own selfish interests, to connect the general good with their own individual success"; governmental provision of relief for the poor violates "the laws of commerce, which are the laws of nature, and consequently the laws of God" (pp. 140–41, 156–57; cf. p. 139).

51. Rosenberg and Birdzell argue that the failures of planned economies derive partly from the planners' assumption that an economy is "a lifeless machine, without the internal capacity to change, adapt, grow, renew, reproduce itself and shape its own future"; a "growth system is like a living organism with impulses of its own" (p. 331). Cf. Friedman, *Free to Choose*, p. 199; and Hayek, pp. 25–26, 29, 61, 110–11.

52. Kristol, *Reflections*, pp. 180, 183–84. Malthus's famous *Essay on Population* in fact incorporates an omniscient God and other Christian concepts: the soul, the Bible, revelation, resurrection, miracles, original sin, and eternal punishment. Chapter XVIII explicitly undertakes to "Vindicate the ways of God to man," and the essay concludes by exhorting man "to fulfill the will of his Creator." On the mixture of optimism and pessimism in *WN*, see Himmelfarb (pp. 57–58), though perhaps she too exaggerates the optimism.

53. Pocock, "Cambridge paradigms," pp. 251–52. On the impetus given to political economy by the Napoleonic Wars, see Winch, "Introduction," pp. 15–16.

54. In expounding Cartesian physics, Smith observes that nature is "rarely . . . mathematically exact," because of the "infinite combination of impulses, which must conspire to the production of each of her effects" (Astronomy IV.64). But Smith's hero is Newton, who was the first to provide a "physical account of the motions of the Planets," built on the "mechanical principle" of gravitation (IV.67,74,76); and Smith himself refers to "laws" of motion (IV.39,56). In WN, see I.iv.12, I.v.5, I.vii.15, I.ix.15, III.i.8–9, III.iv.20, IV.vii.c.80, V.i.a.43, V.iii.10. Viner contrasts the "average" or "statistical" character of the social harmony portrayed in WN with the "universal and perfect" harmony portrayed in TMS. Viner shrewdly points out the prevalence in WN of such phrases as "in most cases," "in general," and "frequently," but misses the profound tensions within TMS (Long View, pp. 222–23). Ricardo's reputation as a determinist is enhanced by statements like the following (on the Poor Laws): "The principle of gravitation is not more certain than the tendency of such laws to change wealth and power into misery and weakness" (V, p. 63). Like Smith, however, Ricardo allows that custom can create the "necessaries" that determine wage rates (V, pp. 52–55; pp. 100, 159). Malthus relentlessly insists on the "inevitability" of nature's laws (X, pp. 74–75), their "fixed and unalterable character" (XIV, p. 92; cf. pp. 19–20, 54, 66, 70–71). Unlike Smith, however, he alleges the existence of a Creator, who can "change one or all of these laws, either suddenly or gradually" (XII, p. 84, IX, p. 61).

55. EPS examines how the different "systems of nature" proposed by philosophers/scientists were "fitted to sooth the imagination" by rendering nature "a more coherent . . . spectacle," not the "agreement" of the systems with "truth and reality" (Astronomy II.12). After a rapturous celebration of Newton's system, moreover, Smith apologizes for implying that its "connecting principles" were "the real chains which Nature makes use of to bind together her several operations" (IV.76). Cf. Smith's remark—drawing on the admittedly "hyperbolical language of Tycho-Brache"—that with Copernicus, "Philosophy . . . moved the Earth from its foundations, stopt the revolution of the Firmament, made the Sun stand still, and subverted the whole order of the Universe" (IV.33).

56. Smith "uses the phrase for vivid effect. . . . He did not believe that the God of theism controlled the working of the economy any more than he believed that Jupiter controlled 'thunder and lightning'" (Raphael, p. 72). "The invisible hand is introduced as a literary embellishment, an elegant way of summarizing an argument already stated" (Letwin, p. 225). Recall Smith's remark that "no system, how well soever in other respects supported, has ever been able to gain any general credit on the world, whose connecting principles were not such as were familiar to all mankind" (Astronomy II.12).

57. "It was the mastery of man over his environment which heralded the dawn of the new age, and it was in the stress of expanding economic energies that this mastery was proved and won" (Tawney, p. 77; cf. Schumpeter, pp. 124–25). According to Caton, the 1780s saw the emergence of the Baco-

nian technological project, a "systematic linkage between science and industry on a commercial basis" (*Politics of Progress*, pp. 32, 323); by 1770 it was "clear that the mainstream of industrial innovation flowed from a linkage of scientific research conducted in universities with engineering research carried out within industrial firms" (pp. 344–45). Rosenberg and Birdzell argue that the economic revolution was not generally fueled by the scientific revolution until after 1800 (p. 23), though many artisans' earlier innovations were abetted by their efforts to adopt Baconian methods. Scientists replaced artisans as the "visible world of the mechanical arts"—e.g., levers, gears, pulleys—yielded in importance to the invisible world of electrons, waves, magnetism, microorganisms, and the like (p. 252).

58. Cf. Dumont, p. 105. It is but a step to Karl Marx, who, from the premise that "all nature" is "man's inorganic body" (Manuscripts of 1844, p. 75 [in Tucker]), tried to construct a science of economics that would wholly eclipse the tradition of philosophy. Arendt argues that modern economics arose as "behavior" replaced "action," and that Marx went further than Smith in expounding a precise science because he conceived its subject matter as "socialized man." Arendt thinks such socialization has in reality been increasing; Smith's resort to the invisible hand reveals that there was "too much unpredictable initiative for the establishment of a science," that the "social realm" of "labor" had not fully supplanted the "public realm" of "action" (Arendt, pp. 41–47, 68–69, 111, 159, 176–77, 198–99, 209, 212).

59. Bourgeois virtue characterizes people on the rise, not people trapped at the bottom or ensconced on top (*WN* II.iii.12, III.ii.7, IV.vii.c.61, V.i.g.42). Cf. Smith's accounts of slavery's inefficiency (*WN* I.viii.41, III.ii.9, III.iii.12), and McNally's remarks on the "progressive" aristocracy (pp. 154, 203–4, 230, 232–33).

60. Does "the great body of the people," those who live by wages, become petit bourgeois who "live by profits," or do they remain privates under the direction of their capitalist generals? See above, pp. 35–36 and 73–76. Marx, of course, insists that we implement what Macpherson calls a "classless struggle with nature" (*Real World*, p. 33).

61. Scholars have neither noticed the uniqueness of the reference in *WN* nor developed the comparison with *TMS*. See pp. 198–202 below on *TMS*.

62. *WN* IV.ix.51, IV.vii.c.54. On the need for *universal* freedom and security, see *WN* III.ii.14, III.iv.4,20, IV.viii.30, V.i.b.25, V.ii.c.18, V.iii.7.

63. Nature's "wisdom . . . seems to have judged that the interest of the great society of mankind would be best promoted by directing the principal attention of each individual to that particular portion of it, which was most within the sphere both of his abilities and of his understanding" (*TMS* VI.ii.2.4). Because humans tend to abuse their "liberty," however, the consummation of nature's agenda requires analytical and rhetorical assistance from philosophers like Smith.

64. On nature's "frugality" and strict "economy," see *TMS* II.i.5.10, III.5.9, VII.iii.3.3; and Hume, *Dialogues*, XI, p. 71. Cf. Blumenberg, pp. 138–39; and Strauss, *Thoughts*, pp. 167, 249.

65. Novak correctly observes that Smith sought "to empower the individual rationality" of all (p. 79), but overlooks the potentially coercive dimensions of this empowerment.

66. Impressed by the *Encyclopedia*'s celebration of the "conquest of nature by Promethean benefactors"—talented merchants, statesmen, philosophers, and inventors—Caton argues that Smith's "populism" and the egalitarianism of his labor theory of value caused him to underestimate the prospects for economic progress ("Preindustrial Economics," pp. 838–89, 841, 850–52; *Politics of Progress*, pp. 325–26, 350, 371, 527). Cf. Himmelfarb's thesis that Smith departed from the French *philosophes* by eschewing recourse to enlightened despots to bring about social progress (p. 53).

67. See the beginning of this chapter for the full quotation from Bossuet.

68. Marx promises a full reconciliation on both scores: communism is "the *genuine* resolution of the conflict between man and nature and between man and man" (Manuscripts of 1844, p. 84 [in Tucker], emphasis in original). Religion and politics disappear along with alienation.

CHAPTER SEVEN *The Atheistic Science of Political Economy*

1. Barbour, pp. 18, 21–22; cf. pp. 53–54 on natural theology, and Blumenberg, p. 476.

2. When Rawls mentions God in his discussion of religious liberty and toleration, he speaks hypothetically (pp. 215, 217–18). The Bible too is passed over, and there is no entry for "God" in the index. Walzer's recent treatise, *Spheres of Justice*, is an exception to these trends; its openness to religion is partly the consequence of its pluralistic deference toward the "caves" constituted by real communities with real histories (pp. 6–9, 26, 28, 87, 197, 314).

3. "What supernatural assistance God was pleased to grant for the increase of his chosen people, does not concern my inquiry" (*Inquiry*, I:iv, p. 36). Steuart's defense of usury, unlike Smith's, is hedged with deferrals toward the religious prohibition (*Inquiry*, IV, pt. 1, ch. iii, pp. 447–48), and Steuart defers to a variety of Christian precepts (I:ix, pp. 73, 80, I:xiv, p. 94). In general, Steuart appears more sympathetic than Smith to religion, government, aristocracy, and charity. According to Campbell and Skinner, Steuart's book—"the previous great treatise on economics"—was not a big seller (*WN*, "General Introduction," p. 42).

4. Flubacher, pp. 78, 80, 83, 426; Halévy, pp. 267–68; McNally, pp. 122–23. For Quesnay, economic laws are among the "lois souveraines instituées par l'Etre Suprême: elles sont immuables et irréfragables et les meilleurs lois possibles" (*Droit Naturel*, quoted in Flubacher, p. 84).

5. Bonar, p. 383; Bryson, pp. 23, 55 (plus notes); Deane, pp. 7–8, 13; Flubacher, pp. 93–94, 111; Lindgren, p. 144; Macfie, p. 79; Novak, p. 45; Tyler, p. 213.

6. Dunn, pp. 128–29; Raphael and Macfie, "Introduction" to *TMS*, p. 19. See pp. 5–6, 8 above and pp. 188–90 below.

7. On the clash between Christianity and "the economic revolution," see Troeltsch, pp. 130–32; and Tawney, pp. 21–22, 24, 30–34, 43–45, 47–48, 52–53, 79–80, 157, 194, 246–47, 272–74.

8. Jesus is mentioned once in the jurisprudence lectures, when Smith states that the clergy had traced their authority to "Jesus Christ and the Pope" (*LJB* 187); there is also a reference to the Jews' expectation of the Messiah (*LJA* iii.99; *LJB* 133). On Smith's discussion of "our Saviour's precept" (*TMS* III.6.13), see pp. 192–96 below.

9. That is, Smith mimics a certain interpretation or kind of Greek philosophy, for it is not clear that Plato, Aristotle, and the Stoics treat God as a "part" of "the great system" analyzed by physics (cf. Logics 2–3,9; and Physics 9–11). Perhaps Smith took his duties as a *philosophe* more seriously than his duties as a historian.

10. Cf. Barbour, pp. 378, 383; and Löwith, p. 158.

11. Hume wrote: "The utmost effort of human reason is to reduce the principles productive of natural phenomena to a greater simplicity, and to resolve the many particular effects into a few general causes, by means of reasonings from analogy, experience, and observation. But . . . [the] ultimate springs and principles are totally shut up from human curiosity and inquiry" (*ICHU*, IV, p. 45; cf. VII, p. 75; and *Dialogues*, VII, p. 46).

12. *TMS* VII.ii.3.3, VII.iv.7,16; *WN* IV.vii.a.15. The first edition of *WN* refers to "the antient constitution of the Roman Catholic church"; Smith took the trouble, in the later editions, to change this phrase to "the antient constitution of the Christian church" (V.i.g.20). Smith also makes sweeping statements about "religion" and "superstition."

13. Smith also refers to a presbyterian election procedure known as "the cure of souls" (*WN* V.i.g.36). Locke's attention to the soul in the *Second Treatise* is likewise minimal: apart from quoting Hooker, Locke refers once to the legislature as the soul of the commonwealth (sec. 212) and once to the debased "souls" of certain writers who defend unconditional obedience (sec. 239). On "Pneumatology," see Bryson, p. 264n2; and Graham, p. 463.

14. When Smith proceeds from education to religion in Book V, he is concerned with priests' influence over the "minds"—not the souls—of the people (*WN* V.i.g.28). Cf. his account of Platonic dualism in *EPS* (Logics 3–5).

15. Locke, *Second Treatise*, secs. 37, 41, 44–45, 51. According to Tawney, the Pauline passage embodied "the fundamental maxim of Christian social ethics" for "countless generations of religious thinkers"; change came with the Puritans, whose goal was not "sufficiency to the needs of daily life, but limitless increase and expansion" (p. 246). Ryan errs by inferring from the citation that Locke "subscribed in a perfectly orthodox way to Saint Paul's dictum that the love of money was the root of all evil" (*Property and Political Theory*, p. 38). In *Some Thoughts Concerning Education*, Locke does claim that covetousness, the desire of possessing "more than we have need of," is

"the Root of all Evil" (sec. 110). Hont and Ignatieff (p. 39) err in attributing this claim to the *Second Treatise*, but provide an otherwise impressive account of the evolution of the Thomistic doctrine of property through Grotius, Pufendorf, and Filmer to Locke (pp. 26–42).

16. The Bible along with God disappears as Locke's chapter proceeds to defend not only "established laws of liberty" but money, inequality, superfluities, and the division of labor (secs. 40–51).

17. Cf. the discussion of *TMS* IV.1.10 on pp. 123–28 above.

18. Ferguson specifies that the "most common acceptation" of the term "interest" involves "those objects of care which refer to our external condition, and the preservation of our animal nature" (*Essay*, I:ii, p. 15). See Hirschman, pp. 32, 35–37, 39–40, 43, 54.

19. Smith faults the "sophistry" and "casuistry" of the modern curriculum, which render it unlikely "to improve the understanding, or to mend the heart" (*WN* V.i.f.32). When the National Conference of U.S. Bishops explains the "moral significance" of work, it invokes not the soul but "the distinctive human capacity for self-expression and self-realization" (*Economic Justice*, par. 97; cf. 137). The language used in the first draft of the letter is still more contemporary (U.S. Bishops Ad Hoc Committee on Catholic Social Teaching and the U.S. Economy, *Draft Letter* [Washington, D.C.: National Catholic News Service, 1984], par. 76). Cf. McGovern, pp. 110, 176–77, 250, 324–25.

20. On the importance of "society and conversation" to "men of the world," see *TMS* I.i.4.10; recall that trade is a form of "persuasion" (*WN* I.ii.1–2). Cf. V.i.f.40; and pp. 76–77 above.

21. The context of *WN*'s sole discussion of immortality, not surprisingly, is pecuniary: analyzing the best means of taxing land-rent.

22. Cf. *WN* II.iii.42 on how a "base and selfish disposition" may contribute more to "publick opulence" than a "liberal or generous spirit"; also see I.x.b.23, III.iv.17, IV.i.1, and pp. 79–81 above.

23. See pp. 82–83 above and 222–23 below on love and benevolence.

24. Löwith remarks that a Christian "lives in a radical tension between present and future. . . . He confidently enjoys what he is anxiously waiting and striving for" (p. 188). Cf. Skinner, p. 172.

25. See Arendt, pp. 87, 207, on the contrary view taken by the ancients.

26. In claiming that "the general character of the inhabitants as to industry or idleness" in "every country" is determined by the proportion in which the annual produce was previously divided between productive and unproductive labor (*WN* II.iii.3,12), Smith attributes the formation of character to economics rather than to religion, politics, and moral education. Cf. Kristol (*Reflections*, p. 203), Rosenberg and Birdzell (pp. 228–29), and Ryan (*Property*, p. 85) on how capitalist institutions, such as corporations, the stock market, and private property, serve to connect past, present, and future.

27. As Bacon pointed out, "The perfection of the sciences is to be looked for not from the swiftness or ability of any one inquirer, but from a succession" ("Prometheus," *Essays*, p. 275). Cf. Rosenberg and Birdzell, p. 252; and Blumenberg, pp. 31–33, 50–51, 238–40, 340, 353, 442–43, 554, 558, 591.

28. Cf. Arendt, p. 102; Pocock, *Machiavellian Moment*, pp. 439–40, 452–59, 490, 496; and Pocock, *Virtue, Commerce*, pp. 68–69, 100, 112–13. In Ernest Becker's words, "Money is the human mode *par excellence* of coolly denying animal boundedness, the determination of nature" (p. 82).

29. Such faith is extolled especially by George Gilder: "Capitalism consists of providing first and getting later" (p. 28); money facilitates making investments without "a predetermined return." From this, Gilder derives his notorious claim that "giving" is "the vital impulse and moral center of capitalism" (p. 30).

30. Religious faith is mentioned in the Article on religion, but is tainted by Smith's resort to Machiavelli's account of the revival of Christian "faith and devotion" (*WN* V.i.g.2). See pp. 167–68 below.

31. By contrast, Locke excludes atheists from toleration because "promises, covenants, and oaths, which are the bonds of human society, can have no hold upon or sanctity" for them (*A Letter on Toleration*, p. 135); "faith and truth, especially in all occasions of attesting it, upon the solemn appeal to heaven by an oath, is the great bond of society" (*Some Considerations*, p. 6). Even Mandeville states that "without the Belief of another World, a Man is under no Obligation for his Sincerity in this: His very Oath is no Tye upon him" (*Fable*, vol. II, p. 314). Cf. Montesquieu, *Spirit of Laws*, VIII:13, XIX:22; and Grotius, *The Law of War and Peace*, II:13.

32. The classic statements on capitalism's debt to Calvinism are those of Weber (pp. 104–5, 112, 114–15, 157, 159–62, 171–72) and Tawney (pp. 105, 113–14, 117, 226, 228–29, 233, 239–40, 244). Both characterize the changes wrought by the Reformation as an extension and secularization of monasticism (Weber, p. 121; Tawney, p. 107). Tawney, however, stresses the continued deference (within Protestantism) to traditional Catholic teachings on social morality and economics (pp. 43–47, 92, 94, 99, 101, 127, 162, 169, 225–26), and criticizes Weber for underemphasizing Machiavelli's contribution to the dissolution of "traditional ethical constraints" (pp. 21, 312–13). Cf. Flubacher, pp. 64–73; Hancock, pp. 20, 28, 91, 95–97, 115–16, 134, 164–77; Strauss, *Natural Right*, pp. 59–61, 317; and Troeltsch, pp. 44–46, 67–68, 75–76, 83–84, 129–32, 136, 139–40.

33. Smith himself would be an exception to this generalization.

34. Cf. *WN* V.iii.8,50,52,56,57,60,61,68,92. Also see Bell (pp. xx, 55, 69) and Novak (p. 165) on the decay of the work ethic.

35. I am indebted to Kevin Conlin for this observation.

36. Smith traces slavery's eventual abolition to considerations of "interest" (*WN* III.ii.12). Montesquieu gives credit to Christianity, but not without hints of a Smithian perspective. Montesquieu states that Christianity had ended slavery "in our climates" (*Spirit of Laws*, XV:7–8), i.e., in Europe. In XV:5, however, he indicates (and ridicules) the Europeans' use of African slaves in the New World (i.e., in other climates) and alludes to its economic advantages; Montesquieu's cynicism is less muted in *The Persian Letters* (#75). Grotius (*The Law of War and Peace*, III.7.6), James Steuart (*Inquiry*, II:xiii, p. 207) and Hegel (*Philosophy of History*, p. 334) defer to the Christian claim.

37. Cf. WN IV.vii.b.61, V.i.d.17, and Montesquieu, *Spirit of Laws*, XV:4.

38. See WN IV.ix.7–8, for comparable uses of the "sacred" by the Physiocrats; and *TMS* III.3.6, on the "sacred rules" of private property. Ricardo too specifies "security of property" as "that principle which should ever be held sacred" (*Principles*, XIV, p. 131).

39. This "holy" and "sacred" character of priests made it very dangerous for the sovereign (in early feudal times) to punish them when they committed crimes (WN V.i.g.22). The third reference to "sacred" occurs when Smith explains the emergence of a distinction between "sacred" and "profane" languages, offering both Europe and ancient Egypt as examples (V.i.f.20). The only other mention of "holy" is a reference to "the holy scriptures" in a context thoroughly indifferent to their holiness or sanctity (f.21).

40. Cf. Deuteronomy 8:3–4, John 6:27, Matthew 4:4, Romans 14:17–18, and 1 Corinthians 15:32.

41. The assessment by Campbell and Skinner of WN's sources is compelling: "The break with the tradition of Christian authority is obvious; even historical parts of the Bible and its apparent relevance to the discussion of a nomadic life are virtually ignored, with only the most incidental of references to the Old Testament" (WN, "General Introduction," p. 51).

42. In none of Smith's writings and lectures is Aquinas even mentioned; Augustine appears (along with Jean La Placette) briefly in a *TMS* footnote (VII.iv.11).

43. Cf. Voltaire: "Whoever has written about our duties has written well in every country of the world, because he wrote only with his reason. They have all said the same thing: Socrates and Epicurus, Confucius and Cicero, Marcus Antoninus and Amurath II" ("On right (Juste) and wrong," PD, p. 273). These positions were partly anticipated by the Deist Matthew Tindal, who in 1730 described Christianity as "one form of the religion of reason whose principles are discoverable by all people in all ages" (quoted in Barbour, p. 60).

44. Proverbs 1:2,7. An unpublished paper of Professor Paul Nelson's called my attention to the relevance here of the original biblical passages. Malthus too retreats from the harshness of Solomon's posture (*Essay*, XIX, p. 126).

45. Genesis (23). See Tawney, p. 138.

46. Smith thus departs from Locke's injunction that "the *instruction* of the people were best still to be left to the precepts and principles of the gospel" (*Reasonableness*, par. 243).

47. Hume's name is mentioned in *none* of the six editions of *TMS* (Teichgraeber, *Free Trade*, p. 132), despite Smith's frequent critiques of Humean doctrine as attributed, for example, to "an ingenious and agreeable philosopher, who joins the greatest depth of thought to the greatest elegance of expression" (*TMS* IV.1.1).

48. Foley says of the education Article (V.i.f): "Perhaps the reader would be sufficiently lulled by a discussion of tax matters not to notice the passing appearance of unorthodoxy" (p. 196). Foley grasps the spirit but not the letter, for the bulk of Smith's discussion of taxation comes later, and there is some

lively material in the first parts (defense and justice) of Book V, chapter 1. Smith's introductory sketch of Book V might indeed deter readers uninterested in tax matters (IV.ix.52); the "very long" (I.xi.p.1) perambulations of the rent chapter might already have weeded out readers prone to superstition, fanaticism, and "enthusiasm."

49. Cf. *WN* V.i.f.34,43,46. But recall Smith's praise of the "beggar" beside the road (*TMS* IV.1.10).

50. Cf. pp. 83–85 and 111–13 above.

51. Smith shows special interest in the death of Socrates (cf. *TMS* I.iii.1.14, VI.ii.1.31). As Raphael and Macfie point out, Smith "deliberately imitated the last sentence of Plato's *Phaedo* by ending his epitaph to Hume with the judgment that Hume had approached 'as nearly to the idea of a perfectly wise and virtuous man, as perhaps the nature of human frailty will permit'" (*TMS* Appendix II, p. 401). With Socrates, of course, there was no general curiosity about the prospects for deathbed repentance.

52. Cf. Strauss, *Spinoza's Critique*, pp. 29, 31; *Political Philosophy*, pp. 38–39; and recall Hume's claim that "the whole is a riddle, an enigma, an inexplicable mystery" (*Natural History*, ch. XV, p. 76). According to Foley, Smith interpreted Plato "almost to the point of abolishing the turn taken in ancient thought by Socrates" (p. xi). Smith does, however, credit Socrates with creating the "form" that introduced philosophy "to the general acquaintance of the world" (Astronomy III.6), and briefly touches on the historical relationship between the study of nature and the pursuit of "ethical, rhetorical, and dialectical questions" (IV.18).

53. Even Smith's friends among the "moderate" Scottish clergy—Hugh Blair, Alexander Carlyle, Adam Ferguson, and William Robertson—did not hesitate to scrutinize "a society's political and economic record for signs of God's judgments" (Sher, pp. 40–43, 102, 183–84, 206–10, 271–72, 325). On the different ways of conceiving the biblical God's relationship to history, see Blumenberg (pp. 30–32, 41–42, 45, 48, 174–75, 468, 484) and Pocock (*Machiavellian Moment*, pp. 7, 31–36).

54. Smith ends the astronomy essay by remarking that Newton's system is "considered . . . the greatest discovery that was ever made by man, the discovery of an immense chain of the most important and sublime truths, all closely connected together, by one capital fact, of the reality of which we have daily experience" (Astronomy IV.76). With the heavens purged of their mystery, one might infer, gravity replaces God as the "one capital fact" (whose reality we "daily experience") that connects "the most important and sublime truths." Cf. Smith's claim that geometry and mechanics introduce the "sublime" as well as the "useful" sciences (*WN* V.i.f.55). On the historical coexistence of Newtonian physics and certain forms of Christianity, see Barbour, pp. 35–43, 288; Hampson, p. 48; Porter, pp. 6, 10, 220n46; and Sher, p. 152n31.

55. Löwith observes about Vico's *New Science* that "nothing is said . . . about Jesus Christ as the turning point in the world's history and almost nothing about the rise and expansion of the Christian Church" in the Middle

Ages (Löwith, p. 129). Locke is more deferential than Smith or Vico. About the Resurrection, he exclaims: "How hath this one truth changed the nature of things in the world?" (*Reasonableness*, par. 245).

56. Montesquieu discusses Constantine and Christianity together (*Spirit of Laws*, XXIII:21).

57. Cf. Löwith, p. 112. The jurisprudence lectures are littered with references to the "introduction" and "establishment" of Christianity, but Smith neither elaborates nor explains these momentous developments; see his offhand reference in *EPS* to "the commencement of the Christian Aera" (Astronomy IV.22).

58. Hence the inappropriateness of Novak's claim that Smith, Montesquieu, Jefferson, and Madison all "saw themselves as agents of the progress which God intended the world to make" (p. 45). According to Löwith, "Modern historical consciousness had discarded the Christian faith in a central event of absolute relevance, yet it maintains its logical antecedents and consequences, viz., the past as preparation and the future as consummation, thus reducing the history of salvation to the impersonal teleology of a progressive evolution in which every present stage is the fulfillment of past preparations" (p. 186).

59. Smith's account of the origins of society abandons the "state of nature" doctrines of Hobbes, Locke, and Rousseau (see pp. 39–41 above), but it preserves their implicit rejections of sacred history. See Rousseau, *Second Discourse*, pp. 97, 102–3, 140, 179–80; Strauss, *Natural Right*, pp. 184–85, 267n32; Meek, *Social Science*, p. 122; and Ryan, *Property and Political Theory*, p. 58. For Alexander Pope, "the State of Nature was the reign of God" (III:148).

60. Locke, *Second Treatise*, secs. 21, 168, 176, 241.

61. Judges 11:23–40. The Lockean appeal differs from the Machiavellian exhortation to rely on "one's own arms" only by the prospect of punishment in the afterlife for the misuse of one's arms.

62. See pp. 41–44 above.

63. In the early days of feudalism, a king "was little more than the greatest proprietor in his dominions" (*WN* III.iv.70). So much for divine right, not to mention the sort of royalty worship Smith flirts with in *TMS* (I.iii.2.3–4).

64. One likewise wonders how many of those who have promulgated Marx's historical materialism really believe it.

65. Burke, *Reflections*, p. 182. Likewise, "nothing is more certain, than that our manners, our civilization, and all the good things" connected with them have depended on "the spirit of a gentleman, and the spirit of religion" (p. 173). Departing conspicuously from Smith, Burke extols religion as a means to "consecrate" the state—in part so that sovereigns (especially a democratic populace) "should have high and worthy notions of their function and destination" and thereby look beyond "the paltry pelf of the moment" (pp. 186–89). Like Burke, Tocqueville parts from Smith in praising aristocracy (including primogeniture) for its contribution to linking the generations. Tocqueville also praises both religion and aristocracy as coun-

terweights to vulgar greed. See, for example, *Democracy in America*, I.i.3, II.i.5,15, II.i.10,17,20, II.ii.10–11, II.iii.14, II.iv.8.

66. Cf. Tocqueville's famous discussion of "democratic historians" (*Democracy in America*, II.i.20) and Gertrude Himmelfarb, "Denigrating the Rule of Reason," *Harper's Magazine* 268 (April 1984): 84–90. As Daniel Bell observes, "The time-dimensions of social change are much slower, and the processes more complex, than the dramaturgic mode of the apocalyptic vision, religious or revolutionary, would have us believe" (p. 8).

67. To appreciate the intense religiosity of eighteenth-century Scotland, especially in the first half-century, see Graham, pp. 149, 160–61, 185, 190–95, 298–99, 302–14, 329–32, 334–43, 355–57, 365–66, 386–88, 400, 405–7, 409–10; and Sher, pp. 31–32, 57–58, 65–66, 70–71, 80–82, 121, 152–54, 158, 281–97. On the religiosity of "enlightened" Scots such as Hugh Blair, James Burnet (Lord Monboddo), Alexander Carlyle, Adam Ferguson, Henry Home (Lord Kames), John Home, William Robertson, and Dugald Stewart, see Sher, pp. 35, 40–44, 63, 102, 125, 175–85, 202, 206–11, 271–72, 305, 323–25; and Bryson, pp. 36, 65, 69, 95–99, 322–23.

68. The list is Barbour's (p. 22).

69. Astronomy IV.19. See pp. 28–32 above.

70. Smith concedes that a "poem may last as long as the world" (*TMS* V.1.4).

71. According to Smith's anonymous letter in the *Edinburgh Review*, Voltaire is "the most universal genius perhaps which France has ever produced" (Letter 17). Also see *TMS* III.3.14, III.6.12, VI.ii.1.22. But recall Smith's complaint about Voltaire's "insolent contempt of all the ordinary decorums of life and conversation" (*TMS* VI.i.10).

72. *WN* I.i.9, V.i.f.51. Cf. V.i.f.28,34; and pp. 83–85 and 111–13 above.

73. In defending economic liberty, Hayek emphasizes the impossibility of achieving comprehensive knowledge: "The more men know, the smaller becomes the share of all that knowledge that any one mind can absorb" (pp. 4, 25–26, 29).

74. *WN* IV.vii.c.44,107, IV.iii.c.2, V.i.a.10, V.i.d.9, V.i.f.15.

75. *WN* I.ii.1, IV.vii.a.2, IV.vii.c.80, IV.ix.51, V.i.g.24.

CHAPTER EIGHT *The Theological-Political Problem*

1. The most strident criticisms indeed occur in the preceding Article (V.i.f.30).

2. "Which is the best Religion is a Question that has caused more Mischief than all other questions together" (Mandeville, *Fable*, vol. II, p. 331).

3. Emphasis in original. Smith's most complete listing of different sects (he mentions Portuguese Jews along with English Puritans, Catholics, and Quakers) is issued to illustrate the effects of religious persecution—i.e., "the disorder and injustice of the European governments"—in peopling America (*WN* IV.vii.b.61).

4. According to Barbour, the "rational religion" of the seventeenth cen-

304 / Notes to Pages 166–67

tury "had been intended as a support for the essentials of Christianity, but by the next century it was to have become a substitute" (p. 40).

5. *WN* V.i.g.23–24,29–30,36; *TMS* VII.iv.16; cf. Physics 9, and pp. 116–20 above. In *EPS*, Smith acknowledges a "mild, just, and religious government"—that of the Muslim "Califfs" in the early Middle Ages (Astronomy IV.21). Voltaire identifies the religion of "Chinese scholars" as the only religion that has "never been sullied by fanaticism" ("Fanaticism," *PD*, p. 203).

6. Cf. Barbour (pp. 60–61) on Tindal and Butler; and recall Smith's counting Solomon among the wise individuals who, in "every age and country of the world," have written down maxims expressing "their own sense" of proper conduct (*WN* V.i.f.25).

7. Smith only once refers to Eastern Orthodoxy: in illustrating the "precarious and insecure" position of a sovereign insufficiently equipped to resist an established clergy, Smith invokes "the revolutions which the turbulence of the Greek clergy was continually occasioning at Constantinople" (*WN* V.i.g.17).

8. Smith acknowledges that English Independents had favored the separation of church and state, and that Pennsylvania had perhaps implemented it. But he describes the Independents as "very wild Enthusiasts" (*WN* V.i.g.8), and nowhere identifies the Quaker religion as "pure and rational."

9. In the very first sentence of the *Letter on Toleration*, Locke identifies toleration as "the chief distinguishing mark of a true church"; is Locke less concerned with the truth of church doctrine? The *Letter* frequently employs provocative phrases—the "true religion," the "orthodox religion," the "true church" (pp. 67, 95, 101, 113, 75)—but never specifies which religion or church is the true one. In the famous chapter in *Du Contrat Social* on civil religion, Rousseau labels the Gospel as "the religion of man" and even as "le vrai théisme." But this apparent concession to the truth of Christianity is subtly belied by Rousseau's identification of the Gospel religion with the "devoirs éternels de la morale" and "le droit divin naturel" (IV:viii, p. 174), concepts that clash with the temporal specificity of biblical revelation. The reference to "natural" divine right, moreover, is implausible because our "natural" state as depicted in the *Second Discourse* dramatically lacks both "right" and divinity. "Vrai" in "le vrai théisme" may thus mean only genuine or essential. Rousseau says that he knows of nothing more contrary to "l'esprit social" than Christian otherworldliness; in denying the possibility of a Christian republic, Rousseau confesses that "chacun de ces deux mots exclut l'autre" (*Du Contrat Social*, IV:viii, pp. 175–77). If any version of Christianity were true in the strict sense, one would presumably accord it higher priority than republicanism or "l'esprit social." The reticence of Locke, Hume, Rousseau, and Smith about "the true religion" might temper sectarianism, but none of them pulls his punches regarding Catholicism.

10. Hegel and Marx, despite the gulf between idealism and materialism, both posit a general logic to history that dictates the development of religion. For Hegel, the Christian principle is "the axis on which the history of the

world turns"; it brings "reconciliation" and historical "completion" (*Philosophy of History*, pp. 319, 324, 342). Marx rejects *Geist* as the engine of history and attempts to derive the religious "superstructure" from the fundamental dialectic in the mode of production. For both Hegel and Marx, there is no place for miraculous divine interventions to disrupt the dialectic of history, and Christianity can be fully explained by or incorporated into that dialectic.

11. Cf. Marsilius of Padua's account of the "singular and obscure cause" that Aristotle could not have addressed. Smith's sole discussion of Greece and Rome in the religion Article is an explicit digression concluding that the poverty of churches benefits society by drawing "men of letters" to their "natural employment" as "teacher[s] of science"; the digression may also serve to remind us that men of letters in antiquity were not priests (*WN* V.i.g.40).

12. According to Hume, "In all ages of the world, priests have been enemies to liberty; and it is certain, that this steady conduct of theirs must have been founded on fixed reasons of interest and ambition" ("Of the Parties of Great Britain," *Essays*, p. 62). Regarding the jurisprudence lectures, Haakonssen observes: "In all cases in which Smith ascribes a significant influence to the clergy, the concern with religion is only part of their motivation, whereas Church policy or private interest . . . are always driving forces" (p. 175). Cf. Tawney's account of how the corruption of the medieval Church displayed "the reality of economic motives in the Age of Faith" (pp. 41–42, 68, 98–99).

13. *Discourses*, III:1; translated by Mansfield, *New Modes and Orders*, p. 304. Unlike Smith, Machiavelli is willing to mention the Dominicans' and Franciscans' exemplification of the "*vita di Cristo*."

14. Spinoza wrote: "The firmest dominion belongs to the sovereign who has most influence over the minds of his subjects" (*Theologico-Political Treatise*, XVII, p. 215), but those who wield "spiritual right and authority . . . have the most complete sway over the popular mind" (XIX, p. 252).

15. Tocqueville says that "Jesus Christ had to come down to earth to make all members of the human race understand that they were naturally similar and equal" (*Democracy in America*, II.i.3, p. 439), and insists that the progress of equality is providentially fated (Introduction). Cf. Hegel, *Philosophy of History*, p. 334; and E. Becker, p. 69.

16. See also Haakonssen, p. 176; *LJB* 133; and *WN* IV.vii.c.77.

17. See Sigmund, pp. 135, 143, 147, 151; Bonar, pp. 51, 53–54; Caton, *Politics of Progress*, p. 111; Lakoff, pp. 115–33; Tawney, pp. 34–38, 69–70; and Troeltsch, p. 151.

18. Spinoza says that Scripture "contains no lofty speculation nor philosophic reasoning, but only very simple matters, such as could be understood by the slowest intelligence" (*TPT*, XIII, p. 175). At the conclusion of *Reasonableness*, Locke describes the basic Christian dogma as "a plain intelligible proposition," and suggests that the Christian religion is suited to "the bulk of mankind . . . to vulgar capacities, and the state of mankind in this world, destined to labour and travail." The gospel preached was "as the poor could understand, plain and intelligible" (par.252).

19. *WN* IV.ix.51, III.iv.20, IV.vii.c.54, IV.viii.30, IV.ix.3, V.i.b.25, V.ii.c.18; cf. pp. 46, 52–56 above.

20. According to Hirschman, "Smith was concerned, far more than earlier writers, with the 'great mob of mankind'" (p. 111). On Smith as proletarian guardian angel, see Danford, pp. 690–92, 695; Himmelfarb, pp. 50–52; Hollander, pp. 245, 249–53; McNally, pp. 225–29, 244, 255–61; Rosenberg, "Smith on Profits" and "Smith and Laissez-Faire," pp. 21, 26; and Viner, *Long View*, p. 245. Within *WN*, consider I.vi.8, I.viii.11–13,44–45, I.ix.24, I.x.c.16, 25,27,34,61, I.xi.a.1, I.xi.p.8–10, III.ii.6,16, III.iii.8, III.iv.10, IV.i.29, IV.ii.16, 18,31,38,43, IV.iii.c.10–11, IV.v.b.3,38, IV.vii.b.3,49,54, IV.vii.c.29,60,66, IV.viii.3–4,17,47,49,53–54, V.i.b.2,12, V.iii.89.

21. *WN* I.x.c.39, IV.vii.b.4, V.i.f.43,45, V.i.g.40.

22. Hence Hume's advice to "bribe" the "indolence" of the clergy (V.i.g.6). Montesquieu describes the clergy as "a family which cannot be extinct" (*Spirit of Laws*, XXV:5).

23. Contrast with Montesquieu, *Spirit of Laws*, XXV:1–4.

24. This passage raises a number of puzzles we will not pursue. For example, why is civilization here identified with hierarchy, when Smith argues that "authority and subordination" are more perfectly established in the shepherd stage of society than in any of the other stages (V.i.b.7)? On the relationship between the two-moralities scheme and *TMS*, see Campbell, p. 176.

25. Cf. *TMS* V.2.5. In his article on Christianity, Voltaire says that "to fetter the people one must appear to wear the same chains as they do" (*PD*, p. 125). Lindgren's interpretation of Smith here is a bit naive: "Laymen accept the doctrines professed by their teachers as true because they believe their teachers to be committed to the same moral convictions which constitute the bonds of their community" (p. 142).

26. See pp. 79–81, 85, and 147–50 above. During the reign of Charles II, Smith indicates, "liberal education" was associated with being a "gentleman and not a puritan" (*TMS* V.2.3).

27. Burke unwittingly provides a tremendous rebuke to *WN* in arguing that "the body of the people must . . . respect that property of which they cannot partake. They must labour to obtain what by labour can be obtained; and when they find, as they commonly do, the success disproportioned to the endeavour, they must be taught their consolation in the final proportions of eternal justice. *Of this consolation whoever deprives them, deadens their industry, and strikes at the root of all acquisition* as of all conservation" (*Reflections*, p. 372). Malthus begins his theodicy chapter (XVIII) by arguing that "the view of human life which results from the contemplation of the constant pressure of distress on man from the difficulty of subsistence, by shewing the little expectation that he can reasonably entertain of perfectibility on earth, seems strongly to point his hopes to the future."

28. See pp. 126–28 above on Smith's ambiguous account of the prospects for long-lasting prosperity; cf. *WN* I.viii.44.

29. The "economy of the rich" is characterized generally by "disorders," as

opposed to the "strict frugality and parsimonious attention of the poor" (*WN* I.viii.41); high profit destroys "that parsimony . . . natural to the character of the merchant" (IV.vii.c.61). Cf. *WN* III.iv.3,19 and III.ii.7 on the virtues of small property; also see Bell, p. 55; Dunn, p. 134; Novak, p. 121; and Rosenberg, "Smith on Profits," p. 388.

30. Even Voltaire criticizes Bayle and argues that it is "absolutely necessary for princes and peoples to have deeply engraved in their minds the notion of a supreme being, creator, ruler, remunerator and avenger" ("Atheist," *PD*, p. 57).

31. In depicting religious toleration as the "first plank of his [Smith's] program" (p. 61), Farr exaggerates Smith's posture as an advocate.

32. "If you have two religions in your midst they will cut each other's throats; if you have thirty, they will live in peace" (Voltaire, "Tolerance," *PD*, p. 390). Cf. the argument in *Federalist* 51 that religious liberty requires a multiplicity of sects.

33. Dunn observes that Hume and Smith in their early works offered their readers "sociological reassurance" rather than "theological reassurance"; each strove "to establish that the bonds of human society, human moral sentiments, neither depended nor needed to depend for either their prevalence or their rationally binding force upon an authority external to human society or to the human race as a whole" (p. 120).

34. According to Weber, however, the Calvinist doctrine of predestination, and the corresponding de-emphasis of the mediating role of Church and Sacraments (among them, transubstantiation, confession, and absolution), produced "a feeling of unprecedented inner loneliness of the single individual . . . forced to follow his path alone to meet a destiny which had been decreed for him from eternity" (pp. 104–6, 116–17).

35. See Farr, on the evolution of the combat between science and enthusiasm in Hume, Locke, Shaftesbury, Ferguson, and Smith.

36. On the religious obstacles to social gaiety in eighteenth-century Scotland, see Graham, pp. 92–96, 122, 137, 142, 188, 270, 314–21, 325, 327, 345–46; and Sher, pp. 33–34, 57–58, 76–78, 82–83.

37. With regard to public diversions, what Smith means by the state's "encouraging" them is just "giving entire liberty to all those who for their own interest" would engage in them (*WN* V.i.g.15). Music and dancing were indeed revealed in the education Article to be "the great amusements of almost all barbarous nations, and the great accomplishments which are supposed to fit any man for entertaining his society" (V.i.f.40). Smith again trusts to the sociological rather than to the theological.

38. Mill puts the matter strongly: "Religious freedom has hardly anywhere been practically realised, except where religious indifference, which dislikes to have its peace disturbed by theological quarrels, has added its weight to the scale" (*On Liberty*, p. 9). Cassirer, by contrast, claims that "tolerance means anything but a recommendation of laxity and indifference to fundamental questions of religion" (p. 164).

39. See pp. 152–53 above.

40. WN alludes to the contribution that confession makes to priestly authority (V.i.g.2), but the account in TMS is more complete (VII.iv.16–17).

41. Fear as a tactic is especially dangerous when employed against a group with "pretensions to independency" (WN V.i.g.19). One wonders how Smith would categorize the tools of Catholic "governing" in terms of violence, fear, expectation, management, and persuasion.

42. In Montesquieu's words, "Penal laws must be avoided in the matter of religion" because fear of them is effaced by the fears inspired by religion. The best way to attack a religion is "by favor, by the comforts of life, by the hope of fortune, not by what reminds one of it, but by what makes one forget it; not by what makes one indignant, but by what leads one to indifference" (Spirit of Laws, XXV:12). Smith's treatment of religion is certainly less shocking than that of Machiavelli, Hobbes, Spinoza, Bayle, Mandeville, Voltaire, Helvétius, Hume, d'Alembert, Diderot, and d'Holbach, and he provides a massive science to turn his reader's thoughts to comforts ("les commodités") and wealth.

43. Smith can thus look back, from the viewpoint of those of "us who live in the present times," and regard the clergy's privileges "in those antient times" as absurd, though these privileges were "the natural or rather the necessary consequence" of the ancient "state of things" (V.i.g.23). By explaining the historical ascendancy of Christianity in terms of "nature," Smith preempts any explanation that invokes the divine or the miraculous; by identifying nature with "the progress of opulence," Smith deprecates politics and the human word.

44. According to Hegel, Wycliffe and Huss failed as reformers (in part) because they "attacked the teaching of the Church chiefly with the weapons of erudition, and consequently failed to excite a deep interest among the people at large" (Philosophy of History, p. 406). To sample the rustic eloquence of Scottish Presbyterian preachers, see Graham, pp. 292–97, 369–70, 400–407.

45. Cf. Hume, "Of the Parties of Great Britain," Essays, p. 67.

46. Hugh Blair, although himself a Presbyterian minister, faulted Smith's account for being "too favourable by much to Presbytery." Presbyterianism "Connects the Teachers too closely with the People; and gives too much aid to that Austere System you Speak of, which is never favourable to the great improvements of mankind" (Smith's Correspondence, #151, 3 April 1776). On the mellowing of the Scottish Presbyterian clergy in the second half of the eighteenth century, see Graham, pp. 121–22, 142, 145, 349–53, 355–57, 374–75, 413–16, 512–24, 530–38; and Sher, pp. 16, 35, 49, 57–60, 64, 68–70, 73, 86, 93, 105, 121, 133, 151, 155–56, 160–61, 191, 319. Phillipson seems to place the origin of the transformation a few years earlier ("Enlightenment," p. 28).

47. Does Smith mean to imply that the austerity of higher clergy is partially feigned and therefore more likely to be excessive? See WN V.i.g.34.

48. Mansfield, "Impersonality," p. 850; similar considerations led Machiavelli to encourage both republics and principalities to exalt worldly gain (p. 855).

49. Wealth and greatness are the "most universal" cause of corruption (*TMS* I.iii.3.1), but it seems that the corruption produced by faction, fanaticism, and religion is "by far the greatest" (III.3.43, III.6.12). Perhaps the "most universal" cause of corruption can be increased in virulence to combat the religious sects that produce the most virulent fanaticism.

50. Cf. pp. 41–45 above, on how age, birth, and, above all, wealth eclipse wisdom and virtue as sources of the "subordination" and "superiority" that secure "the peace and order of society." Also cf. *TMS* VI.ii.1.20, VI.iii.30.

51. Consider Locke's *Second Treatise*, secs. 42, 87, 94, 137, 158, 229, in light of his insistence in the *Letter on Toleration* that "political society was instituted only to preserve for each man his possession of the things of this life" (p. 129) and that government limit its concern to "the public good in earthly or worldly matters, which is the . . . sole object of the commonwealth" (p. 127).

52. *WN* IV.vii.c.75,81,85, V.iii.37,92; cf. I.xi.c.36, III.3.15, IV.i.11,19, V.i.d.16. See pp. 27–32 and 100–109 above.

53. *TMS* I.iii.2.8–9, I.iii.3.2,8, II.iii.2.3, III.2.33, III.3.31,33, IV.1.8,11, VI.i.9,16, VI.ii.2.15, VI.iii.5,13,27–31.

54. Cf. pp. 28–32, 82, 130–38, and 162–64 above. Strauss says of *The Prince* that Machiavelli "tries to divert the adherence of the young from the old to the new teaching by appealing to the taste of the young . . . to the taste of the common people: he displays a bias in favor of the impetuous, the quick, the partisan, the spectacular, and the bloody over and against the deliberate, the slow, the neutral, the silent, and the gentle" (*Thoughts*, p. 82). There is no doubt that Smith elevates the latter group and demotes the former. If, as Strauss asserts, "economism" is "Machiavellianism," it is certainly Machiavellianism "come of age" (*Political Philosophy*, p. 49).

55. Machiavelli, *Prince*, ch. 9. Smith says that religions are begun "among"—not *by*—"the common people" (V.i.g.11), which explains why their susceptibility to enthusiasm and superstition can be reduced if the higher ranks are instructed in science/philosophy (g.14). Smith's account of the two moralities, however, might suggest that he wishes to replace the vices of ambition with "the vices of levity." Also see pp. 27–28 above; and Machiavelli's *Discourses*, I:5 (on maintainers and acquirers) and I:55 (on gentlemen—and priests?).

56. *WN* I.x.a.1, I.xi.c.21, II.v.31–32, IV.ii.4,10, IV.iii.c.2, IV.v.a.3,39, IV.vii.c.43–44,47,89, IV.ix.51, V.i.e.40, V.i.f.3,43,46,49.

57. Arendt, p. 263; Strauss, *Thoughts*, p. 297. On the Romantic rebellion against Newtonianism and deism, see Barbour, pp. 41–42, 57, 62, 65–68.

CHAPTER NINE *Religion and Moral Sentiments I*

1. "Smith in later life experienced greater difficulty in entering into the deity's sentiments" (Dunn, pp. 128–29). According to Raphael and Macfie, Smith "moved away from orthodox Christianity" (Introduction to *TMS*, p. 19). I shall argue that Smith unequivocally rejects orthodox Christianity even in *TMS*. In stating that "certainly Smith never abandoned *natural*

religion," Raphael and Macfie minimize the atheistic tendencies of *WN* (*TMS*, p. 400, emphasis in original).

2. These alterations, because they bring *TMS closer* to the irreligiosity of *WN*, require us to reject Dickey's clever attempt to "historicize" the "Adam Smith Problem" by arguing that the 1790 edition of *TMS* constitutes "a third motivating center" of Smith's thought (p. 609). Dickey goes far astray in contending that Smith ultimately returned to a "quasi-religious conception of nature" and to "mainline Protestant theology shaped in the image of the theology of the divine economy" (pp. 605–8).

3. Dunn too alludes to this possibility (p. 120n5).

4. See pp. 5–6, 8 above.

5. Also recall that the "Principles which lead and direct Philosophical Enquiries" essays were composed, according to Wightman, before the publication of *TMS*, and that the disparaging remarks in Smith's lectures (*LJA* iii.99–100) about the source of Christianity's appeal were first delivered in 1762–63. See p. 169 above.

6. Compare the references to nature's "wisdom" in Part VI of *TMS* (VI.ii.Intro.3, VI.ii.1.4,20, VI.ii.2.4), added in 1790, with the sole reference in *WN* (IV.ix.28).

7. In *TMS*, the sole reference to the invisible hand appears in one of the two Parts (IV and V) that fail to mention God. These two Parts, moreover, contain the book's most sustained defense of economic and technological progress; they are also linked by their brevity and their titles.

8. Although *WN* makes no mention of *TMS*, it says nothing that would prevent *TMS* from continuing to elevate the horizons of its readers—especially the "youth," who exhibit "flexibility" and "natural magnanimity" (*TMS* VII.iv.6; *WN* V.i.f.15,43). Cf. Aristotle, *Nicomachean Ethics*, 1179b6–10.

9. See Matthew 22:32; Mark 12:26; and pp. 124–29 above.

10. *TMS* II.i.5.10, II.iii.Intro.6, II.iii.3.2, III.2.12,31,33, III.3.43, III.5.7, 10,13, VI.ii.3.3,4, VII.ii.1.18,37. Smith designates God as "Architect," "Superintendent," "that superintending Power," or "Physician" only when recounting (or quoting) Stoic views (VII.ii.1.23,26,37,39), with the possible exception of VII.ii.1.46 ("the great Superintendent of the universe"), where Smith seems to glide from a Stoic voice into his own voice.

11. According to Smith, Plato and Timaeus—who seem to be his exemplars of ancient theism—held that "the great Author of all things" formed the universe "out of that matter which had existed from all eternity" (Physics 9).

12. Haakonssen says of Smith's approach: "The first thing to note about religious belief is that it is a consequence of, a function of morality" (p. 75). On the anticipations of Kant in *TMS*, see Oncken, pp. 67–104.

13. Cf. Malthus: "I have never considered the doubts and difficulties that involve some parts of the sacred writings as any argument against their divine original"; "if the scriptural denunciations of eternal punishment were brought home with the same certainty to every man's mind as that the night

will follow the day, this one vast and gloomy idea would take such full possession of the human faculties as to leave no room for any other conceptions" (*Essay*, XIX, p. 127).

14. Locke, *Second Treatise*, secs. 7, 11.

15. Cox, Introduction to the *Second Treatise*, p. xxxi; contrast Locke's interpretation of Cain with Grotius's (*The Law of War and Peace*, I.2.5). The latest research in political science conveys a different view of the Bible: "'Nature' is the only realm the Hebrew knows ('experiences')" (Roelofs, p. 552).

16. "Qui ne voit que la défense naturelle est d'un ordre supérieur à tous les préceptes?" (Montesquieu, *L'Esprit des Lois*, XXVI:7).

17. Thanks are due the Oxford edition editors, Macfie and Raphael, for incorporating passages from Massillon's own text. They interpret Smith's departures from the original as being "minor details" because they are insufficiently attentive to Smith's subterranean combat with Christianity (*TMS*, p. 133n15).

18. The love of self-approbation is "the love of virtue" (*TMS* III.2.8).

19. This sentence and a later reference to "the Roman Catholic superstition" (VII.iv.16) are the only mentions of "Roman Catholic" in *TMS*. Within Smith's corpus, "saint" appears only in a *TMS* footnote reference to Augustine and in the mentions of St. Dominic and St. Francis in *WN*. See pp. 167–68 above, for a discussion of the hostility there exhibited.

20. See pp. 165–67 above on the "true religion" in *WN*. According to Jim Herrick, Voltaire's play emphasized that Islam was based on "false miracles, personal ambition, and ruthless fanaticism," and audiences recognized the intended parallel with Christianity (Herrick, p. 61). In both of his books, Smith mentions Mohammed but not Jesus.

21. See Appendix II of the Oxford *TMS* (esp. p. 399), for an analysis of this passage with reference to other changes Smith made and to a manuscript fragment.

22. Barbour argues, against Freud, that "biblical religion usually sees God's will as the opposite of man's wishes, challenging our conventional morality and destroying our complacency and our pretenses" (p. 256). Strauss (*Spinoza's Critique*, p. 8) states that revelation is an "experience . . . of something undesired, coming from the outside, going against man's grain." The psychological approach of *TMS* at least vindicates religion against the charge of being the self-serving creation of various elites.

23. Smith's claim that belief in the afterlife arises from an intrinsic rather than an instrumental abhorrence of injustice supposes that punishment in the afterlife "cannot serve to deter the rest of mankind, who see it not, who know it not" (*TMS* II.ii.3.12).

24. Smith's closest approach to the Christian vision of Hell is a quotation from Voltaire that ridicules it (*TMS* III.2.35). See pp. 204–5 below; and *WN* V.i.g.1,17.

25. "The concept of original sin is the common opponent against which all the different trends of the philosophy of the Enlightenment join forces"

(Cassirer, p. 141); cf. Smith's other reference to the "depraved state of mankind" (*TMS* II.i.5.8). On the thematic prominence of Fall and Redemption in Scottish Presbyterianism, see Graham, pp. 293–94, 397–98, 400, 410.

26. Even the bishops, in the first draft of the *Letter*, insist that "human life is fulfilled in the knowledge and love of the living God" and that "worship and prayer are the center of Christian existence" (U.S. Bishops Ad Hoc Committee on Catholic Social Teaching and the U.S. Economy, *Draft Letter* [Washington, D.C.: National Catholic News Service, 1984], pars. 27, 325). The language in the final version, however, is less theocentric (National Conference, secs. 329, 332).

27. The stress in *WN* on bettering one's condition and the "natural progress of opulence" would be absurd if "the greatest possible quantity of happiness" always prevailed.

28. See the long quotation from Marcus Aurelius (*TMS* VII.ii.1.37). On the differences between Stoic Providence and the biblical God, see Blumenberg, pp. 34, 37, 132, 157.

29. The mystery in the "secret wheels and springs" (*TMS* I.i.4.2) of "the great machine" is dispelled by science and philosophy, which lay bare the "connecting chains."

30. Stoic cosmology, as portrayed in *EPS*, identifies the deity with nature; in *TMS*, Smith presents the Stoic deity as nature's architect, superintendent, and physician. The eternal "chain of causes and effects" (*TMS* VII.ii.1.37) seems to replace the Stoic doctrine of cyclical destruction (Physics 11). Cf. pp. 112–13 and 141–42 above; and Foley, pp. 29, 43.

31. The closest Smith comes to describing such a relationship is in his account of the Neoplatonists, who recommended imitating the divine virtue of benevolence "till at last we arrived at that immediate converse and communication with the Deity" (*TMS* VII.ii.3.1–2; cf. Logics 5). Smith criticizes this system's rejection of all the self-regarding virtues, pointing out that a human being (unlike the Deity) requires many external things to "support" himself (VII.ii.3.18).

32. *TMS*, p. 136n5. Regarding the impact of the 1755 Lisbon quake on Voltaire's views, see Herrick, pp. 64–65.

33. See especially pp. 49–51, 56–60, 109–13, 123–28, 134–37, and 171–75 above.

34. Viner errs by overlooking the bleaker statements (*Long View*, pp. 217, 229–30).

35. Cf. *TMS* II.i.5.10, III.5.9, on nature's frugality and efficiency. For the other references to nature's "wisdom," see *TMS* II.iii.3.4, VI.ii.Intro.3, VI.ii.1.4,20, VI.ii.2.4; on the "wisdom of God," also see VI.iii.30. In criticizing the argument from design, Hume's Philo invokes "the great frugality with which all powers and faculties are distributed to every particular being"; nature is a "rigid master," not an "indulgent parent" (*Dialogues*, XI, p. 71).

36. As we have seen, Smith's deference toward the "natural" is balanced even in *TMS* by an endorsement of the economic/technological conquest of

nature. This conquest, paradoxically, is itself the manifestation of a "natural progress."

37. Cropsey, *Political Philosophy*, p. 62; cf. pp. 73–74, 87–88; and *Polity*, pp. 38–40. The "roughnesses and inequalities" of nature, according to Malthus, "though they sometimes offend the fastidious microscopic eye of short sighted man, contribute to the symmetry, grace, and fair proportion of the whole" (*Essay*, XIX, p. 125). Cf. Spinoza, *TPT*, XVI (pp. 202, 211); and Pope, I:50–51, IV:149–52.

38. R. H. Coase alludes to the kinship between Smith's thought and Darwin's, but fails to acknowledge that *WN*'s articulation of social harmony abandons the "postulate" of "a divine creator" (pp. 538–41). Although Smith does not suggest that biological species are the fruits of evolution, he displays keen interest in propagation, competition, adaptation, and the survival of the fittest.

39. See pp. 81, 89–93 above.

40. On the soul, also see *TMS* II.iii.3.3, III.6.1. Smith occasionally refers to the "awful futurity" that awaits us. But without stronger endorsement of the reality of the afterlife, that futurity is merely death (I.i.1.13, V.2.5). Soldiers regard death "merely as the loss of life" because familiarity eliminates the "superstitious horror" (VI.iii.7).

41. Characteristically, Smith's use of the word "alone" allows of two interpretations: belief in the afterlife *by itself* can produce the good effects; or the effects cannot occur without the belief.

42. Cf. Arendt's account of the opposition between pagan "action"—the quest to distinguish and immortalize oneself in the public realm—and the Christian vision of immortality and sacredness that ultimately prepared the triumph of the *animal laborans* and the tragic withering of "the political" (Arendt, pp. 41–42, 48–49, 55–56, 126, 129, 135, 159–60, 173, 176–80, 197–99, 247, 313–16, 320–21).

43. Smith translates Massillon's reference to "une vie entière de penitence" as "a whole life of repentance *and mortification*," calling to mind his discussion of "penance and mortification" in *WN*. The French original is provided by the editors of *TMS* (p. 133), who also point out the resemblance to Hume's *ICPM*, IX:i: "Penance, mortification, . . . and the whole train of monkish virtues" are "everywhere rejected by men of sense." Cf. MacIntyre, p. 214. See also Hume's discussion of "the monkish virtues of mortification, penance, humility, and passive suffering," in *Natural History of Religion*, X, p. 52.

44. Cropsey brilliantly diagnoses the dominant project, but not Smith's hesitations and reservations (*Political Philosophy*, pp. 73–74, 87–88).

45. "You *there* burn wise and learned Plato, divine Homer, eloquent Cicero."

46. On the contrast between religion and worldliness, see pp. 143–47 above; also see *WN* V.i.f.35,46, V.i.g.1; *TMS* III.5.13, I.i.4.10.

47. Although the essence of morality is experiencing the sentiment of propriety, Smith acknowledges that the "bulk of mankind," because wrought

of "coarse clay," will be guided by the general rules derived from the sentimental experience (*TMS* III.4.7–10, III.5.1–2).

48. Cf. Hume's famous critique of causality: "As this operation of the mind, by which we infer like effects from like causes, and vice versa, is so essential to the subsistence of all human creatures, it is not probable that it could be trusted to the fallacious deductions of our reason. . . . It is more conformable to the ordinary wisdom of nature to secure so necessary an act of the mind by some instinct . . . independent of all the labored deductions of the understanding" (*ICHU*, V, p. 68).

49. Smith's explanation of how "reasoning and philosophy" ultimately "confirmed" that the rules are the Deity's commands and laws (*TMS* III.5.5–7) is highly complex, but says nothing to indicate that *biblical* rules have been confirmed. And the philosophical confirmation that the Deity "will finally reward the obedient, and punish the transgressors" (III.5.3) invokes only natural phenomena of this world (III.5.6–8).

50. As we have seen, if Socrates had died "quietly in his bed, the glory even of that great philosopher might possibly never have acquired that dazzling splendour in which it has been beheld in all succeeding ages" (*TMS* VI.iii.5). Ajax's death is "beyond the period of true history" (VII.ii.1.31). About the death allegedly by suicide of several Stoics, Smith comments that "their lives have been so very foolishly written, that very little credit is due to the greater part of the tales which are told of them." The reception accorded two different accounts of Zeno's suicide, as opposed to the account that he "died in the natural way," is cited by Smith as an example of "the marvellous" prevailing over "the probable" (VII.ii.1.31).

51. The susceptibility of the followers is partially explained in Smith's famous discussion of the human "disposition to go along with all the passions of the rich and the powerful"; this supports social order and fuels the pursuit of wealth (*TMS* I.iii.2.1–4). We imagine "the great" to exist in a "perfect and happy state" with which it is pleasant to sympathize: "We could even wish them immortal" (I.iii.2.2). Might our love of intelligence, freedom, and goodness lead us to posit indestructible superhuman beings? Cf. *TMS* III.6.7, IV.1.1,11, VI.ii.1.20–21, VI.ii.2.15, VI.ii.3, VI.iii.27,30.

CHAPTER TEN *Religion and Moral Sentiments II*

1. See pp. 46–49, 154–56 above.

2. Mandeville, Introduction to *An Enquiry into the Origin of Moral Virtue*, in *Fable*, vol. I, p. 40.

3. On Hutcheson and Hume, see Teichgraeber (*Free Trade*, p. 85), who likewise points out that this warmth "seemed to dissolve" in *WN* (p. 123). Also see Sher, pp. 166–68.

4. Cropsey, *Polity*, p. 40; cf. *Political Philosophy*, p. 88. Campbell criticizes Smith for "grossly" overusing the vocabulary of "nature," but ignores the possibility that this overuse is deliberate and calls attention to the deepest problems Smith addresses (Campbell, p. 56); Campbell overlooks

the tension between the natural imperative of preservation and the noble (p. 219).

5. "Natural religion has a thousand times prevented citizens from committing crimes. . . . But artificial religion encourages all the cruelties done in association" (Voltaire, "Guerre," *PD*, p. 233).

6. Cf. pp. 183–86 above, on how the "worship" of wealth and greatness may serve as a remedy for the corrupting effects of faction and fanaticism.

7. Marx of course strove to combat the soporific effects of the whole tradition of bourgeois speculation. Without resort to God or heaven, Marx reinfused "the dismal science" with Enlightenment optimism and zeal. Without resort to God or heaven, Nietzsche's doctrine of the eternal return would recreate the earnestness that life derives from a connection to eternity (*The Gay Science*, sec. 341). Communism and National Socialism, unfortunately, demonstrated the extreme heights that non-religious fanaticism can attain.

8. Löwith, p. 163; Christianity has "immensely accentuated and deepened the earnestness of the present instant" (p. 113). According to Troeltsch, Protestantism not only "retained in the strictest fashion the determination of life by the antithesis of heaven and hell," but accentuated the antithesis by rejecting Purgatory (p. 74).

9. See pp. 122–27 above, and recall the passage (excised in 1790) where Smith explains that a vivid and immediate perception of God's "infinite rewards and punishments" would leave humanity "astonished at the immensity of objects so little fitted to its comprehension" and therefore unable to "attend to the little affairs of this world" (*TMS*, p. 128).

10. *TMS* VII.i (title), VII.i.2.

11. Teichgraeber (*Free Trade*, p. 133) quotes this to show that Smith would deny that the Humean enterprise (reducing morality to the passions) had "those dangerous implications for 'virtue' and 'justice'" feared by Hutcheson and others. As we shall see, however, Smith's remark is partly ironic.

12. Part III explains our "judgments concerning our own sentiments and conduct" and the "sense of duty," but two of its chapters are devoted to the subject of "general rules."

13. See above, pp. 29–30, 86–89; and Foley, p. 116.

14. Kristol goes so far as to identify the above passage (I.i.4.5) as "Adam Smith's Mistake," for "what rules the world is ideas" (*Two Cheers*, p. 129). Cf. Montesquieu, *Considerations*, XXII, p. 208.

15. Mill is quite explicit: "The disposition of mankind . . . to impose their own opinions and inclinations as a rule of conduct on others . . . is hardly ever kept under restraint by anything but want of power" ("Introductory," *On Liberty*, p. 15). Cf. Spinoza's argument that "every individual wishes the rest to live after his own mind, and to approve what he approves, and reject what he rejects. . . . As all are equally eager to be first, they fall to strife" (*Political Treatise*, I, p. 289; cf. *TPT*, XVII, p. 216).

16. Cf. pp. 129–38 above. According to Haakonssen, Smith in the lectures seeks natural justice, the standpoint of the impartial spectator, in the con-

crete, precedent-based decisions of "judges and arbiters," because law is otherwise "liable to be guided by political and religious objectives"; Smith therefore prefers case law to statute law (pp. 151–52).

17. Smith is probably referring to the conclusion of *Leviathan*, where Hobbes says the book was "occasioned by the disorders of the present time."

18. Cf. Smith's hints (discussed on pp. 204–5 above) about the "ascetic" doctrines that provoked Mandeville (*TMS* VII.ii.4.12). Smith presents the two apparent enemies of morality, Hobbes and Mandeville, as responding to abuses attributable to religion; he identifies Epicurus—another outspoken critic of religion—as the most flawed ancient theorist.

19. Smith thus passes over the Hobbesian primacy of "natural right" and Hobbes's quasi-moral identification of justice and keeping one's promises. In Smith's defense, one could say that Hobbesian natural right, which permits an individual to do anything he judges conducive to his preservation, is an amoral if not an immoral doctrine; in effect, perhaps, Hobbes's defense of unconditional obedience to the sovereign renders morality wholly conventional. One certainly cannot chastise Smith for claiming that Hobbes reduced the "very ideas of laudable and blameable" to "obedience and disobedience" to the sovereign (*TMS* VII.iii.2.1).

20. For Smith's own extended foray into this "abstract science," see "Of the External Senses" in *EPS*.

21. Hume's famous call "to march up directly to the capital or center of these sciences, to human nature itself" (*Treatise*, Intro., pp. xvi, xvii) may be juxtaposed with his call for "carrying the war into the most secret recesses of the enemy"—for example, into "popular superstitions" and "religious fears and prejudices" (*ICHU*, I, pp. 20–21). In beginning *Leviathan* with the recommendation to "*Read thy self*" rather than books ("Introduction"), Hobbes initiates his campaign against the authority of books—and therewith the Bible (chs. IV, VII). *Leviathan* presents an analysis of "Man" with keen attention to the psychology of religion, and concludes with a detailed biblical "interpretation."

22. *WN* V.i.f.19–35. Cf. V.i.a.21–22,42–44; *TMS* III.2.23.

23. *TMS* VII.ii.4 (title), VII.ii.4.6,14.

24. *TMS* VII.iv (title), VII.iv.2–3,35.

25. "If it were possible" for precept and exhortation to "inspire" fortitude and magnanimity, the ancient systems of propriety "would seem sufficient"; "if it were possible" to inspire humanity and love, the benevolent system "might seem capable" (*TMS* VII.ii.4.5). See VII.ii.2.13 and pp. 88–89 above, on the rhetorical advantages of Epicurean morality.

26. Grotius, *Proleg.*, 37; cf. 1, 30, 38, 48, 56; *The Law of War and Peace*, II.1.4, II.20.39, III.1.4.

27. Grotius, *The Law of War and Peace*, II.20.44–47, III.11.19.

28. See pp. 20–34, 49–51, 60–62, 143–47, and 183–87 above. Also see Grotius, *Proleg.*, 28, 45–46; *The Law of War and Peace*, I.2.2, I.3.6, II.20.9,18,39,44–48, III.1.4, III.15.10–11.

29. See pp. 32–34, 37–39, 51–52, and 60–62 above.

30. See pp. 22–23, 73–74 above, and *TMS* III.5.6 on "what are properly called laws." Regarding the succeeding chapters in *WN*, Smith pleads for his readers' "patience and attention," apologizing for the tedious detail and the obscurity attendant "upon a subject in its own nature extremely abstracted" (*WN* I.iv.18). This abstraction, along with that of the "abstract science of human nature," is apparently preferable to the unpredictability and particularity of the Bible.

31. In *EPS*, Smith describes, in language evocative of revelation, how nature and its author communicate the things human beings need to know. Nature's benevolent purpose in granting us sight is "to inform us concerning the situation and distance of the tangible objects which surround us. Upon the knowledge of this distance and situation depends *the whole conduct of human life*." Smith invokes Berkeley's suggestion that the "objects" of sight "constitute a sort of language which the Author of Nature addresses to our eyes, and by which he informs us of many things, which it is of the utmost importance to us to know" ("Of the External Senses," 60). For Smith, such natural lessons replace revelation.

32. Coase notes that according to Smith's moral theory, "we have to appear worthy in our own eyes" (p. 532), but overlooks the religious implications.

33. *TMS* II.ii.3.12, III.2.33, III.5.3,6,7,12,13.

34. Smith does not here mention the impartial spectator, but his terminology suggests it. The magnanimous man is "most indifferent about what actually are the opinions of mankind with regard to him" but is "delighted with the thoughts of what they should be," i.e., with what they would be "if mankind were cool and candid and consistent with themselves, and properly informed of the motives and circumstances of his conduct" (*TMS* VII.ii.4.10).

35. Cf. *TMS* I.i.5.9 on how virtue implies excellence, not just acceptable action.

36. Consistent with the emphasis in *WN* on the clergy's mode of subsistence, Smith there mentions confession only to suggest the opportunities it afforded for augmenting "the voluntary oblations of the people" (*WN* V.i.g.2). Both books stress this alleged kinship between Catholicism and feudal barbarism.

37. Smith's discussion of casuistry links and to some degree even conflates "the Christian church" and "the rules of Christian purity" with "the Roman Catholic superstition" (*TMS* VII.iv.7,16).

38. Characteristically, Smith labels this credulity as "natural" and provides a sociobiological explanation for it (*TMS* VII.iv.23).

39. *TMS* VII.ii.4.2–4, VII.ii.3.2. On Epicurus, see pp. 86–89 above.

40. Smith claims that "to a man who from his birth was a stranger to society, the objects of his passions, the external bodies which either pleased or displeased him, would occupy the whole of his attention" (*TMS* III.1.3). That is, such a man would have no contact with God; one wonders about Adam.

41. On love and ambition, cf. *TMS* I.iii.2.7 and III.5.8.

42. See pp. 194–95 above.

43. Cf. *TMS* VI.iii.8. Although the natural tendency of "the great mob of mankind" to admire mighty conquerors is "foolish," Smith concedes that it contributes to social stability (VI.iii.30).

44. *TMS* VII.ii.3.1.1,3. In his characteristically delicate way, Smith dances around the historical presence of Jesus. The chapter beings with the remark that the benevolence systems are "not so ancient" as the others. The first adherents Smith mentions are the Neoplatonists "about and after the age of Augustus" (VII.ii.3.1). Cf. pp. 158–59 above on Smith's treatment of Constantine, the initial "establishment" of Christianity, and the first three "great revolution[s]."

45. Hume contrasts the "grandeur" of ancient heroes and the humanity, clemency, tranquillity, and "other social virtues" characteristic of modern government. Hume attributes the difference to "education" rather than nature (*ICPM*, VII, p. 80).

46. Cf. Matthew 22:36–40, 10:34–39; Deuteronomy 4–5; and the *Letter* of the National Conference of U.S. Bishops, pars. 38–39, 43, 365. According to Strauss, "Only by surrendering to God's experienced call which calls for one's loving Him with all one's heart, with all one's soul and with all one's might can one come to see the other human being as one's brother and love him as oneself" (*Spinoza's Critique*, pp. 8–9).

47. *TMS* II.ii.2.1, III.1.3, III.2.32, III.3.3,21–22,25,38, III.4.6,7,12. See pp. 52–56 above.

48. Cf. Hume's famous claim that " 'Tis not contrary to reason to prefer the destruction of the whole world to the scratching of my finger" (*Treatise*, II.iii.3, p. 416). Rather than contradict the claim, Smith provides a psychology to show that its truth is no cause for alarm. One wonders, however, whether *TMS* can account for the behavior of Hitler, Stalin, Pol Pot, and Saddam Hussein. Coase states: "If the man of humanity had been faced with the loss, not of his little finger, but of his arms and legs, and had the number of Chinese who would have been saved by his sacrifice been one hundred rather than one hundred million, he might, indeed probably would, decide differently" (p. 532).

49. Perhaps hesitation arises on the brink of selfish action (in contrast to selfish sentiment) because human beings mete out punishment for actions rather than intentions. See pp. 58–60 above.

50. *TMS* VII.ii.1.29. Cf. VII.ii.1.28, VII.ii.4.10, III.3.27–31.

51. The most extreme version of this position is articulated by Epictetus, who likens a person to a foot; if the "whole" is in order, a "part" should not complain about being amputated (*TMS* VII.ii.1.19–20).

52. *TMS* VII.ii.1.45–46. Smith quotes Alexander Pope (*Essay*, II:87–88) in recounting the Stoic doctrine that all events are equally part of "that great chain of causes and effects" (VII.ii.1.37,39).

53. *TMS* VI.ii.3.2–3, II.i.5.10, II.ii.3.4–5, II.iii.3.2, III.5.7,9, VI.ii.Intro.3, VI.ii.1.20. Compare *TMS* I.ii.3.4 and Pope's remarks about the "Eternal Art educing good from ill" (*Essay*, II:175). On the Stoics and bourgeois virtue, see pp. 89–91 above.

54. "If I could for a moment cease to think that I am a Christian, I would not be able to keep myself from numbering the destruction of Zeno's sect among the misfortunes of human kind" (Montesquieu, *Spirit of Laws*, XXIV:10). By de-emphasizing Fate and passive contemplation, by accentuating the role of Providence in human history, and by incorporating Christ and the afterlife, Scottish thinkers such as Hutcheson, Ferguson, Blair, and Robertson were able to blend Stoicism and Christianity (Sher, pp. 175–86, 325). Smith the political economist was less Stoic and much less Christian than they were. Even in *TMS*, however, Smith equivocates about the afterlife and remarks that it is "Fortune, which governs the world" (II.iii.3.1); also consider the final sentence of Smith's essay on physics (discussed above, p. 312n30).

55. At *TMS* III.3.6, Smith refers to the "truth" of the "great stoical maxim" of never promoting oneself at the expense of others. At VI.ii.3.3, Smith himself says, without reference to the Stoics, that "the wise and virtuous man is at all times willing that his own private interest should be sacrificed to the public interest."

56. Smith's political economy of course meshes better with the Stoic exaltation of world citizenship (*TMS* III.3.11) than it does with the Platonic and Aristotelian exaltation of the polis; cf. *WN* V.i.f.30, on the concern of "ancient moral philosophy" for "the great society of mankind." According to Lowenthal (p. 276) and Pangle (pp. 233–34), the Stoics, compared to Plato and Aristotle, also posit less tension between philosophy and civic devotion.

57. Cropsey errs in arguing that Smith rejects pride in the name of humility (Cropsey, *Polity*, pp. 50–51 and nn. 2, 3).

58. *TMS* VI.iii.16, I.i.5.8, I.ii.3.3, VII.ii.1.4–5,7.

59. "Poor David Hume is dying very fast, but with great cheerfulness and good humour and with more real resignation to the necessary course of things, than any whining Christian ever dyed with pretended resignation to the will of God" (*Correspondence*, #163, 14 August 1776); cf. the letter (#178) subsequently appended to Hume's *Inquiry Concerning Human Understanding*.

60. See pp. 194–96 above, for analysis of Smith's remarks about atonement (*TMS* II.ii.3.12) and the link between virtue and self-approbation (III.6).

61. Kristol thus errs in arguing that Smith "would never have dreamed of repudiating" the classical and biblical distinction between "high" and "low" (*Reflections*, pp. 191–92). The analysis of human nature in *TMS* is of course less reductionist than is the analysis in *Leviathan*.

62. Cf. Danford, pp. 691, 695, and pp. 69–70 above, on the egalitarian dimensions of Smithian pride.

63. Cf. Hume's contrast between Diogenes ("magnanimity, ostentation, pride, and the idea of his own superiority above his fellow creatures") and Pascal ("humility and abasement"). *ICPM*, "A Dialogue," pp. 157–58. Smith likewise faults Aristotle, "that indulgent philosopher," for including ("in the practical parts of his Ethics") "jocularity and good humour" among the virtues even though "the lightness of the approbation which we naturally

bestow upon them should not seem to entitle them to so venerable a name" (*TMS* VII.iv.5).

64. *TMS* I.iii.2.8; cf. III.2.7,24–25,29. Smith is clearly further from Nietzsche than from Aristotle. Nietzsche's "master" morality derives from the "noble type" that "experiences itself as determining values; it does not need approval. . . . It knows itself to be that which first accords honor to things" (*Beyond Good and Evil*, sec. 260, p. 205). To understand vanity, the noble must learn that the commoner (in dependent strata) "*was* only what he was *considered*" (sec. 261, pp. 208–9, emphasis in original).

65. *TMS* I.iii.2.1, VI.iii.22,35, VII.ii.4.10, VII.iv.26–27. See pp. 219–20 above, on the humility and repentance that follow from judging yourself with reference to "exact propriety and perfection" (VI.iii.23–25).

66. Contrast *TMS* I.i.1.13, II.ii.2.21, III.3.33 with I.iii.2.12, III.2.11, III.3.6, VI.iii.7, VII.iv.13.

67. Hume offers similar criticisms ("Of the Populousness of Ancient Nations," *Essays*, pp. 398–99). Invoking suicide as well as exposure, Arendt contrasts the Christian vision of life's "sacredness" with the pagan contempt for life (pp. 315–16).

68. Hutcheson is for Smith both the chief spokesman for the benevolence system and a utilitarian, whereas Hume and Hobbes represent a version of utilitarianism less oriented toward benevolence.

69. Campbell accurately diagnoses Smith's meta-utilitarianism, but too quickly invokes God instead of Hobbesian or Darwinian nature (pp. 205, 217). Campbell is right, however, to identify utility as the principle "necessary for the guidance of those who have to consider the total system of society" (p. 218); utility operates at the "level of contemplation, when men adopt a God's-eye view of society" (p. 219).

70. *TMS* VI.iii.31; cf. pp. 201–2 above. As Campbell puts it, Smith's utilitarianism implies that "most people . . . should concern themselves with their own affairs and adopt an attitude of detachment, even resignation, with respect to the wider world" (p. 220).

71. Smith is especially critical of the consequent Stoic endorsement of suicide, which he of course condemns from nature's point of view, not the Bible's (VII.ii.1.34).

CHAPTER ELEVEN *Karl Marx on the Withering of Religion and Politics*

1. Marx, *GI*, p. 157 (cf. *Capital*, ch. 1, pp. 175–76n35). Marx nevertheless prefers the French and the English—who are blinded by "the political illusion, which is moderately close to reality"—to the German idealists who "make religious illusion the driving force of history" (*GI*, p. 166).

2. "Just as Christ is the intermediary to whom man attributes all his own divinity and all his religious *bonds*, so the state is the intermediary to which man confides all his non-divinity and all his *human freedom*" (Marx, *JQ*, p. 32, emphasis in original; cf. p. 52). In the "misty realm" that is religion,

"the products of the human brain appear as autonomous figures endowed with a life of their own" (*Capital*, ch. 1, p. 165). Marx applies a similar critique to capital and money. See pp. 240–42 below.

3. Marx, *CM*, p. 485. "Marxism is saturated with the optimism of progress, and that alone . . . makes it irreconcilably opposed to religion" (Trotsky, *Revolution Betrayed*, p. 45).

4. *Capital*, ch. 1, p. 173. Cf. 1844, pp. 84–85; JQ, p. 52.

5. Communism is "the *genuine* resolution of the conflict between man and nature and between man and man—the true resolution of the strife between existence and essence . . . between freedom and necessity, between the individual and the species" (Marx, 1844, p. 84, emphasis in original).

6. Marx, JQ, pp. 45, 31; "Contribution to the Critique of Hegel's *Philosophy of Right*: Introduction," p. 54 (in Tucker). In *The Communist Manifesto*, Marx intimates that communism "abolishes all religion" (p. 489).

7. *Capital*, pp. 143; 169; 179; 178–79n2; 197, 203; 197–98, 229, 375–76n72, 746; 199–200, 207, 285, 359, 688n8; 208; 229, 558, 800–801; 252; 256; 314; 337n11; 395, 815; 482; 742; 740.

8. *Capital*, pp. 800–801; 181, 299n16, 359, 496n7, 740n22.

9. Marx, *CM*, pp. 475, 489. Marx correctly describes Smith as "an outspoken enemy of the parsons" (*Capital*, ch. 25, pp. 766–68n6).

10. See pp. 174–79 above. For a more thorough organizational comparison of communism and Catholicism, see Blanshard, pp. 43, 159–63, 168, 172, 206, 244, 287–89.

11. Speech delivered in Amsterdam, 8 September 1872, after a congress of the First International (p. 523). In Lenin's words, there will be "nothing that causes indignation" under communism (V:1, p. 74).

12. Engels, Preface to the English edition of *Capital*, p. 112.

13. Smith denominates the post-feudal European economy as "commercial society," for which he is only occasionally an advocate (as distinguished from a chronicler).

14. Marx describes Smith as "the quintessential political economist of the period of manufacture" (*Capital*, ch. 14, p. 468n19), a period succeeded by the era of "machinery and large-scale industry." Cf. pp. 109, 113 above; Duncan, p. 44; McNally, pp. 12, 265–66; Winch, *Smith's Politics*, p. 142; and John Pocock, "Machiavelli in the Liberal Cosmos," *Political Theory* 13 (November 1985): 573.

15. See pp. 24–26, 40, 116–17, 131, and 186–87 above. Just as there is nothing in Marx of Smith's reliance in *TMS* on God and the other world, there is nothing of the virtues as standards of character that constrain freedom.

16. Capitalism, of course, maintains high "stakes" for the individual insofar as it places responsibility for acquiring necessities such as food, health care, and lodging squarely on his or her shoulders. Cf. Ryan's argument that the security and the moderation traditionally associated with property ownership are compromised by industrialization and the increased scale of the modern economy (*Property*, p. 48).

17. Kristol argues that "scientific" socialism could spawn a mass move-

ment because "it pandered so explicitly to the mass appetites excited—but also, to some degree, at any particular moment, frustrated—by capitalism" (*Reflections*, p. 119).

18. *WN* V.i.f.50,52,54–55,60–61, V.i.g.10–15.

19. Trotsky, *Literature and Revolution*, p. 255.

20. From these premises Wolff brilliantly analyzes the rhetoric of *Capital*, explaining the coexistence of the dry technical analyses not only with the Hegelianisms but with Marx's "richly metaphorical invocation of the religious, political, and literary images of the Western cultural tradition" (*Moneybags*, pp. 4, 41–43, 51, 65, 73, 81).

21. *Capital*, ch. 6, pp. 279–80. Cf. Wolff, *Moneybags*, pp. 28, 38, 43–44, 53, 58–60, 64–65, 75, 79.

22. *Capital*, pp. 672, 680, 729–30. Although "labor-power," like all other commodities, is generally purchased at its full "value" (its cost of production), it is the only commodity whose consumption produces "surplus value" (ch. 6, pp. 270, 274).

23. Whereas the Roman slave was held by chains, the modern laborer, severed from the means of production, is "bound to his owner by invisible threads. The appearance of independence is maintained by a constant change in the person of the individual employer, and by the legal fiction of a contract" (*Capital*, ch. 23, p. 719; cf. p. 799). Thus, "the silent compulsion of economic relations sets the seal on the domination of the capitalist" (ch. 28, p. 899).

24. *Capital*, pp. 325, 345, 425, 486–88. Thus the bourgeoisie "has been the first to show what man's activity can bring about" (*CM*, p. 476).

25. Marx, *CM*, pp. 479–83; *Capital*, ch. 32, p. 929. To comprehend the controversial "immiseration thesis," also see *Capital*, ch. 25, esp. secs. 3 and 4.

26. *Capital*, pp. 477–78, 635. "In manufacturing, the social productive power of the collective worker, hence of capital, is enriched through the impoverishment of the worker in individual productive power" (14:5, p. 483; cf. pp. 470, 481–82, 486, 549).

27. The capitalist "ruthlessly forces the human race to produce for production's sake. In this way he spurs on the development of society's productive forces" to a point "which *alone* can form the real basis of a higher form of society, a society in which the full and free development of every individual forms the ruling principle" (*Capital*, 24:3, p. 739).

28. By introducing the Hegelian dialectic to political economy, Marx provides "an organic and not merely mechanical interpretation of human society" (Deane, pp. 127–28); he likewise consummates the protean Darwinism of Smith's political economy. In the Preface to *Capital*, Marx likens his investigation to biology as well as to physics.

29. Marx, Gotha, p. 531. The dominance of exchange value over use value will likewise be inverted; cf. pp. 73–76 above. Arendt points out a fundamental tension in Marx's thought between two views of labor: labor as an eternal necessity that defines our species-being; and labor as a necessity we gradually overcome in our approach to the "realm of freedom" (Arendt, p. 104). See *Capital*, 7:1; *Capital*, vol. III, p. 820.

30. Communist countries, however, failed in eliminating an underground economy, including bribery and the black market, at least as much as they failed in eliminating religion and "domination." Smith recommends the exchange relationship, in which self-interest is channeled into "management and persuasion," as the alternative to the violence and enslavement that flow from our "natural insolence" (*WN* III.ii.10, V.i.g.19). See pp. 69–72 above.

31. Smith contrasts the division of labor in a commercial society with the well-rounded though undistinguished lives led by the bulk of people in the previous stages. Neither Smith nor Marx encourages his readers to dwell on the desirable features of these more primitive arrangements.

32. *Capital*, vol. III, p. 820. Cf. Trotsky: communism's "highest goal is to free finally and once for all the creative forces of mankind from all pressure, limitation and humiliating dependence. Personal relations, science and art will not know any externally imposed 'plan', nor even any shadow of compulsion" (*Revolution Betrayed*, p. 180).

33. Trotsky apparently was unworried on this score: "The average human type will rise to the heights of an Aristotle, a Goethe, or a Marx. And above this ridge new peaks will rise" (*Literature and Revolution*, p. 256). Karl Kautsky likewise claims that the "*Übermensch*" will exist "not as an exception but as a rule" (quoted in Flubacher, pp. 267–68). For a post-Marxian defense of a pyramidal society, see Nietzsche, *Beyond Good and Evil*, secs. 257–58, and *The Antichrist*, sec. 57; cf. Engels, p. 714.

34. This strange remark about "Christian qualities" is perhaps clarified by Marx's argument that "Christianity, with its religious cult of man in the abstract, more particularly in its bourgeois development, i.e. in Protestantism, Deism, etc., is the most fitting form of religion" for a society of commodity producers (*Capital*, p. 172); the capitalist's imperative or function is "the appropriation of ever more wealth in the abstract" (p. 254). Both Marx and Smith must strain to explicate Christianity's unique historical impact in terms of *general* socioeconomic forces. Cf. Marx, JQ, pp. 32, 39, 51; and pp. 162–68, 194–97 above.

35. *Capital*, 24:3, p. 742. As Marx says in *The Poverty of Philosophy*, "No antagonism, no progress" (p. 53).

36. As we have seen, Smith thus departs conspicuously from his friend Edmund Burke, who laments the Enlightenment enterprise of stripping life's "pleasing illusions" and "decent drapery." Wolff fails to acknowledge that Smith, not to mention Machiavelli, Hobbes, Spinoza, Locke, and Gibbon, may have provided the essentials of Feuerbach's revelation of "the church in its true nature as a secular institution, created by man as an instrument of domination" (Wolff, *Moneybags*, p. 39).

37. Cf. pp. 34–36, 170–82 above. Heilbroner, in *Behind the Veil*, pp. 137–40, states: in insisting that government avoid "superintending the industry of private people," Smith is requiring not the elimination of such superintendence but its delegation to the private sector where it is "performed under the aegis of market forces and the universalized quest for income." Heil-

broner goes on to challenge the whole Enlightenment view that "societies and civilizations rose and fell, but the subordination of the lower classes remained" (p. 159). Marx modifies this doctrine by promising that the lower classes will rise to enjoy eternal freedom and civilization.

38. The masters can hold out longer, "combine" more easily, and summon the assistance of government (*WN* I.viii.12–13). Cf. *Capital*, pp. 344, 394–95, 412. To explain how the proletarian's enslavement coexists with his right to quit, if not to strike, Marx can invoke only the worker's dependence on the capitalist class as a whole. The "law which always holds the relative surplus-population or industrial reserve army in equilibrium with the extent and energy of accumulation rivets the worker to capital more firmly than the wedges of Hephaestus held Prometheus to the rock" (*Capital*, 25:4, p. 799; cf. pp. 380, 531–32, 719). Cf. pp. 126–27 above, on Smith's analysis of wages.

39. Rousseau, like Marx, denounces both commercialism and the oppression of the poor. In the last two books of the *Social Contract*, however, Rousseau outdoes Marx in explaining how the "public power" may be appropriately exercised.

40. Marx chides "utopian" socialists who seek a new social science to create the material prerequisites for the proletariat's emancipation and who speculate about "the best possible plan of the best possible state of society" (*CM*, III:3). Cf. *The Poverty of Philosophy*, pp. 108–10.

41. Marx, *CM*, pp. 475–76, 478, 483, 488–89; *GI*, p. 185; *CW*, pp. 636, 639; *Capital*, pp. 453, 518–23, 620–21, 739, and all of ch. 32. Cf. Engels, pp. 713–14. Recent events, of course, have highlighted communism's failure to vanquish nationalism and ethnic identity in the Soviet bloc.

42. Arendt, p. 60; cf. pp. 43–44, 131n82, 321.

43. *Capital*, pp. 91, 348, 353, 377, 382–83, 390–99, 405–16, 523, 607, 610, 613–14, 620, 635.

44. Marx, *CM*, p. 491; *Capital*, 24:3, p. 739.

45. Engels, pp. 712, 717. Engels poses the riddle thus: "In proportion as anarchy in social production vanishes, the political authority of the state dies out" (p. 717).

46. Marx, *CW*, p. 635; *Capital*, 1:4, p. 171. The early Marx belittles modern liberty, "the right to do everything which does not harm others," because "it leads every man to see in other men, not the *realization*, but rather the *limitation* of his own liberty" (JQ, p. 42, emphasis in original). Marx's seriousness about modern individuality, however, is shown by his deprecation of ancient modes of production founded on "the immaturity of man as an individual, when he has not yet torn himself loose from the umbilical cord of his natural species-connection with other men" (*Capital*, p. 173), that is, from his "tribe or community"; "common ownership of the conditions of production" is not enough if the individual is a bee in a hive (ch. 13, p. 452). Rousseau's social contract likewise struggles to combine the extremes of freedom and association. Cf. David Miller's penetrating discussion of capitalist and communist individualism (pp. 190–95).

47. Marx, *CM*, p. 490; Gotha, p. 531. Engels explains that deliverance from

capitalism's bonds, and from the "senseless extravagance" with which the ruling class consumes, is "the one precondition for . . . a practically unlimited increase of production itself" (p. 715). Cf. Lenin, V:4, p. 79.

48. Like the Rousseauean legislator who must think himself capable of "changing human nature, so to speak" (*Social Contract*, II:vii), Marx recommends revolution as a means to purge "all the muck of ages" (*GI*, p. 193). Cf. Lenin, III:3, p. 43, V:4, p. 80.

49. See *Capital*, 15:9, p. 618, for a vision of well-rounded laboring in a more industrial setting. Marx acknowledges that "all directly social or communal labor on a large scale requires, to a greater or lesser degree, a directing authority, in order to secure the harmonious co-operation of the activities of individuals, and to perform the general functions that have their origin in the motion of the total productive organism." Thus differs a violinist from an orchestra (*Capital*, ch. 13, pp. 448–49). Cf. Lenin, IV:2, p. 52.

50. Marx, *CM*, p. 490. Cf. *The Poverty of Philosophy*, II:5, p. 151.

51. Marx, *CM*, pp. 484, 490. Philip Kain astutely points out that Marx, in *The Civil War in France*, seemed to abandon this vision of enlarging "the State." Because the state machinery—the standing army and the bureaucracy—will be smashed by the proletariat, there is no danger that the state will dominate society "as a separate and independent power out of the control of its citizens" (Kain, pp. 509, 512). Kain argues that the dominating role of the state can be dispensed with where the proletariat is truly a majority, but he acknowledges the difficulties posed by Marx's use (in "Gotha") of the term "dictatorship" to characterize the first phase of communism (pp. 513–15).

52. The ambiguous reference to democracy—translated by Engels and Samuel Moore in the International Publishers edition as "the establishment of democracy"—implies both that the agenda might be initiated by roughly democratic means, for example, legislation passed by elected parliaments, and that these mechanisms might continue in place. In an 1872 speech, Marx said that the manner in which the proletariat seized political power in a particular country would reflect its "institutions, mores, and traditions." Thus, in England, America, and perhaps Holland, the "workers can attain their goal by peaceful means" (p. 523). Engels, in his 1895 Introduction to Marx's "Class Struggles in France," argues that the 1848 model of revolution via "street fighting" is largely obsolete, and emphasizes the prospects for the German workers to emancipate themselves by utilizing universal suffrage. Engels concludes by invoking the Christians' conquest of Rome (pp. 560–67, 570–71). Cf. Lenin, pp. 14, 17–18, 33, 48, 59–60, 72, 82–83.

53. Although communism utterly excludes private ownership of capital goods, it will allow, at least within certain limits, the private ownership of items for personal consumption: "We by no means intend to abolish this personal appropriation of the products of labor, an appropriation that is made for the maintenance and reproduction of human life, and that leaves no surplus wherewith to command the labor of others" (Marx, *CM*, pp. 485–86). Whereas capital is the "first negation" of individual private property (the

peasant's land or the artisan's tool), it inexorably "begets . . . its own negation": "individual property," communist style (*Capital*, ch. 32, pp. 927–29;
cf. pp. 452, 730, 734, and Gotha, pp. 528–31).

54. Marx, *CM*, pp. 494–95. Germany is "on the eve of a bourgeois revolution" that "will be but the prelude to an immediately following proletarian
revolution" (p. 500).

55. Engels made this remark (in his preface to the text published as a
separate pamphlet in 1891) in order to assuage the terror invoked in the
"Social-Democratic philistine" by the prospect of proletarian dictatorship
(p. 629).

56. What if Marx had died in 1869? There are remarks favorable to democracy—for example, that "democracy is the solved riddle of all constitutions"—in his critique of Hegel's *Philosophy of Right* (p. 20), but Marx
neither finished nor published this critique. Lenin amusingly explains why
Marx's pre-1852 writings failed to resolve the question of what will replace
the state machinery destroyed by the revolution: "Experience had not yet
yielded material for the solution of this problem which history placed on the
order of the day later on, in 1871" (II:2, p. 28).

57. The standing army was replaced by "the armed people." Cf. Lenin,
pp. 23, 37, 43, 74–75, 83, who also emphasizes the dissolution of the bureaucracy (III:3, p. 41).

58. Marx does not specify whether the national delegates were to be
elected by the people at large or by the district delegates.

59. Marx consistently emphasizes the extension of public education. One
wonders, however, whether the expertise necessary even to operate and
repair modern equipment—to say nothing about the expertise needed by
inventors and planners—can be inculcated and employed without such
"alienating" consequences as specialization, coercion, financial incentives,
and the creation of a privileged class. Cf. Lenin, pp. 38, 43, 83–84.

60. *Capital*, 10:7, p. 416. Marx elsewhere criticizes "the rights of man"
because of their intrinsic connection to the egoism of civil society (*bür-
gerliche Gesellschaft*) (JQ, pp. 40–44). Under communism, human beings
will behave themselves even though natural rights and sacred commandments will have been relegated to the "ash heap of history."

61. Cf. pp. 183–87, 209–16 above; and Smith, *TMS* I.i.4.5.

62. *Federalist* 10, 51. Because they strive so hard to unmask the hidden
and harsh truths of capitalism, Marxists are prone to overlook Marx's be-
comingly modest statement that he had discovered not the existence of class
conflict in modern society but the historical necessity of its ultimate eclipse
(letter to Joseph Weydemeyer, 5 March 1852, p. 220). In this sense, Marx
is distinctive for his idealism rather than his realism. Arendt understates
Marx's originality by overstating the degree to which classical political
economy posited that the ongoing socialization of man would produce a
fundamental harmony of interests (pp. 43–44).

63. One classical synthesis is Marcuse's *Eros and Civilization*, but the
Freudian vocabulary is amply displayed in recent work by the philosopher

Wolff (*Moneybags*, p. 35) and the economist Heilbroner (*Behind the Veil*, pp. 18–20, 24, 34, 37, 197).

64. Cf. Marx, *CW* (pp. 632, 634), on the representation of workers and peasants in the Paris Commune. Although Lenin insists that even the democratic state will ultimately wither, the interim will require "the strictest control, by society and by the state, of the quantity of labor and the quantity of consumption" (V:4, p. 80).

65. Although communist elites have tended toward vigorous pursuit of "place, pelf, and patronage," they have been aware of the dangers of *displaying* their material perquisites.

66. Marx, *GI*, p. 162; cf. his disparagement of the "*Weltverbesserer*" (*CM*, p. 484).

67. Lenin, III:2, p. 38; cf. pp. 42–43, 52–53, 68, 83–84. Lenin also makes the eminently sane prediction that "excesses on the part of *individual persons*" will continue; but these will be dealt with by "the armed people itself," as when a crowd "parts a pair of combatants or does not allow a woman to be outraged" (V:2, pp. 74–75).

68. Marx, *CM*, pp. 481, 484. Lenin's vanguard theory, and its augmentation into both Maoist militarism and the "*foco*" extolled by Che Guevara and Regis Debray, is an assertion of the old-fashioned tools of specialization, organization, violence, and dogged determination to smash the fetters imposed by the mode of production. Cf. Semmel, pp. 8–12, 28, 49–50, 53, 57, 112–28, 191, 262–72.

69. In defending market socialism, David Miller argues that "the market should be an object of collective *choice*. . . . There is an important difference between recognizing as justified something that exists independently of our choice, and seeing that thing as an expression of our will" (p. 201, emphasis in original). Adam Smith, by contrast, strives to discourage his readers from viewing social arrangements as the product of human will or choice. When Miller argues that market socialism might overcome alienation, however, he unwittingly draws on Smith: work, despite its instrumental appearance, would be seen as "communal, because everyone would understand that the system of exchange led to beneficial results. Again, social relations would appear competitive, but it would be understood that competition was the most effective way for each to contribute to the welfare of the rest" (Miller, p. 200; cf. pp. 186–88).

70. *Capital*, pp. 612, 617n29, 619, 635, 929, 930n2.

71. Marx himself cited "the cooperative movement" as an invaluable "social experiment" ("Inaugural Address," the First International, 1864, p. 518). Cf. the remarks on Robert Owen in *Capital* (pp. 614, 635).

72. Cropsey, *Political Philosophy*, p. 109. Contemporary Marxists generally invoke two considerations against the argument that Marxism is refuted by the manifest prosperity of the Western proletariat: capitalism is periodically rent by "crises," which will continue and worsen; exploitation has been exported to the Third World.

73. *Capital*, ch. 6, p. 275; cf. pp. 341, 376. The subsistence theory of wages

was pioneered by Smith and Ricardo, with a similar proviso about the historical character of "necessity."

74. For Marx, this struggle embodies "an antinomy, of right against right, both equally bearing the seal of the law of exchange" and is therefore settled by force and "class struggle" not economic science (*Capital*, 10:1, p. 344; cf. pp. 394–95, 412). According to Ryan, Mill's political economy followed Smith instead of Marx by emphasizing bargaining rather than exploitation and surplus value (*Property and Political Theory*, pp. 147–48).

75. See pp. 109–13, 122–28 above. Cf. Plato, *Laws*, 803b; *Phaedo*, 64a; *Republic*, 485a–486b, 604b–c.

76. On the difficulties capitalism has in engendering ideological and moral support, see Kristol, *Reflections*, pp. 27–42; *Two Cheers*, pp. 59, 83, 96–97, 126–30, 174; Bell, pp. 3–84; and Novak, pp. 19–20, 182–86. All three stress the threat posed to capitalism by the decline of religion. Perhaps this decline has served to make Marx's eschatology more attractive as an intergenerational vision of human destiny.

77. Capitalism disturbs the "metabolic interaction between man and the earth" that "originated in a merely natural and spontaneous fashion" and thus "compels its systematic restoration as a regulative law of social production," a "new and higher synthesis" of town and country (*Capital*, 15:10, pp. 637–38). Cf. *GI*, p. 168, and Marx's famous passage on pretechnological production (p. 160).

78. People who exalt reproductive freedom are often silent about reproductive responsibility.

79. The economist E. F. Schumacher pioneered the ecological critique of economics in his famous *Small is Beautiful*. Although Schumacher is a socialist, he does not look beyond "the realm of necessity," and his religiosity further distances him from Marx.

80. Their empiricism differs most strikingly from contemporary social science because of its ubiquitous incorporation of "history."

81. Whereas positivistic social science is in danger of "fiddling while Rome burns," ethics severed from science (natural and social) can decay into arrogant moralizing.

82. The above definition is generally credited to Lionel Robbins, who formulated the scarcity postulate as follows: "We have been turned out of Paradise. We have neither eternal life nor unlimited means of gratification. Everywhere we turn, if we choose one thing we must relinquish others" (quoted in Xenos, p. 235). Xenos demonstrates that Hume and Smith developed "a political, historical, and social theory of scarcity . . . before there was any formal postulate of scarcity in the economic theory" (p. 233).

83. Although "contradictions" are for Marx the essence of humanity's present and past, indeed the motor of historical development, he promises they will be overcome by communism. Heilbroner thus offers a definition of economics that removes the implication of essential trade-offs (*Behind the Veil*, p. 14). Even the anti-Marxist Cropsey too quickly accommodates the Marxian critique in this respect (*Political Philosophy*, p. 98).

84. Unlike Marx, Smith stresses that the best may be enemy to the good (*WN* IV.v.b.53; *TMS* VI.ii.2.16,18), and occasionally recommends that reforms be implemented with "reserve and circumspection" (*WN* IV.ii.39–44, IV.vii.c.44). On moderation, also see *WN* V.i.f.40.

85. Marxism "works like a stencil applied to every grievance in human affairs" (Novak, p. 195).

86. The challenge is to purge Marx of his dogmatic utopianism and materialism without destroying the integrity and rigor of his intellectual enterprise. One thus wonders whether liberation theology can avoid corrupting both Catholicism and Marxism.

87. Cf. Minowitz, "Machiavellianism." According to Irving Kristol, neoconservatism tries to combine the spirit of Friedman and Hayek with that of Leo Strauss and "pre-modern political philosophy" (*Two Cheers*, pp. 54, 158, 253; *Reflections*, p. xii), but the difficulty of this enterprise is revealed in part by Kristol's unseemly disparagement of environmentalists' doubts about the conquest of nature (*Two Cheers*, pp. 40–50). Michael Novak's attempted marriage of Christianity and Adam Smith, as we have seen, is likewise problematic. Cf. Bell, pp. xii, xiv, xv.

88. In the Preface to the first French edition of *Capital*, Marx does state that "there is no royal road to science, and only those who do not dread the fatiguing climb of its steep path have a chance of gaining its luminous summits" (p. 104).

89. In trying to harmonize capitalism and biblical religion, both Gilder and Novak argue that they share existentialist values such as commitment, creativity, diversity, pluralism, chance, risk, emptiness, and nothingness (Gilder, pp. 279, 286, 299, 307, 312; Novak, pp. 49, 55, 62, 64–65, 67–68, 123).

Works Cited

Alt, James E., and K. Alec Chrystal. *Political Economics.* Berkeley: Univ. of California Press, 1983.

Anspach, Ralph. "The Implications of the *Theory of Moral Sentiments* for Adam Smith's Economic Thought." *History of Political Economy* 4 (1972): 176–206.

Arendt, Hannah. *The Human Condition.* Chicago: Univ. of Chicago Press, 1958.

Aristotle. *Politics.* Trans. Carnes Lord. Chicago: Univ. of Chicago Press, 1984.

Bacon, Francis. *The Essays.* Ed. J. Pitcher. Harmondsworth, Eng.: Penguin Books, 1985.

Barbour, Ian. *Issues in Science and Religion.* New York: Harper & Row, 1966.

Becker, Carl L. *The Heavenly City of the Eighteenth-Century Philosophers.* New Haven, CT: Yale Univ. Press, 1932.

Becker, Ernest. *Escape from Evil.* New York: The Free Press, 1975.

Bell, Daniel. *The Cultural Contradictions of Capitalism.* New York: Basic Books, 1976.

Berger, Peter L. *The Capitalist Revolution.* New York: Basic Books, 1986.

Bitterman, H. J. "Adam Smith's Empiricism and the Law of Nature." *Journal of Political Economy* 48 (1940): 487–520.

Blanshard, Paul. *Communism, Democracy, and Catholic Power.* Boston: Beacon Press, 1951.

Blaug, Mark. *Economic Theory in Retrospect.* Homewood, IL: Richard D. Irwin, 1968.

Blumenberg, Hans. *The Legitimacy of the Modern Age.* Trans. Robert M. Wallace. Cambridge, MA: M.I.T. Press, 1983.

Bonar, James. *Philosophy and Political Economy*. London: Swan Sonnenschein, 1893.

Bryson, Gladys. *Man and Society: The Scottish Inquiry of the 18th Century*. Princeton, N.J.: Princeton Univ. Press, 1945.

Burke, Edmund. *Reflections on the Revolution in France*. Ed. C. C. O'Brien. Harmondsworth, Eng.: Penguin Books, 1968.

———. "Thoughts and Details on Scarcity." In Burke's *Works*, vol. V, pp. 133–69. Boston: Little, Brown, 1871.

Burrow, John, Stefan Collini, and Donald Winch. *That Noble Science of Politics*. Cambridge, Eng.: Cambridge Univ. Press, 1983.

Campbell, Thomas D. *Adam Smith's Science of Morals*. London: George Allen & Unwin, 1971.

Campbell, T. D., and I. S. Ross. "The Utilitarianism of Adam Smith's Policy Advice." *Journal of the History of Ideas* 42 (1981): 73–92.

Cassirer, Ernst. *The Philosophy of the Enlightenment*. Princeton, N.J.: Princeton Univ. Press, 1951.

Caton, Hiram. *The Politics of Progress*. Gainesville: Univ. of Florida Press, 1988.

———. "The Preindustrial Economics of Adam Smith." *Journal of Economic History* 45 (December 1985): 833–53.

Chitnis, Anand. *The Scottish Enlightenment and Early Victorian English Society*. London: Croom Helm, 1986.

Coase, Ronald H. "Adam Smith's View of Man." *Journal of Law and Economics* 19 (October 1976): 529–46.

Cropsey, Joseph. *Political Philosophy and the Issues of Politics*. Chicago: Univ. of Chicago Press, 1977.

———. *Polity and Economy*. The Hague: Martinus Nijhoff, 1957.

Danford, John. "Adam Smith, Equality, and the Wealth of Sympathy." *American Journal of Political Science* 24 (November 1980): 674–95.

Deane, Phyllis. *The Evolution of Economic Ideas*. Cambridge, Eng.: Cambridge Univ. Press, 1978.

Dickey, Laurence. "Historicizing the 'Adam Smith Problem.'" *Journal of Modern History* 58 (September 1986): 579–609.

Dumont, Louis. *From Mandeville to Marx: The Genesis and Triumph of Economic Ideology*. Chicago: Univ. of Chicago Press, 1977.

Duncan, Graeme. *Marx and Mill*. Cambridge, Eng.: Cambridge Univ. Press, 1973.

Dunn, John. "From applied theology to social analysis: the break between John Locke and the Scottish Enlightenment." In Istvan Hont and Michael Ignatieff, eds., *Wealth and Virtue*, pp. 119–35. Cambridge, Eng.: Cambridge Univ. Press, 1983.

Earle, Edward M. "Adam Smith, Alexander Hamilton, Friedrich List: The Economic Foundations of Military Power." In Peter Paret, ed., *Makers of Modern Strategy*, pp. 217–61. Princeton, N.J.: Princeton Univ. Press, 1986.

Engels, Friedrich. *Socialism: Utopian and Scientific*. In Robert C. Tucker, ed., *The Marx-Engels Reader*, 2d ed., pp. 683–717. New York: W. W. Norton, 1978.

Farr, James. "Political Science and the Enlightenment of Enthusiasm." *American Political Science Review* 82 (March 1988): 51–69.

Ferguson, Adam. *An Essay on the History of Civil Society.* Ed. Duncan Forbes. Edinburgh: Edinburgh Univ. Press, 1966.

Flubacher, Joseph. *The Concept of Ethics in the History of Economics.* New York: Vantage Press, 1950.

Foley, Vernard. *The Social Physics of Adam Smith.* Lafayette, IN: Purdue Univ. Press, 1976.

Forbes, Duncan. "Skeptical Whiggism, Commerce, and Liberty." In A. S. Skinner and T. Wilson, eds., *Essays on Adam Smith*, pp. 179–201. Oxford: Oxford Univ. Press, 1976.

Friedman, Milton. *Capitalism and Freedom.* Chicago: Univ. of Chicago Press, 1962.

——. *Free to Choose.* New York: Avon Books, 1981.

Gay, Peter. *The Enlightenment: An Interpretation: The Rise of Modern Paganism.* New York: W. W. Norton, 1977.

Gilder, George. *Wealth and Poverty.* New York: Bantam Books, 1981.

Graham, H. Grey. *The Social Life of Scotland in the 18th Century.* London: Adam & Charles Black, 1901.

Grotius, Hugo. *De Jure Belli Et Pacis.* Ed. William Whewell. 2 vols. Cambridge, Eng.: Cambridge Univ. Press, 1845.

——. *Of the Law of War and Peace.* Trans. F. W. Kelsey. 2 vols. Oxford: Oxford Univ. Press, 1927.

Gunnell, John. *Between Philosophy and Politics.* Amherst: Univ. of Massachusetts Press, 1986.

——. "The Myth of the Tradition." *APSR* 72 (March 1978): 122–34.

——. "Political Theory and Politics." *Political Theory* 13 (August 1985): 339–61.

Haakonssen, Knud. *The Science of a Legislator: The Natural Jurisprudence of David Hume and Adam Smith.* Cambridge, Eng.: Cambridge Univ. Press, 1981.

Halévy, Elie. *The Growth of Philosophic Radicalism.* Trans. Mary Morris. New York: Kelley & Millman, 1928.

Hampson, Norman. "The Enlightenment in France." In R. Porter and M. Teich, eds., *The Enlightenment in National Context*, pp. 41–53. Cambridge, Eng.: Cambridge Univ. Press, 1981.

Hancock, Ralph. *Calvin and the Foundations of Modern Politics.* Ithaca, N.Y.: Cornell Univ. Press, 1989.

Harpham, Edward. "Liberalism, Civic Humanism, and the Case of Adam Smith." *American Political Science Review* 78 (September 1984): 764–74.

Hartwell, R. M. "Comment." In Thomas Wilson and Andrew S. Skinner, eds., *The Market and The State*, pp. 33–41. Oxford: Oxford Univ. Press, 1976.

Hayek, Friedrich. *The Constitution of Liberty.* Chicago: Univ. of Chicago Press, 1959.

Hegel, G. W. F. *The Philosophy of History*. Trans. J. Sibree. New York: Dover, 1956.

———. *The Philosophy of Right*. Trans. T. M. Knox. Oxford: Oxford Univ. Press, 1967.

Heilbroner, Robert L. *Behind the Veil of Economics*. New York: W. W. Norton, 1988.

———. "The Paradox of Progress: Decline and Decay in *The Wealth of Nations*." In A. S. Skinner and T. Wilson, eds., *Essays on Adam Smith*, pp. 524–39. Oxford: Oxford Univ. Press, 1976.

———. "Review of Donald McCloskey, *The Rhetoric of Economics*." *New York Review of Books*, December 1986, pp. 46–48.

———. *The Worldly Philosophers*. 4th ed. New York: Simon & Schuster, 1972.

Heilbroner, Robert, and Lester Thurow. *Economics Explained*. New York: Simon & Schuster, 1982.

Herrick, Jim. *Against the Faith: Essays on Deists, Skeptics and Atheists*. Buffalo, NY: Prometheus Books, 1985.

Himmelfarb, Gertrude. *The Idea of Poverty: England in the Early Industrial Age*. New York: Random House, 1983.

Hirschman, Albert O. *The Passions and the Interests*. Princeton, N.J.: Princeton Univ. Press, 1977.

Hobbes, Thomas. *Leviathan*. Ed. C. B. Macpherson. Harmondsworth, Eng.: Penguin Books, 1968.

Hollander, Samuel. *The Economics of Adam Smith*. Toronto: Univ. of Toronto Press, 1973.

Holmes, Stephen T. "Self-Interest in *The Wealth of Nations*." Paper presented at the 1985 convention of the American Political Science Association.

Hont, Istvan, and Michael Ignatieff. "Needs and Justice in the *Wealth of Nations*." In Hont and Ignatieff, eds., *Wealth and Virtue*, pp. 1–44. Cambridge, Eng.: Cambridge Univ. Press, 1983.

Hume, David. *Dialogues Concerning Natural Religion*. Ed. R. Popkin. Indianapolis, IN: Hackett Publishing Company, 1980.

———. *Essays: Moral, Political and Literary*. Ed. Eugene F. Miller. Indianapolis, IN: Liberty Classics, 1985.

———. *An Inquiry Concerning Human Understanding*. Ed. C. Handel. Indianapolis, IN: Bobbs-Merrill, 1955.

———. *An Inquiry Concerning the Principles of Morals*. Ed. C. Handel. Indianapolis, IN: Bobbs-Merrill, 1957.

———. *The Natural History of Religion*. Ed. H. E. Root. Stanford, CA: Stanford Univ. Press, 1956.

———. *A Treatise of Human Nature*. Ed. P. H. Nidditch. Oxford: Oxford Univ. Press, 1978.

Hutcheson, Francis. *Illustrations on the Moral Sense*. Cambridge, MA: Harvard Univ. Press, 1971.

————. *An Inquiry Concerning Moral Good and Evil.* In L. A. Selby-Bigge, ed., *British Moralists,* vol. I, pp. 69–177. New York: Dover, 1965.

Ignatieff, Michael. *The Needs of Strangers.* Harmondsworth, Eng.: Penguin Books, 1986.

Kain, Philip. "Estrangement and the Dictatorship of the Proletariat." *Political Theory* 7 (November 1979): 509–20.

Kant, Immanuel. "Conjectural Beginnings of Human History." Trans. E. Fackenheim. In Kant, *On History,* pp. 53–68. Ed. Lewis White Beck. Indianapolis, IN: Bobbs-Merrill, 1963.

————. *Critique of Practical Reason.* Trans. L. W. Beck. Indianapolis, IN: Bobbs-Merrill, 1956.

————. "Idea for a Universal History from a Cosmopolitan Point-of-View." Trans. L. W. Beck. In Kant, *On History,* pp. 11–26. Ed. Lewis White Beck. Indianapolis, IN: Bobbs-Merrill, 1963.

Kindleberger, C. P. "The Historical Background: Adam Smith and the Industrial Revolution." In Thomas Wilson and Andrew S. Skinner, eds., *The Market and The State,* pp. 1–32. Oxford: Oxford Univ. Press, 1976.

Kirzner, Israel M. "The 'Austrian' perspective on the crisis." In Daniel Bell and Irving Kristol, eds., *The Crisis in Economic Theory,* pp. 111–22. New York: Basic Books, 1981.

Kristol, Irving. *Reflections of a Neoconservative.* New York: Basic Books, 1983.

————. *Two Cheers for Capitalism.* New York: Mentor Books, 1978.

Kuttner, Robert. "The Poverty of Economics." *The Atlantic Monthly* (February 1985): 74–84.

Lakoff, Sanford. "Christianity and Equality." In John Chapman and J. Roland Pennock, eds., *Nomos IX: Equality,* pp. 115–33. New York: Atherton Press, 1967.

Lane, Robert E. "Market Justice, Political Justice." *American Political Science Review* 80 (June 1986): 383–402.

Lenin, V. I. *State and Revolution.* New York: International Publishers, 1971.

Letwin, William. *The Origins of Scientific Economics.* London: Methuen, 1963.

Lindbloom, Charles E. *Politics and Markets.* New York: Basic Books, 1977.

Lindgren, J. Ralph. *The Social Philosophy of Adam Smith.* The Hague: Martinus Nijhoff, 1973.

Locke, John. *An Essay Concerning Human Understanding.* Ed. A. C. Fraser. New York: Dover, 1959.

————. *A Letter on Toleration.* Trans. J. W. Gough. Oxford: Oxford Univ. Press, 1968.

————. *The Reasonableness of Christianity.* Ed. I. T. Ramsey. Stanford, CA: Stanford Univ. Press, 1958.

————. *The Second Treatise of Government.* Ed. Richard Cox. Arlington Heights, IL: Harlan Davidson, 1982.

————. *Some Considerations of the Consequences of the Lowering of Inter-*

est, and the Raising the Value of Money. In Locke's *Works,* vol. V, pp. 2–206. London: Thomas Tegg, 1823.

———. *Some Thoughts Concerning Education.* In James Axtell, ed., *The Educational Writings of John Locke,* pp. 111–325. Cambridge, Eng.: Cambridge Univ. Press, 1968.

———. *Two Treatises of Government.* Ed. P. Laslett. Cambridge, Eng.: Cambridge Univ. Press, 1963.

Lowenthal, David. "Montesquieu and the Classics." In Joseph Cropsey, ed., *Ancients and Moderns,* pp. 258–82. New York: Basic Books, 1964.

Löwith, Karl. *Meaning in History.* Chicago: Univ. of Chicago Press, 1949.

Lucretius. *The Nature of Things.* Trans. Frank Copley. New York: W. W. Norton, 1977.

Macfie, Alec L. *The Individual in Society.* London: George Allen & Unwin, 1967.

Machiavelli, Niccolò. *The Prince.* Trans. Harvey C. Mansfield, Jr. Chicago: Univ. of Chicago Press, 1985.

———. *Il Principe E Discorsi.* Ed. S. Bertelli. Milan: Giangiacomo Feltrinelli Editore, 1960.

MacIntyre, Alasdair. *After Virtue.* South Bend, IN: Univ. of Notre Dame Press, 1981.

Macpherson, C. B. *Democratic Theory: Essays in Retrieval.* Oxford: Oxford Univ. Press, 1973.

———. *The Political Theory of Possessive Individualism.* Oxford: Oxford Univ. Press, 1962.

———. *The Real World of Democracy.* Oxford: Oxford Univ. Press, 1972.

Madison, James, Alexander Hamilton, and John Jay. *The Federalist Papers.* New York: Modern Library, 1937.

Malthus, Thomas Robert. *An Essay on the Principle of Population.* Ed. P. Appleman. New York: W. W. Norton, 1976.

Mandeville, Bernard. *Fable of the Bees.* Ed. F. B. Kaye. 2 vols. Oxford: Oxford Univ. Press, 1924.

Mansfield, Harvey C., Jr. *Machiavelli's New Modes and Orders.* Ithaca, NY: Cornell Univ. Press, 1979.

———. "On the Impersonality of the Modern State." *American Political Science Review* 77 (December 1983): 849–57.

Marx, Karl. *Capital,* vol. I. Trans. Ben Fowkes. New York: Random House, 1976.

———. *Capital,* vol. II. Trans. David Fernbach. New York: Random House, 1981.

———. *Capital,* vol. III. Trans. Ernest Untermann. New York: International Publishers, 1967.

———. *The Marx-Engels Reader.* 2d ed. Robert C. Tucker, ed. New York: W. W. Norton, 1978.

———. *The Poverty of Philosophy.* Moscow: Progress Publishers, 1955.

McCloskey, Donald N. *The Rhetoric of Economics.* Madison: Univ. of Wisconsin Press, 1985.

McGovern, Arthur F. *Marxism: An American Christian Perspective*. Maryknoll, NY: Orbis Books, 1980.

McNally, David. *Political Economy and the Rise of Capitalism*. Berkeley: Univ. of California Press, 1988.

Medick, Hans. *Naturzustand und Naturgeschichte der bürgerlichen Gesellschaft: Die Ursprunge der bürgerlichen Sozialtheorie als Geschichtsphilosophie und Sozialwissenschaft bei Samuel Pufendorf, John Locke und Adam Smith*. Göttingen: Vandenhoeck & Ruprecht, 1973.

Meek, Ronald. *Economics and Ideology*. London: Chapman & Hall, 1967.

———. *Smith, Marx, and After*. London: Chapman & Hall, 1977.

———. *Social Science and the Ignoble Savage*. Cambridge, Eng.: Cambridge Univ. Press, 1976.

Mill, John Stuart. *On Liberty*. Ed. D. Spitz. New York: W. W. Norton, 1975.

Miller, David. "Marx, Communism, and Markets." *Political Theory* 15 (May 1987): 182–204.

Minowitz, Peter. "Invisible Hand, Invisible Death: Adam Smith on War and Socioeconomic Development." *Journal of Political and Military Sociology* 17 (Winter 1989): 305–15.

———. "Machiavellianism Come of Age?" *The Political Science Reviewer* 22 (1993).

Montesquieu. *Considerations on the Causes of the Greatness of the Romans and their Decline*. Trans. David Lowenthal. Ithaca, NY: Cornell Univ. Press, 1968.

———. *Oeuvres Complètes*. Ed. D. Oster. Paris: Editions du Seuil, 1964.

———. *The Spirit of the Laws*. Trans. Anne Cohler, Basia Miller, and Harold Stone. Cambridge, Eng.: Cambridge Univ. Press, 1989.

Myers, Milton L. *The Soul of Modern Economic Man*. Chicago: Univ. of Chicago Press, 1983.

National Conference of U.S. Bishops. *Economic Justice for All*. Washington, DC: U.S. Catholic Conference, 1986.

Nietzsche, Friedrich. *Beyond Good and Evil*. Trans. Walter Kaufmann. New York: Random House, 1966.

Novak, Michael. *The Spirit of Democratic Capitalism*. New York: Simon & Schuster, 1982.

Nozick, Robert. *Anarchy, State, and Utopia*. New York: Basic Books, 1974.

Oncken, August. *Adam Smith und Immanuel Kant*. Leipzig: Duncker & Humblot, 1877.

Pangle, Thomas L. *Montesquieu's Philosophy of Liberalism*. Chicago: Univ. of Chicago Press, 1973.

Phillipson, Nicholas. "Adam Smith as civic moralist." In Istvan Hont and Michael Ignatieff, eds., *Wealth and Virtue*, pp. 179–202. Cambridge, Eng.: Cambridge Univ. Press, 1983.

———. "The Enlightenment in Scotland." In R. Porter and M. Teich, eds., *The Enlightenment in National Context*, pp. 19–40. Cambridge, Eng.: Cambridge Univ. Press, 1981.

Plato. *Laws*. Trans. Thomas Pangle. New York: Basic Books, 1980.

———. *Republic*. Trans. Allan Bloom. New York: Basic Books, 1968.

Pocock, John. "Cambridge paradigms and Scotch philosophers: a study of the relations between the civic humanist and the civil jurisprudential interpretation of eighteenth-century social thought." In Istvan Hont and Michael Ignatieff, eds., *Wealth and Virtue*, pp. 235–52. Cambridge, Eng.: Cambridge Univ. Press, 1983.

———. "Civic Humanism and Its Role in Anglo-American Thought." In his *Politics, Language and Time*, pp. 80–103. New York: Atheneum, 1973.

———. *The Machiavellian Moment*. Princeton, NJ: Princeton Univ. Press, 1975.

———. *Virtue, Commerce, and History*. Cambridge, Eng.: Cambridge Univ. Press, 1985.

Pope, Alexander. *An Essay on Man*. Ed. M. Mack. New Haven, CT: Yale Univ. Press, 1950.

Porter, Roy. "The Enlightenment in England." In R. Porter and M. Teich, eds., *The Enlightenment in National Context*, pp. 1–18. Cambridge, Eng.: Cambridge Univ. Press, 1981.

Porter, Roy, and Mikulas Teich, eds. *The Enlightenment in National Context*. Cambridge, Eng.: Cambridge Univ. Press, 1981.

Rae, John. *Life of Adam Smith*. New York: Augustus M. Kelly, 1965.

Raphael, D. D. *Adam Smith*. Oxford: Oxford Univ. Press, 1985.

Rawls, John. *A Theory of Justice*. Cambridge, MA: Harvard Univ. Press, 1971.

Ricardo, David. *The Principles of Political Economy and Taxation*. London: Everyman's Library, 1973.

Roelofs, H. Mark. "Liberation Theology: The Recovery of Biblical Radicalism." *American Political Science Review* 82 (June 1988): 549–66.

Rosenberg, Nathan. "Adam Smith and Laissez-Faire Revisited." In Gerald P. O'Driscoll, ed., *Adam Smith and Modern Political Economy*, pp. 19–34. Ames: Iowa State Univ. Press, 1979.

———. "Adam Smith on Profits—Paradox Lost and Regained." In A. S. Skinner and T. Wilson, eds., *Essays on Adam Smith*, pp. 377–89. Oxford: Oxford Univ. Press, 1976.

———. "Adam Smith on the Division of Labor: Two Views or One?" *Economica* 32 (1965): 127–39.

Rosenberg, Nathan, and L. E. Birdzell. *How the West Grew Rich: The Economic Transformation of the Industrial World*. New York: Basic Books, 1986.

Rousseau, Jean-Jacques. *Du Contrat Social*. Paris: Garnier-Flammarion, 1966.

———. *The First and Second Discourses*. Trans. Roger Masters and Judith Masters. New York: St. Martin's Press, 1964.

———. *On the Social Contract & "Political Economy"*. Trans. Roger Masters and Judith Masters. New York: St. Martin's Press, 1978.

Ryan, Alan. *Property*. Minneapolis: Univ. of Minnesota Press, 1987.

———. *Property and Political Theory*. Oxford: Basil Blackwell, 1984.

Schumacher, E. F. *Small is Beautiful*. New York: Harper & Row, 1973.

Schumpeter, Joseph. *Capitalism, Socialism and Democracy*. New York: Harper Torchbooks, 1942.

Semmel, Bernard. *Marxism and the Science of War*. Oxford: Oxford Univ. Press, 1981.

Sher, Richard B. *Church and University in the Scottish Enlightenment*. Princeton, NJ: Princeton Univ. Press, 1985.

Shklar, Judith N. *Montesquieu*. Oxford: Oxford Univ. Press, 1987.

Sigmund, Paul. "Hierarchy, Equality, and Consent in Medieval Christian Thought." In John Chapman and J. Roland Pennock, eds., *Nomos IX: Equality*, pp. 134–53. New York: Atherton Press, 1967.

Skinner, Andrew S. *A System of Social Science*. Oxford: Oxford Univ. Press, 1979.

Skinner, Andrew S., and Thomas Wilson, eds. *Essays on Adam Smith*. Oxford: Oxford Univ. Press, 1976.

Small, Albion. *Adam Smith and Modern Sociology*. Chicago: Univ. of Chicago Press, 1907.

Spinoza, Benedict. *A Theologico-Political Treatise and A Political Treatise*. Trans. R. H. M. Elwes. New York: Dover, 1951.

Steuart, Sir James. *An Inquiry into the Principles of Political Oeconomy*. Ed. A. S. Skinner. London: Oliver & Boyd, 1966.

Stewart, Dugald. "Account of the Life and Writings of Adam Smith." In Adam Smith, *Essays on Philosophical Subjects*, pp. 265–351. Ed. W. P. D. Wightman, J. C. Bryce, and I. S. Ross. Oxford: Oxford Univ. Press, 1980.

Strauss, Leo. *Natural Right and History*. Chicago: Univ. of Chicago Press, 1950.

——. *Spinoza's Critique of Religion*. New York: Schocken Books, 1965.

——. *Thoughts on Machiavelli*. New York: The Free Press, 1958.

——. *What is Political Philosophy?* New York: The Free Press, 1959.

Tawney, Richard H. *Religion and the Rise of Capitalism*. Harmondsworth, Eng.: Penguin Books, 1984.

Teichgraeber, Richard, III. *Free Trade and Moral Philosophy*. Durham, NC: Duke Univ. Press, 1986.

——. "Rethinking *Das Adam Smith Problem*." *Journal of British Studies* 20 (Spring 1981): 106–23.

Thurow, Lester C. *Dangerous Currents: The State of Economics*. New York: Vintage Books, 1984.

Tocqueville, Alexis de. *Democracy in America*. Trans. George Lawrence. New York: Doubleday, 1969.

Troeltsch, Ernst. *Protestantism and Progress*. Boston: Beacon Press, 1958.

Trotsky, Leon. *Literature and Revolution*. New York: Russell & Russell, 1957.

——. *The Revolution Betrayed*. New York: Pathfinder Press, 1937.

Tucker, Robert C., ed. *The Marx-Engels Reader*. 2d ed. New York: W. W. Norton, 1978.

Tyler, Gus. "The Myth of Free Trade." *Dissent* (Spring 1988): 212–18.

Viner, Jacob. *The Long View and the Short*. New York: The Free Press, 1958.

———. *The Role of Providence in the Social Order*. Philadelphia, PA: The American Philosophical Society, 1972.

Voltaire. *Philosophical Dictionary*. Trans. T. Besterman. Harmondsworth, Eng.: Penguin Books, 1972.

Walzer, Michael. *Spheres of Justice*. New York: Basic Books, 1983.

Weber, Max. *The Protestant Ethic and the Spirit of Capitalism*. New York: Charles Scribner, 1958.

West, E. G. "Adam Smith and Rousseau's *Discourse on Inequality*: Inspiration or Provocation?" *Journal of Economic Issues* 5 (1971): 56–70.

Winch, Donald. "Adam Smith's 'enduring particular result': a political and cosmopolitan perspective." In Istvan Hont and Michael Ignatieff, eds., *Wealth and Virtue*, pp. 253–69. Cambridge, Eng.: Cambridge Univ. Press, 1983.

———. *Adam Smith's Politics: An Essay in Historiographic Revision*. Cambridge, Eng.: Cambridge Univ. Press, 1978.

———. "Introduction" to John Stuart Mill, *Principles of Political Economy*. Harmondsworth, Eng.: Penguin Books, 1970.

Wolff, Robert Paul. *Moneybags Must be so Lucky*. Amherst: Univ. of Massachusetts Press, 1988.

———. *Understanding Marx*. Princeton, NJ: Princeton Univ. Press, 1984.

Xenos, Nicholas. "Liberalism and the Postulate of Scarcity." *Political Theory* 15 (May 1987): 225–43.

Index of Names

McNally, David, 262n8, 264n25, 266n9, 268n24, 270n45
Medick, Hans, 162, 262n5, 263n22
Meek, Ronald, 274–75n27
Mill, James, 25
Mill, John Stuart, 18, 149, 261n4, 307n38, 315n15, 328n74
Millar, John, 266n9
Miller, David, 324n46, 327n69
Mohammed, 143, 194, 311n20
Montesquieu, 6, 12, 19, 21, 26, 33, 39, 78, 135, 158, 183, 217f, 266nn8, 9, 267n15, 271n64, 277n6, 279n33, 280nn35, 38, 282n7, 292n44, 299n36, 302n56, 306n22, 308n42, 311n16, 319n54
Moses, 2, 156, 158, 181, 236, 290n20
Myers, Milton, 279n31

National Conference of U.S. Bishops, 298n19, 312n26
Newton, Isaac, 6, 133, 134, 294nn54, 55, 301n54
Nietzsche, Friedrich, 83, 233, 234, 315n7, 320n64, 323n33
Noah, 192
Novak, Michael, 11, 276n50, 288n10, 293n47, 296n65, 302n58, 328n76, 329nn87, 89
Nozick, Robert, 18, 139–40, 270n44

Pangle, Thomas, 266n8, 277n6, 319n56
Parmenides, 232, 233
Pascal, 229, 319n63
Paul, Saint, 144, 297–98n15
Philip of Macedon, 110, 142, 158
Phillipson, Nicholas, 266n6, 270n52, 276n51, 308n46
Plato, 6, 19, 22, 34, 37, 50, 53, 61, 64–65, 72–73, 83–88 *passim*, 94–95, 98, 102, 115, 119, 129, 156, 160, 205, 215, 217, 223, 226, 232, 233, 254, 264–65n31, 270n50, 271n55, 275–76n43, 277n1, 278n15, 280n38, 281–82n56, 289n17, 290n25, 297nn9, 14, 301n51, 310n11, 319n56
Pocock, John, 10, 61, 133, 157, 264n25, 270–71n52, 276n51, 285n35
Polybius, 19, 156, 264–65n31

Pope, Alexander, 183, 290n21, 302n59, 318nn52, 53
Posner, Richard, 4
Prometheus, 75, 324n38
Pufendorf, Samuel, 6, 12, 213

Quesnay, François, 28–29, 129, 136, 296n4

Raphael, D. D., 5, 133–34, 198, 291n29, 294n56, 300n51, 309–10n1, 311n17
Rawls, John, 4, 18, 139–40, 285n37, 296n2
Ricardo, David, 3, 12, 23, 25, 133, 139, 147, 149, 256, 264n25, 265n3, 269n35, 278n15, 280n43, 292nn37, 41, 294n54, 300n38, 327–28n73
Robbins, Lionel, 328n82
Robertson, William, 301n53, 303n67, 319n54
Roelofs, H. Mark, 311n15
Rosenberg, Nathan, 103, 272–73n11, 293n51, 295n57
Ross, I. S., 276n48
Rousseau, Jean-Jacques, 6, 12, 23, 25, 30, 33, 39–41, 69, 83, 88, 98, 145, 173, 186–87, 217, 228, 239, 243, 269n32, 271nn55, 56, 272nn10, 11, 273n12, 275n34, 279n23, 280n38, 283n10, 284n21, 285n37, 289n14, 302n59, 304n9, 324n39, 325n48
Ryan, Alan, 297n15, 321n16, 328n74

Say, Jean-Baptiste, 23, 25, 82, 261n3, 264n25
Schumacher, E. F., 328n79
Schumpeter, Joseph, 82, 279n22
Scipio Nasica, 108
Shaftesbury, 226, 307n35
Sher, Richard, 307n36, 308n46
Skinner, Andrew, 296n3, 300n41
Skinner, Quentin, 10
Small, Albion, 265n2
Socrates, 37, 48, 84, 154, 156–57, 207, 243, 257, 277n1, 290n25, 301n51, 314n50
Solomon, 154–55, 300n44, 304n6
Spinoza, Benedict, 135, 222, 224, 289n15, 290n20, 305nn14, 18, 308n42, 315n15, 323n36

Library of Congress Cataloging-in-Publication Data

Minowitz, Peter, 1955–
    Profits, priests, and princes : Adam Smith's emancipation
    of economics from politics and religion / Peter
    Minowitz.
        p.   cm.
    Includes bibliographical references.
    ISBN 0–8047–2166–1 (cloth : alk. paper) :
    1. Economics—Moral and ethical aspects.
    2. Economics—Philosophy.   3. Smith, Adam. 1723–
    1790.   I. Title.
    HB72.M53   1993
    330.15'3—dc 20   93-18798
                                                      CIP

⊗ This book is printed on acid-free paper